DrMaster
Publications Inc.
www.DrMasterbooks.com

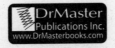

IRON WOK JAN!

Translator / Michiko Nakayama
English Adaptation / Sandra Mak
Editor / Benjamin Stone
Supervising Editor / Ken Li
Production Artists / Bryce Gunkel / Stephanie Zhu
V.P. of Operations / Yuki Chung
President / Jennifer Chen

DrMaster Publications, Inc.
4044 Clipper Ct.
Fremont, CA 94538
www.DrMasterbooks.com

First Edition: October 2005
ISBN 1-59796-033-0

15

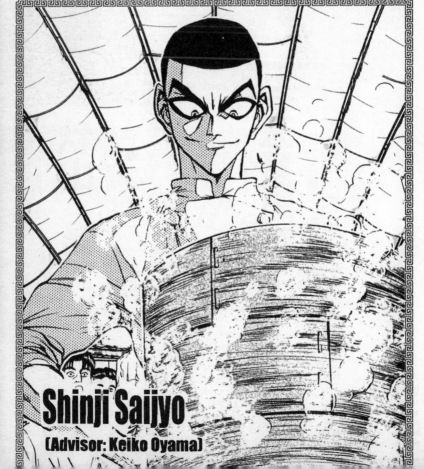

Shinji Saijyo
(Advisor: Keiko Oyama)

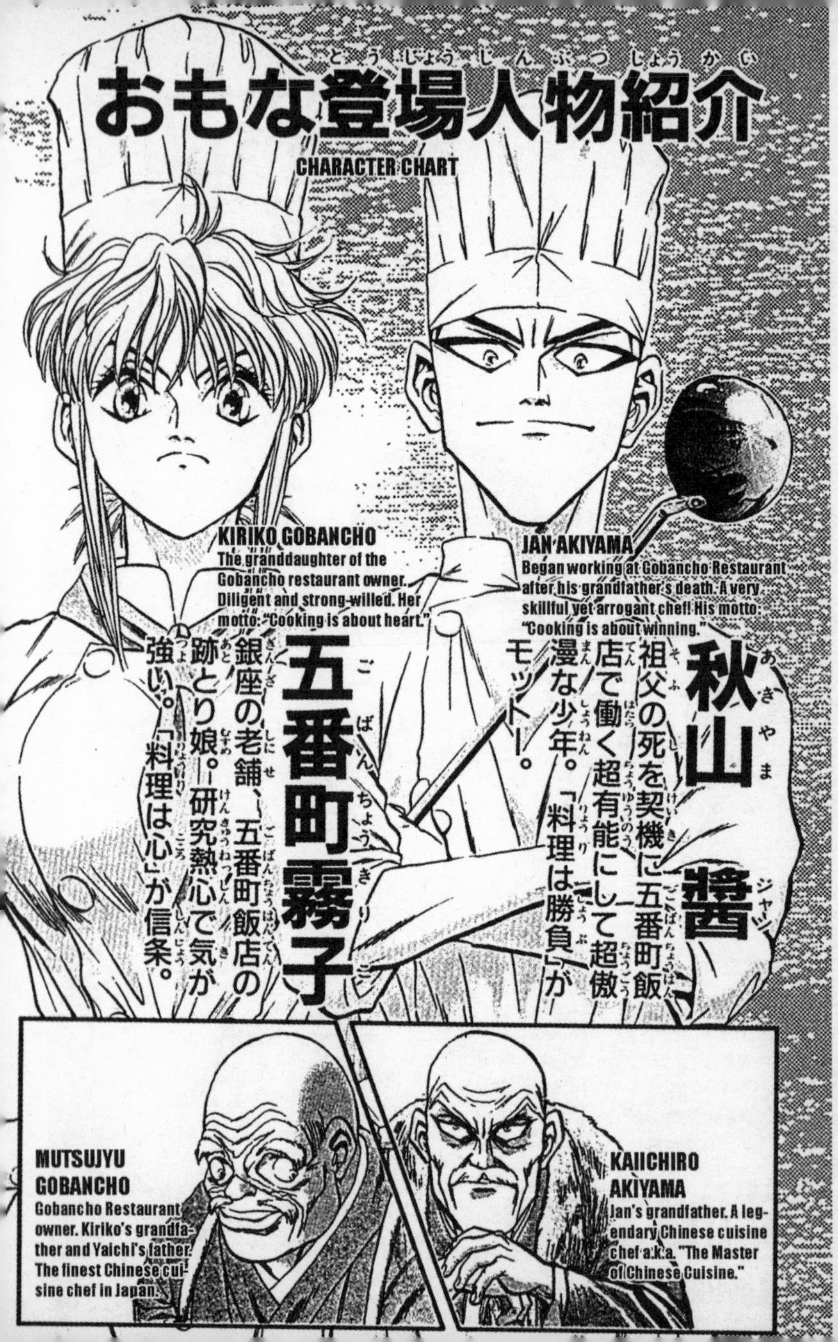
おもな登場人物紹介
CHARACTER CHART
秋山醬
祖父の死を契機に五番町飯店で働く超有能にして超傲漫な少年。「料理は勝負」がモットー。
JAN AKIYAMA
Began working at Gobancho Restaurant after his grandfather's death. A very skillful yet arrogant chef! His motto: "Cooking is about winning."
五番町霧子
銀座の老舗、五番町飯店の跡とり娘。研究熱心で気が強い。「料理は心」が信条。
KIRIKO GOBANCHO
The granddaughter of the Gobancho restaurant owner. Diligent and strong-willed. Her motto: "Cooking is about heart."
KAIICHIRO AKIYAMA
Jan's grandfather. A legendary Chinese cuisine chef a.k.a. "The Master of Chinese Cuisine."
MUTSUJYU GOBANCHO
Gobancho Restaurant owner. Kiriko's grandfather and Yaichi's father. The finest Chinese cuisine chef in Japan.

CELINE YANG

Jan and Kiriko's coworker. Her father is from Hong Kong and her mother is French. She is developing a new form of Chinese Cuisine which she calls "Nouvelle Chinoise." Her Philosophy - "Cooking is about abundance."

TAKAO OKONOGI

Gobancho Restaurant trainee who constantly screws up and is the only person Jan opens up to.

YAICHI GOBANCHO

A highly respected Chinese cuisine chef. Head of the kitchen at the Gobancho Restaurant and is Kiriko's uncle, as well as her understanding mentor. He possesses a wide knowledge of cooking.

NICHIDO OTANI

A food critic with the tongue of god. Has been humiliated by Jan many times and is plotting to eliminate Jan from the cooking industry.

IRON WOK JAN!

VOL. 15 TABLE OF CONTENTS

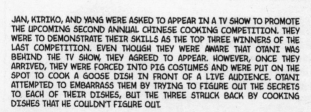

JAN, KIRIKO, AND YANG WERE ASKED TO APPEAR IN A TV SHOW TO PROMOTE THE UPCOMING SECOND ANNUAL CHINESE COOKING COMPETITION. THEY WERE TO DEMONSTRATE THEIR SKILLS AS THE TOP THREE WINNERS OF THE LAST COMPETITION. EVEN THOUGH THEY WERE AWARE THAT OTANI WAS BEHIND THE TV SHOW, THEY AGREED TO APPEAR. HOWEVER, ONCE THEY ARRIVED, THEY WERE FORCED INTO PIG COSTUMES AND WERE PUT ON THE SPOT TO COOK A GOOSE DISH IN FRONT OF A LIVE AUDIENCE. OTANI ATTEMPTED TO EMBARRASS THEM BY TRYING TO FIGURE OUT THE SECRETS TO EACH OF THEIR DISHES, BUT THE THREE STRUCK BACK BY COOKING DISHES THAT HE COULDN'T FIGURE OUT.

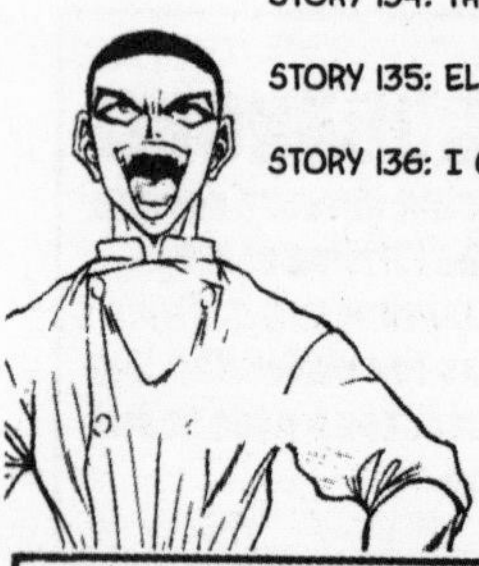

S
Y
N
O
P
S
I
S

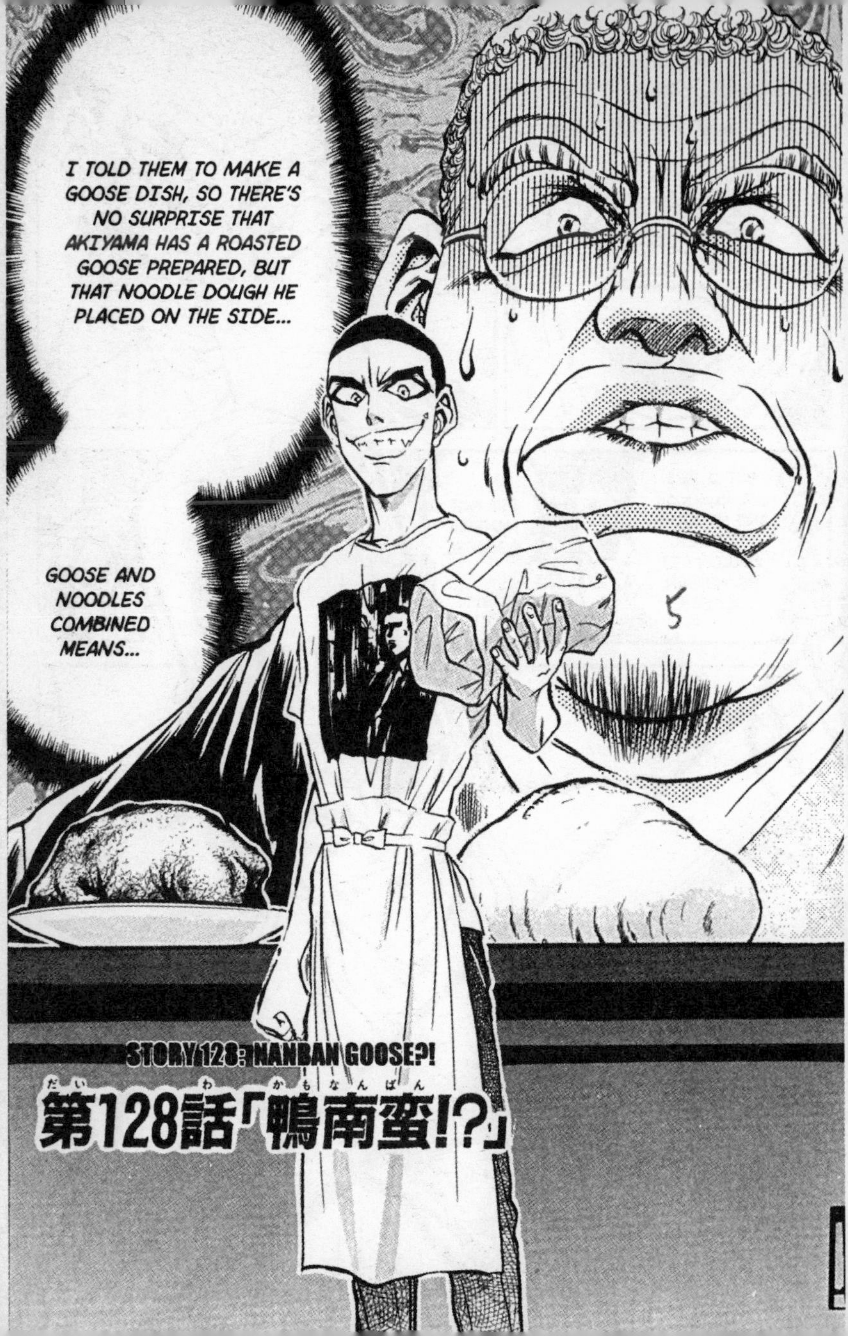
I TOLD THEM TO MAKE A GOOSE DISH, SO THERE'S NO SURPRISE THAT AKIYAMA HAS A ROASTED GOOSE PREPARED, BUT THAT NOODLE DOUGH HE PLACED ON THE SIDE...
GOOSE AND NOODLES COMBINED MEANS...
STORY 128: NANBAN GOOSE?!
第128話「鴨南蛮!?」

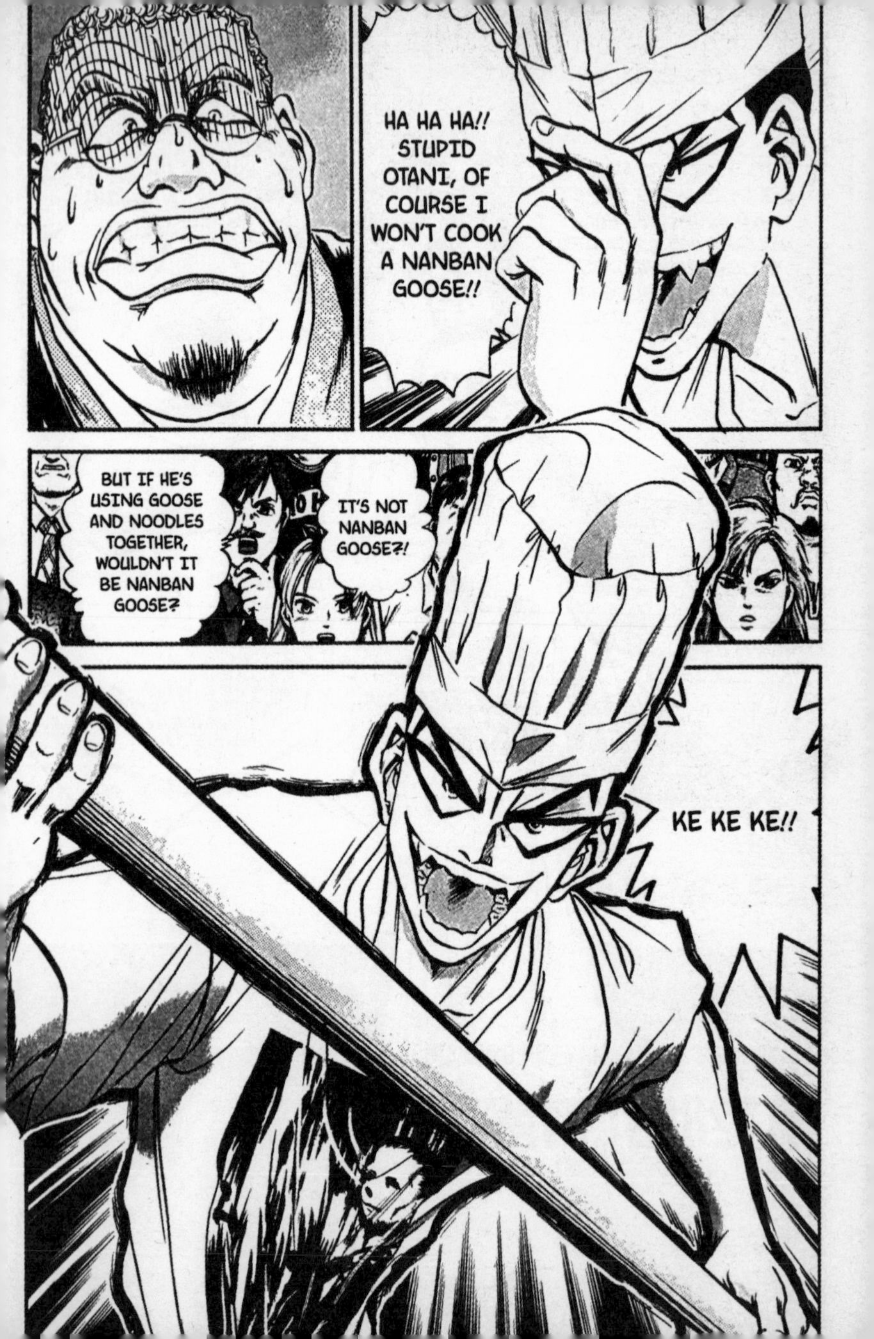
HA HA HA!! STUPID OTANI, OF COURSE I WON'T COOK A NANBAN GOOSE!!
IT'S NOT NANBAN GOOSE?!
BUT IF HE'S USING GOOSE AND NOODLES TOGETHER, WOULDN'T IT BE NANBAN GOOSE?
KE KE KE!!

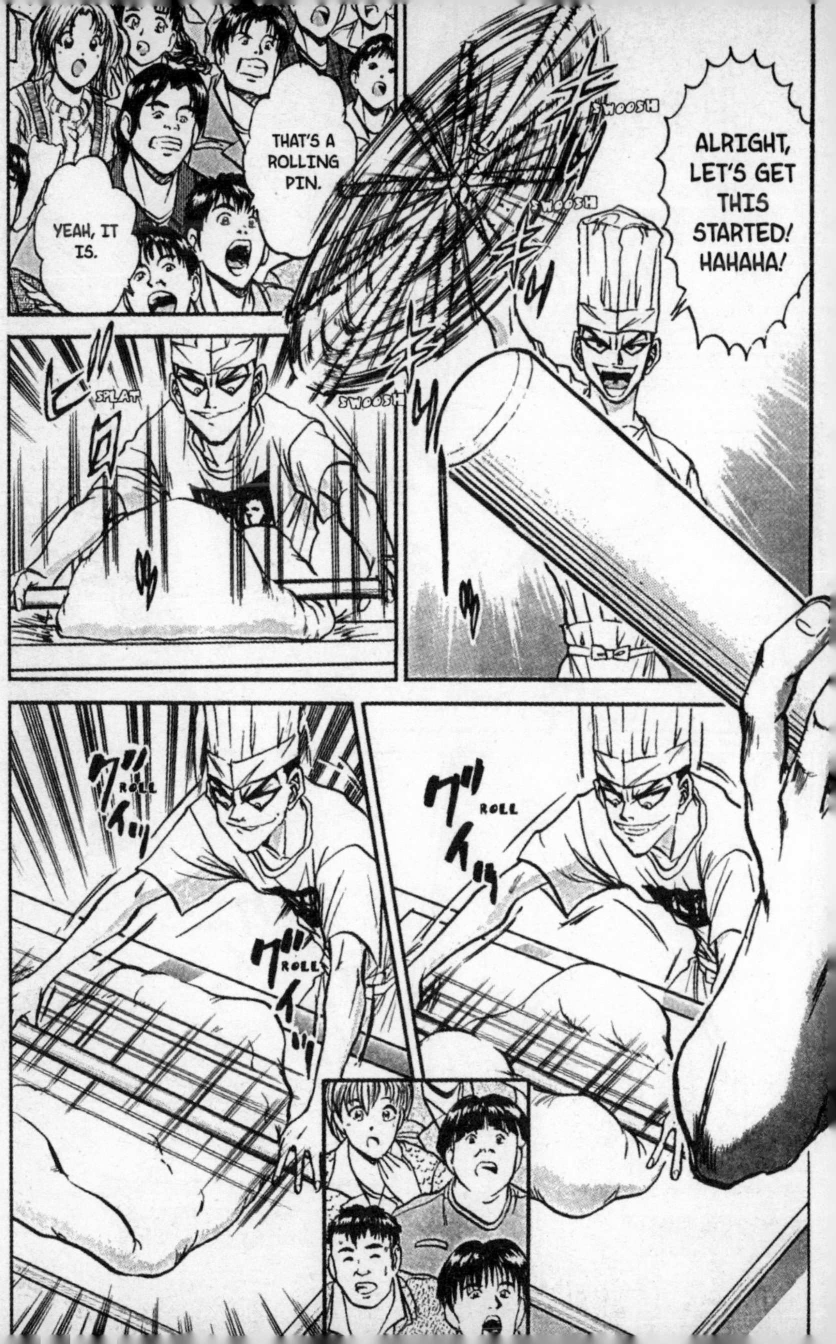
THAT'S A ROLLING PIN.
YEAH, IT IS.
SWOOSH
ALRIGHT, LET'S GET THIS STARTED! HAHAHA!
SWOOSH
SWOOSH
SPLAT
ROLL
ROLL
ROLL

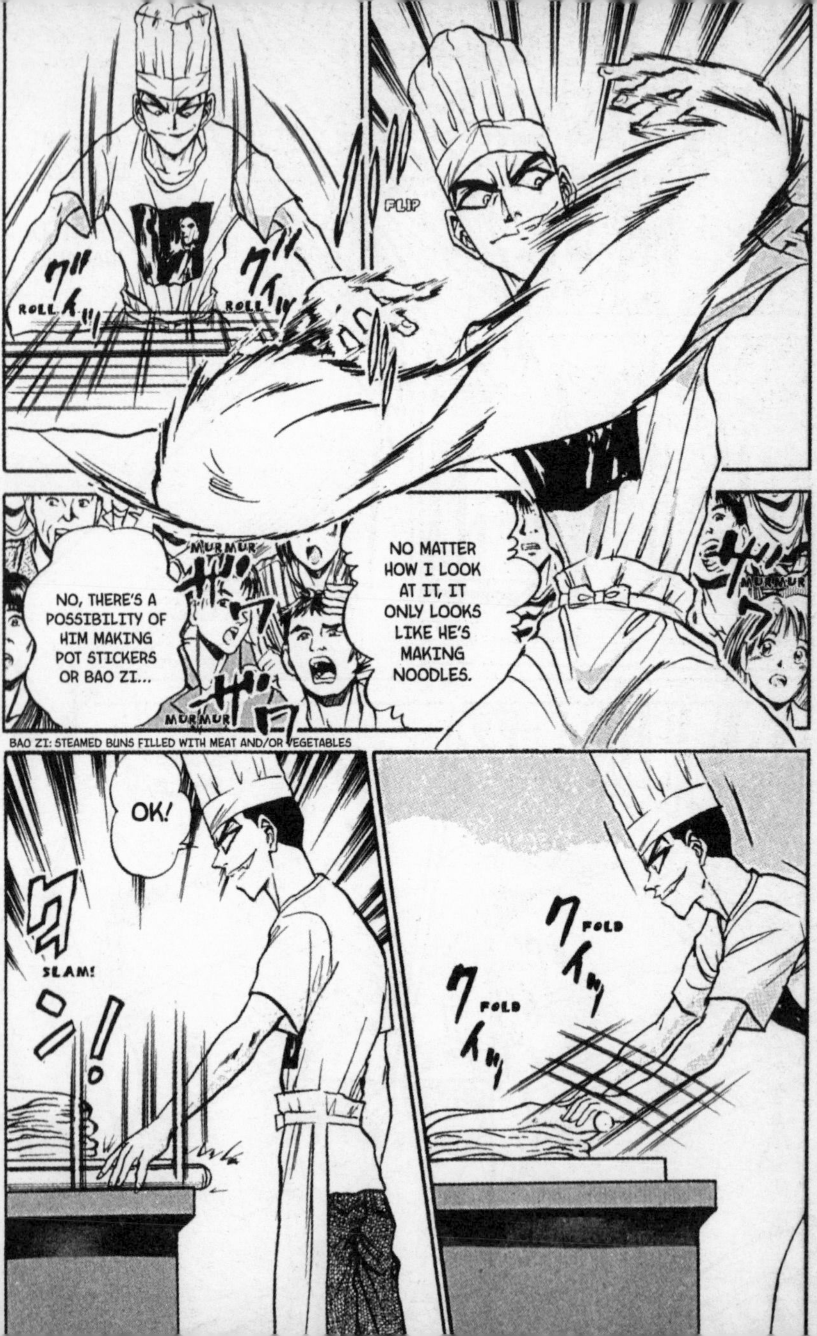
FLIP
ROLL
ROLL
MURMUR
NO MATTER HOW I LOOK AT IT, IT ONLY LOOKS LIKE HE'S MAKING NOODLES.
MURMUR
NO, THERE'S A POSSIBILITY OF HIM MAKING POT STICKERS OR BAO ZI...
MURMUR
FOLD
FOLD
OK!
SLAM!

BAO ZI: STEAMED BUNS FILLED WITH MEAT AND/OR VEGETABLES

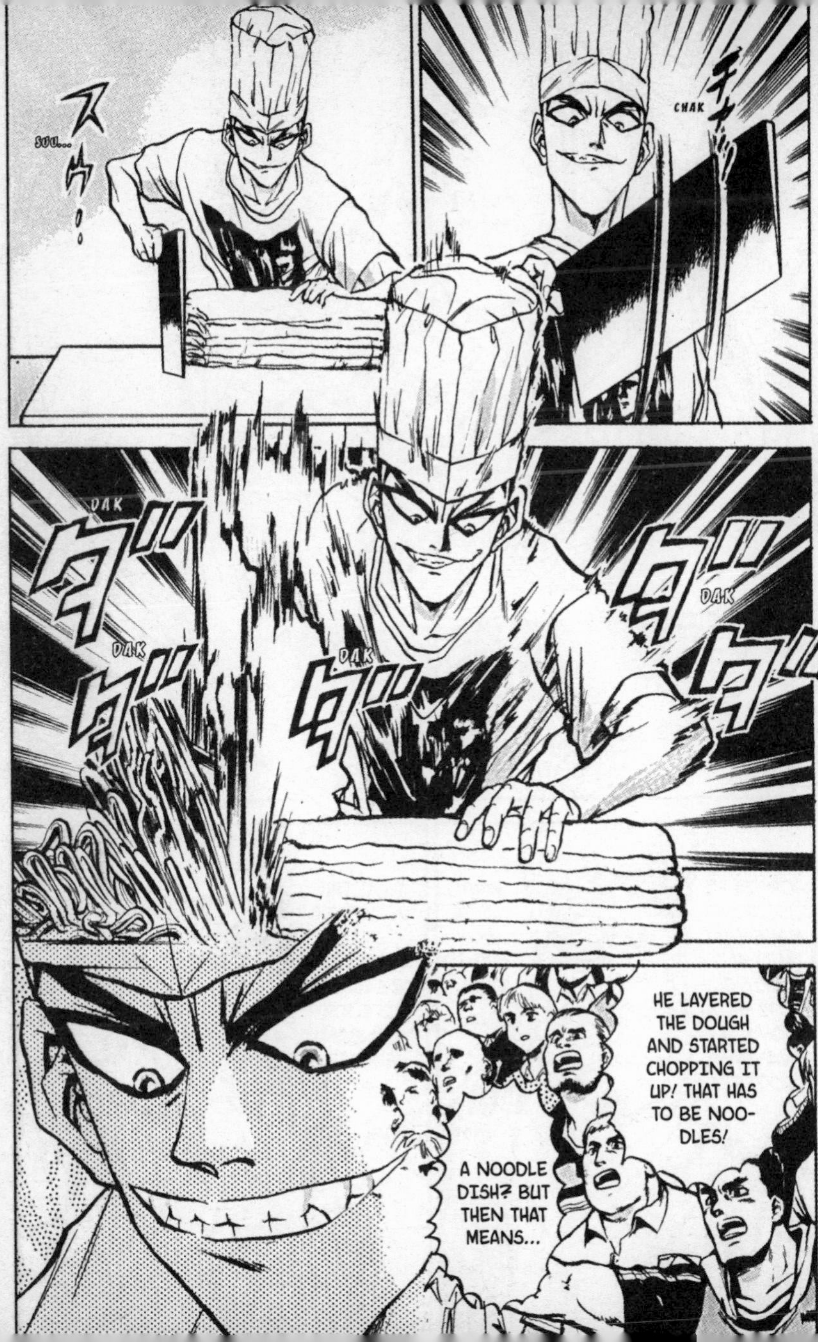
CHAK
SUU...
DAK
DAK
DAK
DAK
HE LAYERED THE DOUGH AND STARTED CHOPPING IT UP! THAT HAS TO BE NOO-DLES!
A NOODLE DISH? BUT THEN THAT MEANS...

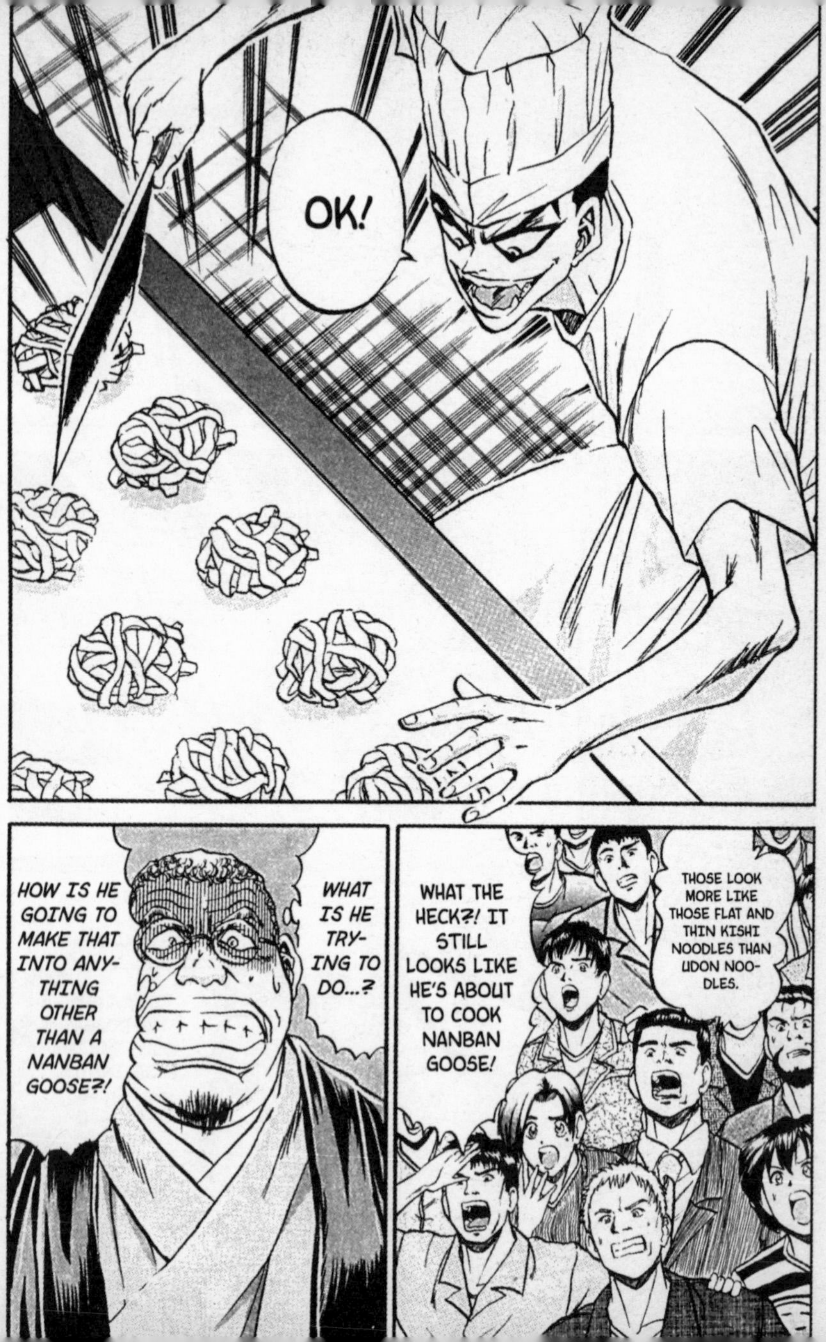
OK!
THOSE LOOK MORE LIKE THOSE FLAT AND THIN KISHI NOODLES THAN UDON NOODLES.
WHAT THE HECK?! IT STILL LOOKS LIKE HE'S ABOUT TO COOK NANBAN GOOSE!
WHAT IS HE TRYING TO DO...?
HOW IS HE GOING TO MAKE THAT INTO ANYTHING OTHER THAN A NANBAN GOOSE?!

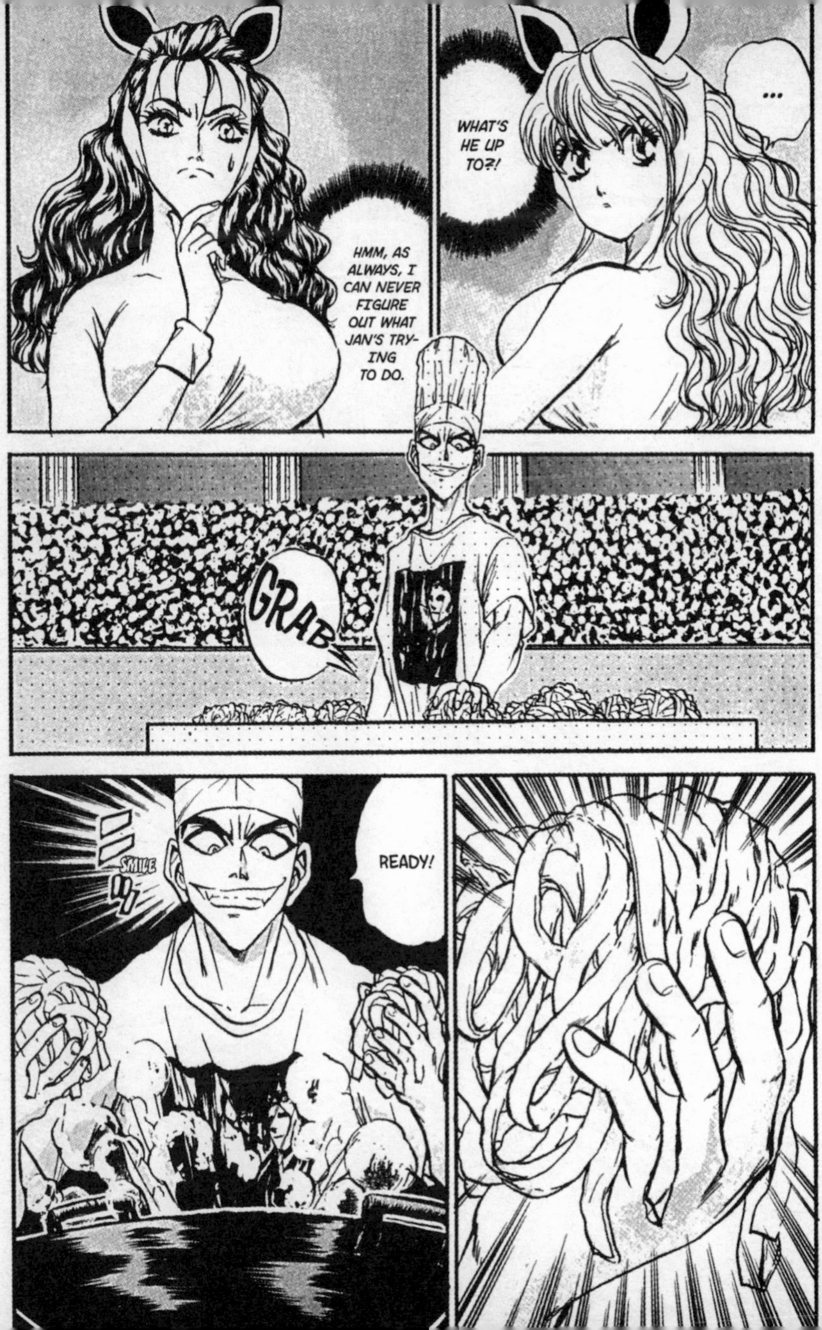
...
WHAT'S HE UP TO?!
HMM, AS ALWAYS, I CAN NEVER FIGURE OUT WHAT JAN'S TRY-ING TO DO.
GRAB
READY!
SMILE

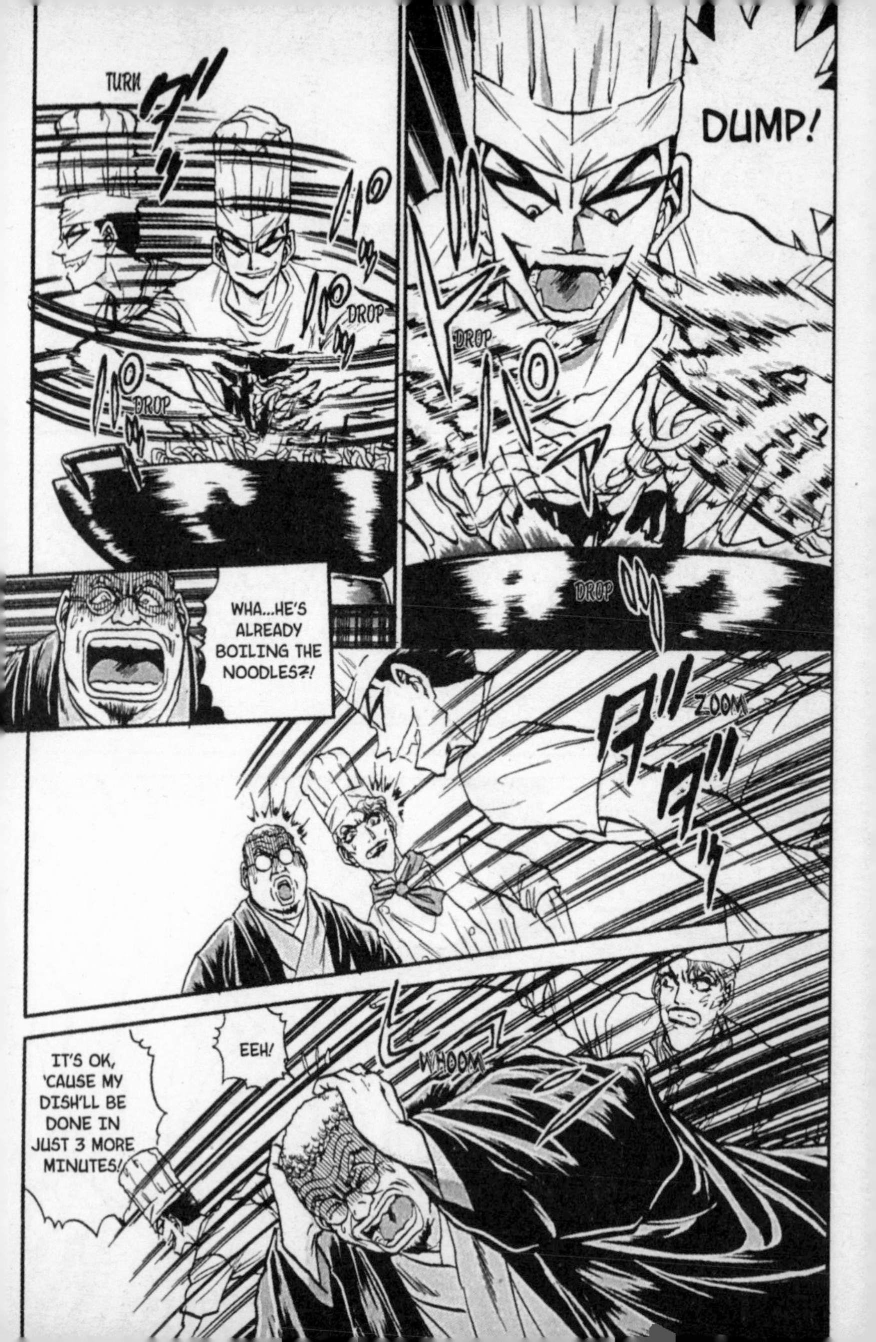
DUMP!
DROP
DROP
TURN
DROP
DROP
WHA...HE'S ALREADY BOILING THE NOODLES?!
ZOOM
EEH!
WHOOM
IT'S OK, 'CAUSE MY DISH'LL BE DONE IN JUST 3 MORE MINUTES!

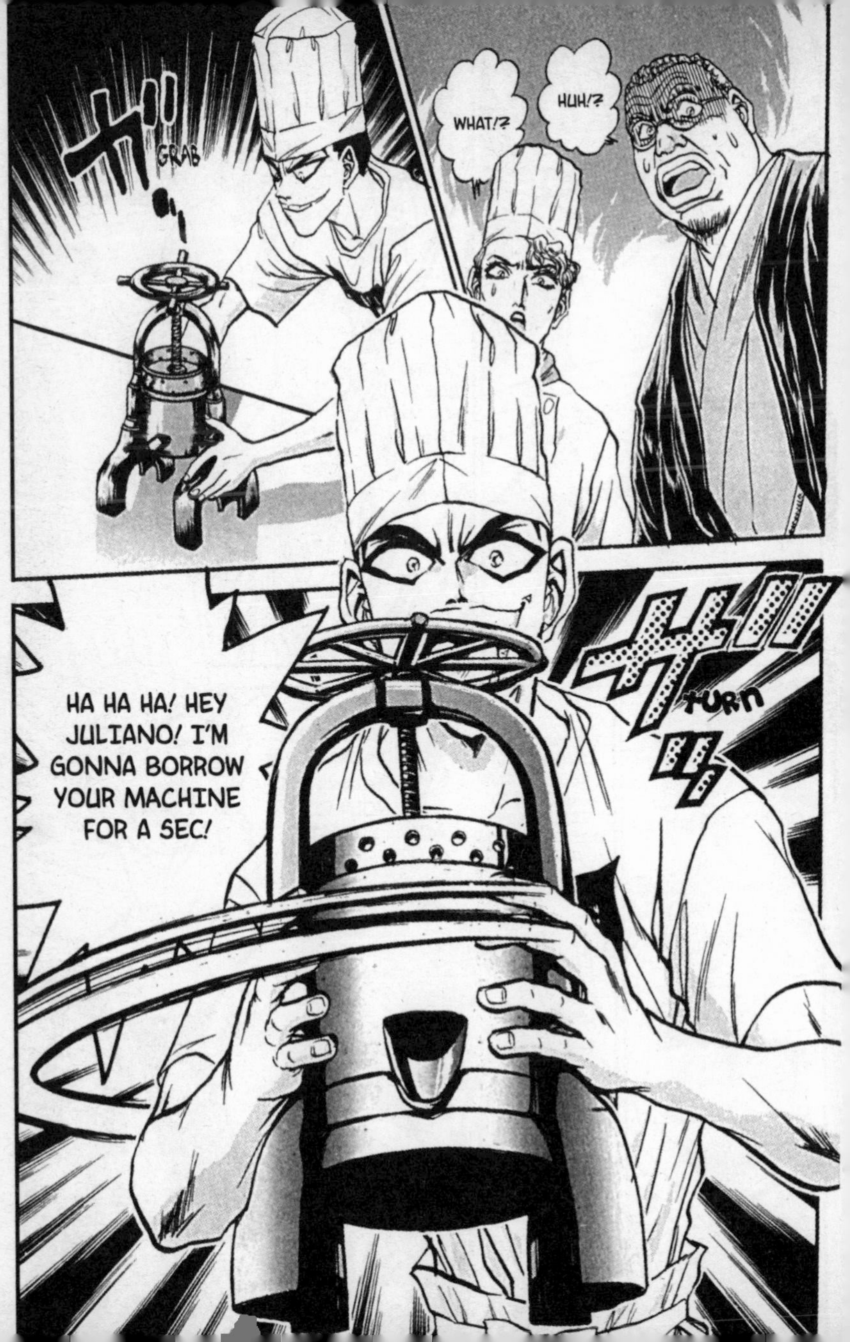
HUH!?
WHAT!?
GRAB
TURN
HA HA HA! HEY JULIANO! I'M GONNA BORROW YOUR MACHINE FOR A SEC!

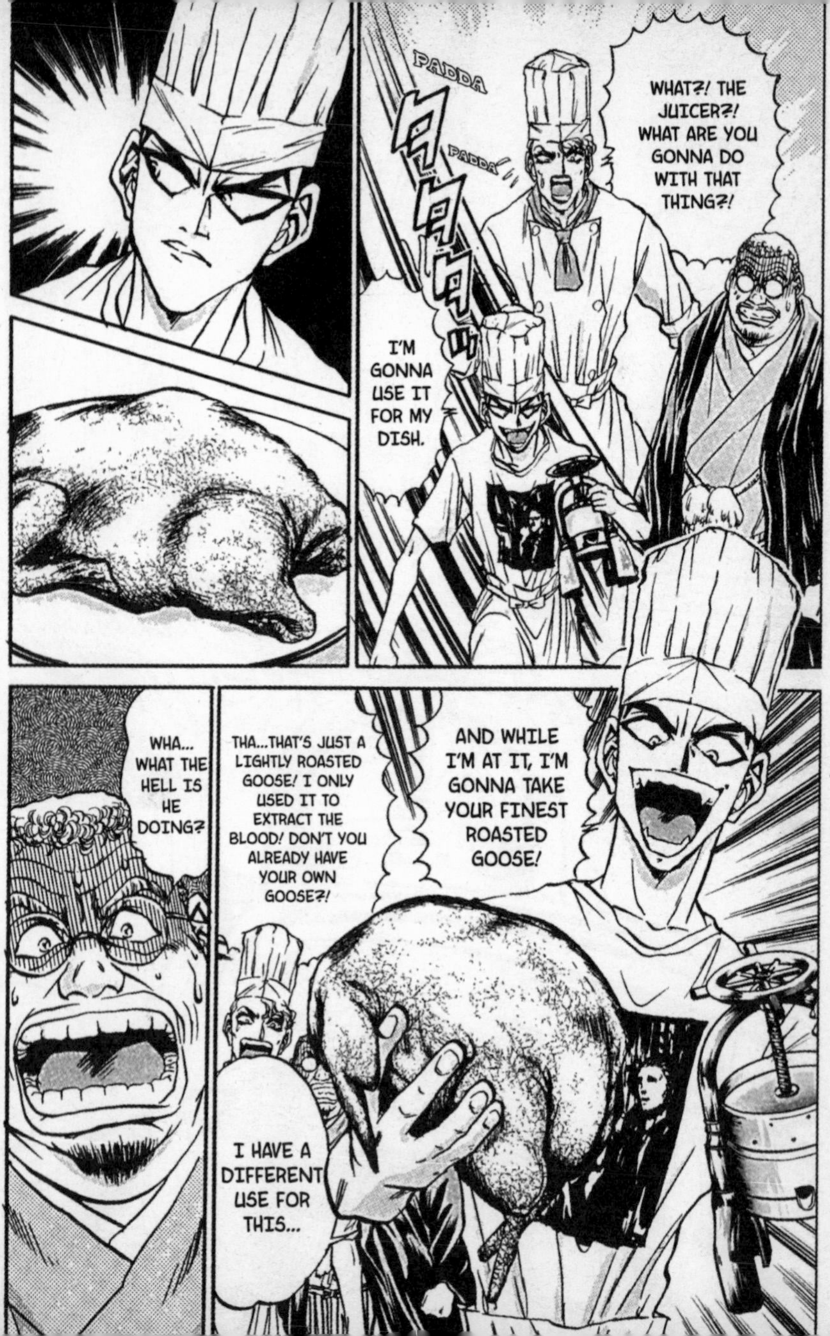
WHAT?! THE JUICER?! WHAT ARE YOU GONNA DO WITH THAT THING?!
PADDA
PADDA
I'M GONNA USE IT FOR MY DISH.
AND WHILE I'M AT IT, I'M GONNA TAKE YOUR FINEST ROASTED GOOSE!
THA...THAT'S JUST A LIGHTLY ROASTED GOOSE! I ONLY USED IT TO EXTRACT THE BLOOD! DON'T YOU ALREADY HAVE YOUR OWN GOOSE?!
I HAVE A DIFFERENT USE FOR THIS...
WHA... WHAT THE HELL IS HE DOING?

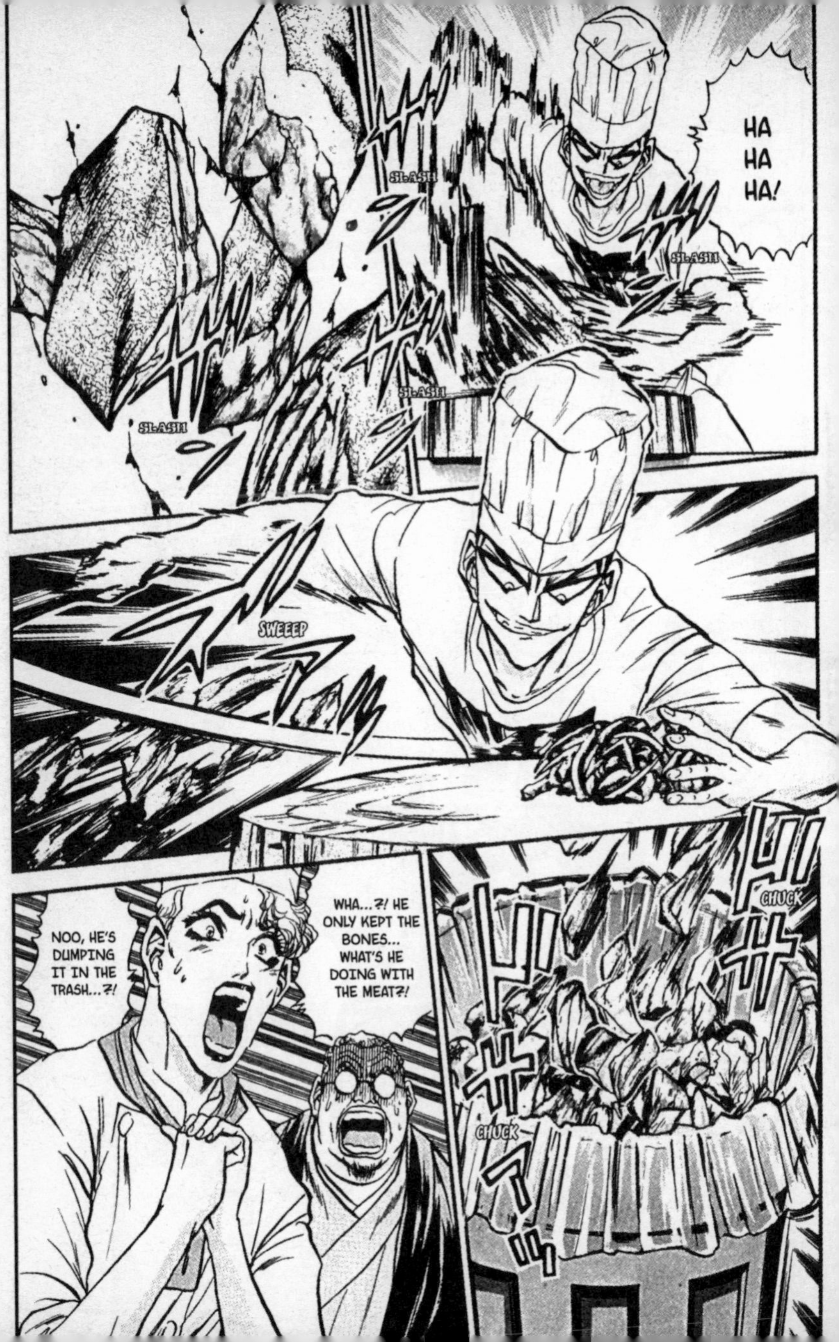
HA HA HA!
SLASH
SLASH
SLASH
SLASH
SWEEEP
CHUCK
CHUCK
WHA...?! HE ONLY KEPT THE BONES... WHAT'S HE DOING WITH THE MEAT?!
NOO, HE'S DUMPING IT IN THE TRASH...?!

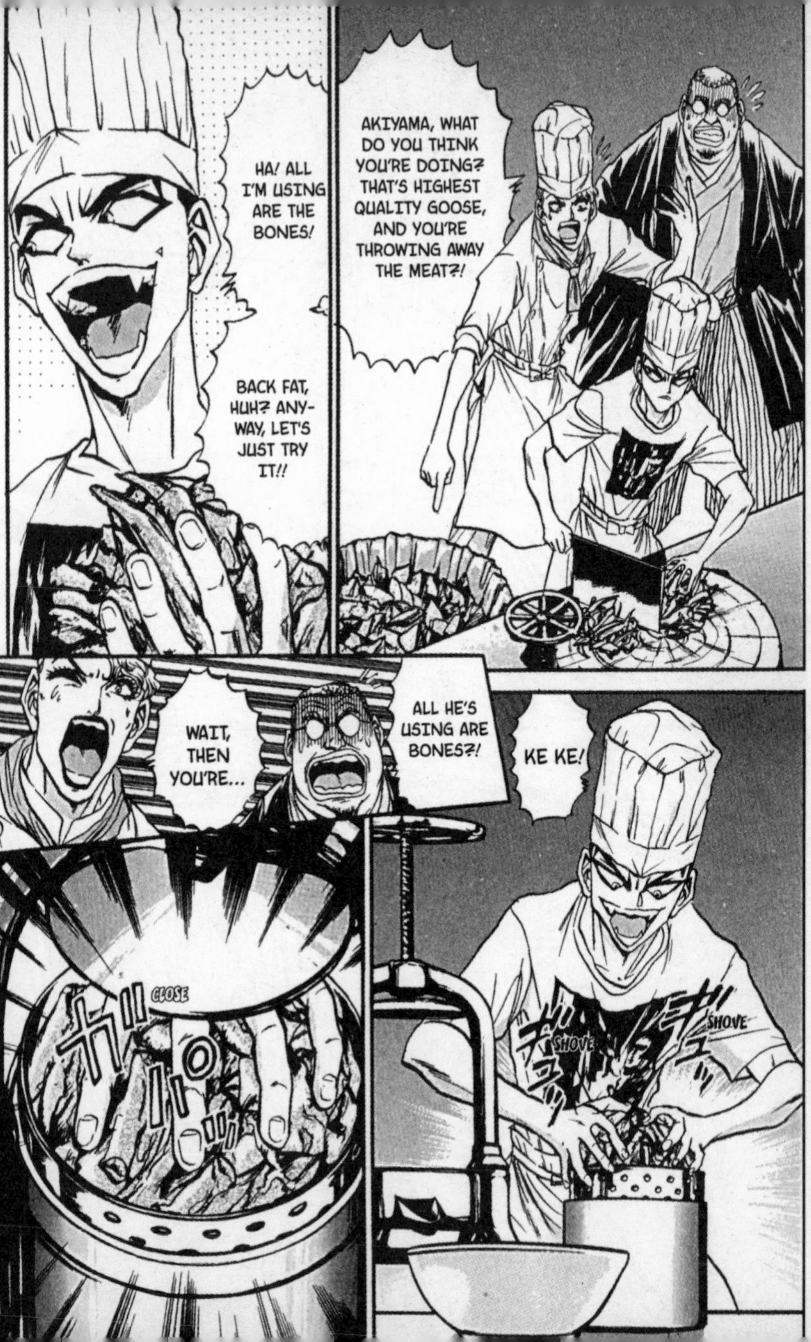
AKIYAMA, WHAT DO YOU THINK YOU'RE DOING? THAT'S HIGHEST QUALITY GOOSE, AND YOU'RE THROWING AWAY THE MEAT?!
HA! ALL I'M USING ARE THE BONES!
BACK FAT, HUH? ANY-WAY, LET'S JUST TRY IT!!
KE KE!
SHOVE
SHOVE
ALL HE'S USING ARE BONES?!
WAIT, THEN YOU'RE...
CLOSE

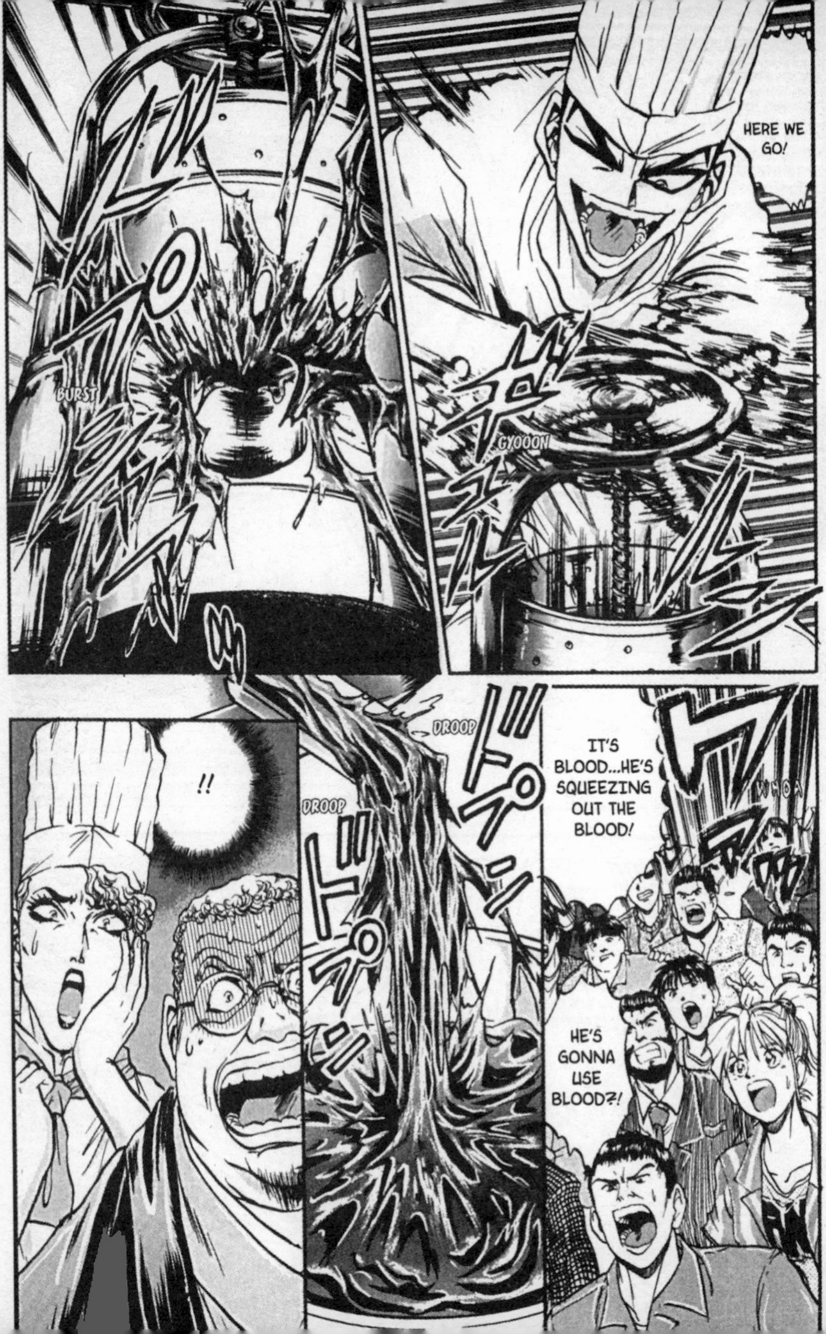
HERE WE GO!
GYOOON
BURST
WHOA
IT'S BLOOD...HE'S SQUEEZING OUT THE BLOOD!
HE'S GONNA USE BLOOD?!
DROOP
DROOP
!!

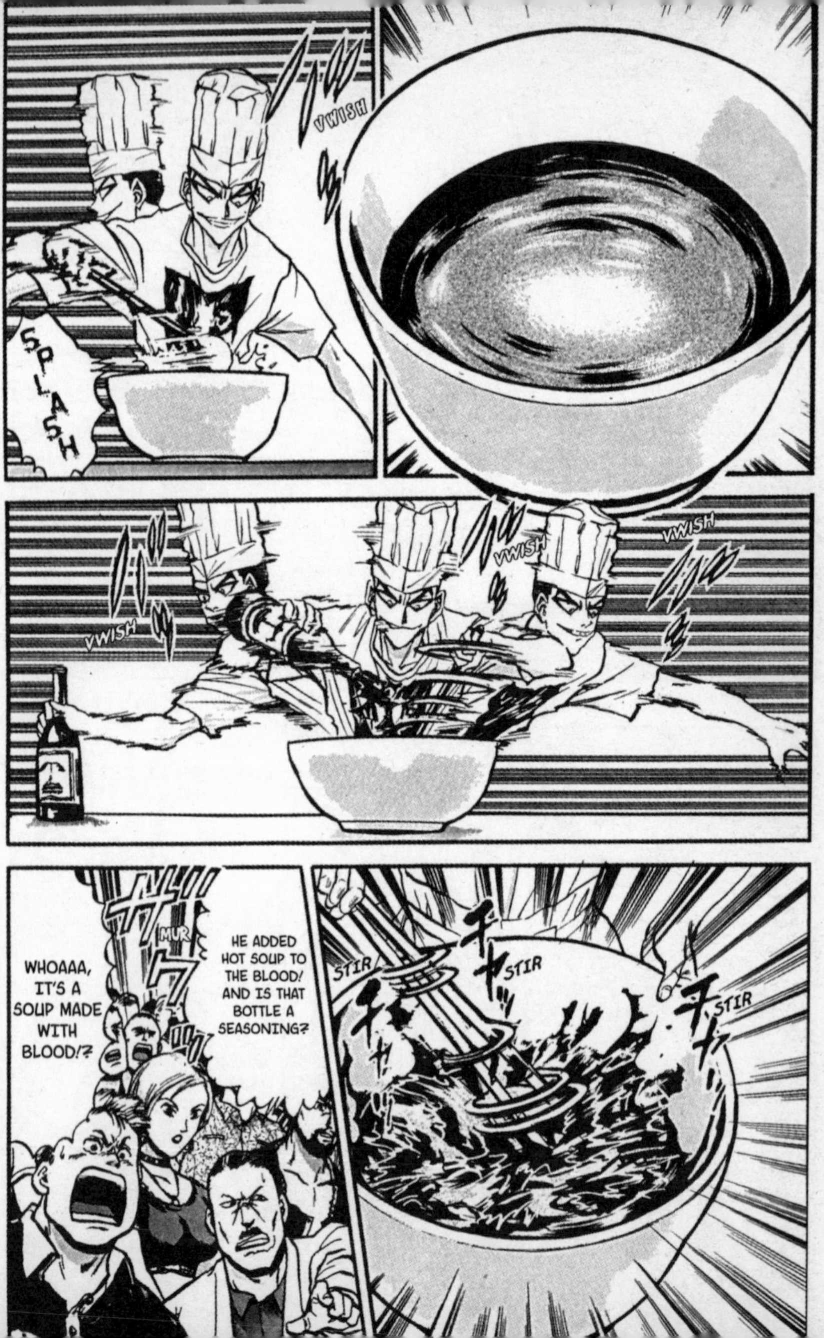
VWISH
SPLASH
VWISH
VWISH
VWISH
STIR
STIR
STIR
HE ADDED HOT SOUP TO THE BLOOD! AND IS THAT BOTTLE A SEASONING!?
MUR
WHOAAA, IT'S A SOUP MADE WITH BLOOD!?

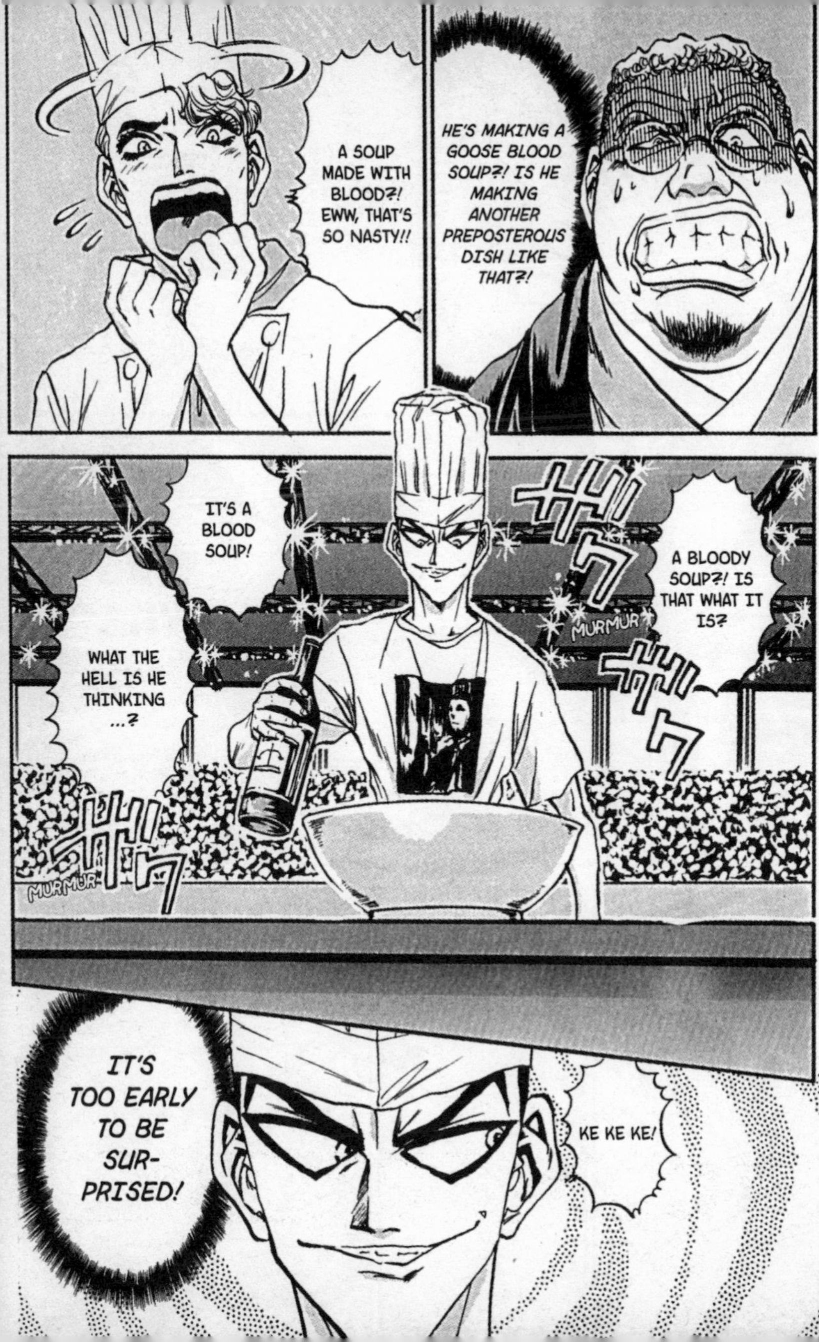
HE'S MAKING A GOOSE BLOOD SOUP?! IS HE MAKING ANOTHER PREPOSTEROUS DISH LIKE THAT?!
A SOUP MADE WITH BLOOD?! EWW, THAT'S SO NASTY!!
A BLOODY SOUP?! IS THAT WHAT IT IS?
MURMUR
IT'S A BLOOD SOUP!
WHAT THE HELL IS HE THINKING ...?
MURMUR
KE KE KE!
IT'S TOO EARLY TO BE SUR-PRISED!

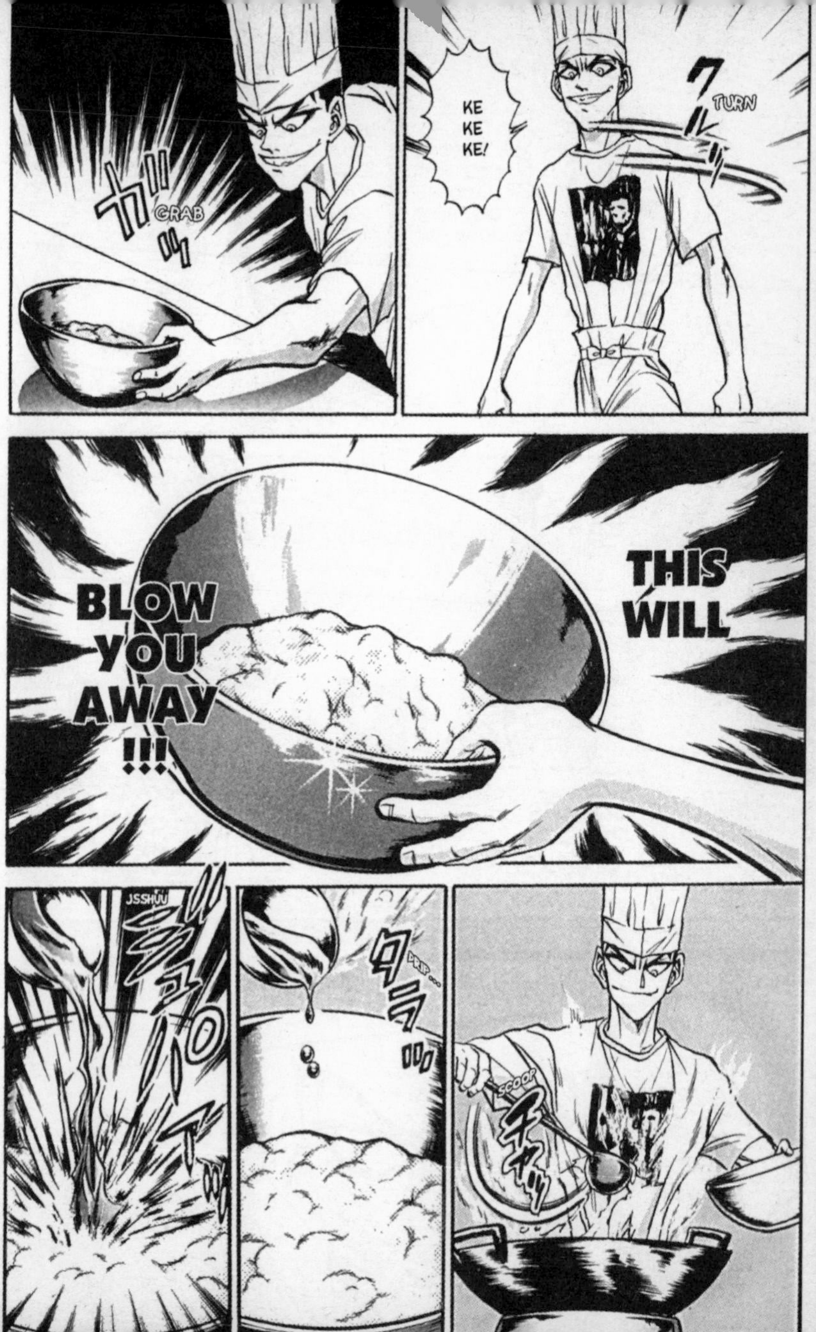
KE KE KE!
TURN
GRAB
THIS WILL
BLOW YOU AWAY!!!
SCOOP
DRIP...
JSSHUU

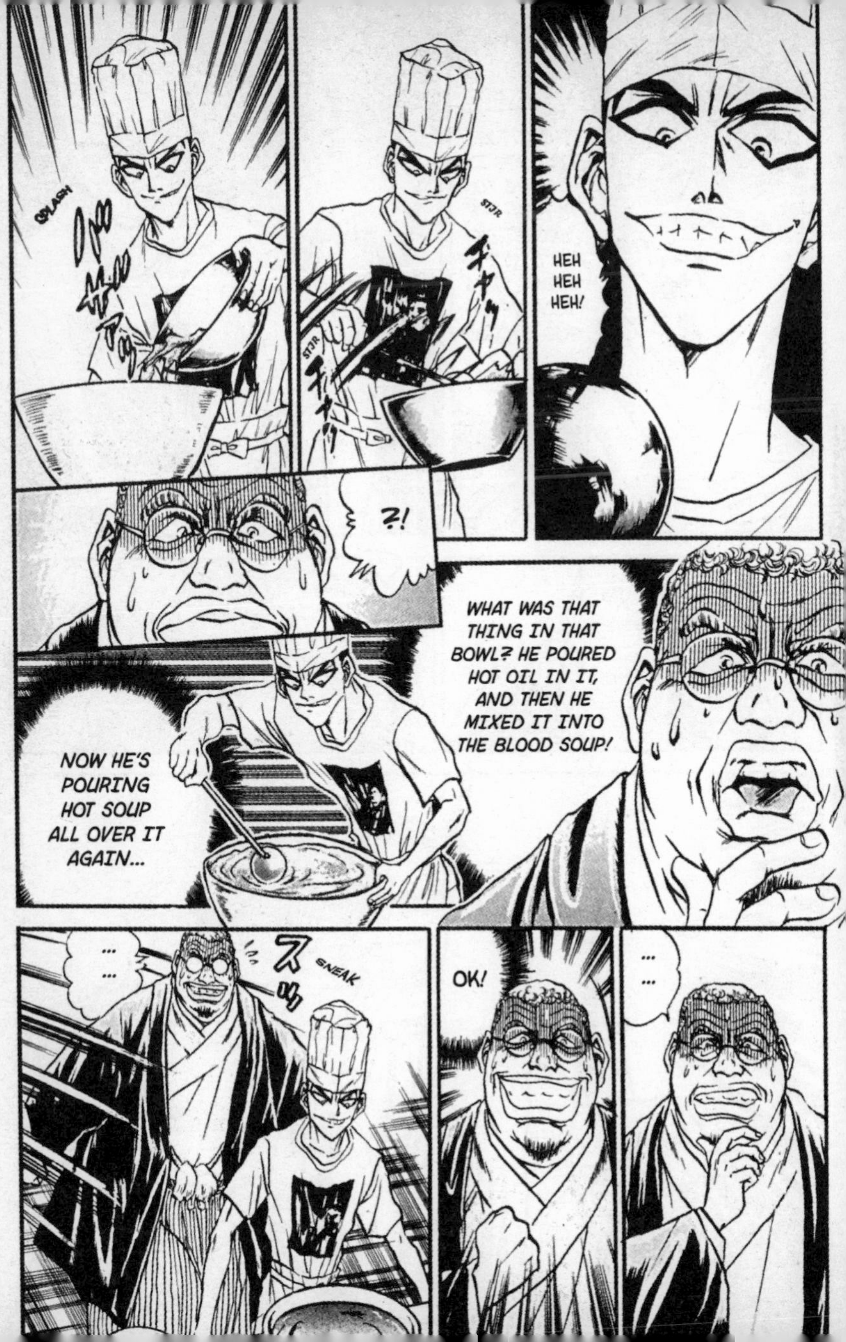
HEH HEH HEH!
STIR
STIR
SPLASH
?!
WHAT WAS THAT THING IN THAT BOWL? HE POURED HOT OIL IN IT, AND THEN HE MIXED IT INTO THE BLOOD SOUP!
NOW HE'S POURING HOT SOUP ALL OVER IT AGAIN...
... ...
OK!
... ...
SNEAK

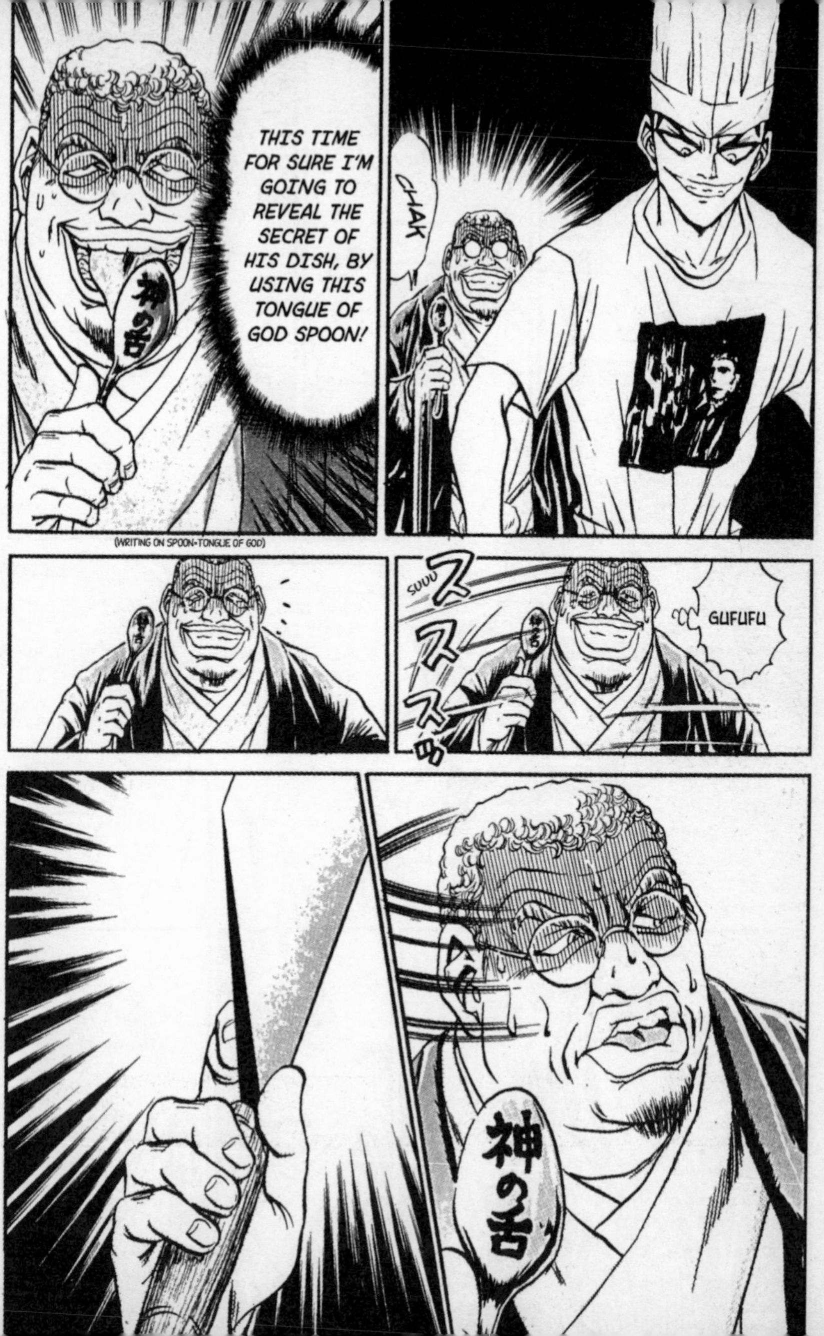
CHAK
THIS TIME FOR SURE I'M GOING TO REVEAL THE SECRET OF HIS DISH, BY USING THIS TONGUE OF GOD SPOON!
神の舌
(WRITING ON SPOON=TONGUE OF GOD)
GUFUFU
SUUU
神の舌

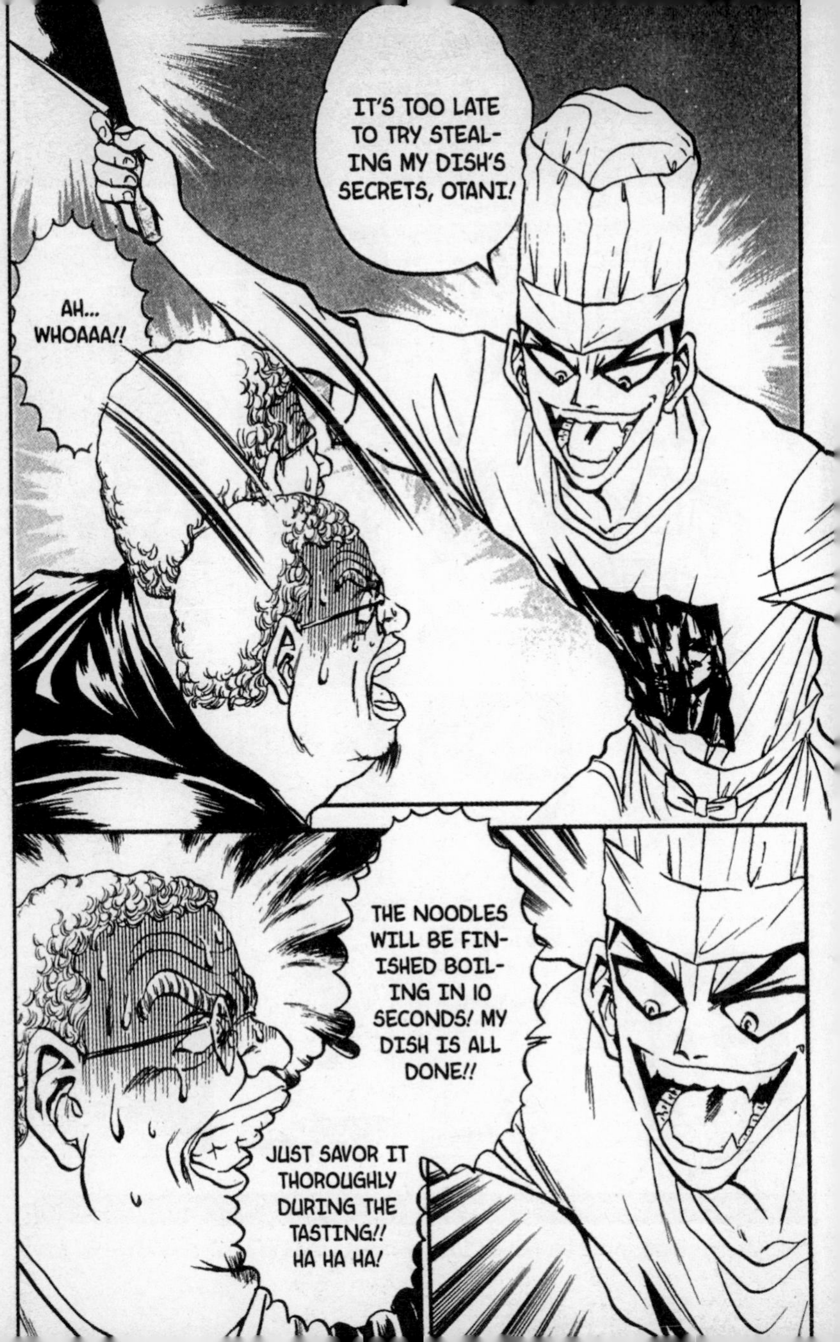
IT'S TOO LATE TO TRY STEAL-ING MY DISH'S SECRETS, OTANI!
AH... WHOAAA!!
THE NOODLES WILL BE FIN-ISHED BOIL-ING IN 10 SECONDS! MY DISH IS ALL DONE!!
JUST SAVOR IT THOROUGHLY DURING THE TASTING!! HA HA HA!

FAN ART EXHIBITION PARTY!!

PRESENTING DRAWINGS SUBMITTED BY THE FANS TO THE READERS PAGE IN *WEEKLY SHONEN CHAMPION!!*

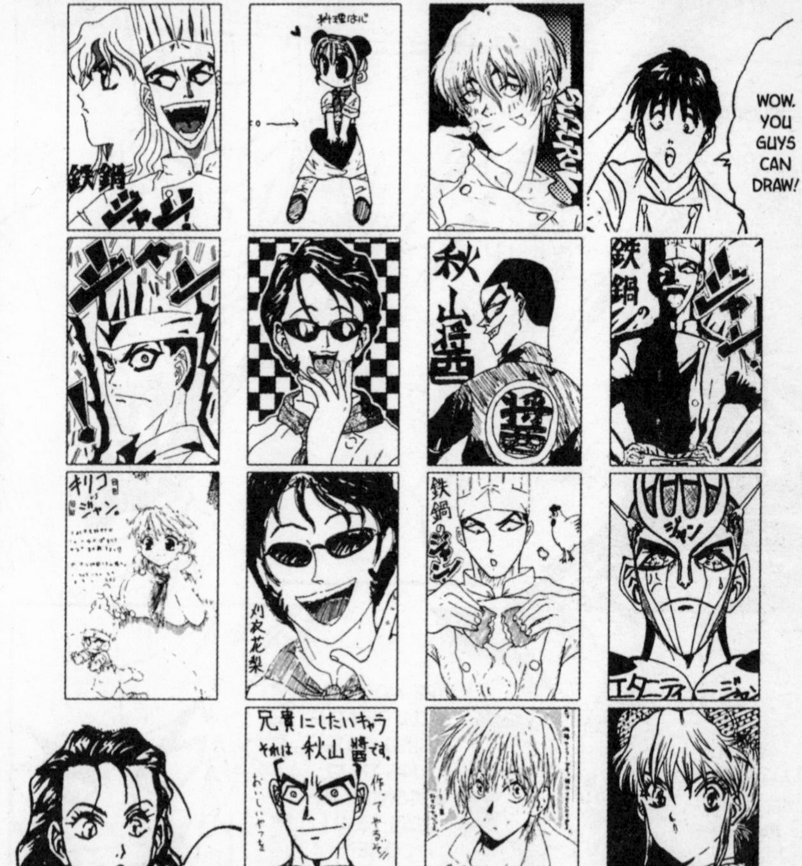
WOW. YOU GUYS CAN DRAW!
鉄鍋のジャン
秋山醤
刈衣花梨
兄貴にしたいキャラ
それは秋山醤です。
毎日おいしい料理を作ってくれそう。
YUP, THEY SURE CAN!

MR. SAIJO IS HAPPY TO SEE EVERYONE'S ILLUSTRATIONS. KUDOS TO SAIJO SENSEI'S WORK TOO!

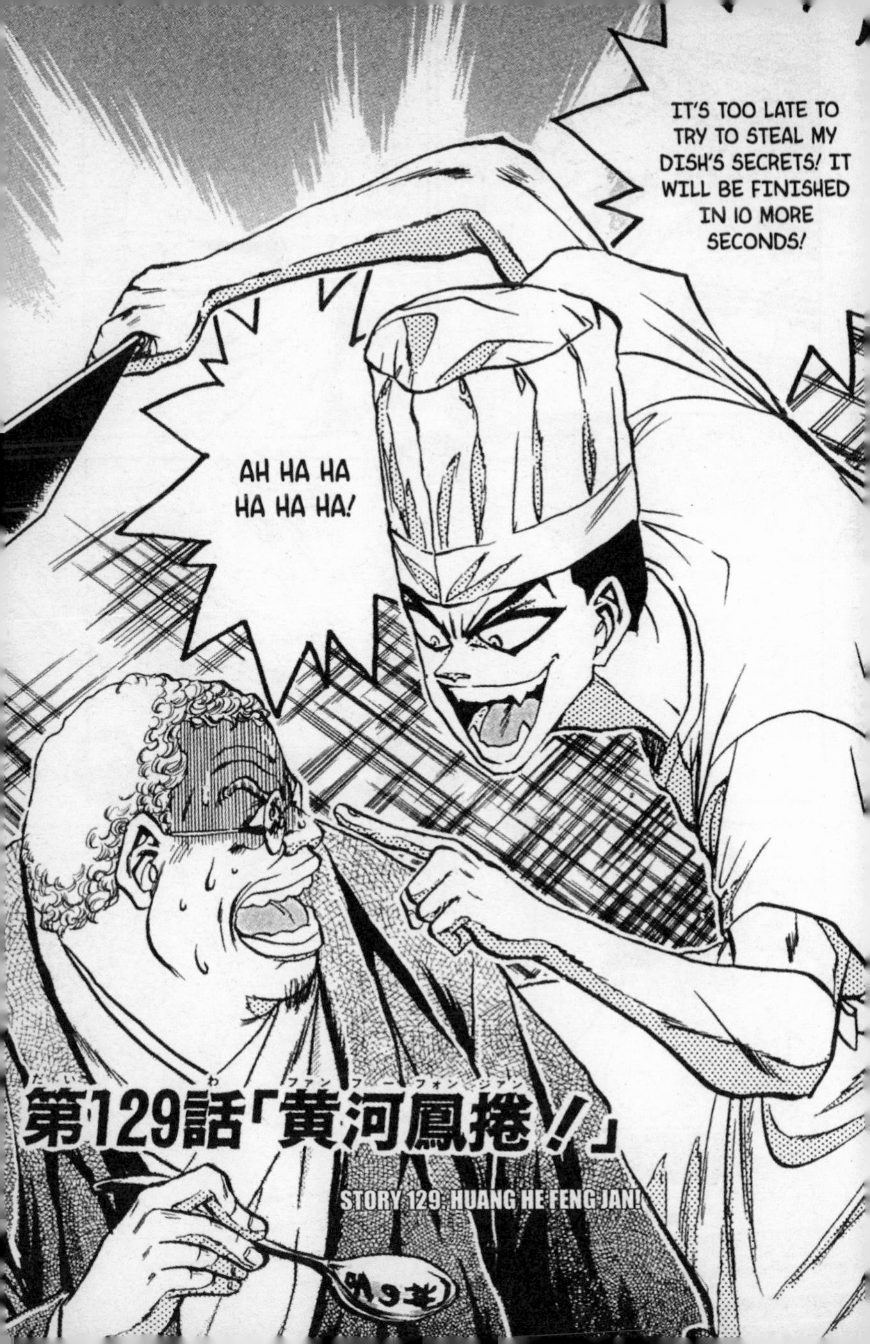
IT'S TOO LATE TO TRY TO STEAL MY DISH'S SECRETS! IT WILL BE FINISHED IN 10 MORE SECONDS!
AH HA HA HA HA HA!
第129話「黄河鳳捲！」
STORY 129: HUANG HE FENG JAN!

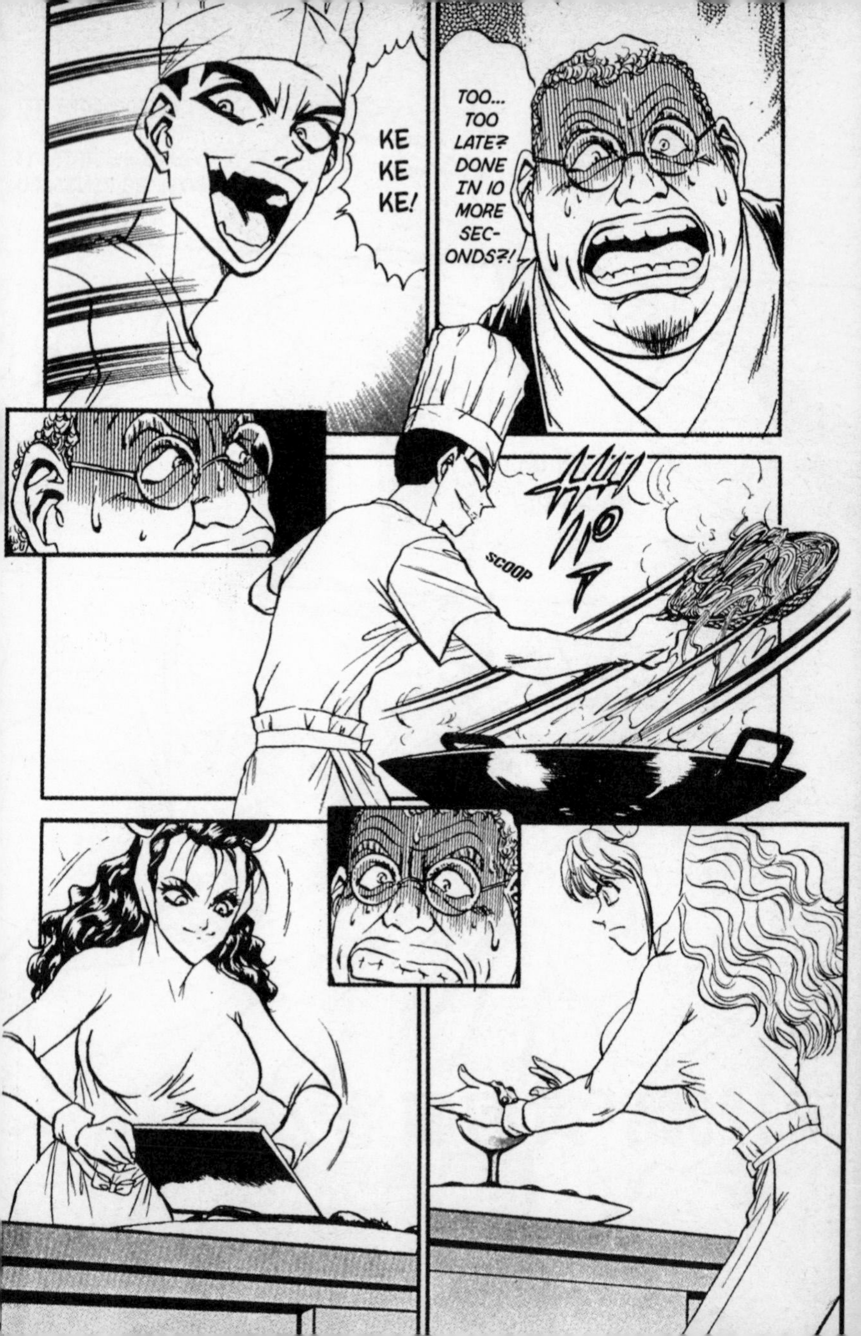
TOO... TOO LATE? DONE IN 10 MORE SEC- ONDS?!
KE KE KE!
SCOOP

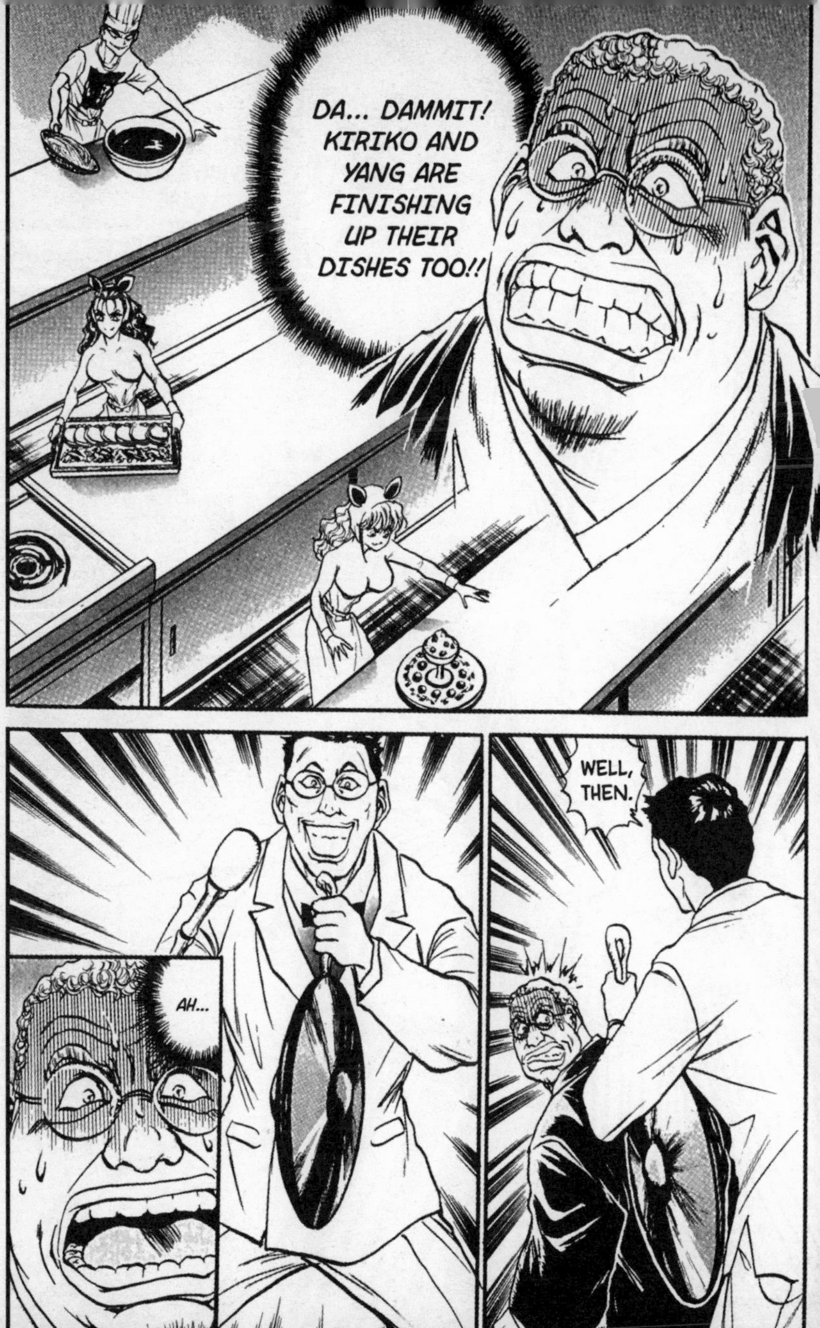
DA... DAMMIT! KIRIKO AND YANG ARE FINISHING UP THEIR DISHES TOO!!
WELL, THEN.
AH...

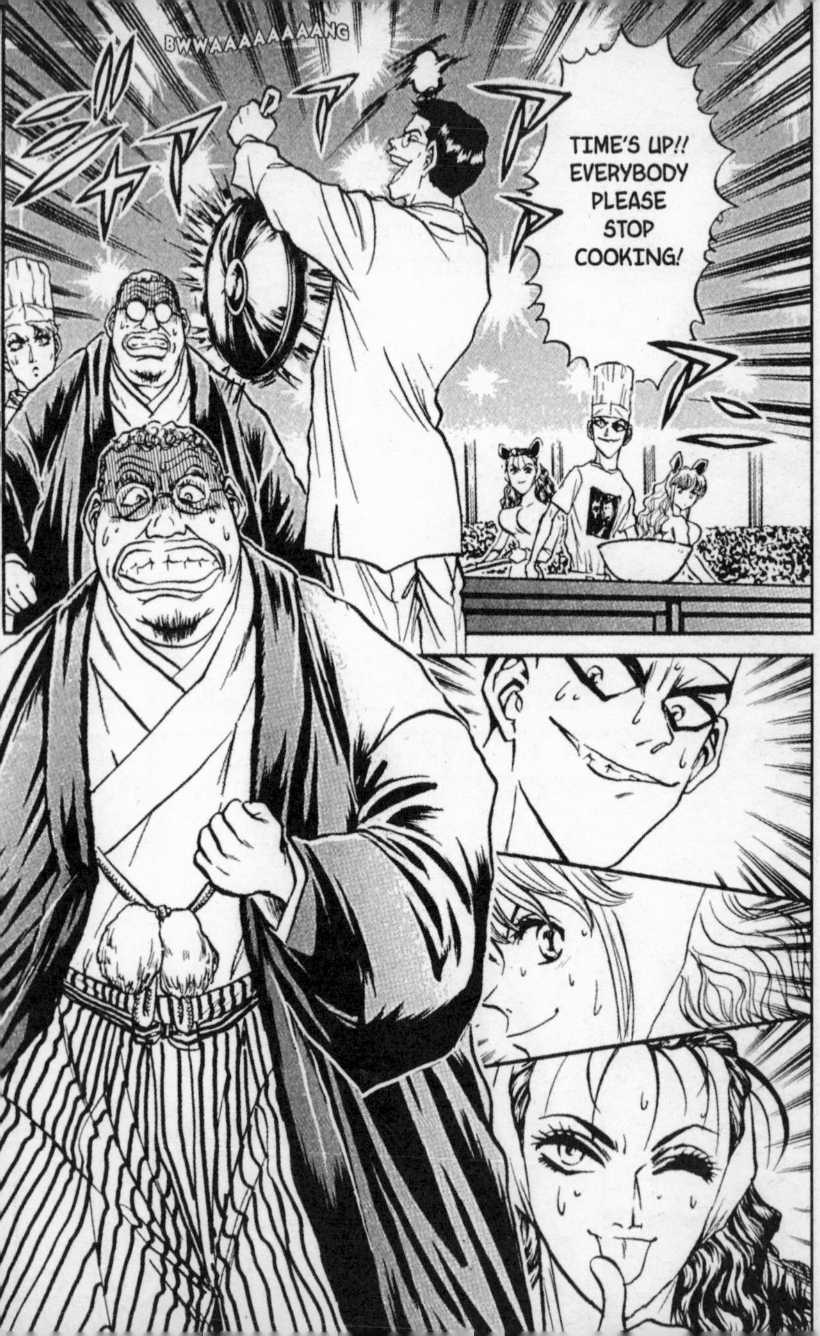
BWWAAAAAAAANG
TIME'S UP!! EVERYBODY PLEASE STOP COOKING!

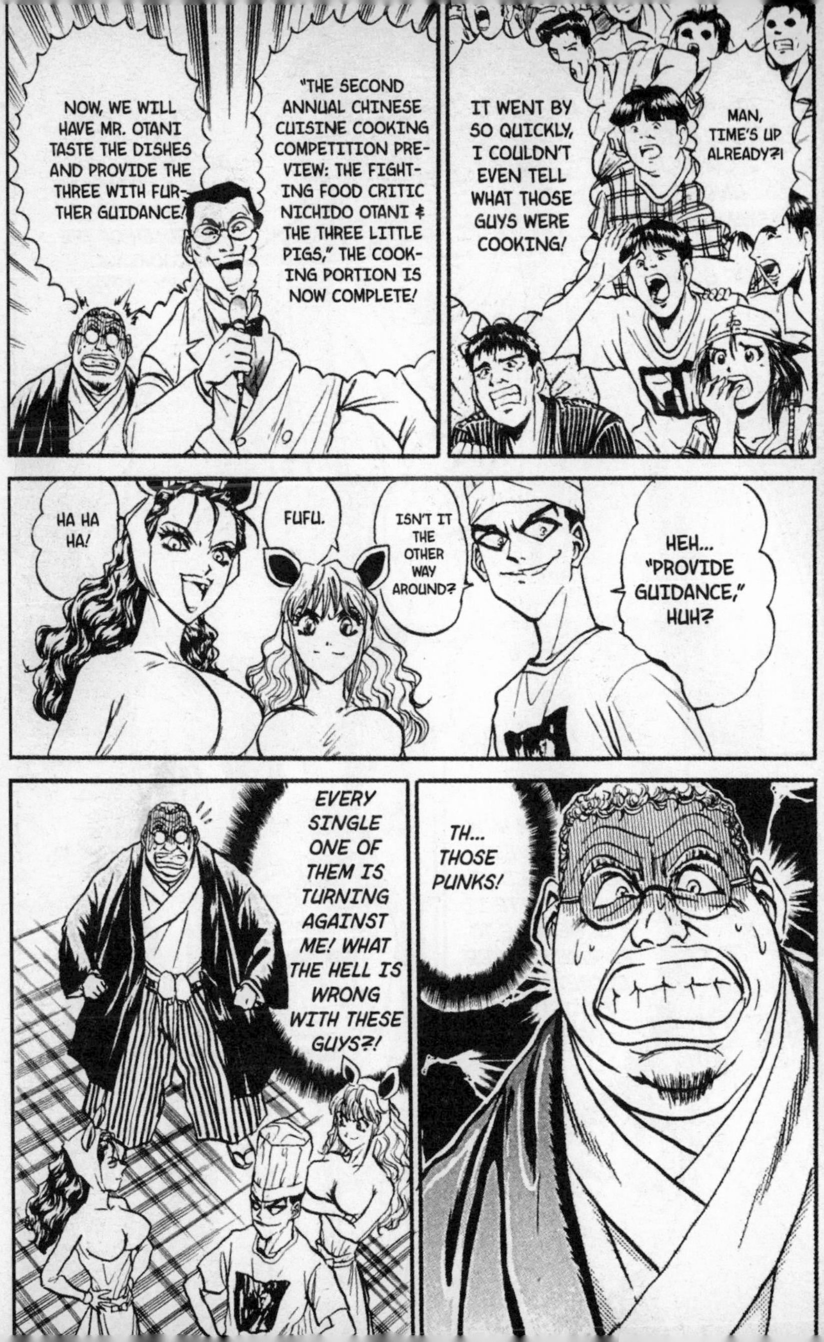
MAN, TIME'S UP ALREADY?!
IT WENT BY SO QUICKLY, I COULDN'T EVEN TELL WHAT THOSE GUYS WERE COOKING!
"THE SECOND ANNUAL CHINESE CUISINE COOKING COMPETITION PREVIEW: THE FIGHTING FOOD CRITIC NICHIDO OTANI & THE THREE LITTLE PIGS," THE COOKING PORTION IS NOW COMPLETE!
NOW, WE WILL HAVE MR. OTANI TASTE THE DISHES AND PROVIDE THE THREE WITH FURTHER GUIDANCE!
HEH... "PROVIDE GUIDANCE," HUH?
ISN'T IT THE OTHER WAY AROUND?
FUFU.
HA HA HA!
TH... THOSE PUNKS!
EVERY SINGLE ONE OF THEM IS TURNING AGAINST ME! WHAT THE HELL IS WRONG WITH THESE GUYS?!

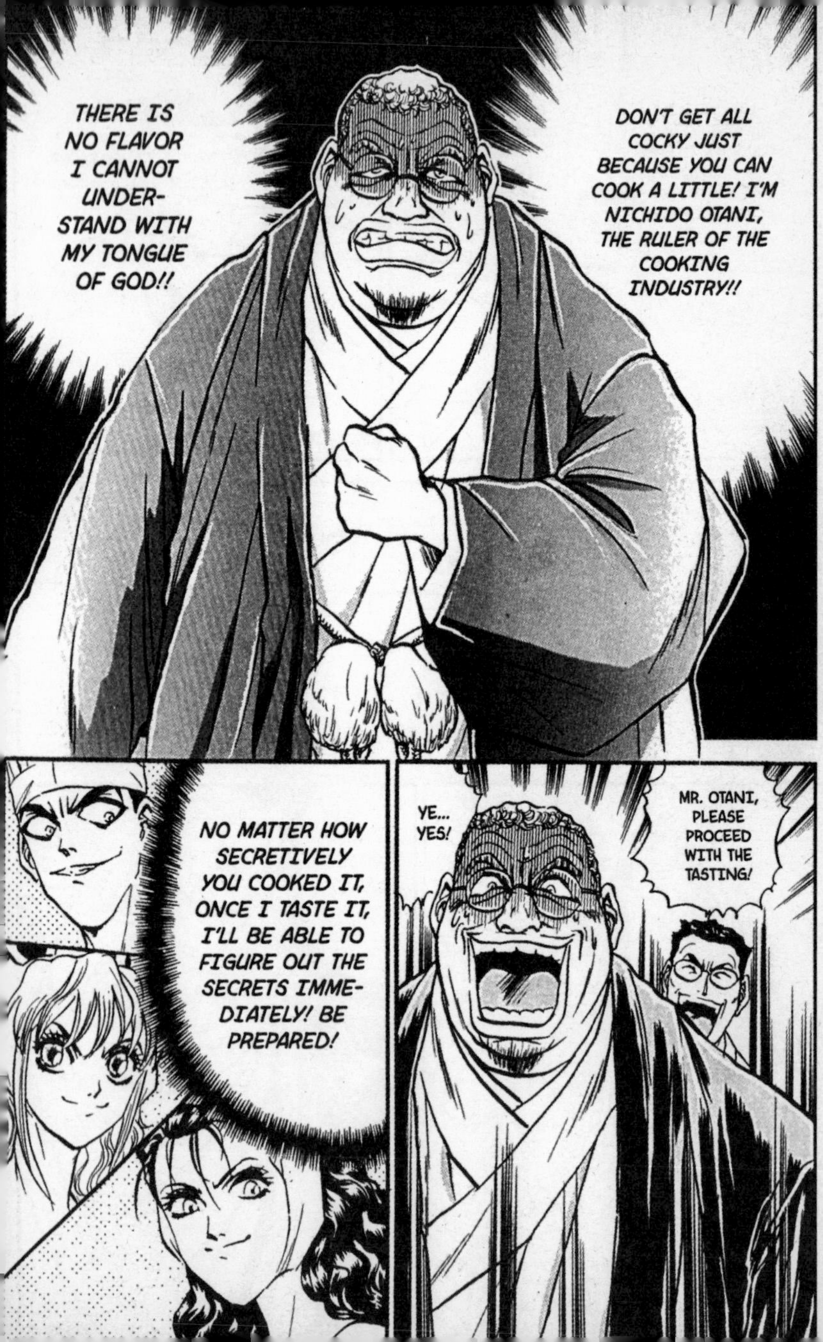
DON'T GET ALL COCKY JUST BECAUSE YOU CAN COOK A LITTLE! I'M NICHIDO OTANI, THE RULER OF THE COOKING INDUSTRY!!
THERE IS NO FLAVOR I CANNOT UNDER-STAND WITH MY TONGUE OF GOD!!
MR. OTANI, PLEASE PROCEED WITH THE TASTING!
YE... YES!
NO MATTER HOW SECRETIVELY YOU COOKED IT, ONCE I TASTE IT, I'LL BE ABLE TO FIGURE OUT THE SECRETS IMME-DIATELY! BE PREPARED!

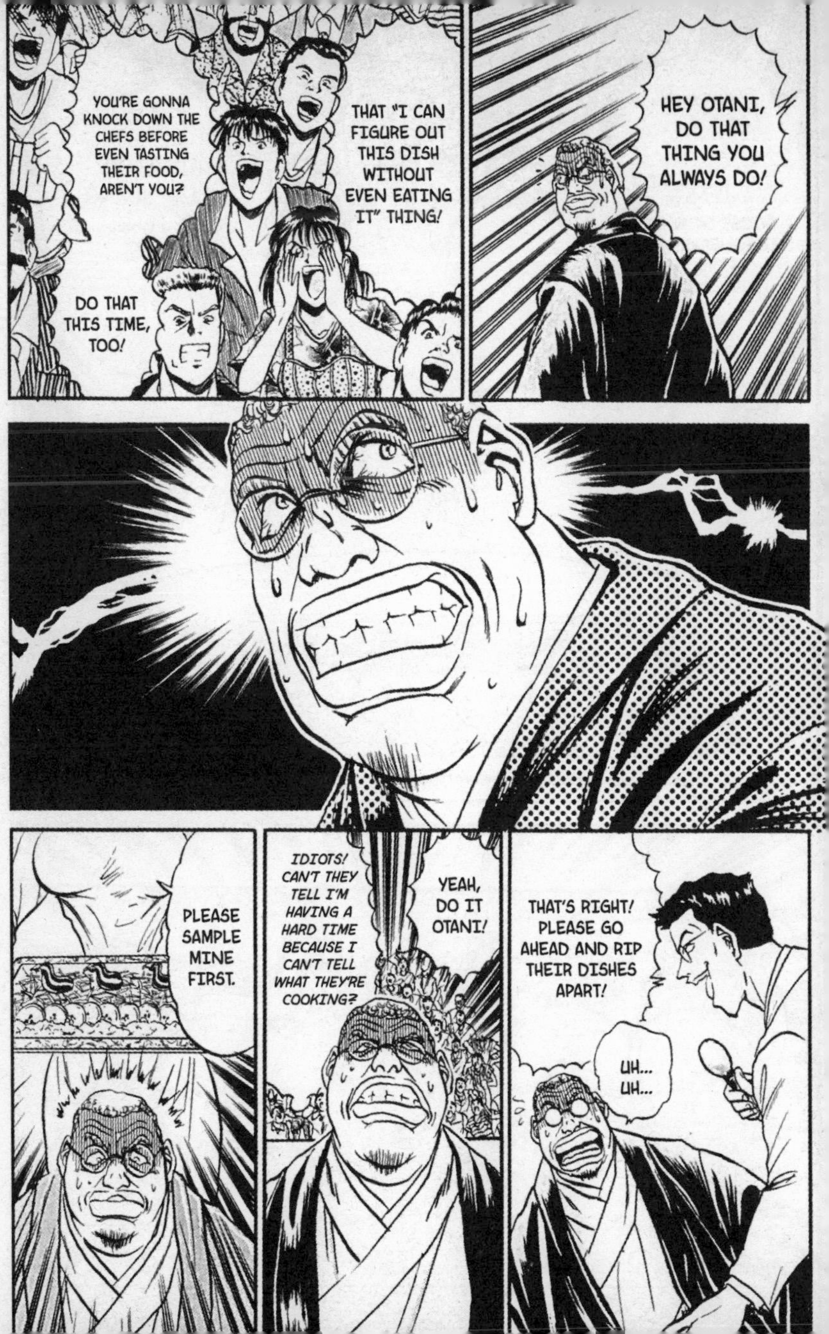
HEY OTANI, DO THAT THING YOU ALWAYS DO!
THAT "I CAN FIGURE OUT THIS DISH WITHOUT EVEN EATING IT" THING!
YOU'RE GONNA KNOCK DOWN THE CHEFS BEFORE EVEN TASTING THEIR FOOD, AREN'T YOU?
DO THAT THIS TIME, TOO!
THAT'S RIGHT! PLEASE GO AHEAD AND RIP THEIR DISHES APART!
UH... UH...
YEAH, DO IT OTANI!
IDIOTS! CAN'T THEY TELL I'M HAVING A HARD TIME BECAUSE I CAN'T TELL WHAT THEY'RE COOKING?
PLEASE SAMPLE MINE FIRST.

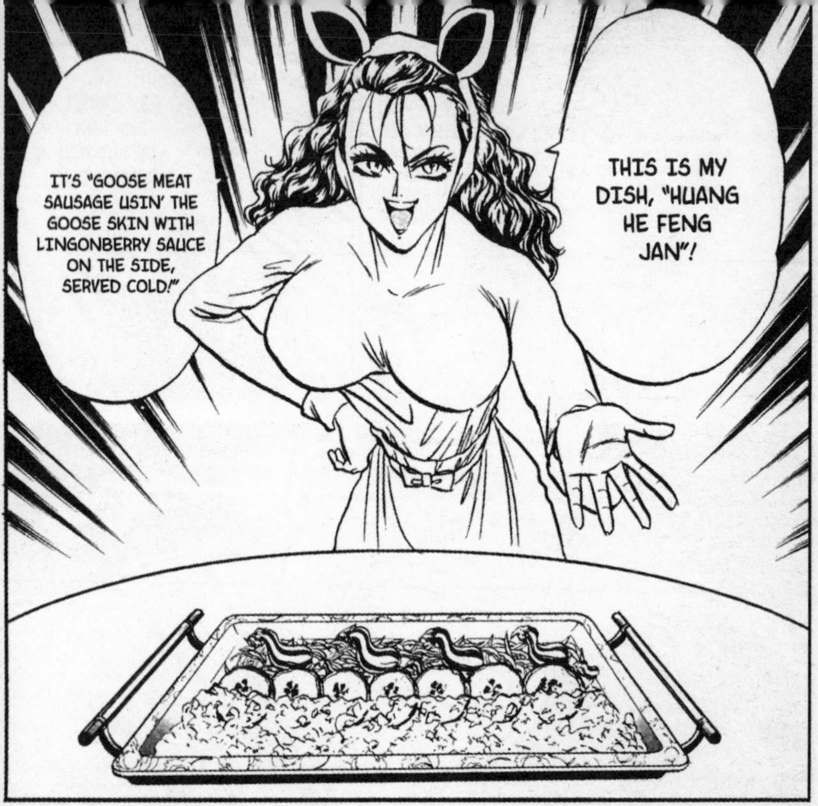
THIS IS MY DISH, "HUANG HE FENG JAN"!
IT'S "GOOSE MEAT SAUSAGE USIN' THE GOOSE SKIN WITH LINGONBERRY SAUCE ON THE SIDE, SERVED COLD!"
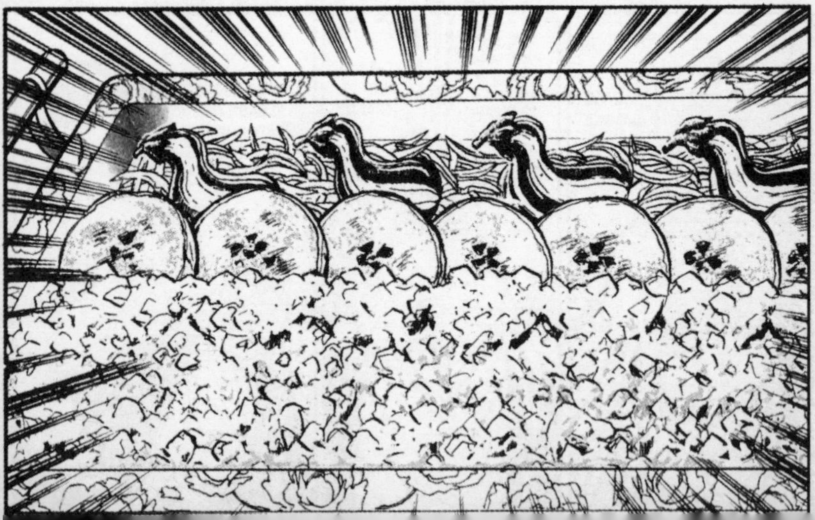

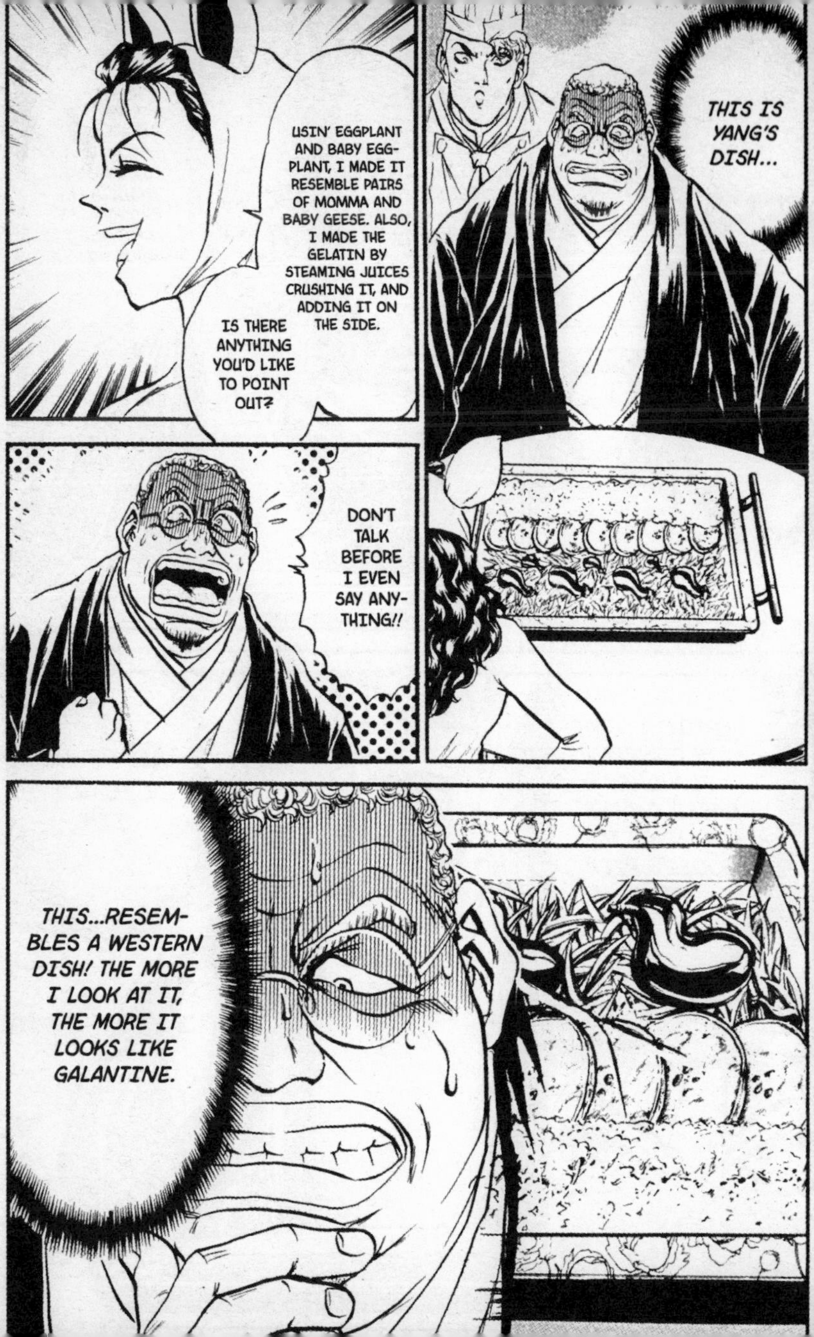
THIS IS YANG'S DISH...
USIN' EGGPLANT AND BABY EGG-PLANT, I MADE IT RESEMBLE PAIRS OF MOMMA AND BABY GEESE. ALSO, I MADE THE GELATIN BY STEAMING JUICES CRUSHING IT, AND ADDING IT ON THE SIDE.
IS THERE ANYTHING YOU'D LIKE TO POINT OUT?
DON'T TALK BEFORE I EVEN SAY ANY-THING!!
THIS...RESEM-BLES A WESTERN DISH! THE MORE I LOOK AT IT, THE MORE IT LOOKS LIKE GALANTINE.

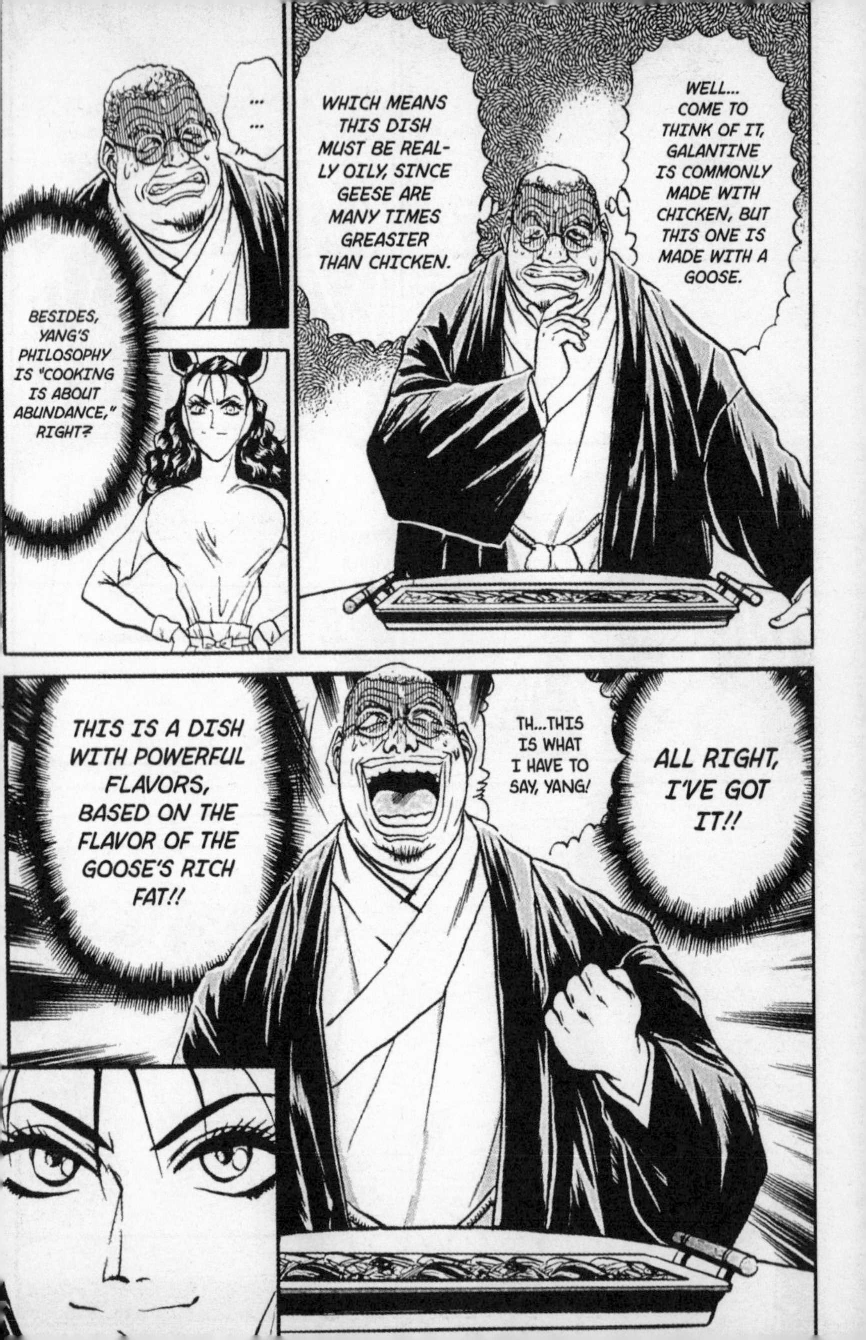
WELL... COME TO THINK OF IT, GALANTINE IS COMMONLY MADE WITH CHICKEN, BUT THIS ONE IS MADE WITH A GOOSE.
WHICH MEANS THIS DISH MUST BE REALLY OILY, SINCE GEESE ARE MANY TIMES GREASIER THAN CHICKEN.
... ...
BESIDES, YANG'S PHILOSOPHY IS "COOKING IS ABOUT ABUNDANCE," RIGHT?
ALL RIGHT, I'VE GOT IT!!
TH...THIS IS WHAT I HAVE TO SAY, YANG!
THIS IS A DISH WITH POWERFUL FLAVORS, BASED ON THE FLAVOR OF THE GOOSE'S RICH FAT!!

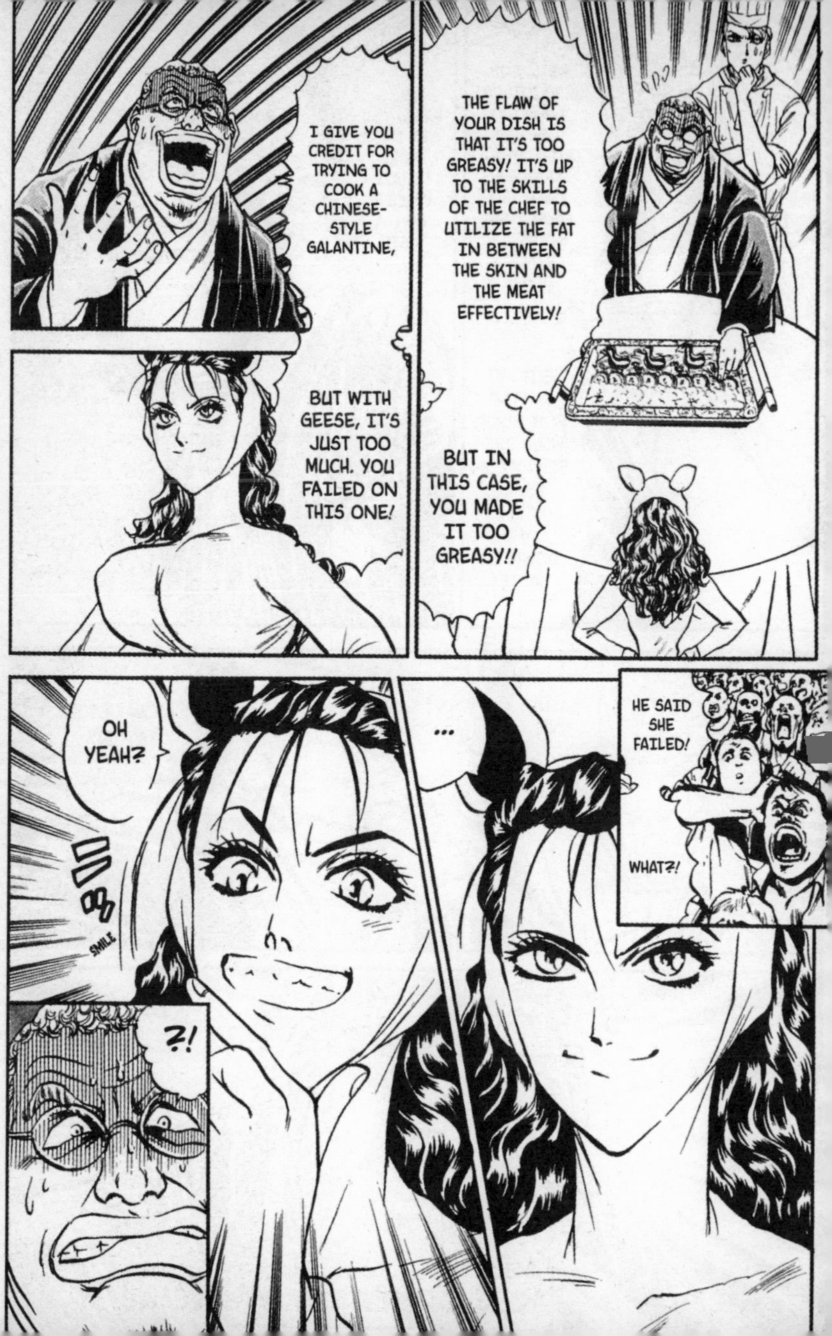
THE FLAW OF YOUR DISH IS THAT IT'S TOO GREASY! IT'S UP TO THE SKILLS OF THE CHEF TO UTILIZE THE FAT IN BETWEEN THE SKIN AND THE MEAT EFFECTIVELY!
BUT IN THIS CASE, YOU MADE IT TOO GREASY!!
I GIVE YOU CREDIT FOR TRYING TO COOK A CHINESE-STYLE GALANTINE,
BUT WITH GEESE, IT'S JUST TOO MUCH. YOU FAILED ON THIS ONE!
HE SAID SHE FAILED!
WHAT?!
...
OH YEAH?
SMILE
?!

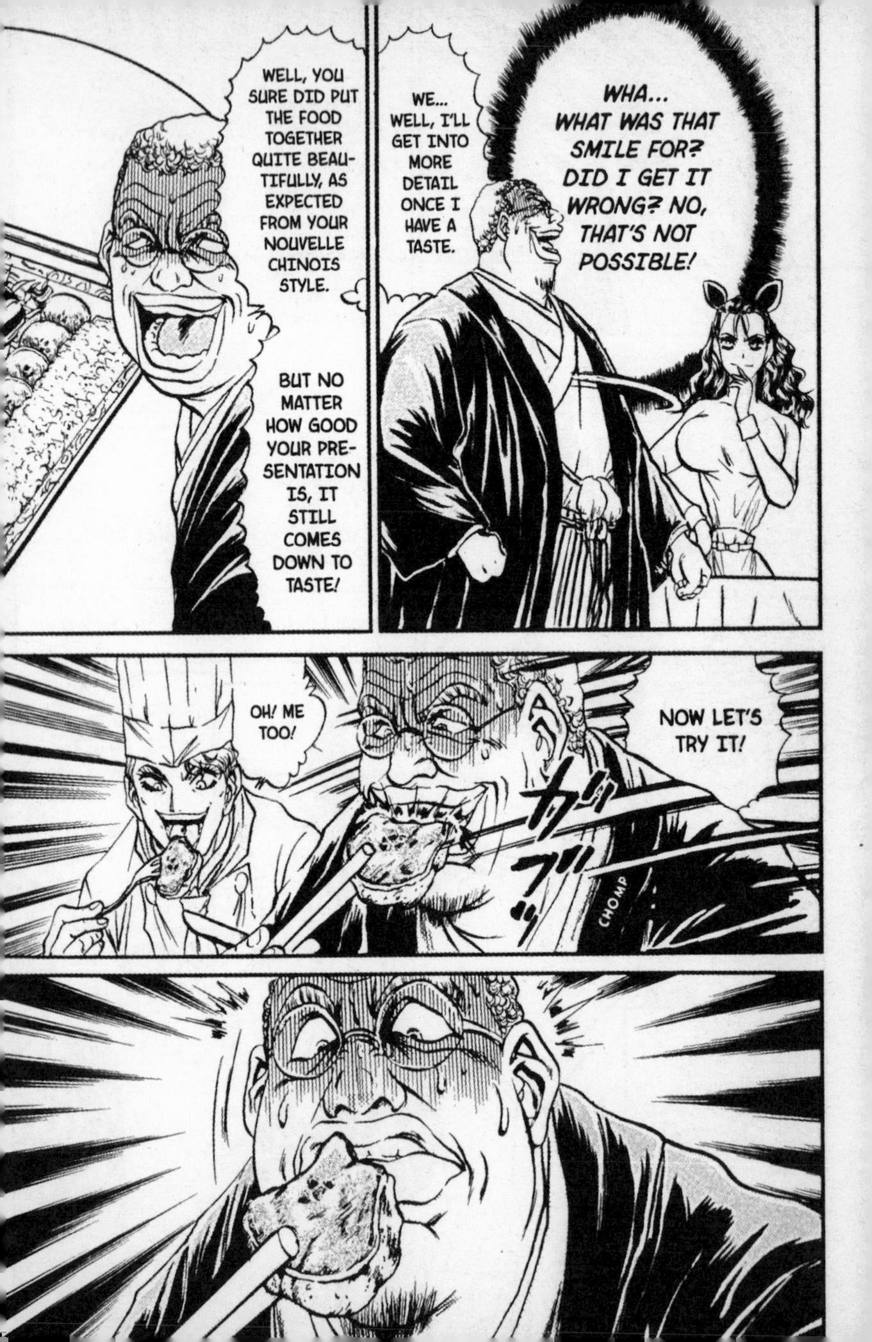
WHA... WHAT WAS THAT SMILE FOR? DID I GET IT WRONG? NO, THAT'S NOT POSSIBLE!
WE... WELL, I'LL GET INTO MORE DETAIL ONCE I HAVE A TASTE.
WELL, YOU SURE DID PUT THE FOOD TOGETHER QUITE BEAUTIFULLY, AS EXPECTED FROM YOUR NOUVELLE CHINOIS STYLE.
BUT NO MATTER HOW GOOD YOUR PRESENTATION IS, IT STILL COMES DOWN TO TASTE!
NOW LET'S TRY IT!
CHOMP
OH! ME TOO!

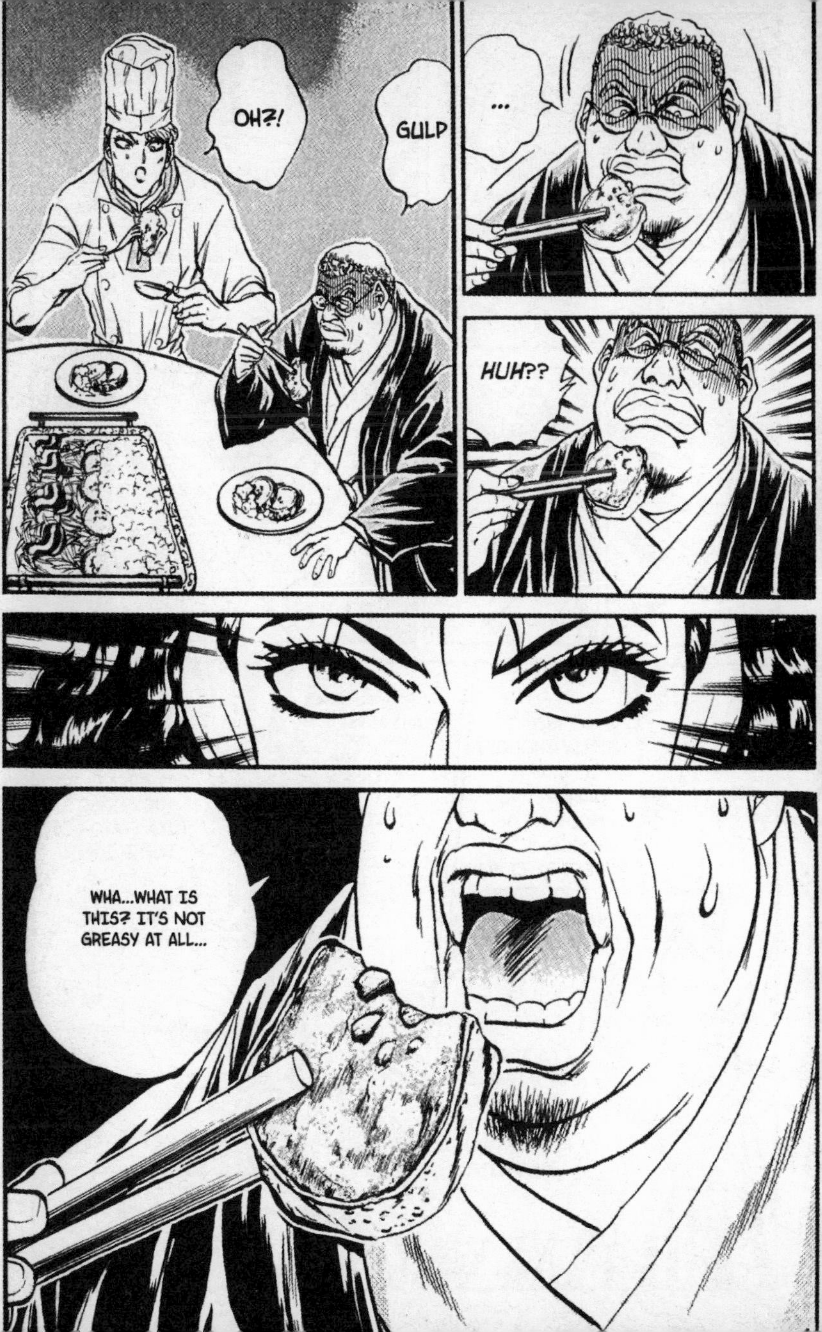
...
HUH??
GULP
OH?!
WHA...WHAT IS THIS? IT'S NOT GREASY AT ALL...

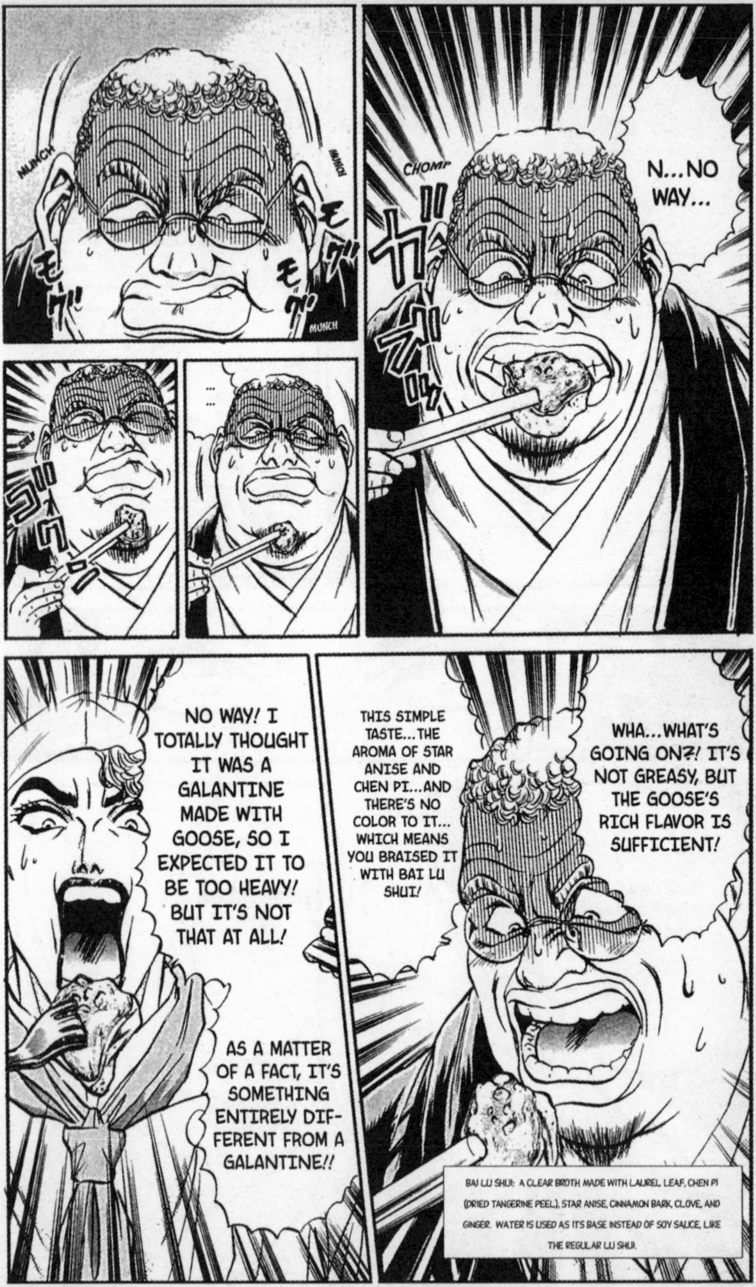
CHOMP
N...NO WAY...
MUNCH
MUNCH
MUNCH
...
...
WHA...WHAT'S GOING ON?! IT'S NOT GREASY, BUT THE GOOSE'S RICH FLAVOR IS SUFFICIENT!
THIS SIMPLE TASTE...THE AROMA OF STAR ANISE AND CHEN PI...AND THERE'S NO COLOR TO IT... WHICH MEANS YOU BRAISED IT WITH BAI LU SHUI!
BAI LU SHUI: A CLEAR BROTH MADE WITH LAUREL LEAF, CHEN PI (DRIED TANGERINE PEEL), STAR ANISE, CINNAMON BARK, CLOVE, AND GINGER. WATER IS USED AS ITS BASE INSTEAD OF SOY SAUCE, LIKE THE REGULAR LU SHUI.
NO WAY! I TOTALLY THOUGHT IT WAS A GALANTINE MADE WITH GOOSE, SO I EXPECTED IT TO BE TOO HEAVY! BUT IT'S NOT THAT AT ALL!
AS A MATTER OF A FACT, IT'S SOMETHING ENTIRELY DIF-FERENT FROM A GALANTINE!!

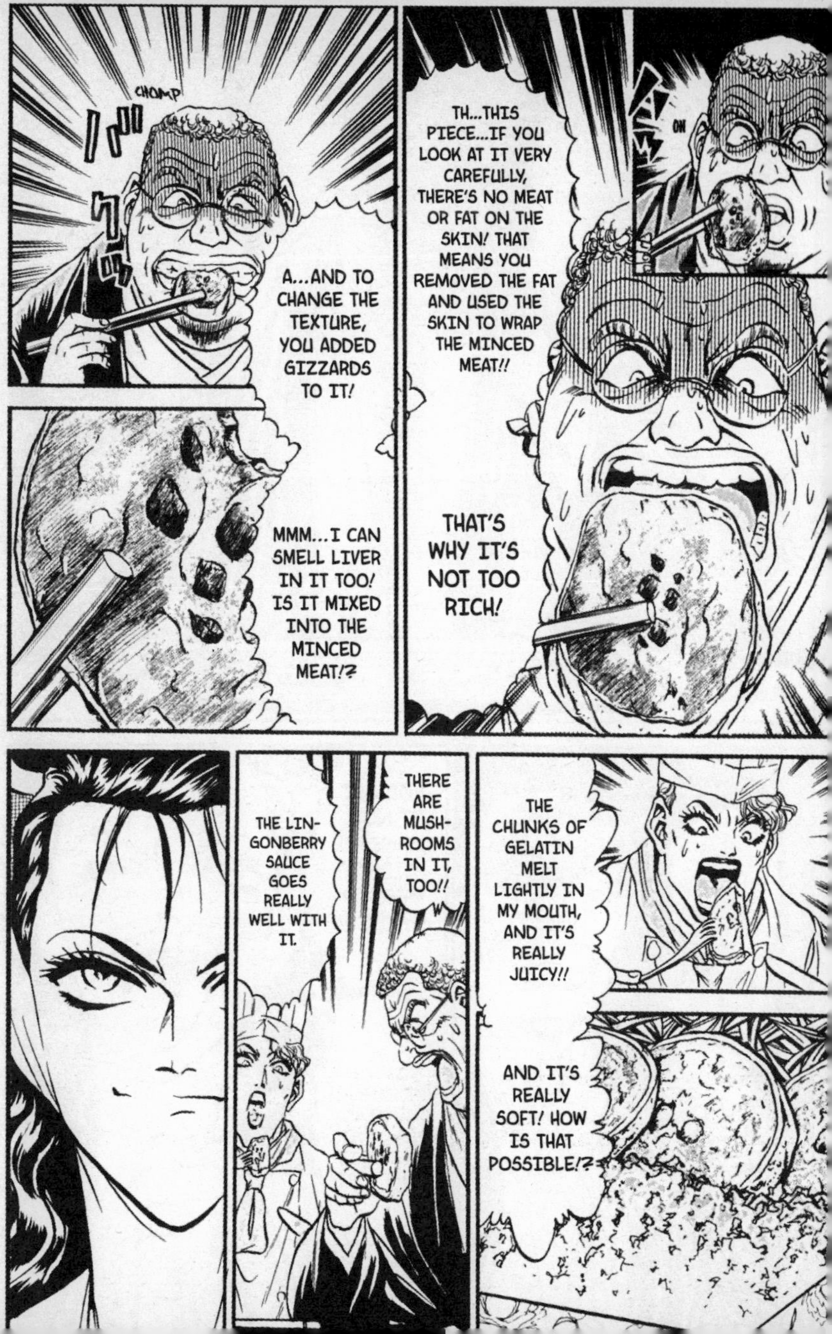
ON
TH...THIS PIECE...IF YOU LOOK AT IT VERY CAREFULLY, THERE'S NO MEAT OR FAT ON THE SKIN! THAT MEANS YOU REMOVED THE FAT AND USED THE SKIN TO WRAP THE MINCED MEAT!!
THAT'S WHY IT'S NOT TOO RICH!
CHOMP
A...AND TO CHANGE THE TEXTURE, YOU ADDED GIZZARDS TO IT!
MMM...I CAN SMELL LIVER IN IT TOO! IS IT MIXED INTO THE MINCED MEAT!?
THE CHUNKS OF GELATIN MELT LIGHTLY IN MY MOUTH, AND IT'S REALLY JUICY!!
AND IT'S REALLY SOFT! HOW IS THAT POSSIBLE!?
THERE ARE MUSH-ROOMS IN IT, TOO!!
THE LIN-GONBERRY SAUCE GOES REALLY WELL WITH IT.

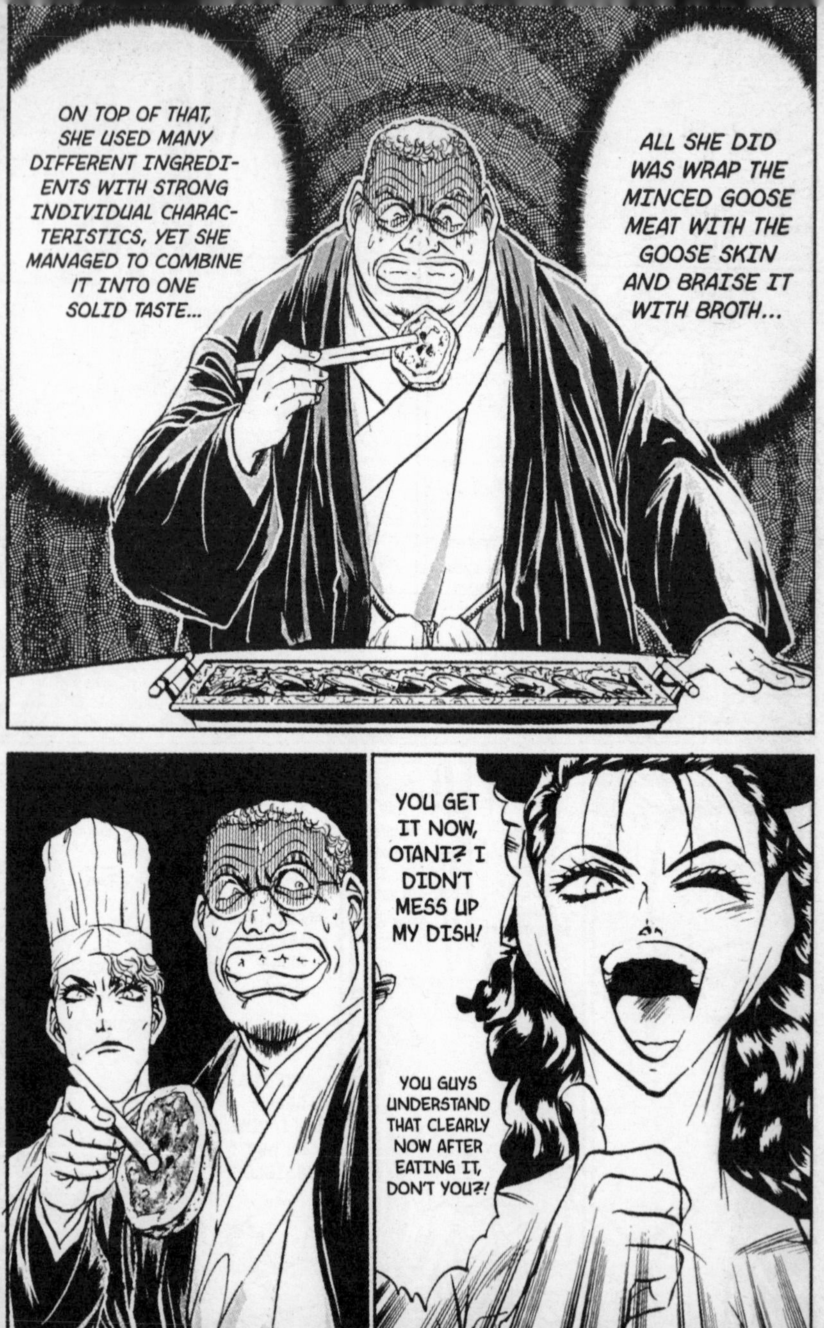
ALL SHE DID WAS WRAP THE MINCED GOOSE MEAT WITH THE GOOSE SKIN AND BRAISE IT WITH BROTH...
ON TOP OF THAT, SHE USED MANY DIFFERENT INGREDI- ENTS WITH STRONG INDIVIDUAL CHARAC- TERISTICS, YET SHE MANAGED TO COMBINE IT INTO ONE SOLID TASTE...
YOU GET IT NOW, OTANI?! I DIDN'T MESS UP MY DISH!
YOU GUYS UNDERSTAND THAT CLEARLY NOW AFTER EATING IT, DON'T YOU?!

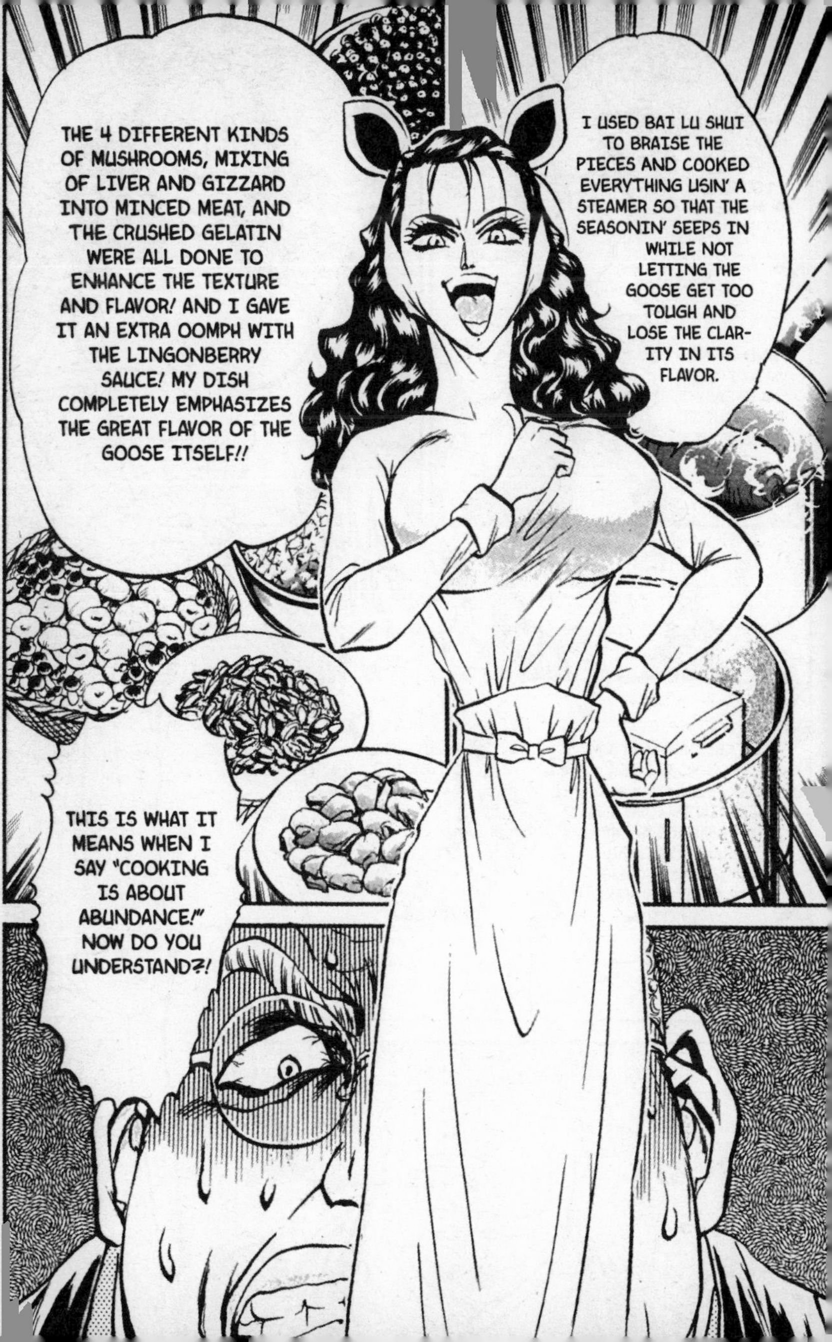
I USED BAI LU SHUI TO BRAISE THE PIECES AND COOKED EVERYTHING USIN' A STEAMER SO THAT THE SEASONIN' SEEPS IN WHILE NOT LETTING THE GOOSE GET TOO TOUGH AND LOSE THE CLAR-ITY IN ITS FLAVOR.
THE 4 DIFFERENT KINDS OF MUSHROOMS, MIXING OF LIVER AND GIZZARD INTO MINCED MEAT, AND THE CRUSHED GELATIN WERE ALL DONE TO ENHANCE THE TEXTURE AND FLAVOR! AND I GAVE IT AN EXTRA OOMPH WITH THE LINGONBERRY SAUCE! MY DISH COMPLETELY EMPHASIZES THE GREAT FLAVOR OF THE GOOSE ITSELF!!
THIS IS WHAT IT MEANS WHEN I SAY "COOKING IS ABOUT ABUNDANCE!" NOW DO YOU UNDERSTAND?!

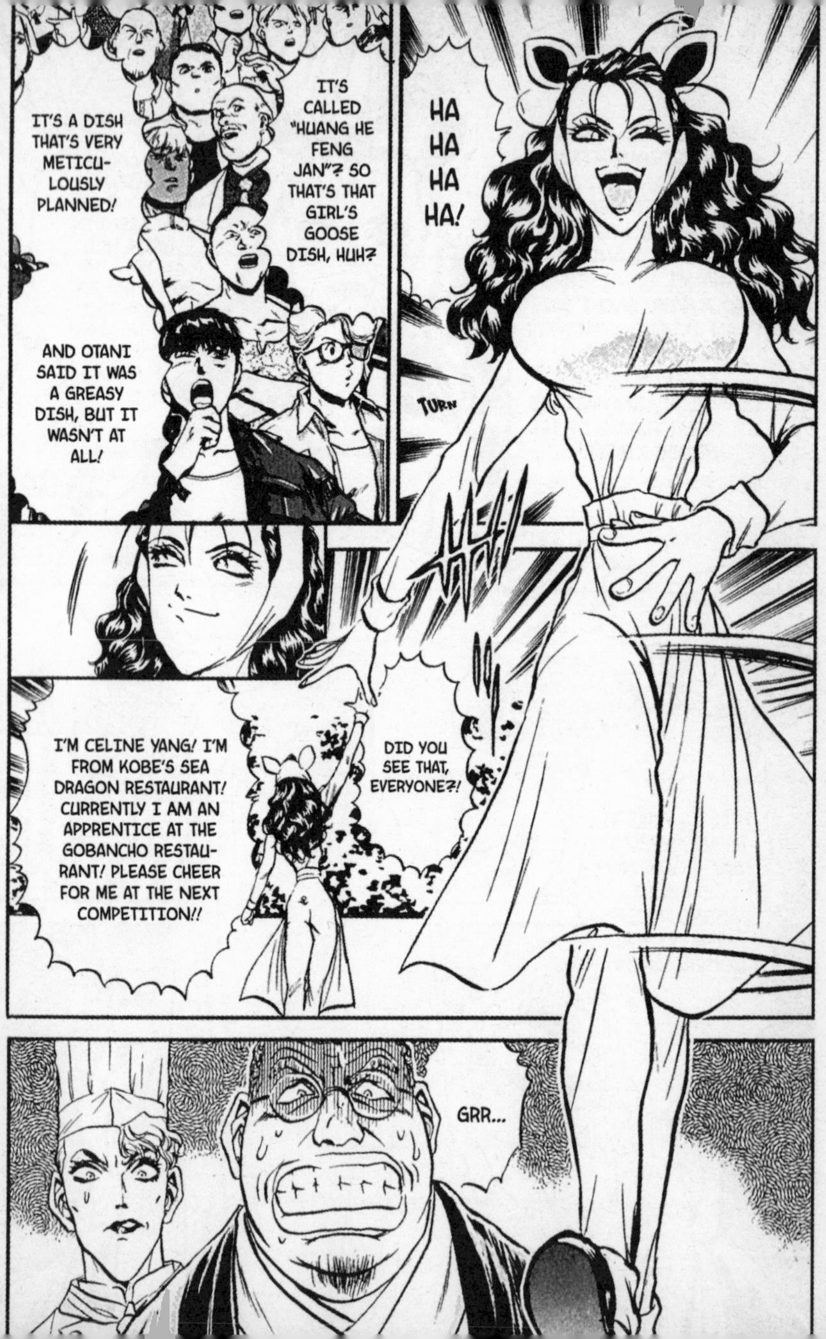
IT'S CALLED "HUANG HE FENG JAN"? SO THAT'S THAT GIRL'S GOOSE DISH, HUH?
IT'S A DISH THAT'S VERY METICU-LOUSLY PLANNED!
AND OTANI SAID IT WAS A GREASY DISH, BUT IT WASN'T AT ALL!
HA HA HA HA!
TURN
DID YOU SEE THAT, EVERYONE?!
I'M CELINE YANG! I'M FROM KOBE'S SEA DRAGON RESTAURANT! CURRENTLY I AM AN APPRENTICE AT THE GOBANCHO RESTAU-RANT! PLEASE CHEER FOR ME AT THE NEXT COMPETITION!!
GRR...

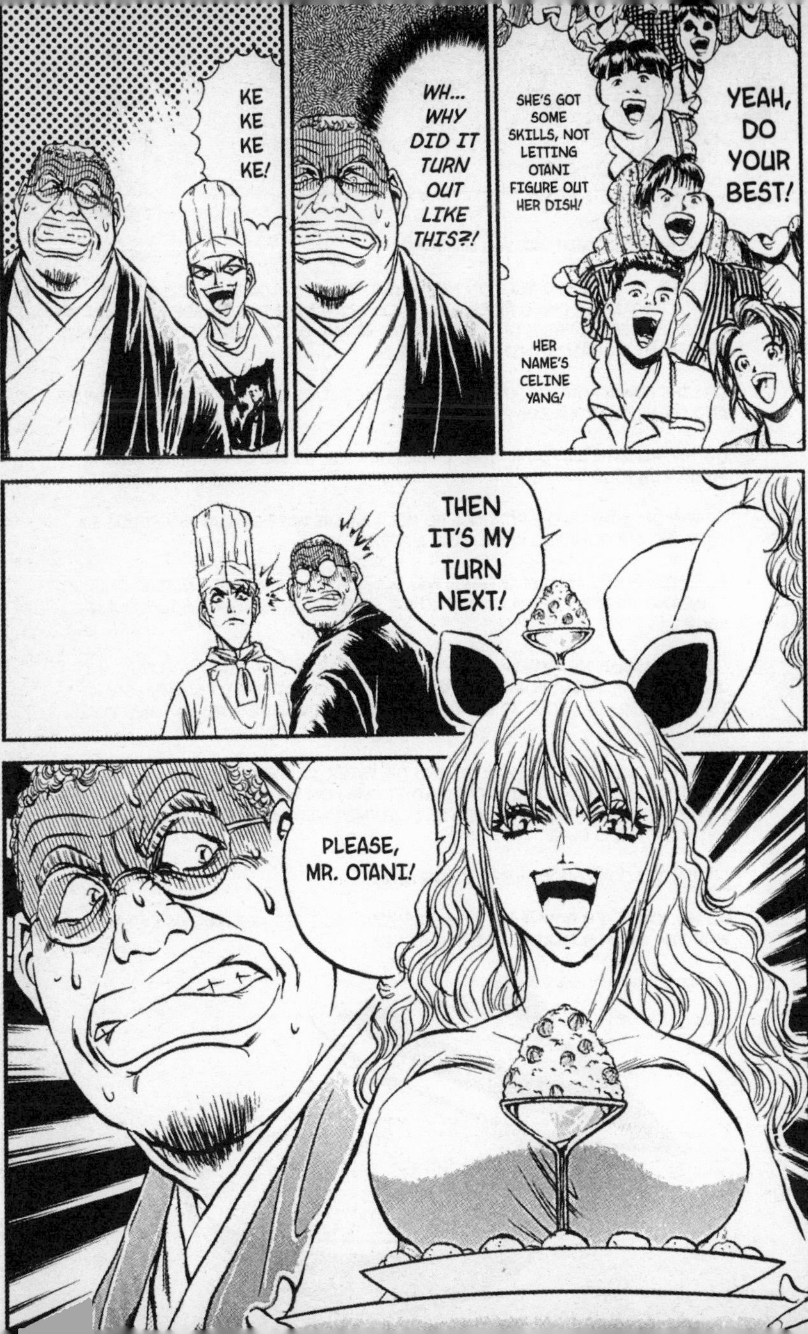
YEAH, DO YOUR BEST!
SHE'S GOT SOME SKILLS, NOT LETTING OTANI FIGURE OUT HER DISH!
HER NAME'S CELINE YANG!
WH... WHY DID IT TURN OUT LIKE THIS?!
KE KE KE KE!
THEN IT'S MY TURN NEXT!
PLEASE, MR. OTANI!

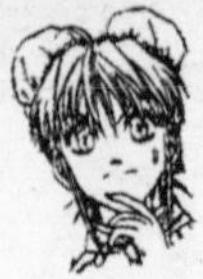

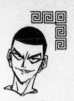

KIRIKO AND JAN'S

YUI ZHOU (POTATO PORRIDGE)

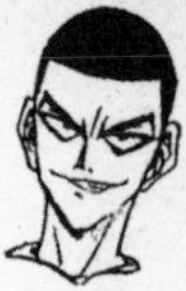

(J) HEY KIRIKO, WHAT ARE YOU MAKING?

(K) I ATE A LITTLE TOO MUCH ON NEW YEARS...BUT THE BLOATED FEELING IN MY STOMACH WILL BE SOLVED AFTER I EAT THIS. IT'S A DISH THAT I MADE BASED ON THE CHINESE CUISINE PRINCIPLE THAT MEDICINE AND ONE'S DAILY FOOD ARE EQUALLY IMPORTANT IN MAINTAINING ONE'S HEALTH.

(J) LIKE HOW A BOWL OF PORRIDGE IN THE MORNING WILL NURTURE YOUR STOMACH AND CLEAN OUT YOUR BOWELS?

(K) YUP! TO MAKE IT, YOU'LL NEED 2 CUPS OF RICE, 8 CUPS OF WATER, 300 GRAMS OF SWEET POTATO...

(J) WHY DO WOMEN LIKE POTATOES SO MUCH, BY THE WAY? IS THAT WHY YOU'RE SO DULL AND UNCOOL? YOU KNOW, LIKE A POTATO.

(K) ...*IGNORES*...ANYWAY, AKIYAMA, WHY DON'T YOU HELP ME OUT INSTEAD OF JUST STANDING THERE? I BET YOU WANT TO EAT SOMETHING REFRESHING TOO, DON'T YOU?

(J) IF YOU WANT ME TO HELP, WHY DON'T YOU JUST SAY SO? FIRST, YOU PEEL AND JULIENNE* THE SWEET POTATOES ABOUT THE SIZE OF MATCHSTICKS. THEN SOAK IT IN THE WATER FOR ABOUT 30 MINUTES, CHANGING THE WATER TWO TO THREE TIMES. OK, I DID IT.

(K) GET A CLAY POT, POUR THE RICE AND THE WATER IN THERE, AND ADD THE SWEET POTATO AS WELL, ONCE YOU'VE DRAINED IT. TURN ON THE HEAT, AND ONCE THE CONTENTS BOIL, SKIM THE FOAM AND LET IT SIMMER WITH LOW HEAT FOR A LITTLE WHILE. NOW IT'S DONE.

(J) HEY, IT LOOKS GOOD. HURRY, GIMME SOME.

(K) NO. 'CAUSE I'M GONNA EAT THIS. IT'S YOUR FAULT FOR NOT MAKING EXTRA. THAT'S WHAT YOU GET FOR TALKING CRAP ABOUT ME!

JULIENNE: CUTTING INTO LONG THIN STRIPS

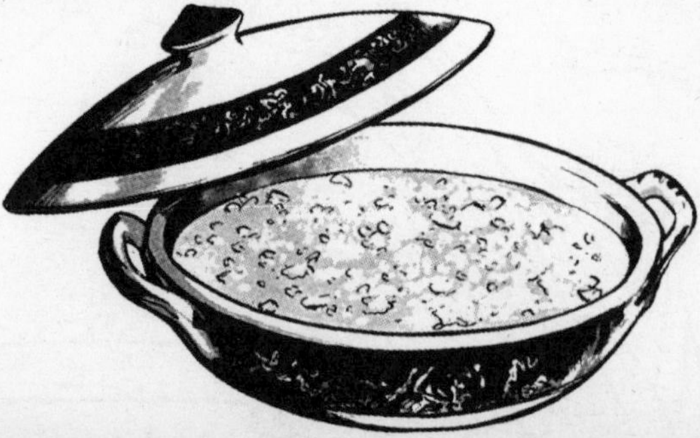

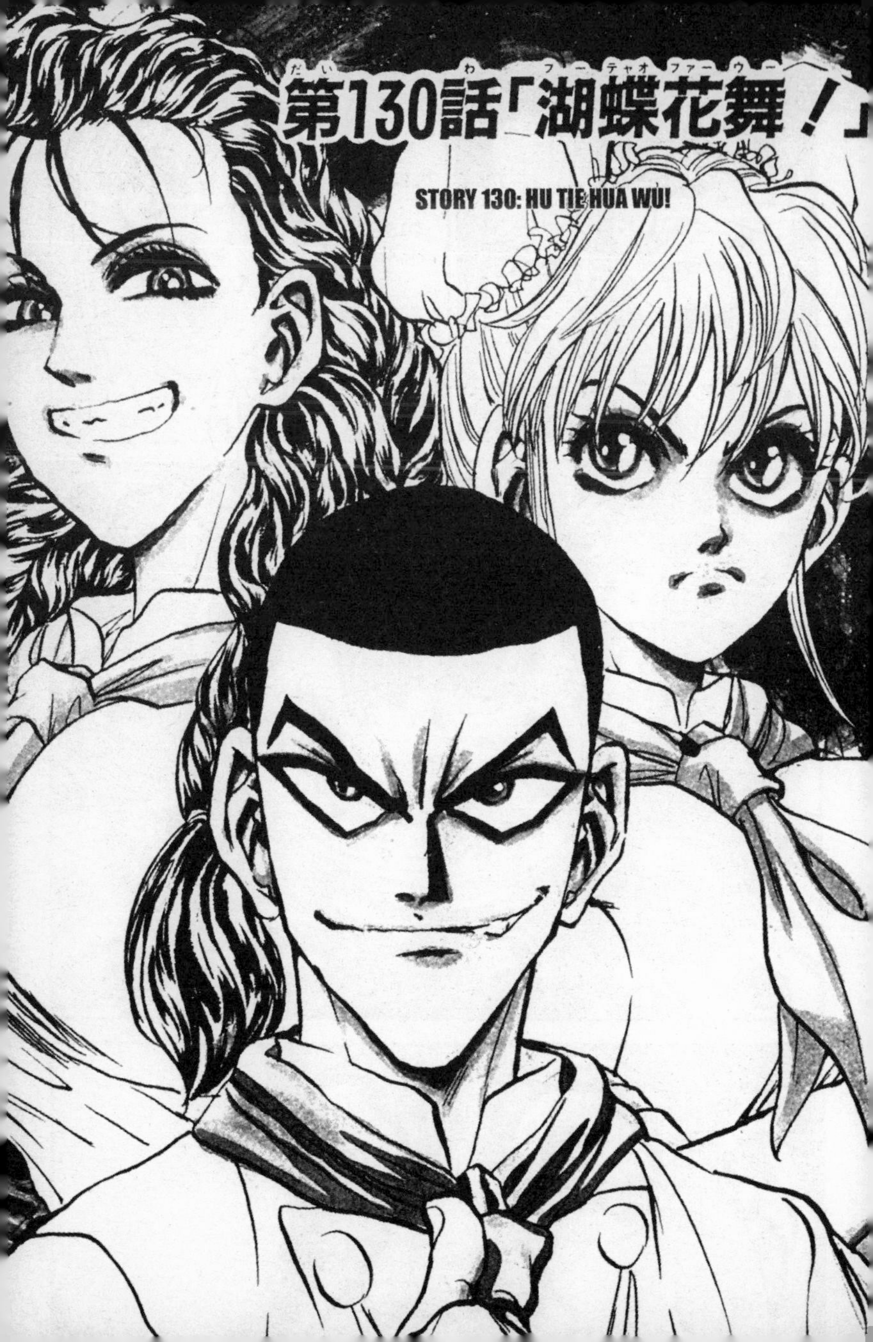
第130話「湖蝶花舞！」
STORY 130: HU TIE HUA WU!

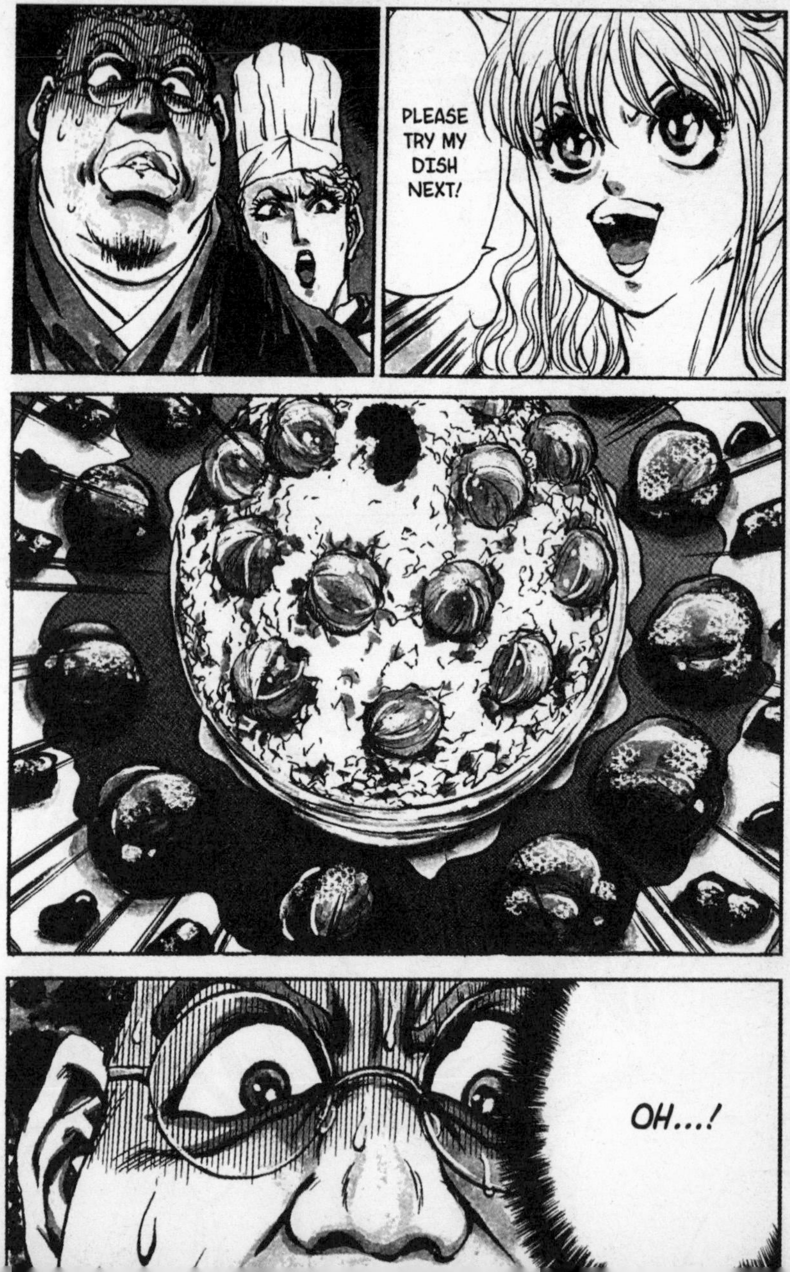
PLEASE TRY MY DISH NEXT!
OH...!

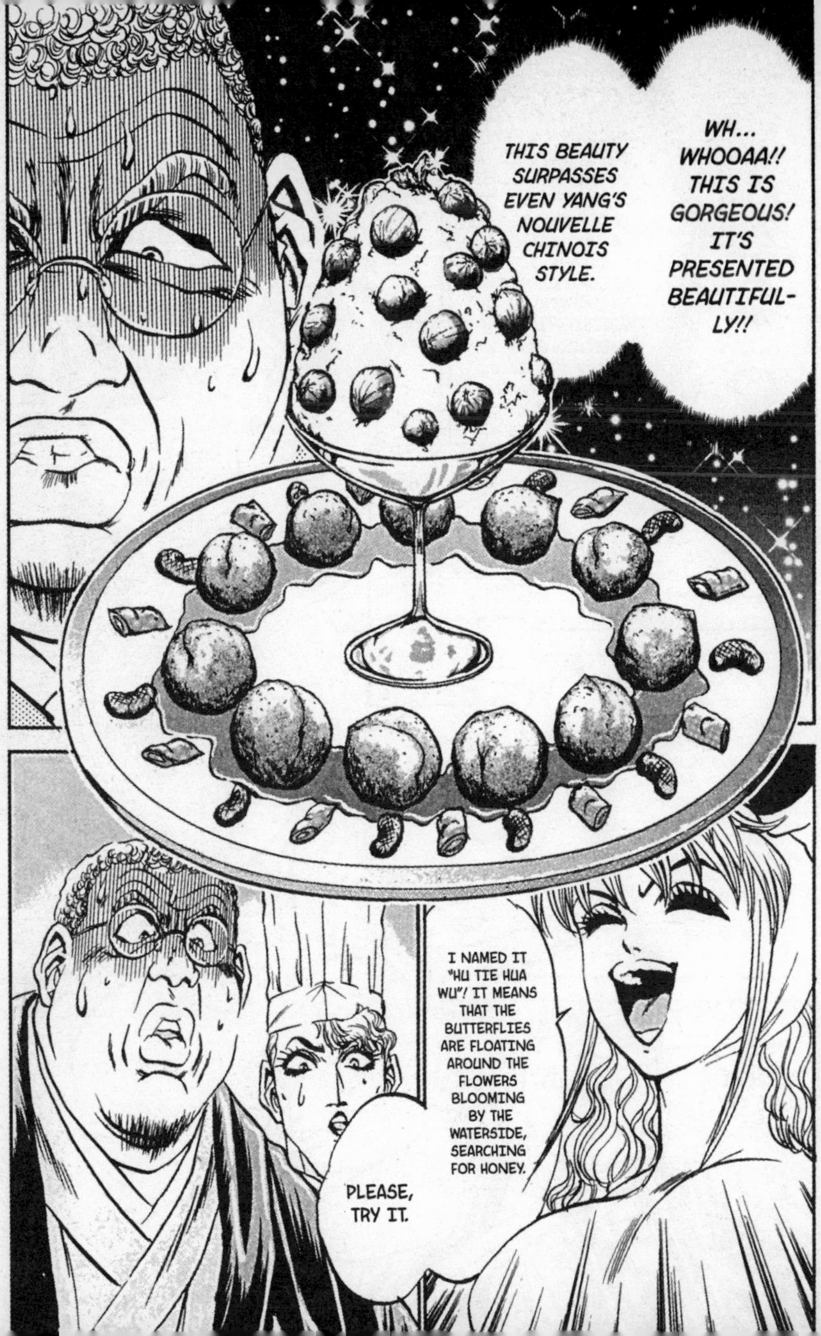
WH... WHOOAA!! THIS IS GORGEOUS! IT'S PRESENTED BEAUTIFUL-LY!!
THIS BEAUTY SURPASSES EVEN YANG'S NOUVELLE CHINOIS STYLE.
I NAMED IT "HU TIE HUA WU"! IT MEANS THAT THE BUTTERFLIES ARE FLOATING AROUND THE FLOWERS BLOOMING BY THE WATERSIDE, SEARCHING FOR HONEY.
PLEASE, TRY IT.

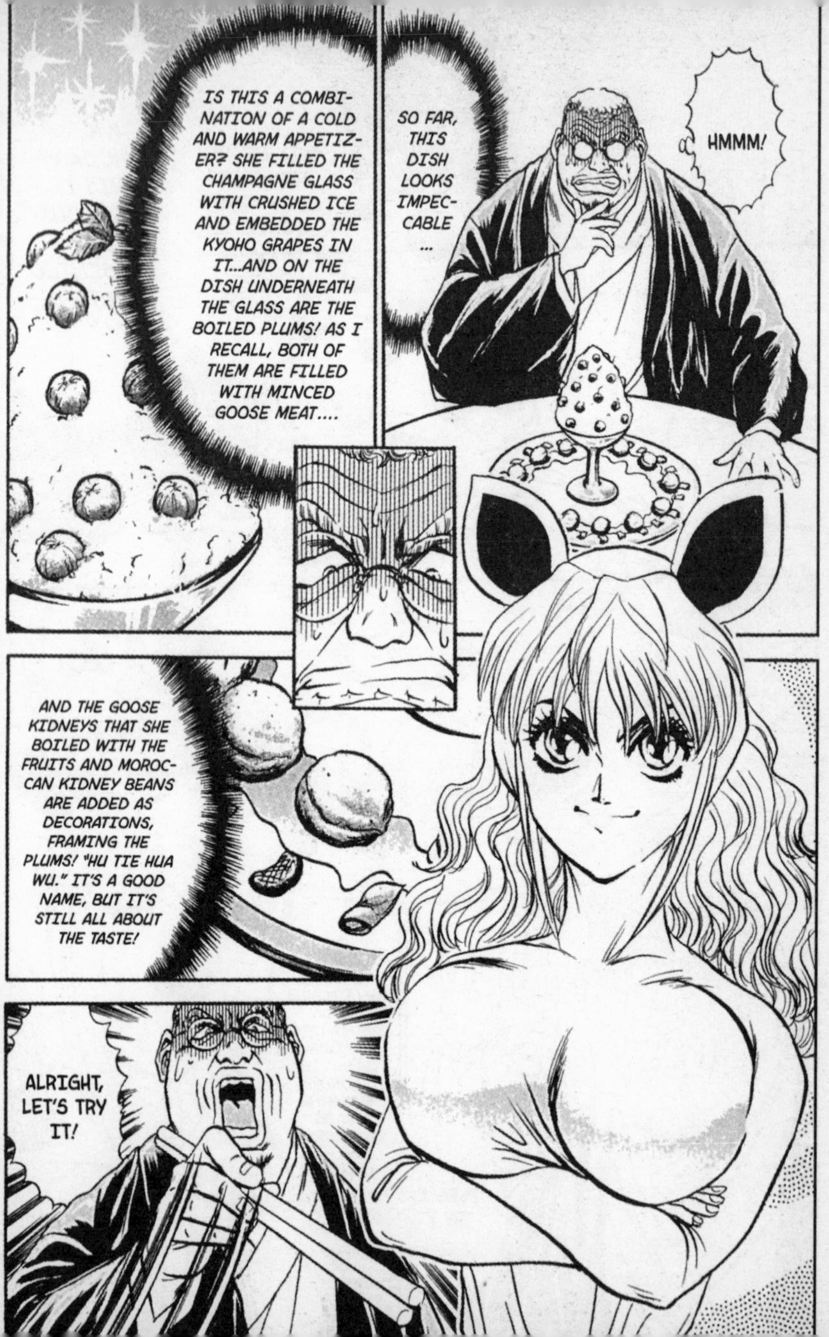
HMMM!
SO FAR, THIS DISH LOOKS IMPECCABLE...
IS THIS A COMBINATION OF A COLD AND WARM APPETIZER? SHE FILLED THE CHAMPAGNE GLASS WITH CRUSHED ICE AND EMBEDDED THE KYOHO GRAPES IN IT...AND ON THE DISH UNDERNEATH THE GLASS ARE THE BOILED PLUMS! AS I RECALL, BOTH OF THEM ARE FILLED WITH MINCED GOOSE MEAT....
AND THE GOOSE KIDNEYS THAT SHE BOILED WITH THE FRUITS AND MOROCCAN KIDNEY BEANS ARE ADDED AS DECORATIONS, FRAMING THE PLUMS! "HU TIE HUA WU." IT'S A GOOD NAME, BUT IT'S STILL ALL ABOUT THE TASTE!
ALRIGHT, LET'S TRY IT!

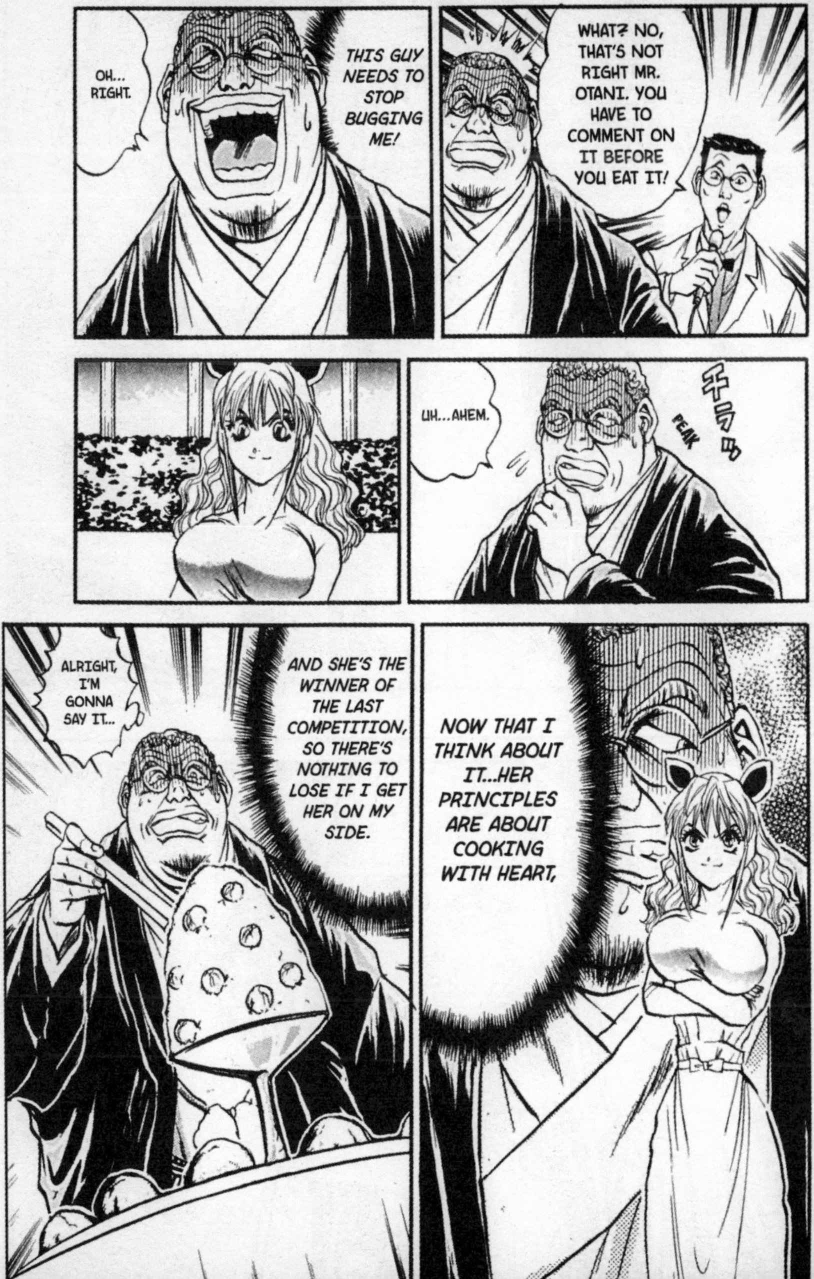
WHAT? NO, THAT'S NOT RIGHT MR. OTANI. YOU HAVE TO COMMENT ON IT BEFORE YOU EAT IT!
THIS GUY NEEDS TO STOP BUGGING ME!
OH... RIGHT.
チラッ
PEAK
UH...AHEM.
NOW THAT I THINK ABOUT IT...HER PRINCIPLES ARE ABOUT COOKING WITH HEART,
AND SHE'S THE WINNER OF THE LAST COMPETITION, SO THERE'S NOTHING TO LOSE IF I GET HER ON MY SIDE.
ALRIGHT, I'M GONNA SAY IT...

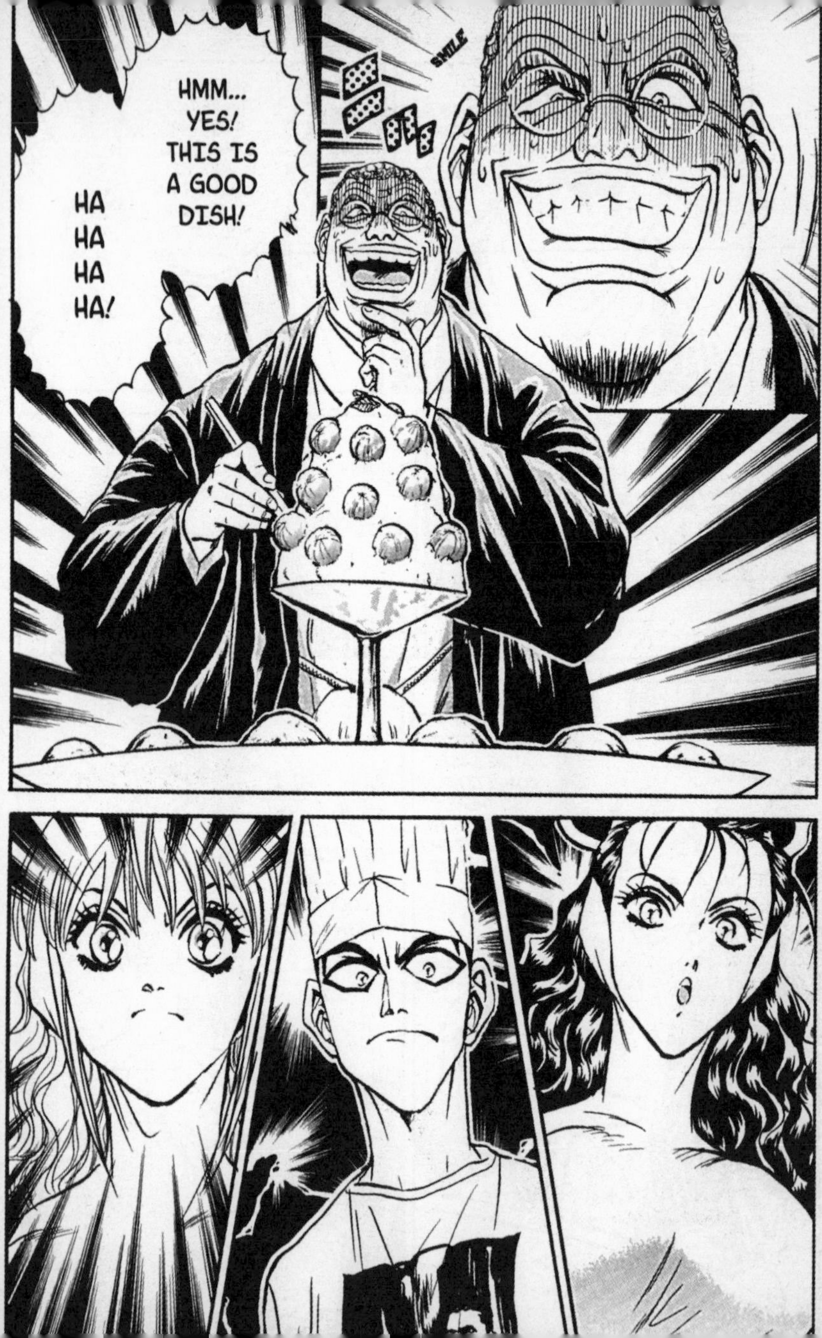
SMILE
HMM... YES! THIS IS A GOOD DISH!
HA HA HA HA!

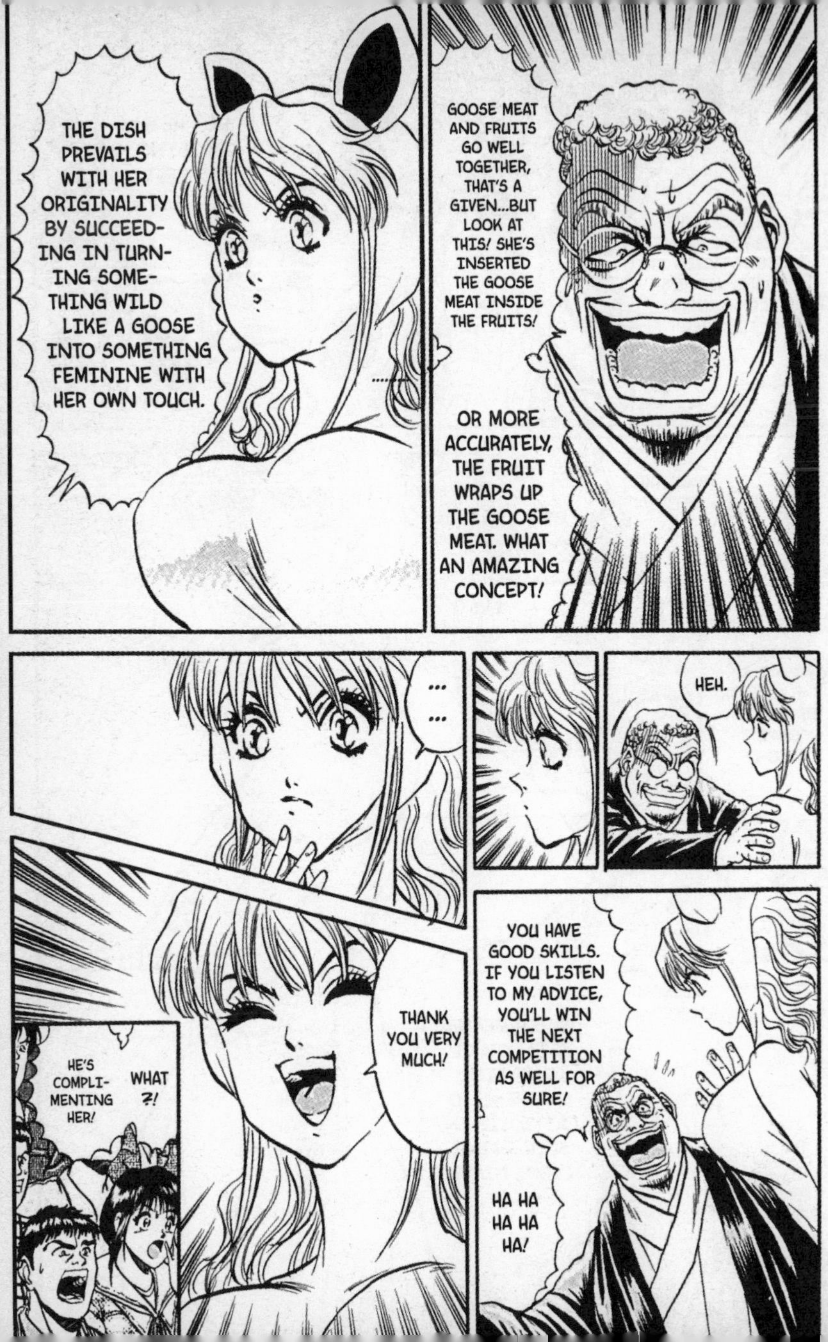
GOOSE MEAT AND FRUITS GO WELL TOGETHER, THAT'S A GIVEN...BUT LOOK AT THIS! SHE'S INSERTED THE GOOSE MEAT INSIDE THE FRUITS!
OR MORE ACCURATELY, THE FRUIT WRAPS UP THE GOOSE MEAT. WHAT AN AMAZING CONCEPT!
THE DISH PREVAILS WITH HER ORIGINALITY BY SUCCEEDING IN TURNING SOMETHING WILD LIKE A GOOSE INTO SOMETHING FEMININE WITH HER OWN TOUCH.
......
HEH.
... ...
YOU HAVE GOOD SKILLS. IF YOU LISTEN TO MY ADVICE, YOU'LL WIN THE NEXT COMPETITION AS WELL FOR SURE!
HA HA HA HA HA!
THANK YOU VERY MUCH!
WHAT?!
HE'S COMPLIMENTING HER!

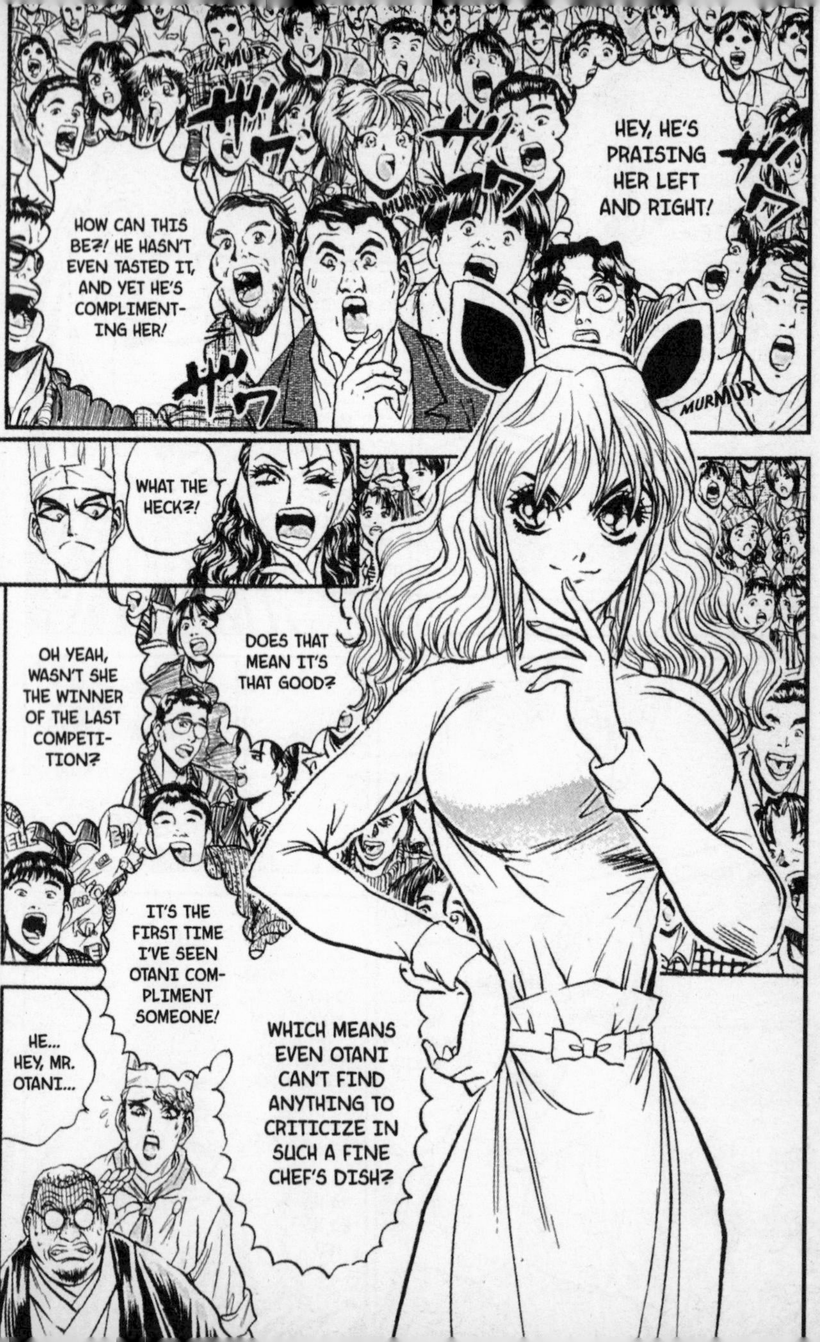
MURMUR
MURMUR
HEY, HE'S PRAISING HER LEFT AND RIGHT!
HOW CAN THIS BE?! HE HASN'T EVEN TASTED IT, AND YET HE'S COMPLIMENTING HER!
MURMUR
WHAT THE HECK?!
DOES THAT MEAN IT'S THAT GOOD?
OH YEAH, WASN'T SHE THE WINNER OF THE LAST COMPETITION?
IT'S THE FIRST TIME I'VE SEEN OTANI COMPLIMENT SOMEONE!
WHICH MEANS EVEN OTANI CAN'T FIND ANYTHING TO CRITICIZE IN SUCH A FINE CHEF'S DISH?
HE... HEY, MR. OTANI...

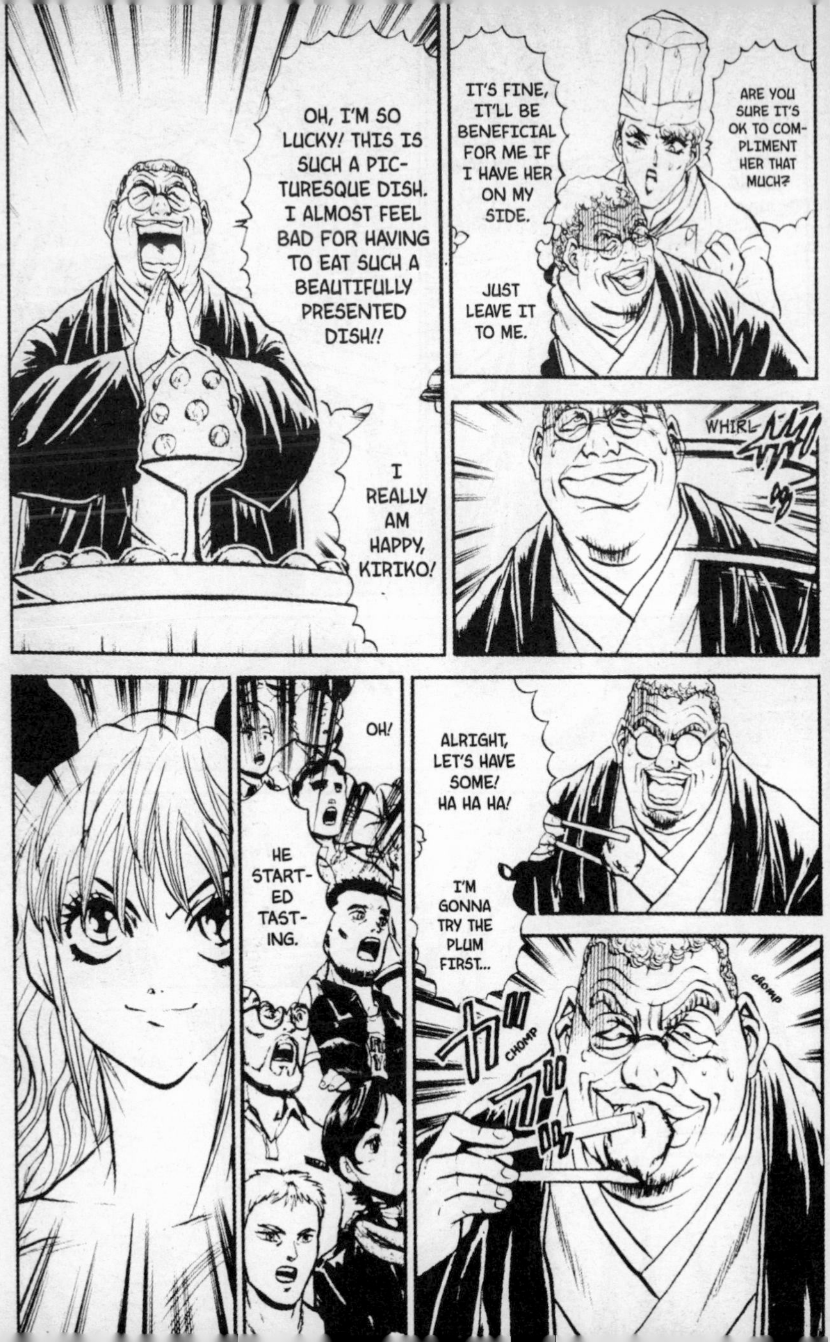
ARE YOU SURE IT'S OK TO COMPLIMENT HER THAT MUCH?
IT'S FINE, IT'LL BE BENEFICIAL FOR ME IF I HAVE HER ON MY SIDE.
JUST LEAVE IT TO ME.
WHIRL
OH, I'M SO LUCKY! THIS IS SUCH A PICTURESQUE DISH. I ALMOST FEEL BAD FOR HAVING TO EAT SUCH A BEAUTIFULLY PRESENTED DISH!!
I REALLY AM HAPPY, KIRIKO!
ALRIGHT, LET'S HAVE SOME! HA HA HA!
I'M GONNA TRY THE PLUM FIRST...
CHOMP
CHOMP
OH!
HE STARTED TASTING.

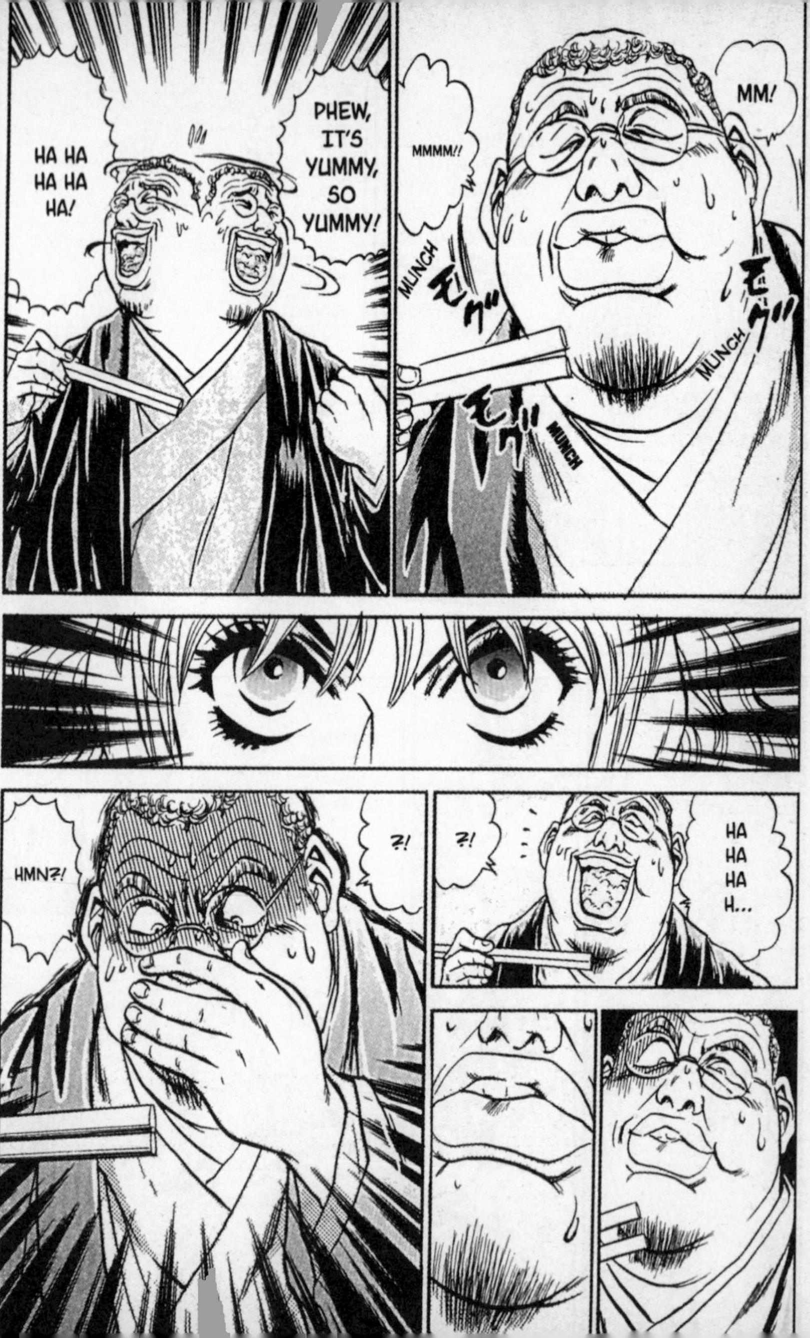
MM!
MMMM!!
MUNCH
MUNCH
MUNCH
PHEW, IT'S YUMMY, SO YUMMY!
HA HA HA HA HA!
HA HA HA H...
?!
?!
HMN?!

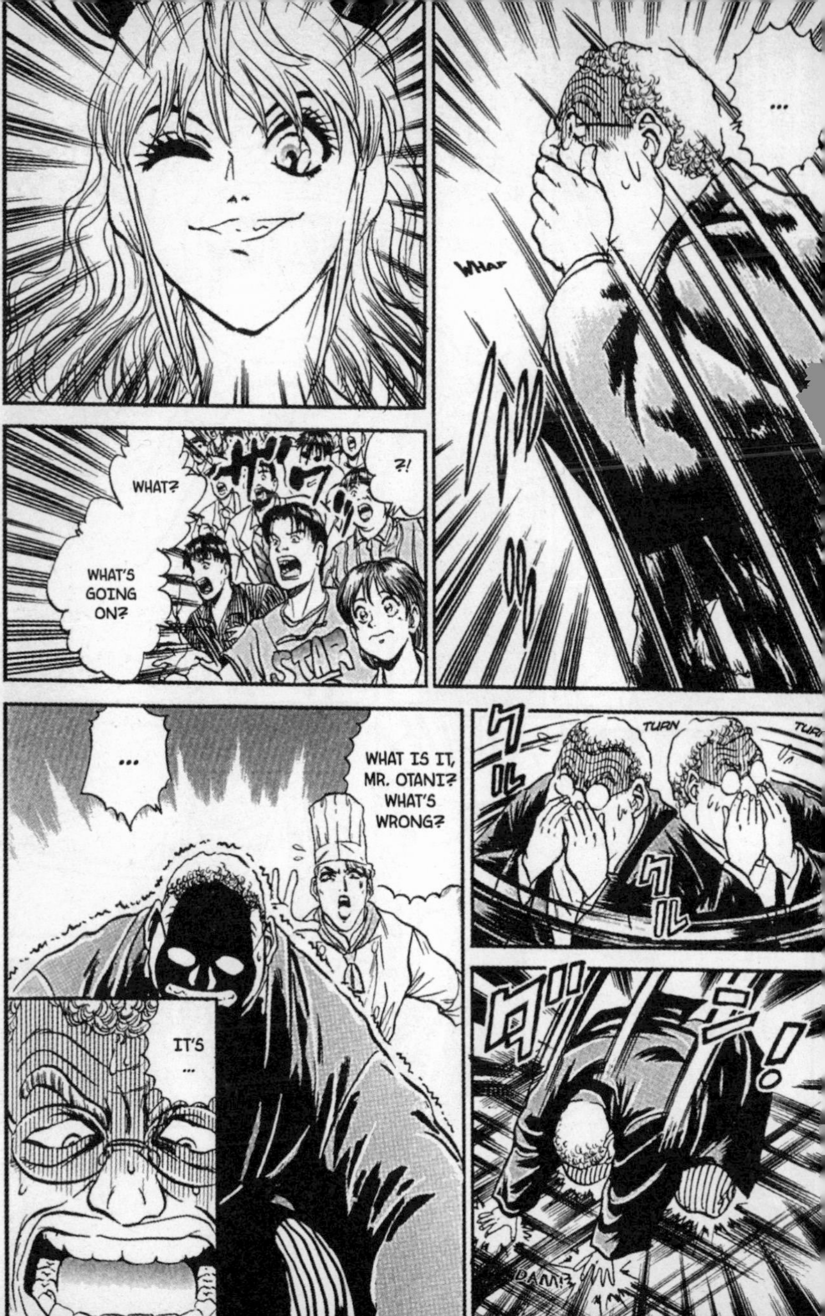
...
WHAP
?!
WHAT?
WHAT'S GOING ON?
TURN
TURN
DAM!?
WHAT IS IT, MR. OTANI? WHAT'S WRONG?
...
IT'S ...

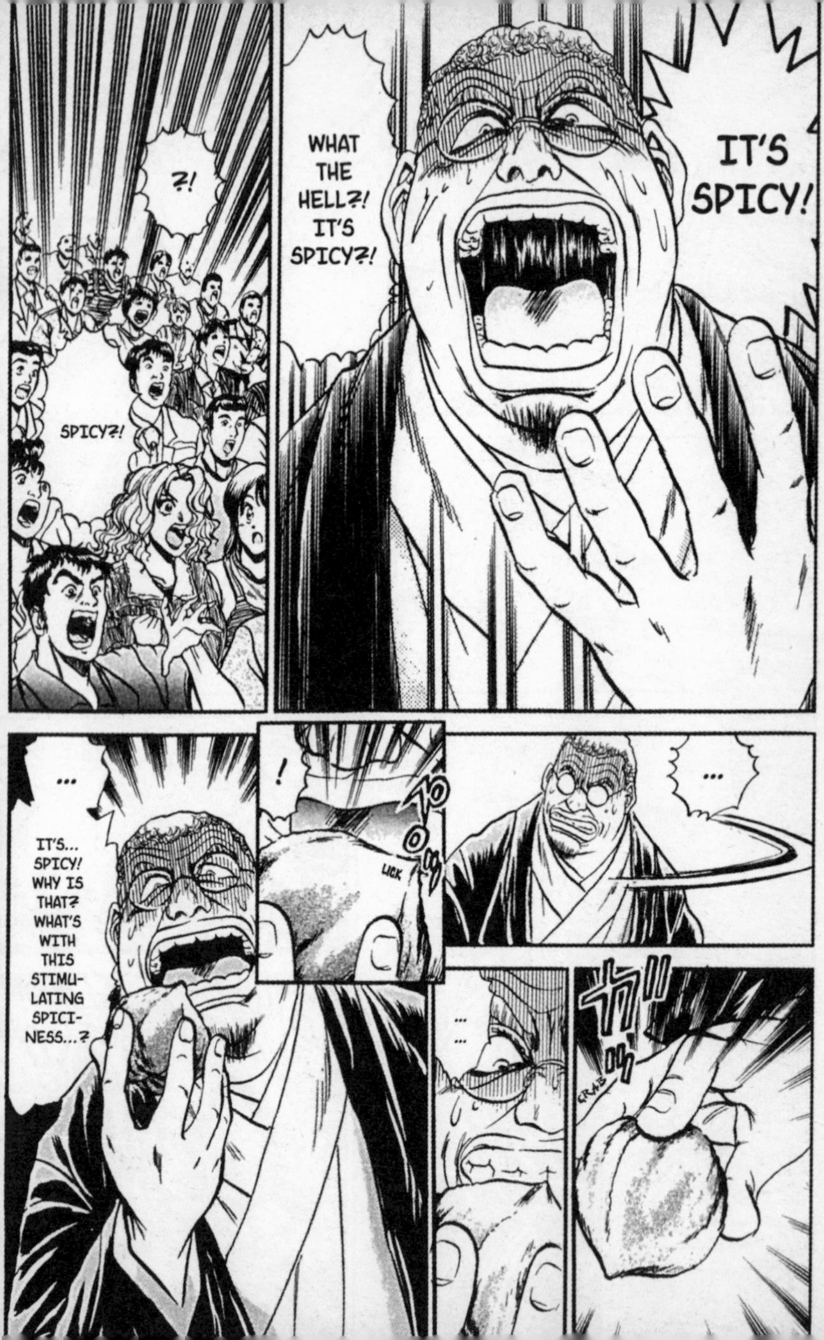
IT'S SPICY!
WHAT THE HELL?! IT'S SPICY?!
?!
SPICY?!
...
!
LICK
GRAB
... ...
...
IT'S... SPICY! WHY IS THAT? WHAT'S WITH THIS STIMULATING SPICINESS...?

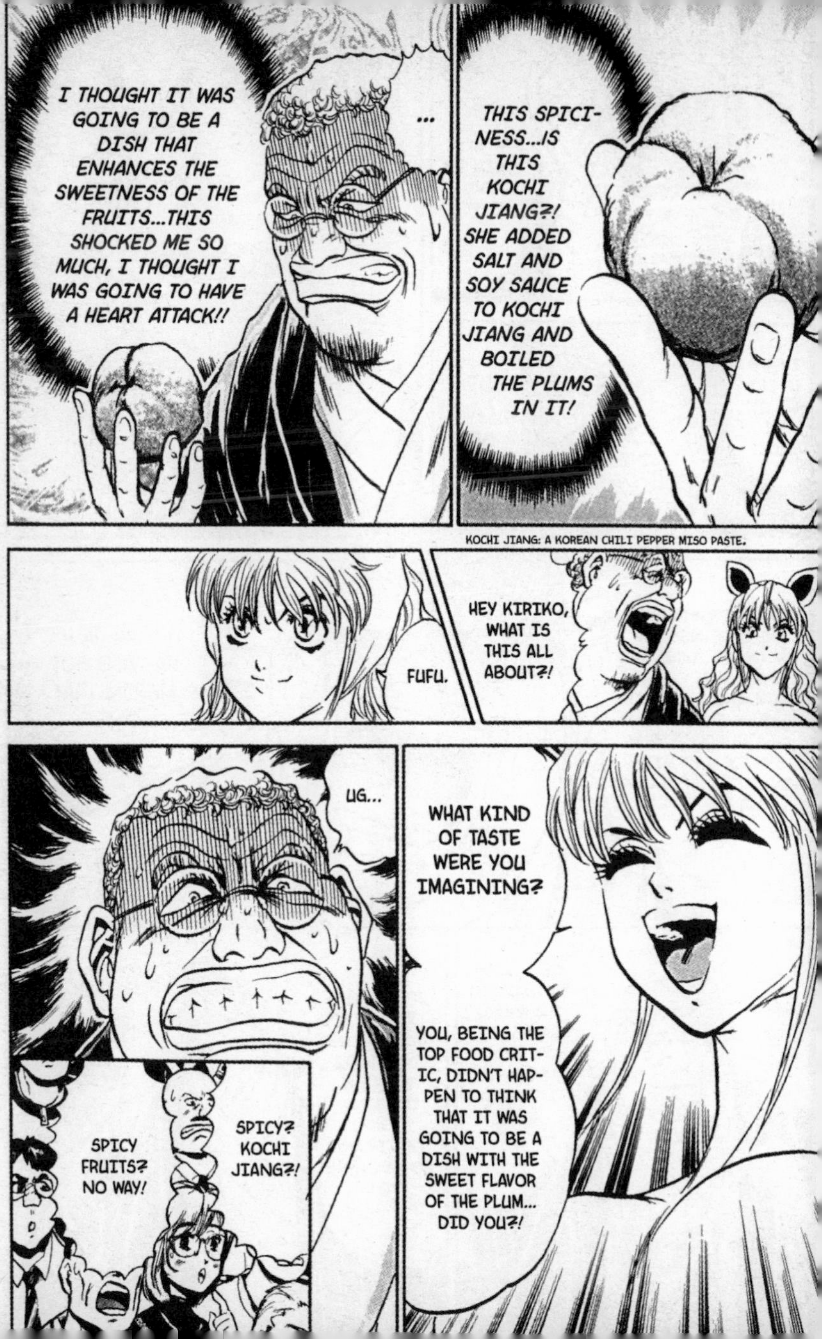
THIS SPICINESS...IS THIS KOCHI JIANG?! SHE ADDED SALT AND SOY SAUCE TO KOCHI JIANG AND BOILED THE PLUMS IN IT!
...
I THOUGHT IT WAS GOING TO BE A DISH THAT ENHANCES THE SWEETNESS OF THE FRUITS...THIS SHOCKED ME SO MUCH, I THOUGHT I WAS GOING TO HAVE A HEART ATTACK!!
KOCHI JIANG: A KOREAN CHILI PEPPER MISO PASTE.
HEY KIRIKO, WHAT IS THIS ALL ABOUT?!
FUFU.
WHAT KIND OF TASTE WERE YOU IMAGINING?
YOU, BEING THE TOP FOOD CRITIC, DIDN'T HAPPEN TO THINK THAT IT WAS GOING TO BE A DISH WITH THE SWEET FLAVOR OF THE PLUM... DID YOU?!
UG...
SPICY? KOCHI JIANG?!
SPICY FRUITS? NO WAY!

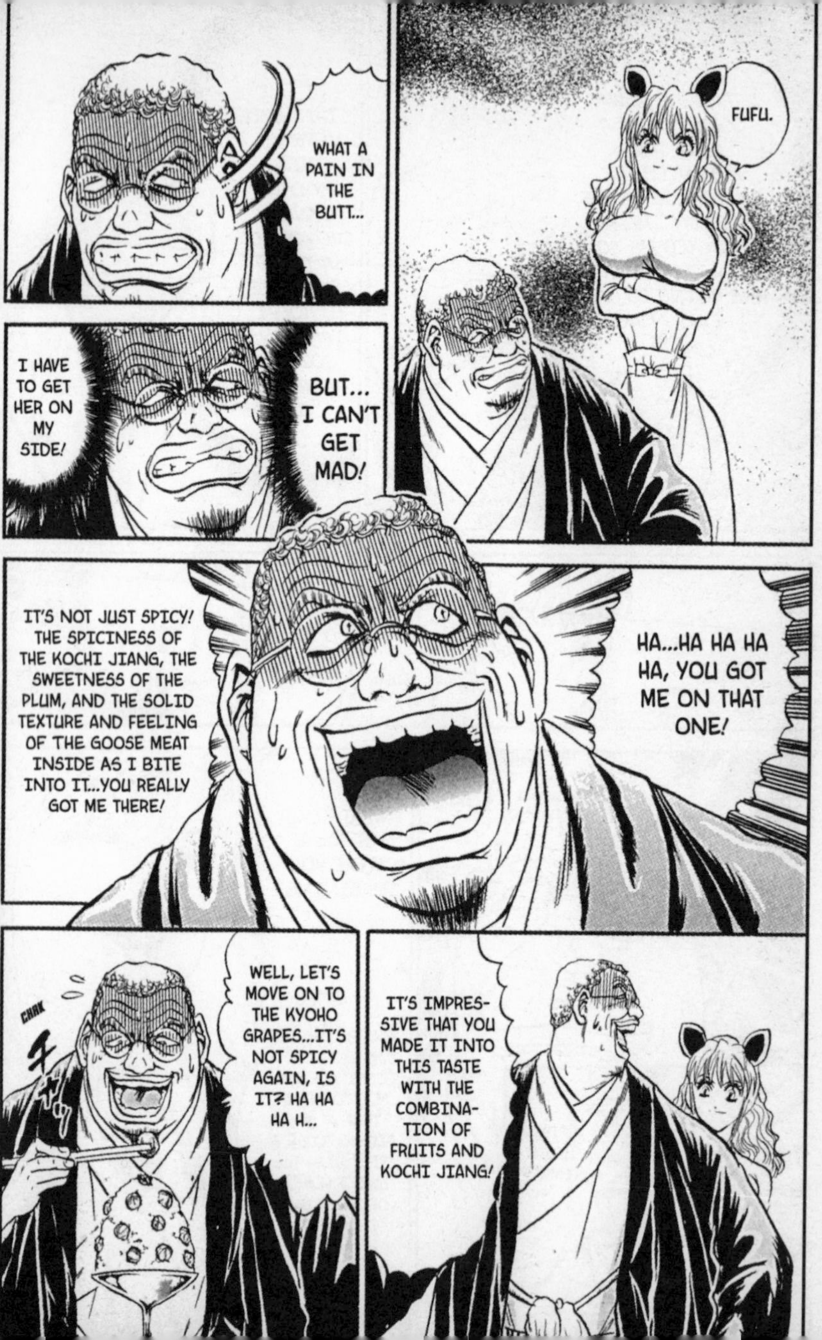
FUFU.
WHAT A PAIN IN THE BUTT...
BUT... I CAN'T GET MAD!
I HAVE TO GET HER ON MY SIDE!
HA...HA HA HA HA, YOU GOT ME ON THAT ONE!
IT'S NOT JUST SPICY! THE SPICINESS OF THE KOCHI JIANG, THE SWEETNESS OF THE PLUM, AND THE SOLID TEXTURE AND FEELING OF THE GOOSE MEAT INSIDE AS I BITE INTO IT...YOU REALLY GOT ME THERE!
IT'S IMPRES-SIVE THAT YOU MADE IT INTO THIS TASTE WITH THE COMBINA-TION OF FRUITS AND KOCHI JIANG!
WELL, LET'S MOVE ON TO THE KYOHO GRAPES...IT'S NOT SPICY AGAIN, IS IT? HA HA HA H...
CHAK

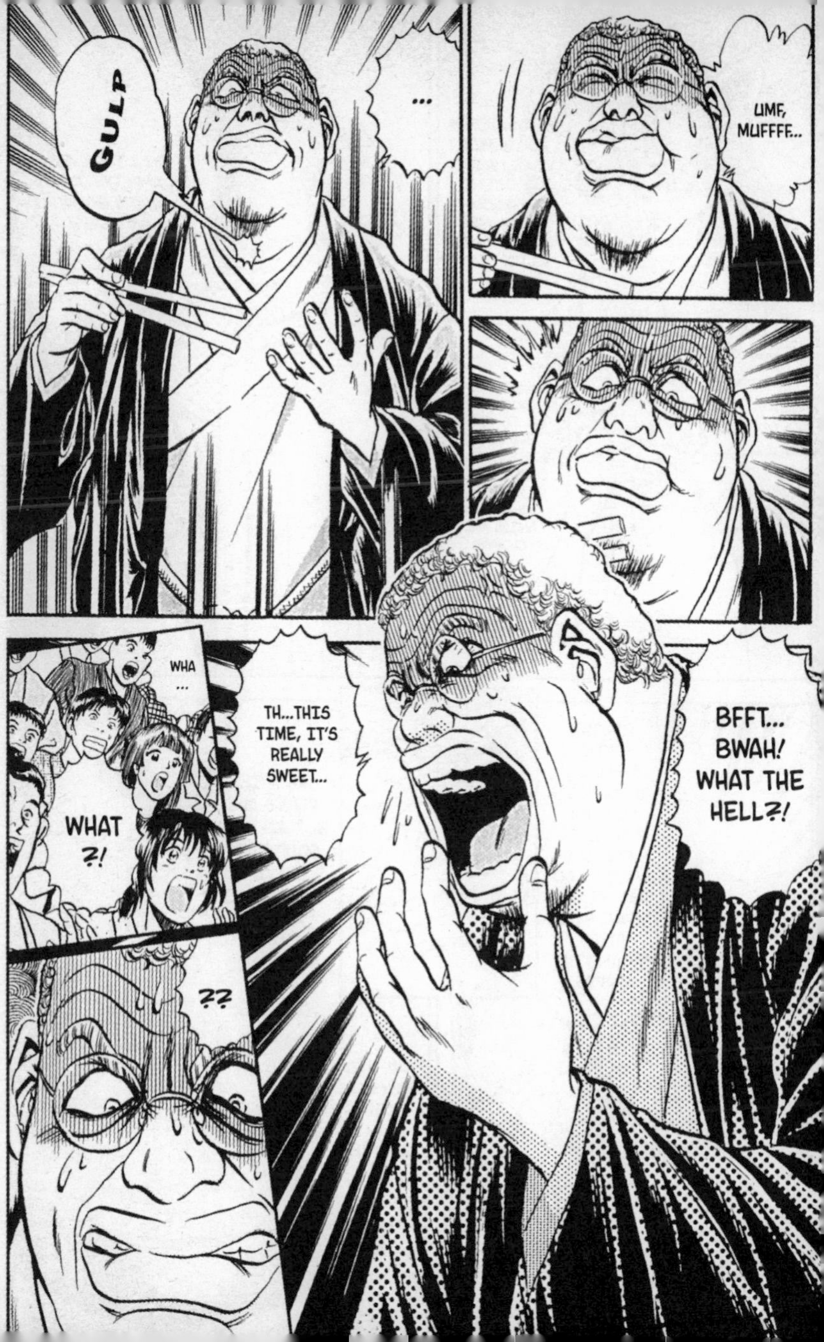
UMF, MUFFFF...
...
GULP
BFFT... BWAH! WHAT THE HELL?!
TH...THIS TIME, IT'S REALLY SWEET...
WHA ...
WHAT ?!
??

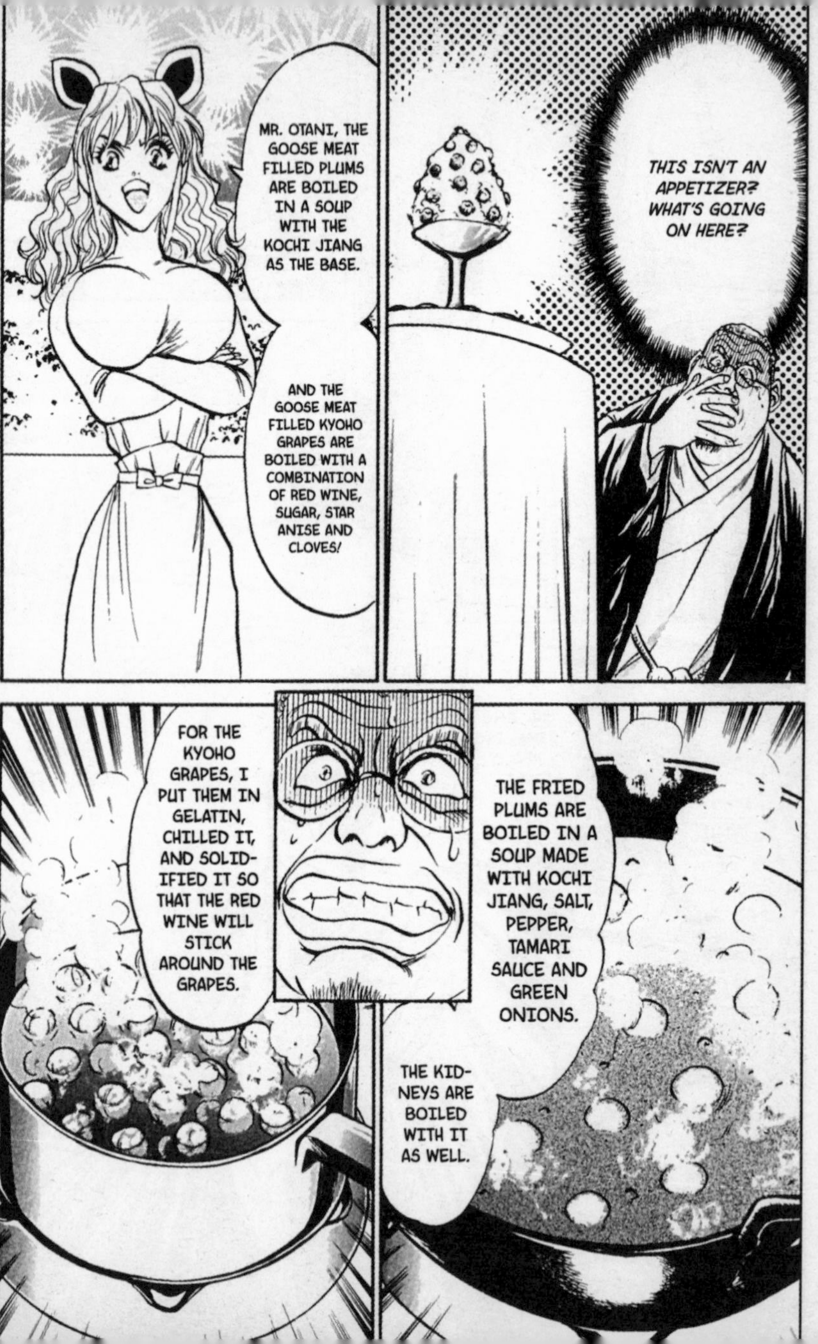
THIS ISN'T AN APPETIZER? WHAT'S GOING ON HERE?
MR. OTANI, THE GOOSE MEAT FILLED PLUMS ARE BOILED IN A SOUP WITH THE KOCHI JIANG AS THE BASE.
AND THE GOOSE MEAT FILLED KYOHO GRAPES ARE BOILED WITH A COMBINATION OF RED WINE, SUGAR, STAR ANISE AND CLOVES!
THE FRIED PLUMS ARE BOILED IN A SOUP MADE WITH KOCHI JIANG, SALT, PEPPER, TAMARI SAUCE AND GREEN ONIONS.
THE KID-NEYS ARE BOILED WITH IT AS WELL.
FOR THE KYOHO GRAPES, I PUT THEM IN GELATIN, CHILLED IT, AND SOLID-IFIED IT SO THAT THE RED WINE WILL STICK AROUND THE GRAPES.

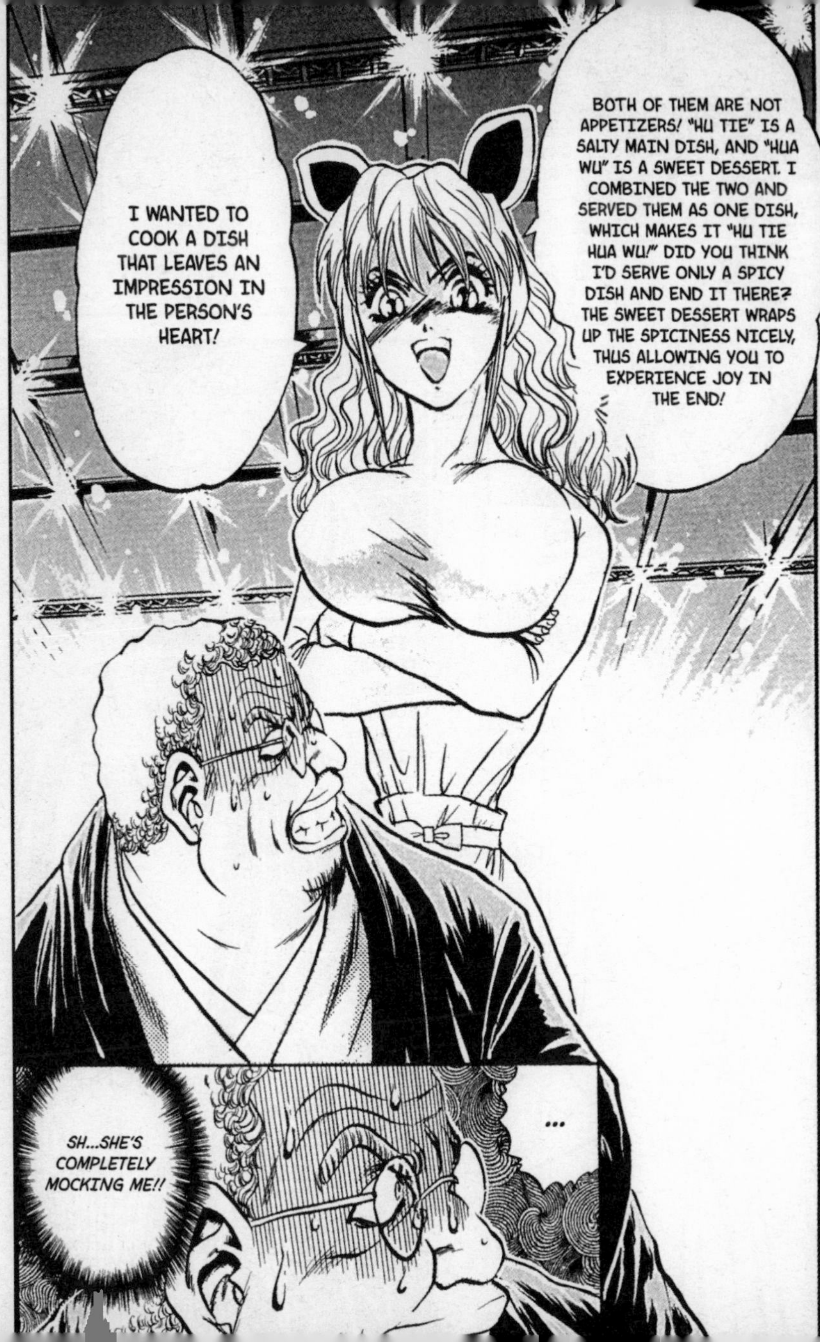
BOTH OF THEM ARE NOT APPETIZERS! "HU TIE" IS A SALTY MAIN DISH, AND "HUA WU" IS A SWEET DESSERT. I COMBINED THE TWO AND SERVED THEM AS ONE DISH, WHICH MAKES IT "HU TIE HUA WU!" DID YOU THINK I'D SERVE ONLY A SPICY DISH AND END IT THERE? THE SWEET DESSERT WRAPS UP THE SPICINESS NICELY, THUS ALLOWING YOU TO EXPERIENCE JOY IN THE END!
I WANTED TO COOK A DISH THAT LEAVES AN IMPRESSION IN THE PERSON'S HEART!
...
SH...SHE'S COMPLETELY MOCKING ME!!

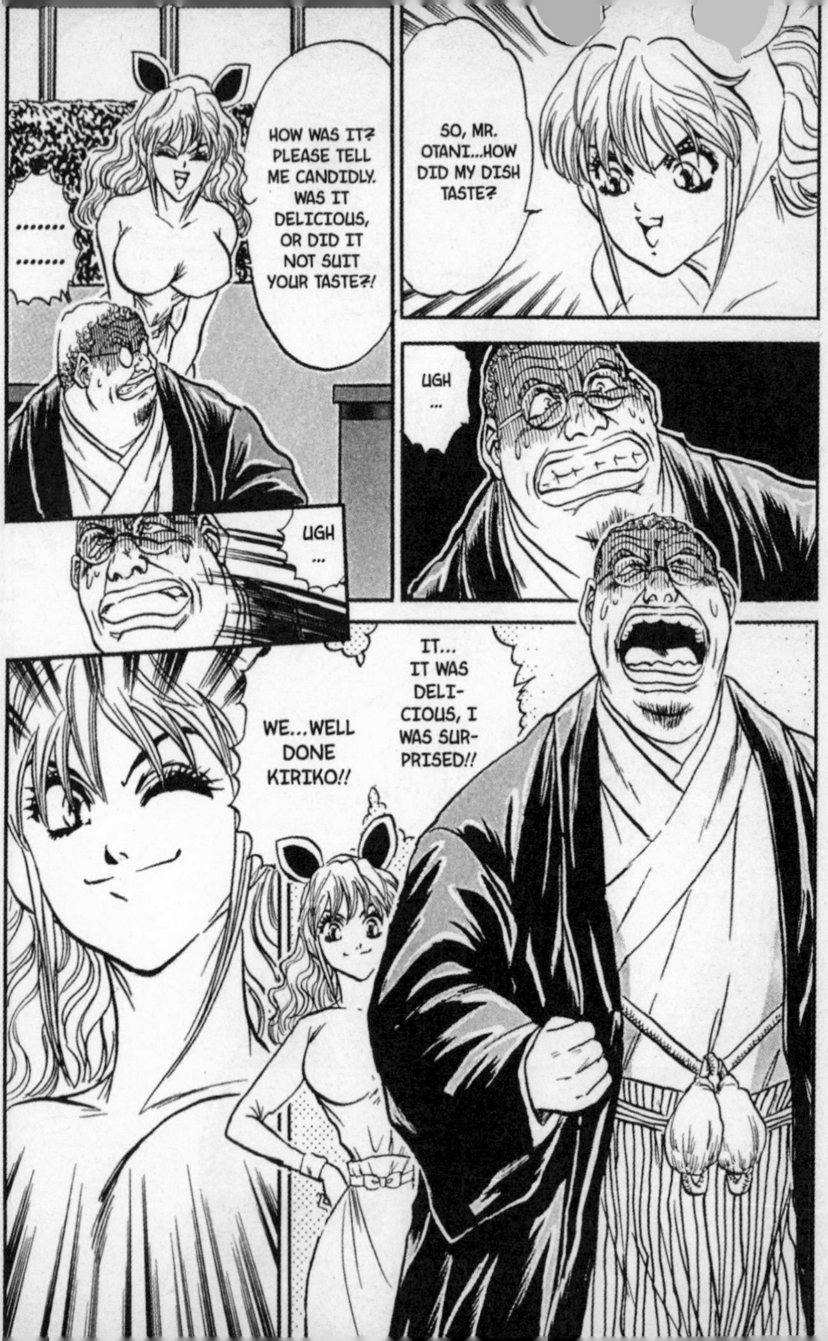
SO, MR. OTANI...HOW DID MY DISH TASTE?
HOW WAS IT? PLEASE TELL ME CANDIDLY. WAS IT DELICIOUS, OR DID IT NOT SUIT YOUR TASTE?!
....
....
UGH ...
UGH ...
IT... IT WAS DELICIOUS, I WAS SURPRISED!!
WE...WELL DONE KIRIKO!!

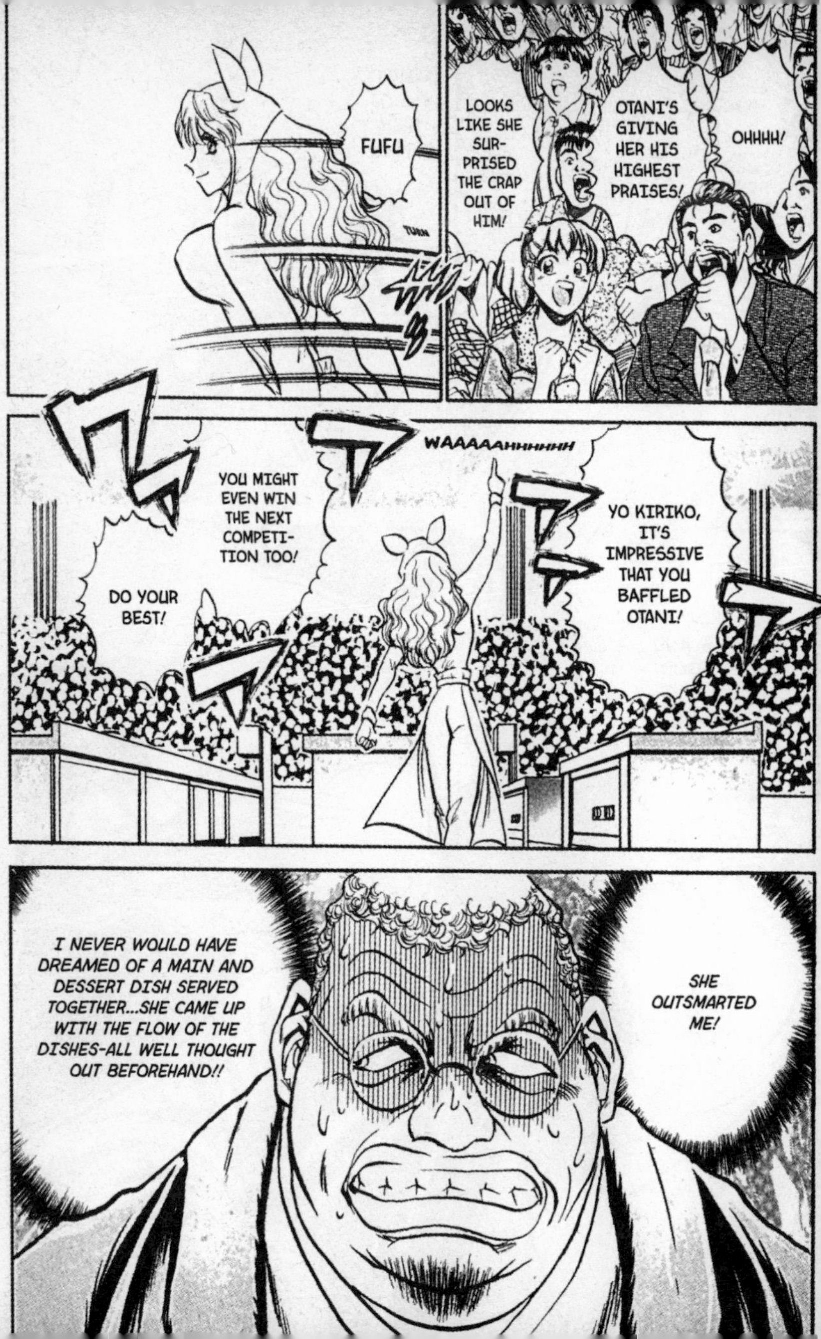
OHHHH!
OTANI'S GIVING HER HIS HIGHEST PRAISES!
LOOKS LIKE SHE SURPRISED THE CRAP OUT OF HIM!
FUFU
YO KIRIKO, IT'S IMPRESSIVE THAT YOU BAFFLED OTANI!
WAAAAAHHHHHH
YOU MIGHT EVEN WIN THE NEXT COMPETITION TOO!
DO YOUR BEST!
SHE OUTSMARTED ME!
I NEVER WOULD HAVE DREAMED OF A MAIN AND DESSERT DISH SERVED TOGETHER...SHE CAME UP WITH THE FLOW OF THE DISHES-ALL WELL THOUGHT OUT BEFOREHAND!!

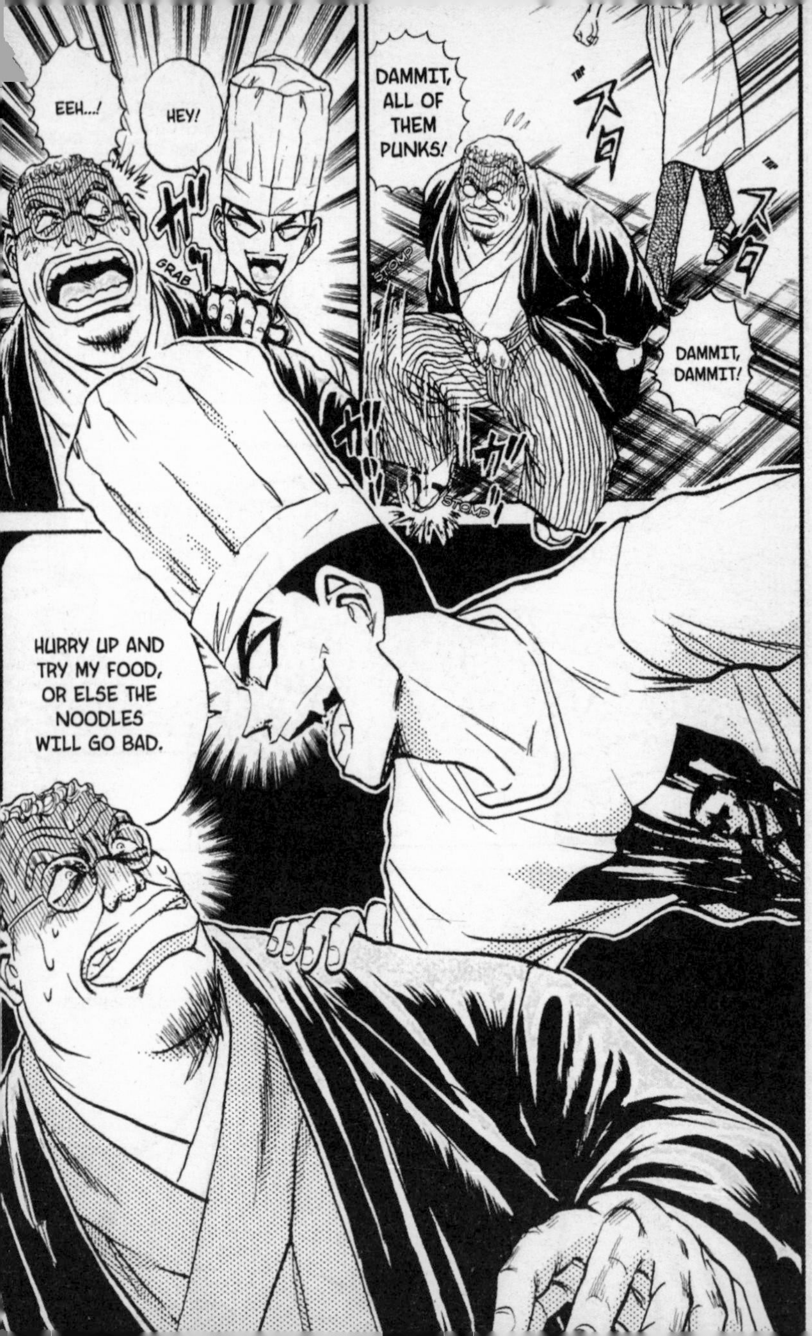
DAMMIT, ALL OF THEM PUNKS!
STOMP
STOMP
DAMMIT, DAMMIT!
HEY!
EEH...!
GRAB
HURRY UP AND TRY MY FOOD, OR ELSE THE NOODLES WILL GO BAD.

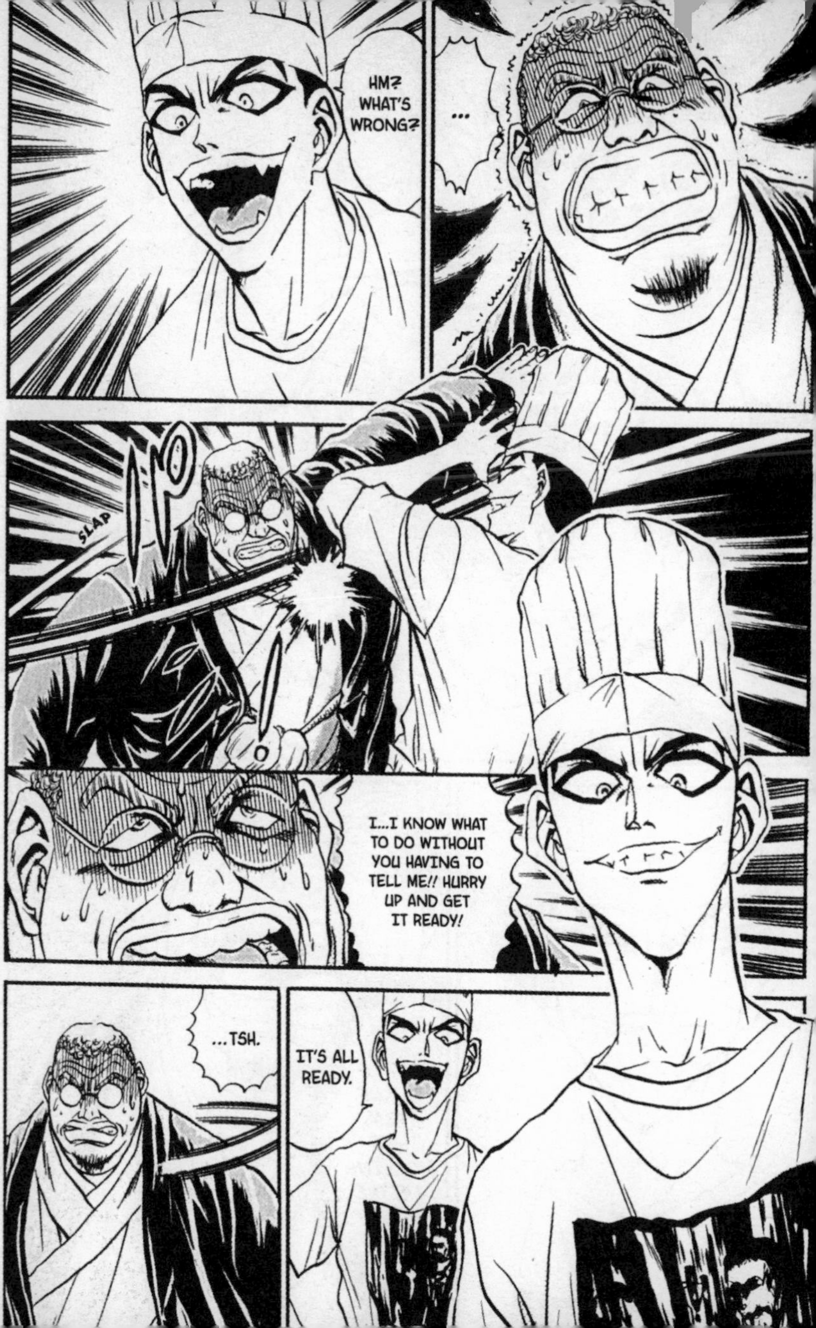
...
HM? WHAT'S WRONG?
SLAP
I...I KNOW WHAT TO DO WITHOUT YOU HAVING TO TELL ME!! HURRY UP AND GET IT READY!
IT'S ALL READY.
...TSH.

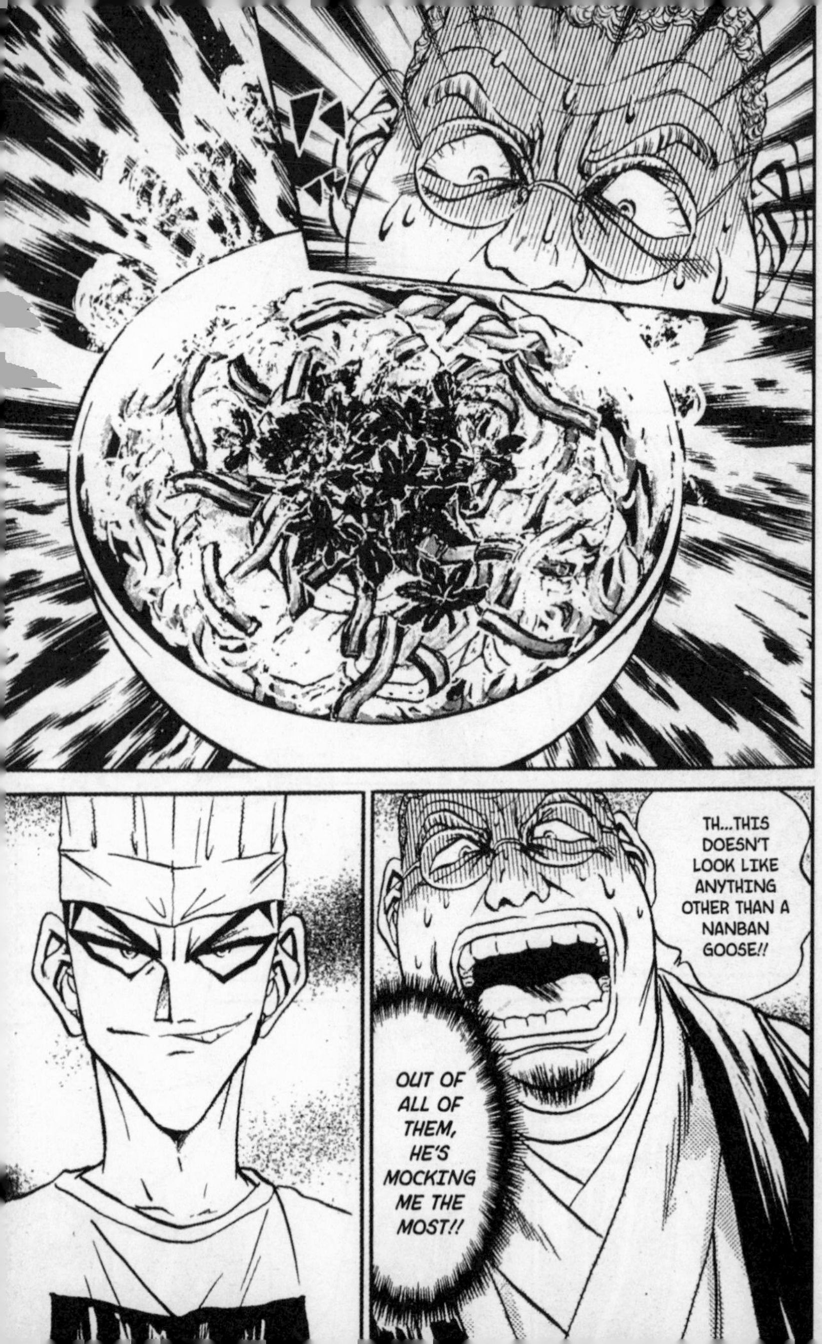
TH...THIS DOESN'T LOOK LIKE ANYTHING OTHER THAN A NANBAN GOOSE!!
OUT OF ALL OF THEM, HE'S MOCKING ME THE MOST!!

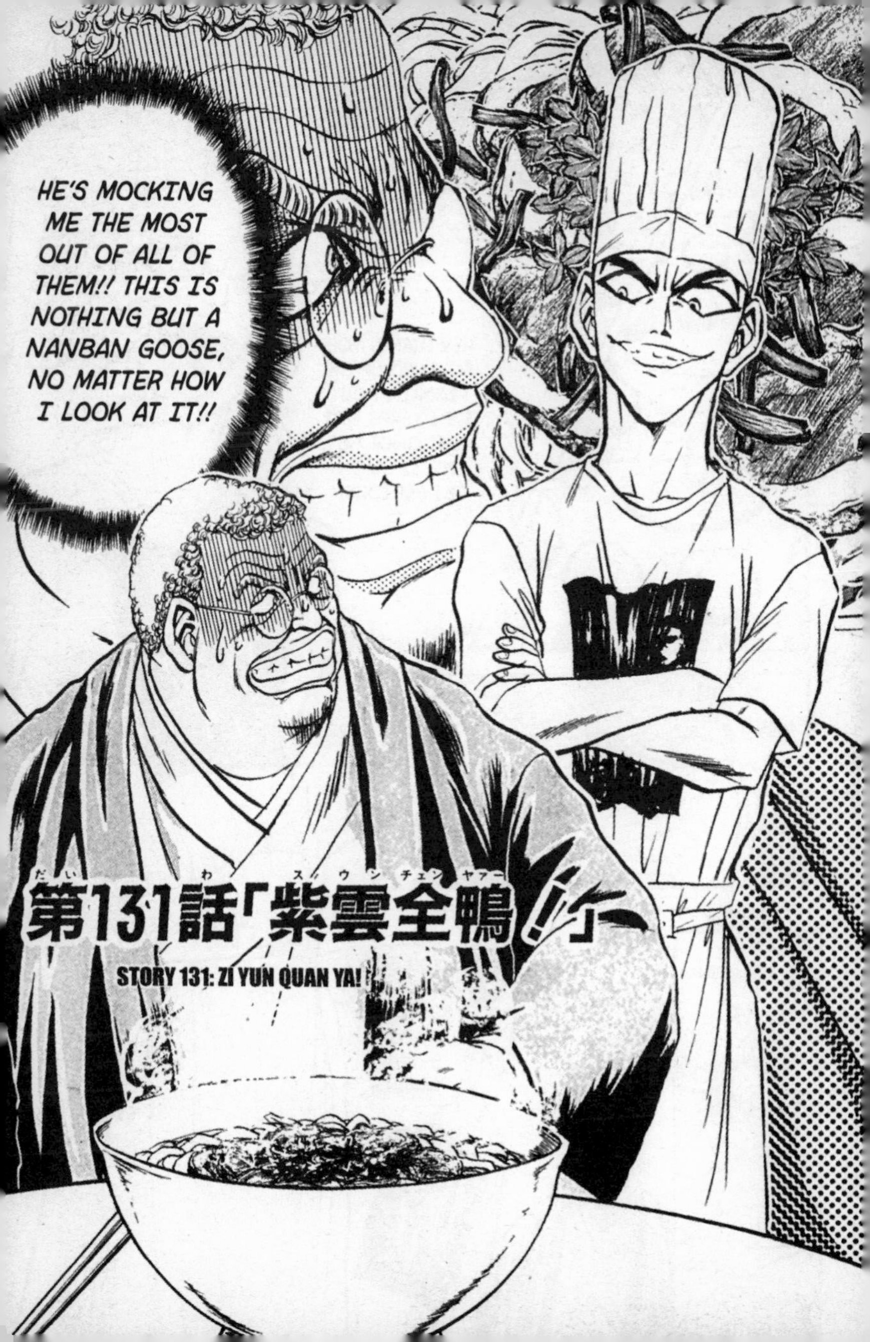
HE'S MOCKING ME THE MOST OUT OF ALL OF THEM!! THIS IS NOTHING BUT A NANBAN GOOSE, NO MATTER HOW I LOOK AT IT!!
第131話「紫雲全鴨!」
STORY 131: ZI YUN QUAN YA!

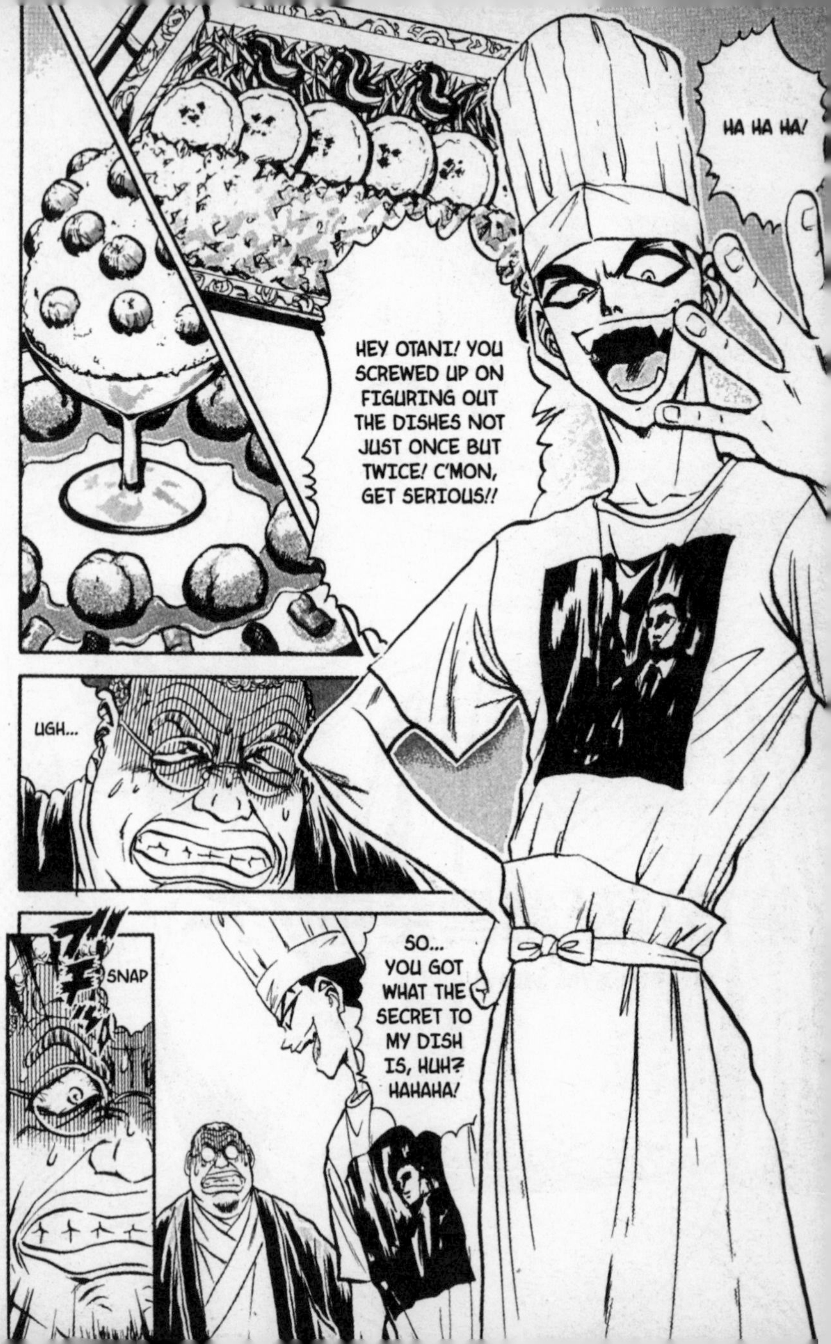
HA HA HA!
HEY OTANI! YOU SCREWED UP ON FIGURING OUT THE DISHES NOT JUST ONCE BUT TWICE! C'MON, GET SERIOUS!!
UGH...
SO... YOU GOT WHAT THE SECRET TO MY DISH IS, HUH? HAHAHA!
SNAP

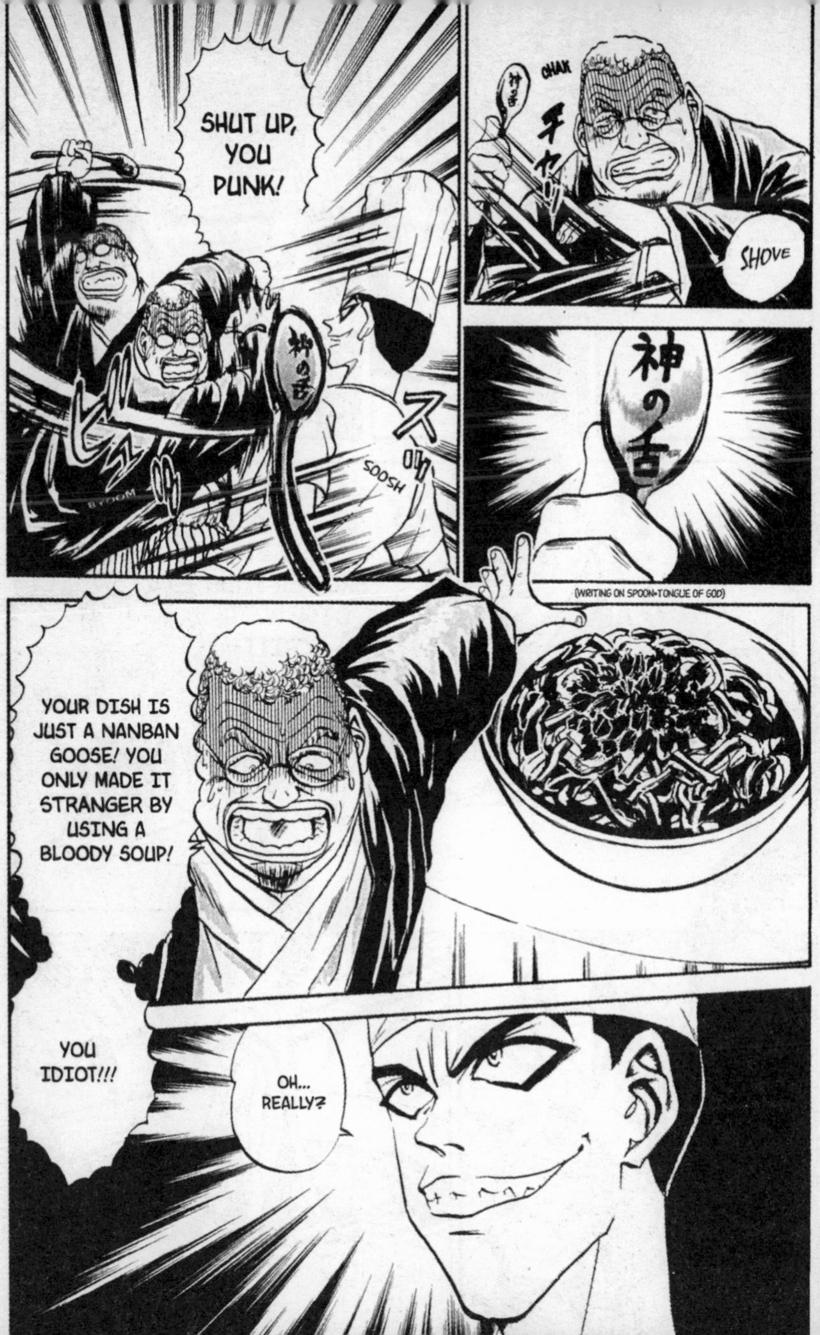

CHAK
SHOVE
SHUT UP, YOU PUNK!
SOOSH
BYOOM
(WRITING ON SPOON=TONGUE OF GOD)
神の舌
YOUR DISH IS JUST A NANBAN GOOSE! YOU ONLY MADE IT STRANGER BY USING A BLOODY SOUP!
YOU IDIOT!!!
OH... REALLY?

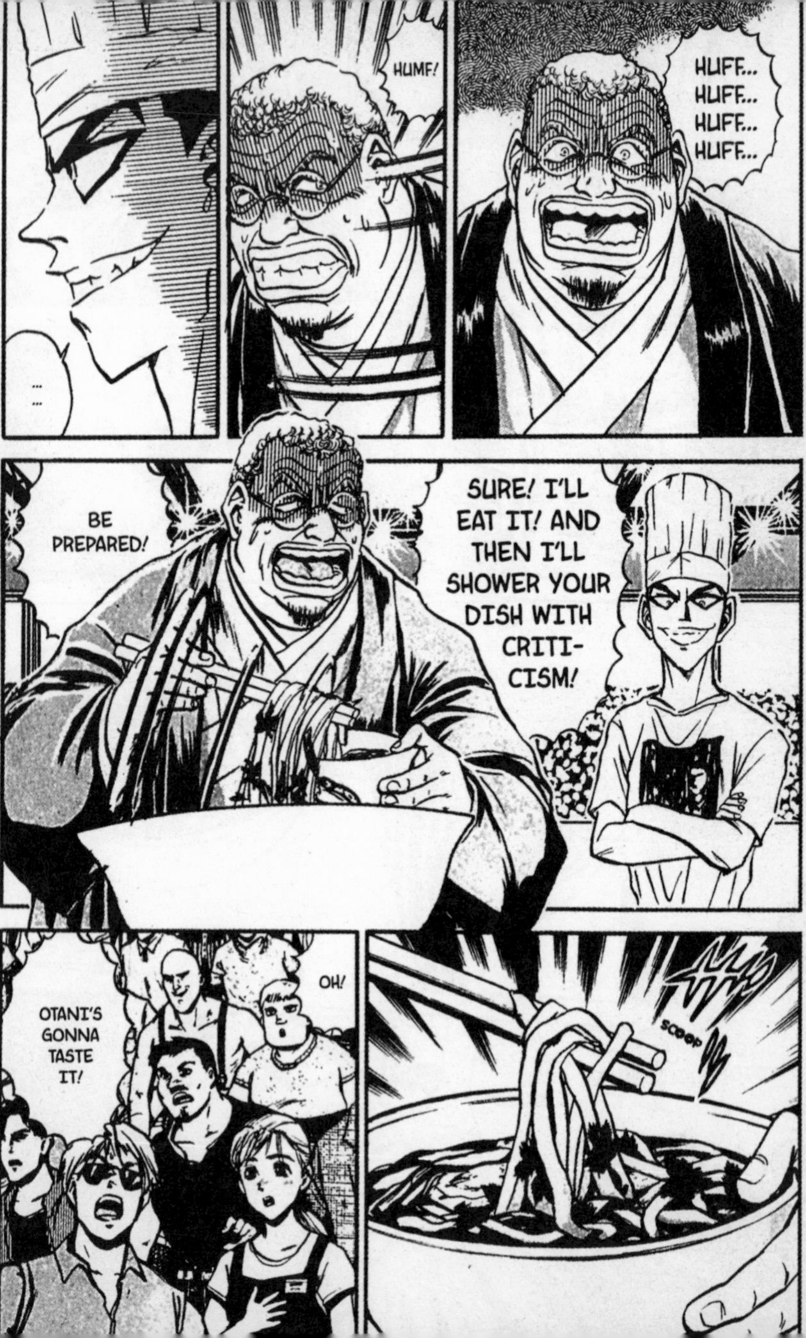
HUFF... HUFF... HUFF... HUFF...
HUMF!
... ...
SURE! I'LL EAT IT! AND THEN I'LL SHOWER YOUR DISH WITH CRITI- CISM!
BE PREPARED!
SCOOP
OH!
OTANI'S GONNA TASTE IT!

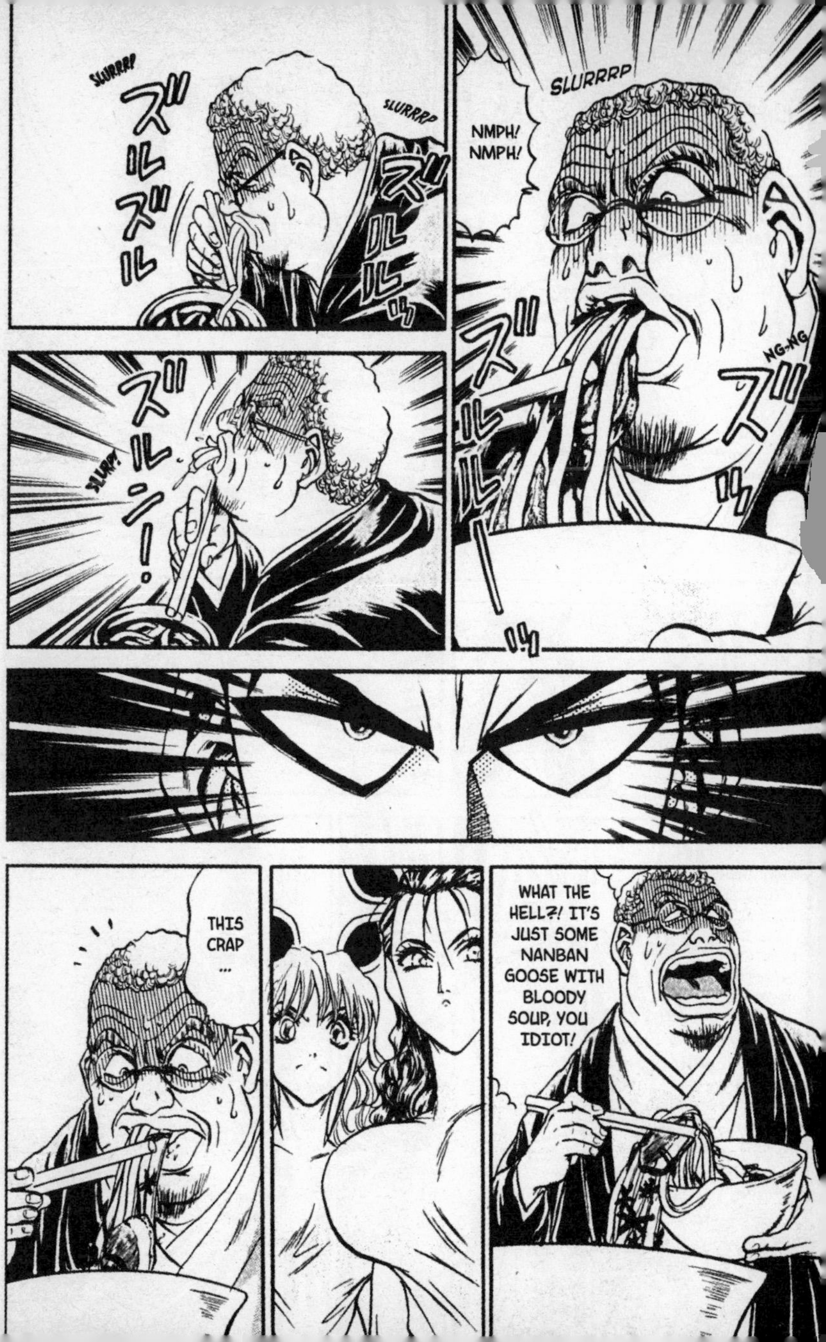
SLURRRP
NMPH! NMPH!
NG-NG
SLURRP
SLURRRP
SLURP!
WHAT THE HELL?! IT'S JUST SOME NANBAN GOOSE WITH BLOODY SOUP, YOU IDIOT!
THIS CRAP ...

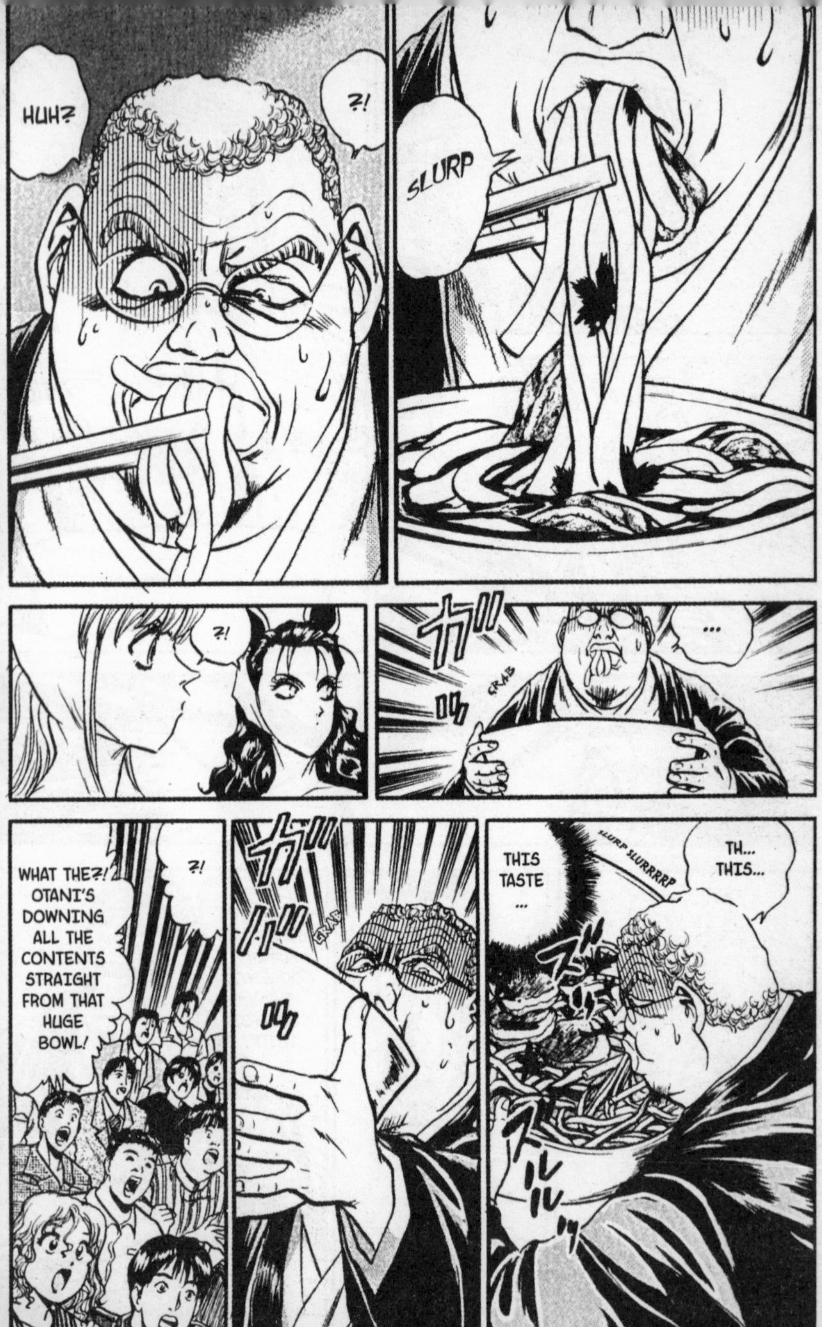
SLURP
?!
HUH?
...
GRAB
?!
TH... THIS...
SLURP SLURRRRP
THIS TASTE ...
GRAB
?!
WHAT THE?! OTANI'S DOWNING ALL THE CONTENTS STRAIGHT FROM THAT HUGE BOWL!

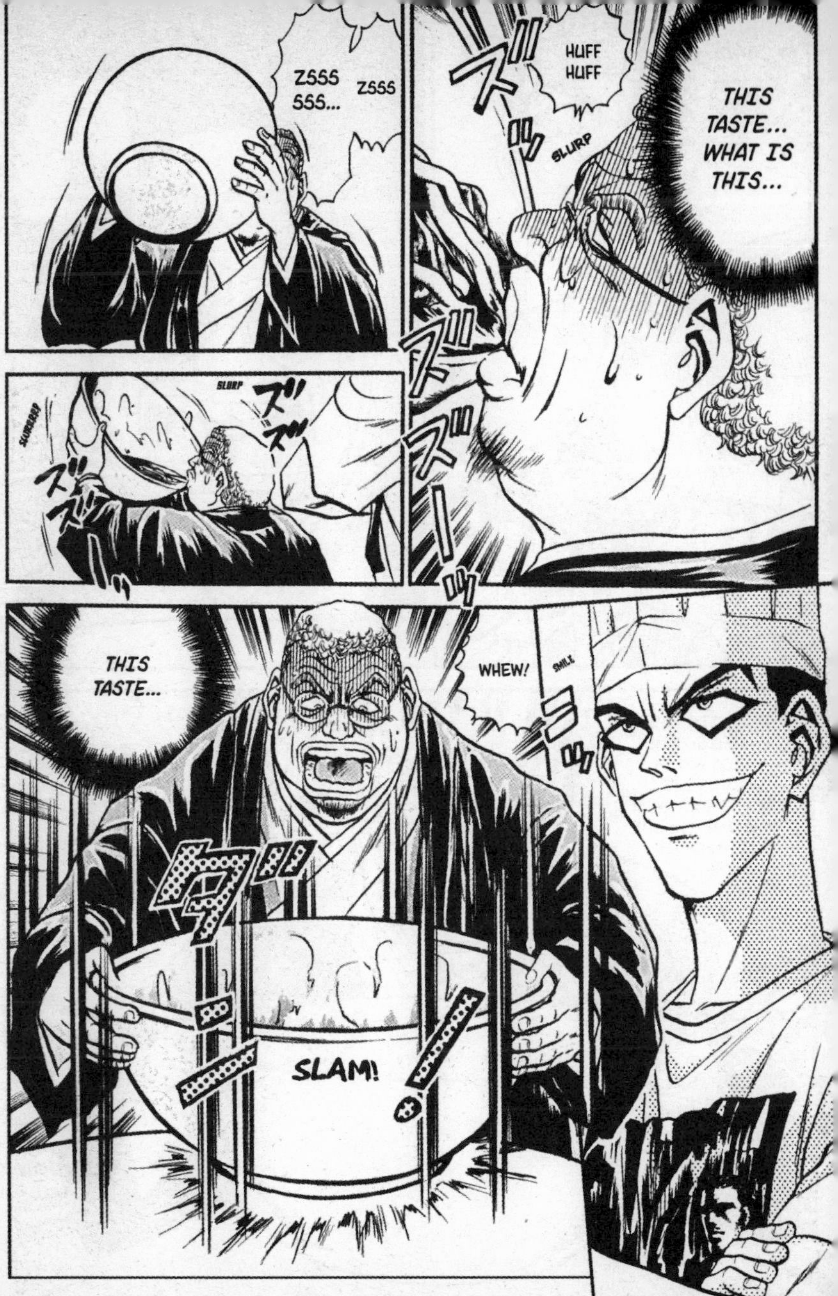
HUFF HUFF
SLURP
THIS TASTE... WHAT IS THIS...
ZSSS SSS...
ZSSS
SLURP
SLURRRP
WHEW!
SMILE
THIS TASTE...
SLAM!

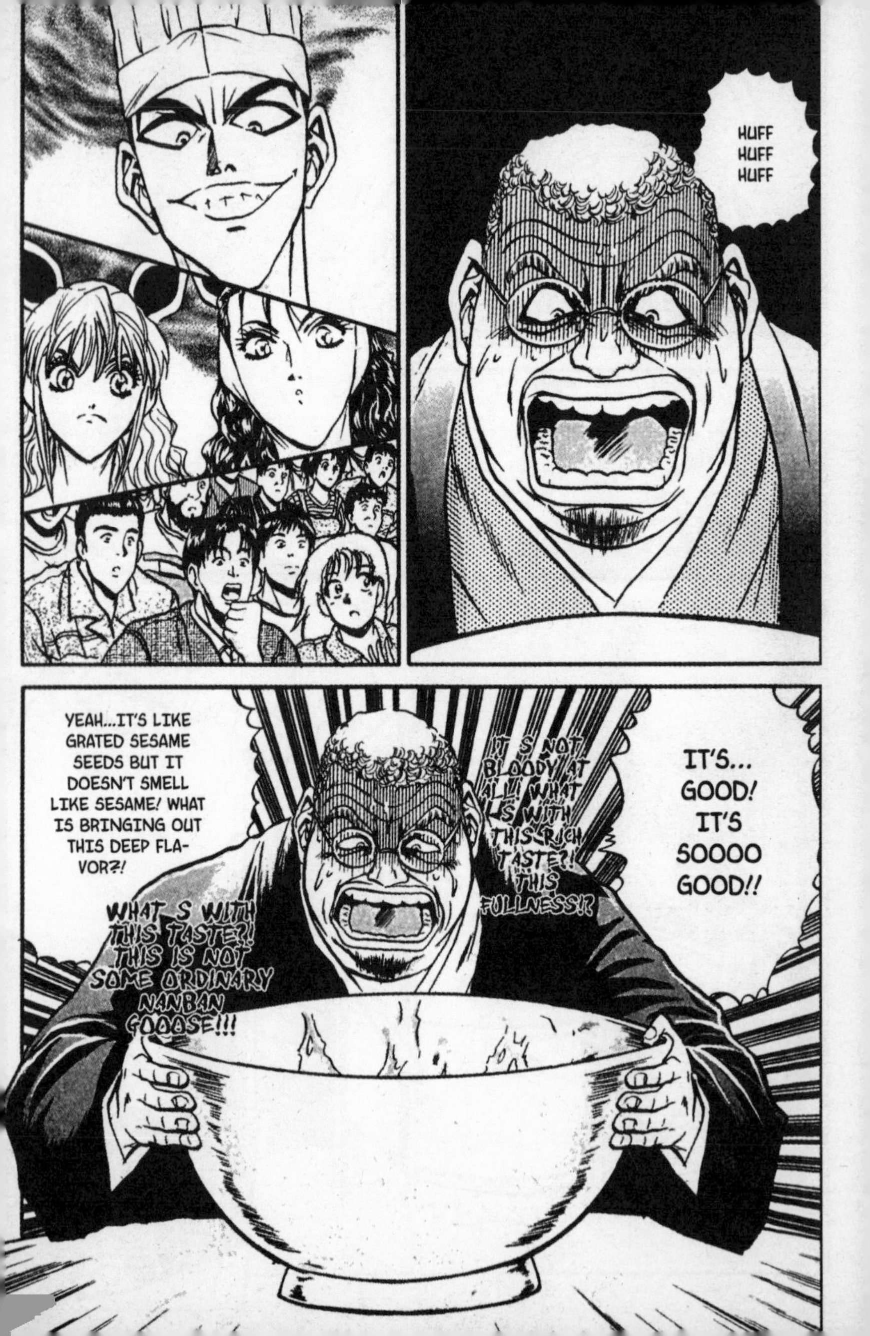
HUFF HUFF HUFF
IT'S... GOOD! IT'S SOOOO GOOD!!
IT'S NOT BLOODY AT ALL! WHAT IS WITH THIS RICH TASTE?! THIS FULLNESS!?
YEAH...IT'S LIKE GRATED SESAME SEEDS BUT IT DOESN'T SMELL LIKE SESAME! WHAT IS BRINGING OUT THIS DEEP FLAVOR?!
WHAT'S WITH THIS TASTE?! THIS IS NOT SOME ORDINARY NANBAN GOOOSE!!!

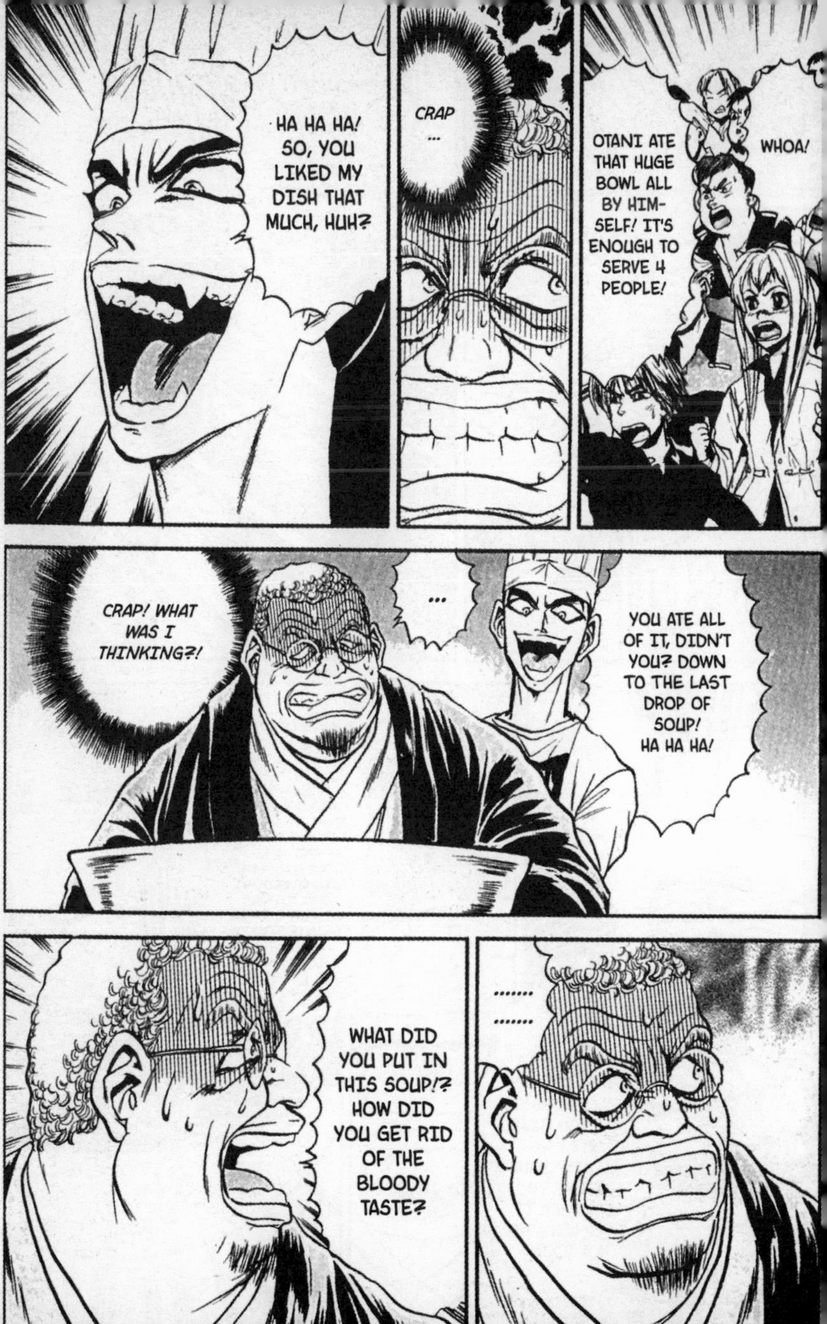
WHOA!
OTANI ATE THAT HUGE BOWL ALL BY HIM-SELF! IT'S ENOUGH TO SERVE 4 PEOPLE!
CRAP ...
HA HA HA! SO, YOU LIKED MY DISH THAT MUCH, HUH?
YOU ATE ALL OF IT, DIDN'T YOU? DOWN TO THE LAST DROP OF SOUP! HA HA HA!
...
CRAP! WHAT WAS I THINKING?!
....
WHAT DID YOU PUT IN THIS SOUP!? HOW DID YOU GET RID OF THE BLOODY TASTE?

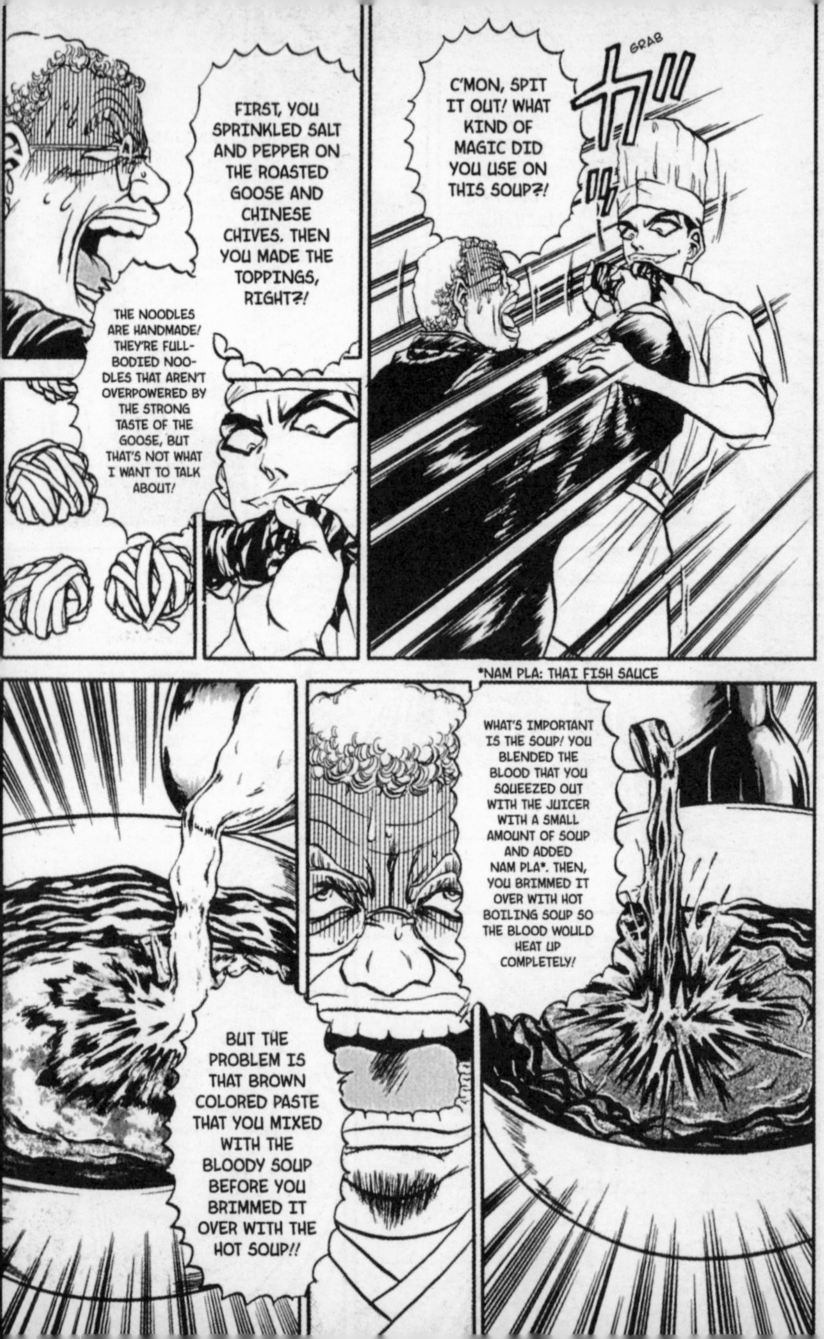
GRAB
C'MON, SPIT IT OUT! WHAT KIND OF MAGIC DID YOU USE ON THIS SOUP?!
FIRST, YOU SPRINKLED SALT AND PEPPER ON THE ROASTED GOOSE AND CHINESE CHIVES. THEN YOU MADE THE TOPPINGS, RIGHT?!
THE NOODLES ARE HANDMADE! THEY'RE FULL-BODIED NOODLES THAT AREN'T OVERPOWERED BY THE STRONG TASTE OF THE GOOSE, BUT THAT'S NOT WHAT I WANT TO TALK ABOUT!
*NAM PLA: THAI FISH SAUCE
WHAT'S IMPORTANT IS THE SOUP! YOU BLENDED THE BLOOD THAT YOU SQUEEZED OUT WITH THE JUICER WITH A SMALL AMOUNT OF SOUP AND ADDED NAM PLA*. THEN, YOU BRIMMED IT OVER WITH HOT BOILING SOUP SO THE BLOOD WOULD HEAT UP COMPLETELY!
BUT THE PROBLEM IS THAT BROWN COLORED PASTE THAT YOU MIXED WITH THE BLOODY SOUP BEFORE YOU BRIMMED IT OVER WITH THE HOT SOUP!!

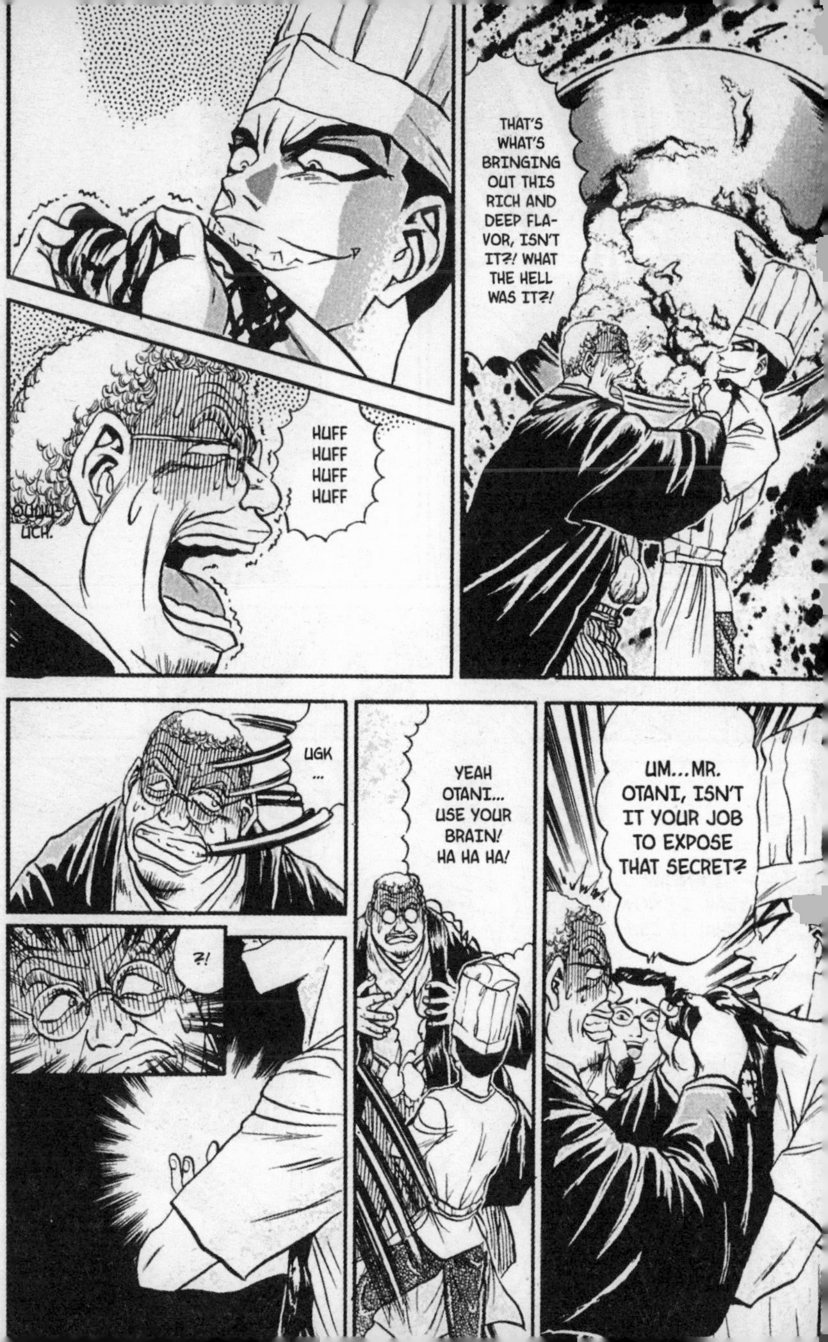
THAT'S WHAT'S BRINGING OUT THIS RICH AND DEEP FLAVOR, ISN'T IT?! WHAT THE HELL WAS IT?!
HUFF HUFF HUFF HUFF
UCH.
UM...MR. OTANI, ISN'T IT YOUR JOB TO EXPOSE THAT SECRET?
YEAH OTANI... USE YOUR BRAIN! HA HA HA!
UGK ...
?!

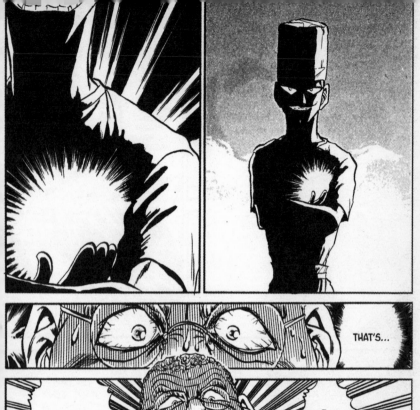

THAT'S...

I...

I KNOW! YEAH, I KNOW WHAT IT IS!!

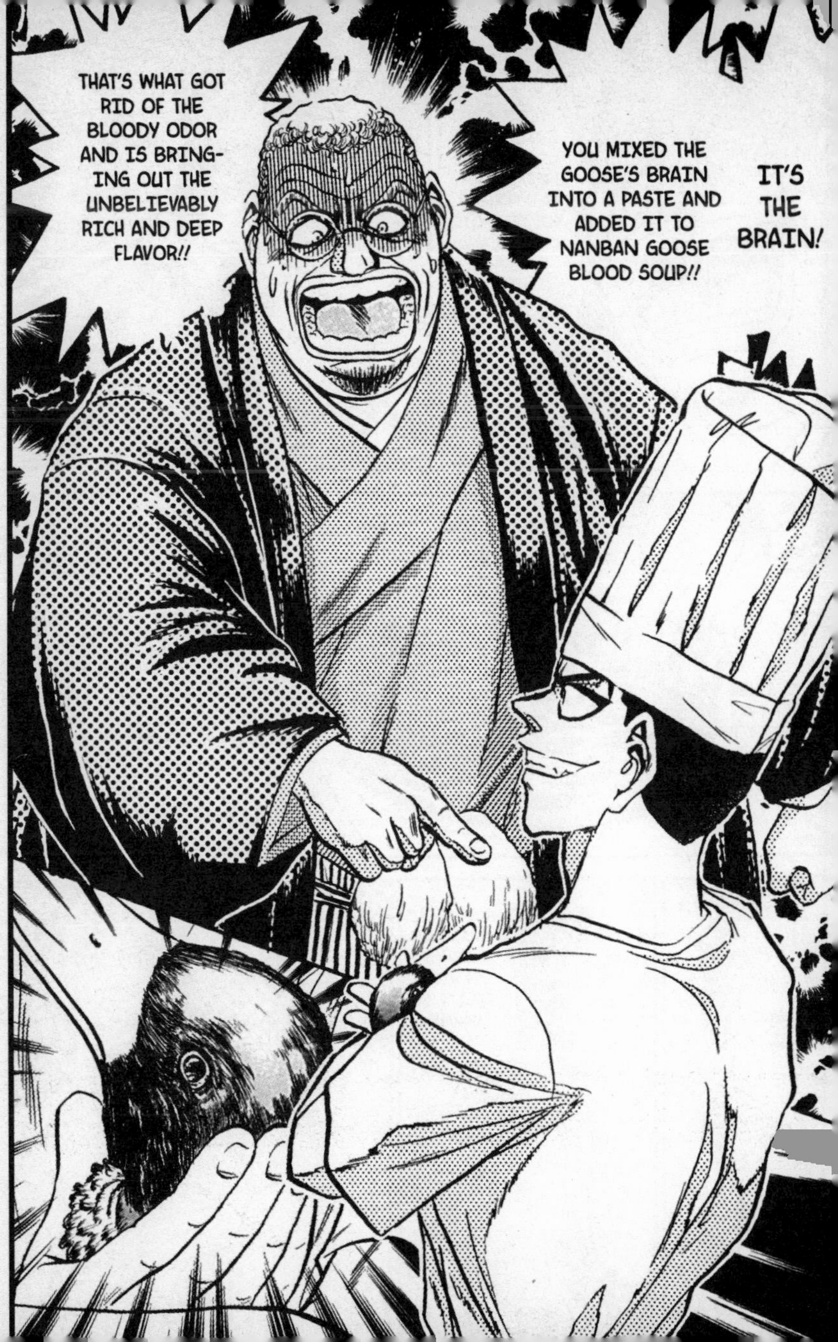
IT'S THE BRAIN!
YOU MIXED THE GOOSE'S BRAIN INTO A PASTE AND ADDED IT TO NANBAN GOOSE BLOOD SOUP!!
THAT'S WHAT GOT RID OF THE BLOODY ODOR AND IS BRING-ING OUT THE UNBELIEVABLY RICH AND DEEP FLAVOR!!

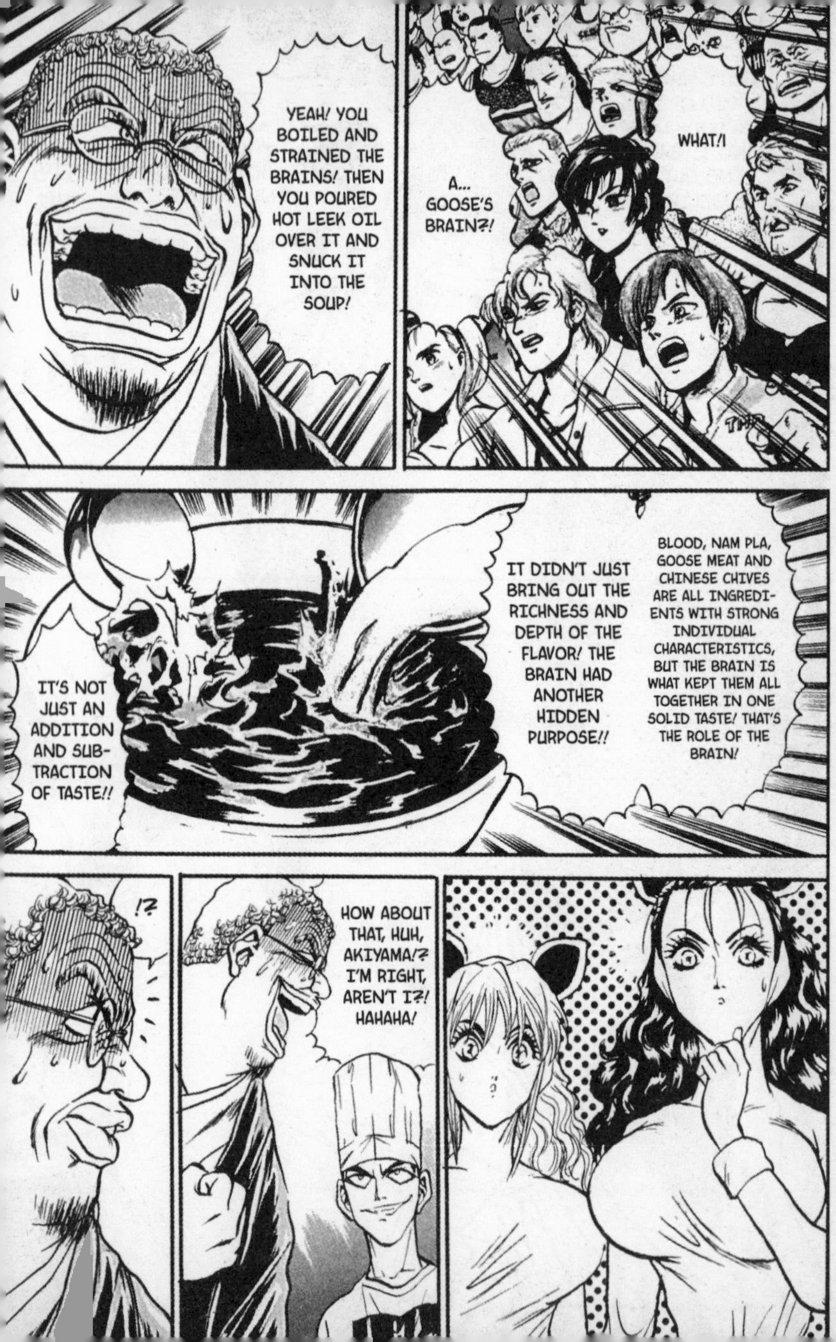
YEAH! YOU BOILED AND STRAINED THE BRAINS! THEN YOU POURED HOT LEEK OIL OVER IT AND SNUCK IT INTO THE SOUP!
A... GOOSE'S BRAIN?!
WHAT?!
IT'S NOT JUST AN ADDITION AND SUB-TRACTION OF TASTE!!
IT DIDN'T JUST BRING OUT THE RICHNESS AND DEPTH OF THE FLAVOR! THE BRAIN HAD ANOTHER HIDDEN PURPOSE!!
BLOOD, NAM PLA, GOOSE MEAT AND CHINESE CHIVES ARE ALL INGREDI-ENTS WITH STRONG INDIVIDUAL CHARACTERISTICS, BUT THE BRAIN IS WHAT KEPT THEM ALL TOGETHER IN ONE SOLID TASTE! THAT'S THE ROLE OF THE BRAIN!
!?
HOW ABOUT THAT, HUH, AKIYAMA!? I'M RIGHT, AREN'T I?! HAHAHA!

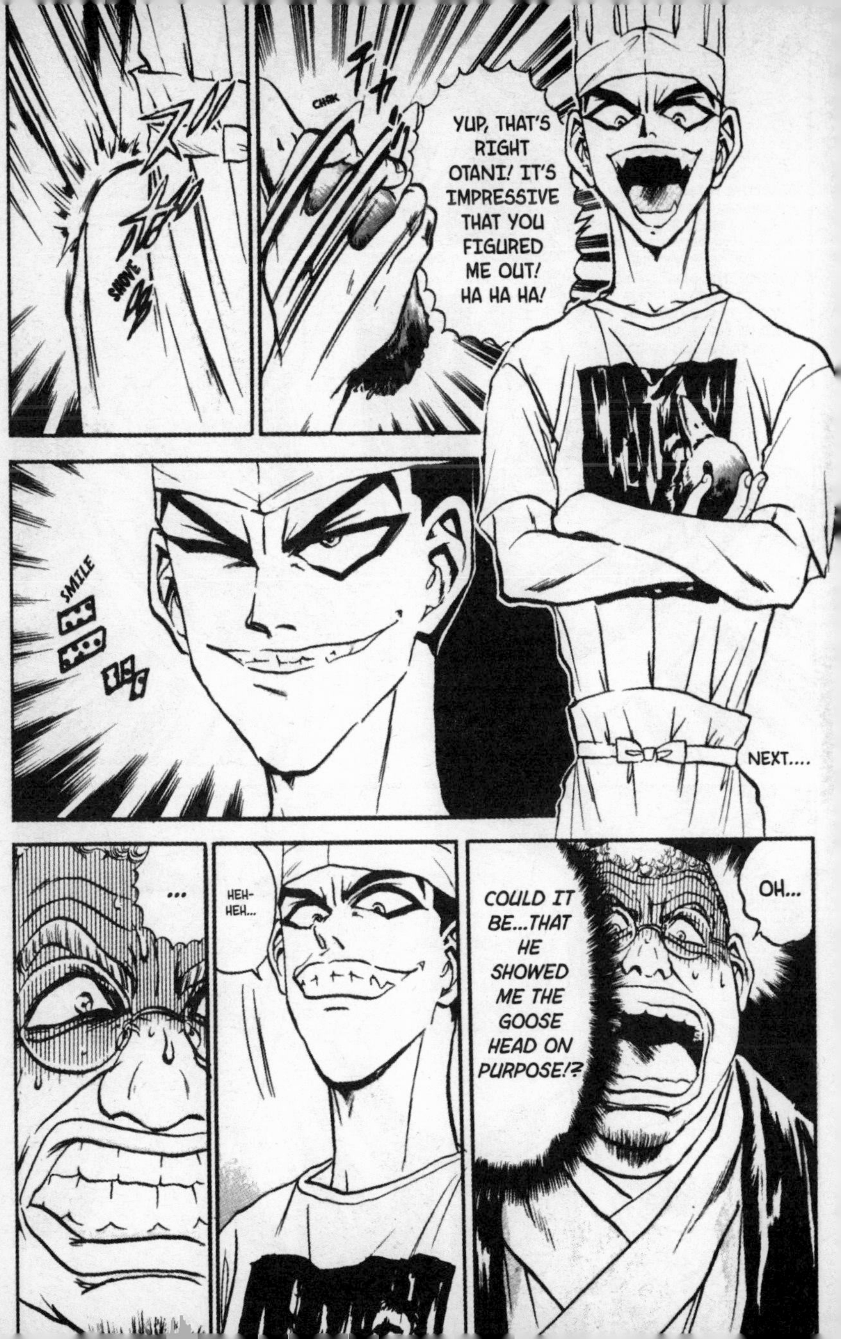
YUP, THAT'S RIGHT OTANI! IT'S IMPRESSIVE THAT YOU FIGURED ME OUT! HA HA HA!
NEXT....
CHAK
SHOVE
SMILE
OH...
COULD IT BE...THAT HE SHOWED ME THE GOOSE HEAD ON PURPOSE!?
HEH-HEH...
...

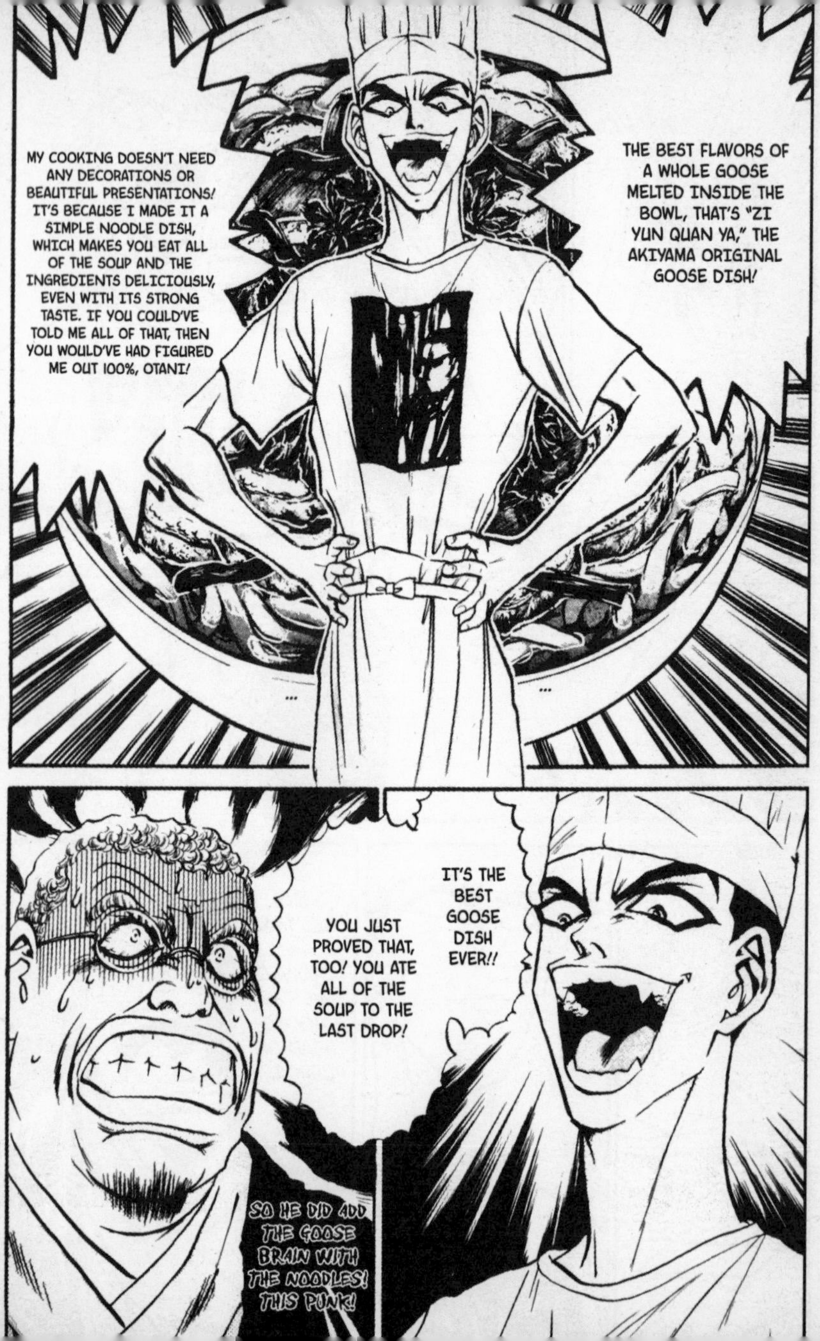
THE BEST FLAVORS OF A WHOLE GOOSE MELTED INSIDE THE BOWL, THAT'S "ZI YUN QUAN YA," THE AKIYAMA ORIGINAL GOOSE DISH!
MY COOKING DOESN'T NEED ANY DECORATIONS OR BEAUTIFUL PRESENTATIONS! IT'S BECAUSE I MADE IT A SIMPLE NOODLE DISH, WHICH MAKES YOU EAT ALL OF THE SOUP AND THE INGREDIENTS DELICIOUSLY, EVEN WITH ITS STRONG TASTE. IF YOU COULD'VE TOLD ME ALL OF THAT, THEN YOU WOULD'VE HAD FIGURED ME OUT 100%, OTANI!
...
...
IT'S THE BEST GOOSE DISH EVER!!
YOU JUST PROVED THAT, TOO! YOU ATE ALL OF THE SOUP TO THE LAST DROP!
SO HE DID ADD THE GOOSE BRAIN WITH THE NOODLES! THIS PUNK!

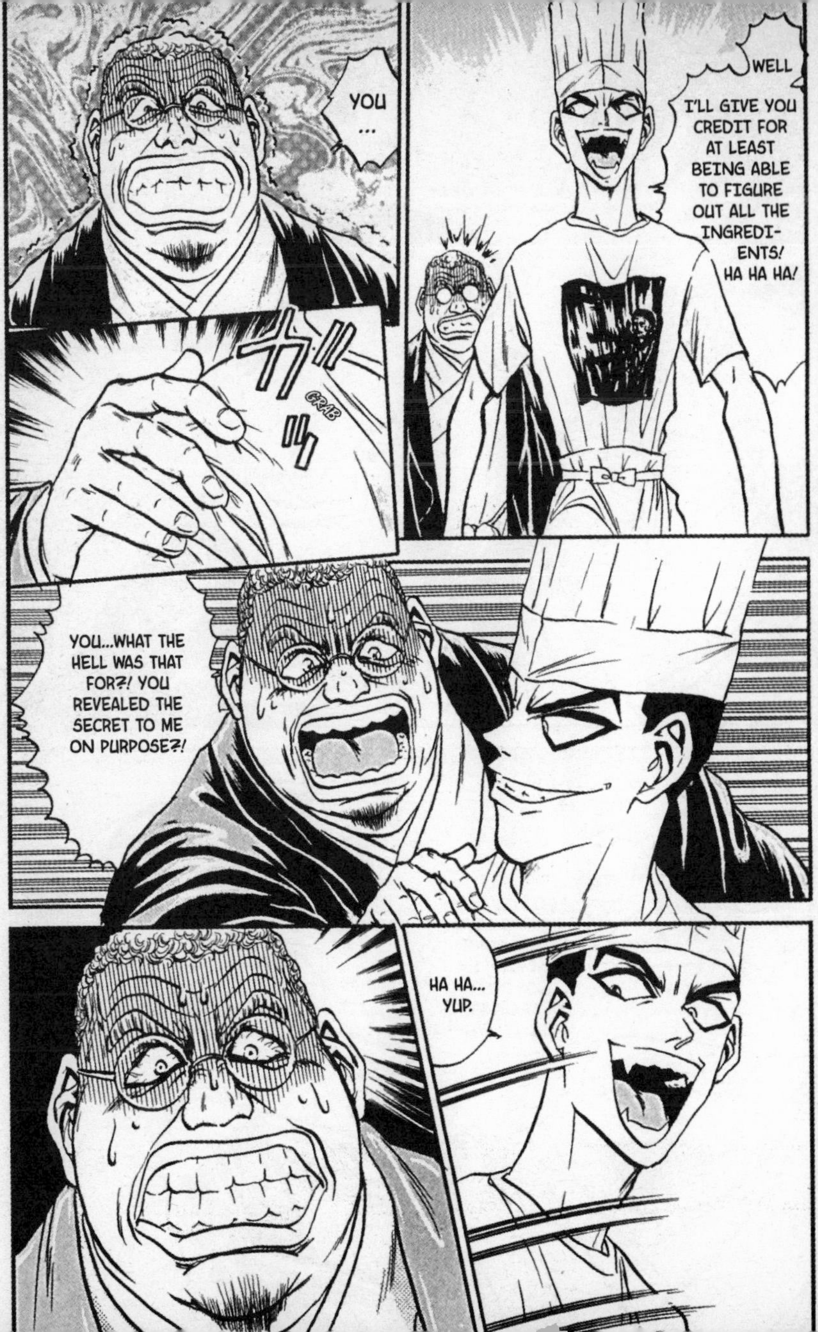
WELL
I'LL GIVE YOU CREDIT FOR AT LEAST BEING ABLE TO FIGURE OUT ALL THE INGREDI- ENTS! HA HA HA!
YOU ...
GRAB
YOU...WHAT THE HELL WAS THAT FOR?! YOU REVEALED THE SECRET TO ME ON PURPOSE?!
HA HA... YUP.

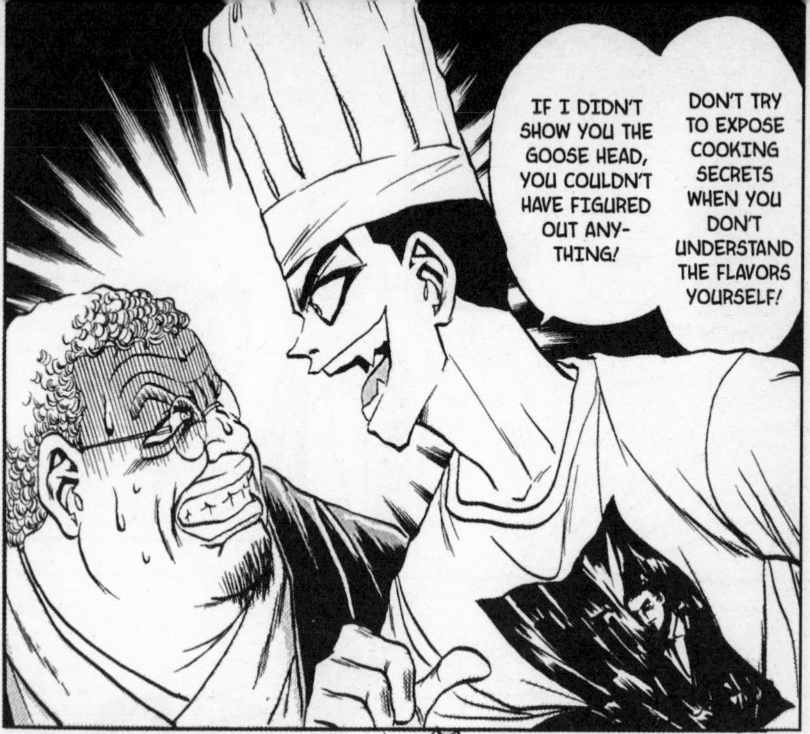
DON'T TRY TO EXPOSE COOKING SECRETS WHEN YOU DON'T UNDERSTAND THE FLAVORS YOURSELF!
IF I DIDN'T SHOW YOU THE GOOSE HEAD, YOU COULDN'T HAVE FIGURED OUT ANY-THING!
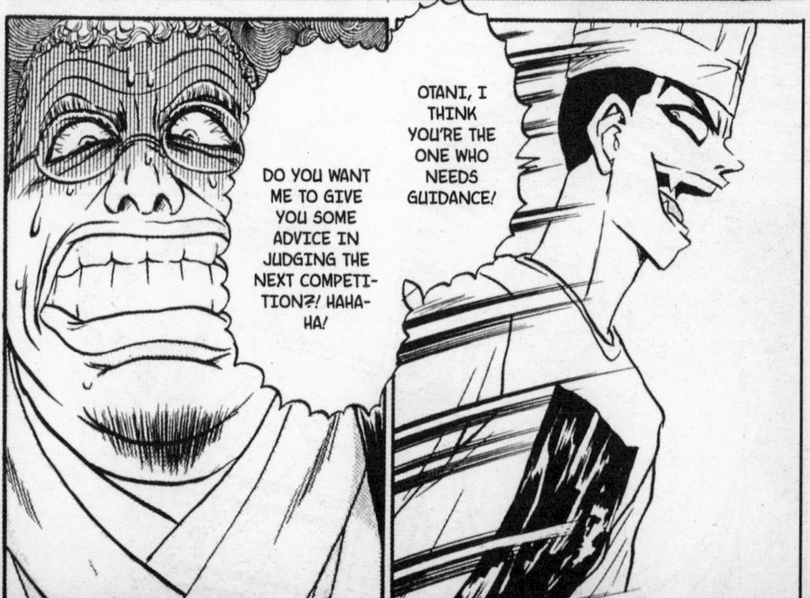
OTANI, I THINK YOU'RE THE ONE WHO NEEDS GUIDANCE!
DO YOU WANT ME TO GIVE YOU SOME ADVICE IN JUDGING THE NEXT COMPETI-TION?! HAHA-HA!

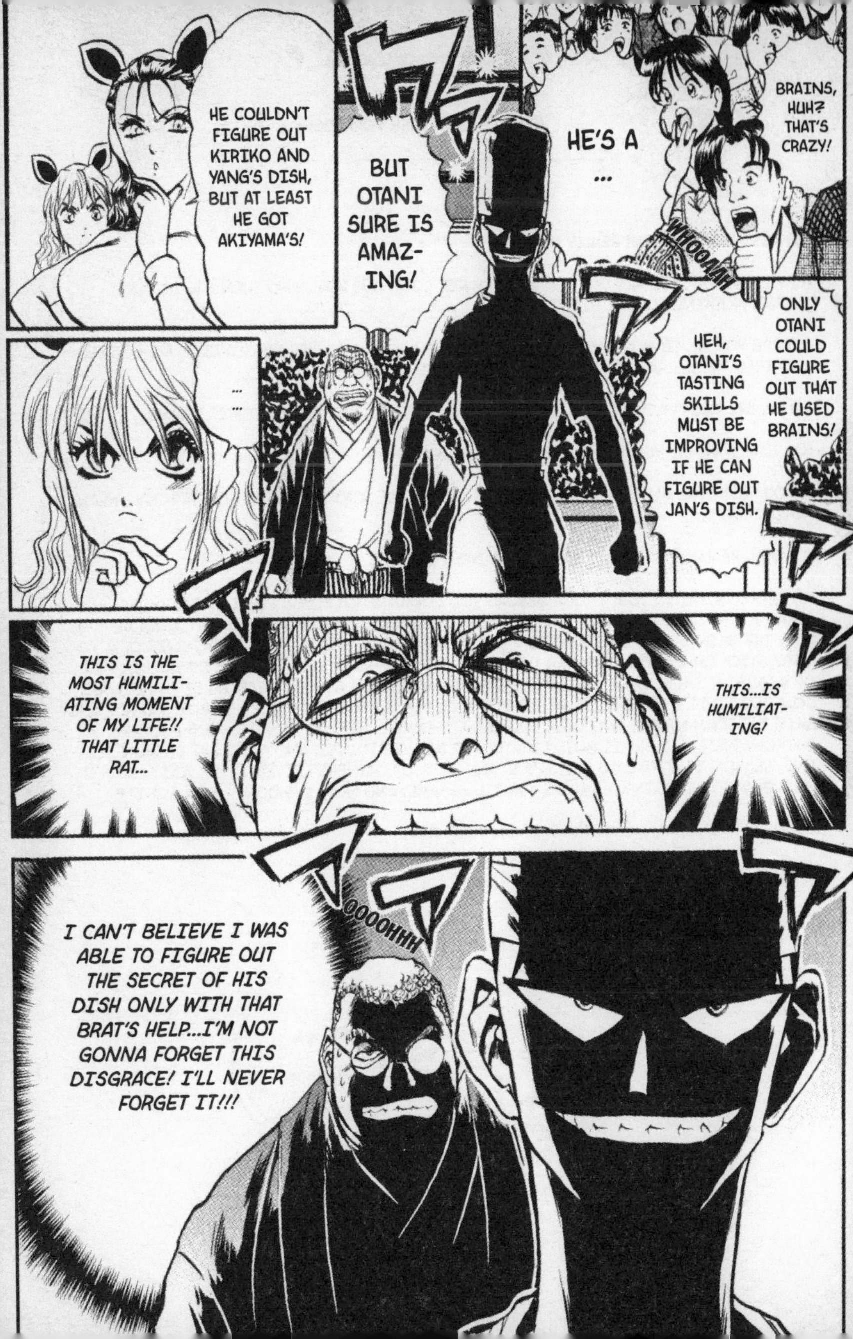
BRAINS, HUH? THAT'S CRAZY!
WHOOOAAH
HE'S A ...
BUT OTANI SURE IS AMAZ-ING!
HE COULDN'T FIGURE OUT KIRIKO AND YANG'S DISH, BUT AT LEAST HE GOT AKIYAMA'S!
ONLY OTANI COULD FIGURE OUT THAT HE USED BRAINS!
HEH, OTANI'S TASTING SKILLS MUST BE IMPROVING IF HE CAN FIGURE OUT JAN'S DISH.
... ...
THIS...IS HUMILIAT-ING!
THIS IS THE MOST HUMILI-ATING MOMENT OF MY LIFE!! THAT LITTLE RAT...
OOOOHHH
I CAN'T BELIEVE I WAS ABLE TO FIGURE OUT THE SECRET OF HIS DISH ONLY WITH THAT BRAT'S HELP...I'M NOT GONNA FORGET THIS DISGRACE! I'LL NEVER FORGET IT!!!

JAN AND OKONOGI'S

LUO BO JIU CAI ZHOU
(DAIKON AND LEEK PORRIDGE)

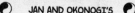

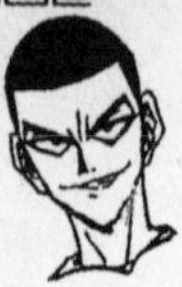

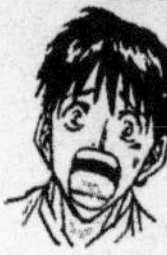

(O) HEY JAN, YOU LOOK REALLY MAD.

(J) KIRIKO TRICKED ME. SHE HAD ME HELP HER COOK HER MEAL, AND THEN SHE TOLD ME THERE'S NOTHING FOR ME TO EAT.

(O) ARE YOU TALKING ABOUT THAT SWEET POTATO PORRIDGE? SHE JUST CAME TO ME EARLIER AND TOLD ME SHE HAS SOME LEFTOVERS AND GAVE ME SOME.

(J) AH, SHE MUST'VE BEEN REALLY PISSED ABOUT MY "YOU'RE LIKE A POTATO" REMARK.

(O) HUH? WHAT DO YOU MEAN, SHE'S LIKE A POTATO?

(J) OH, NOTHING. ANYWAY, OKONOGI, I'LL LET YOU EAT SOMETHING EVEN BETTER THAN WHAT KIRIKO MADE.

(O) OOH, REALLY?! I'LL HELP YOU IN ANY WAY POSSIBLE.

(J) THIRTY MINUTES TO AN HOUR BEFORE YOU COOK THE RICE, YOU POUR IT THROUGH A STRAINER TO DRAIN OFF THE WATER AND DRIZZLE 1 TABLESPOON OF SALAD OIL OVER IT. PEEL THE SKIN OF THE DAIKON AND CHOP IT INTO LONG THIN STRIPS IN THE SIZE OF A MATCHSTICK OR A LITTLE THICKER THAN THAT. CHOP UP THE CHINESE CHIVES IN THE LENGTH OF ABOUT AN INCH. BOIL THE SOUP IN A POT FIRST THEN ADD THE RICE IN IT TO BOIL, BUT DON'T COVER IT WITH THE LID. AT FIRST YOU'LL USE STRONG HEAT. AFTER IT BOILS ONCE, YOU SKIM THE FOAM NEATLY, AND THEN YOU LET IT SIMMER. AFTER 10 MINUTES, YOU ADD THE DAIKON. THEN, YOU LET IT BOIL LIGHTLY FOR 30-40 MINUTES, AND AFTER THE DAIKON SOFTENS, SEASON IT WITH SALT, SOY SAUCE, AND STIR IN CHINESE CHIVES. AFTER YOU SCOOP IT IN A BOWL, YOU SPRINKLE PARCHED WHITE SESAME, AND NOW IT'S DONE. YOU GOT IT?

(O) NEVER MIND, JAN. JUST MAKE IT ON YOUR OWN.

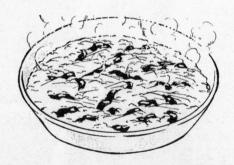

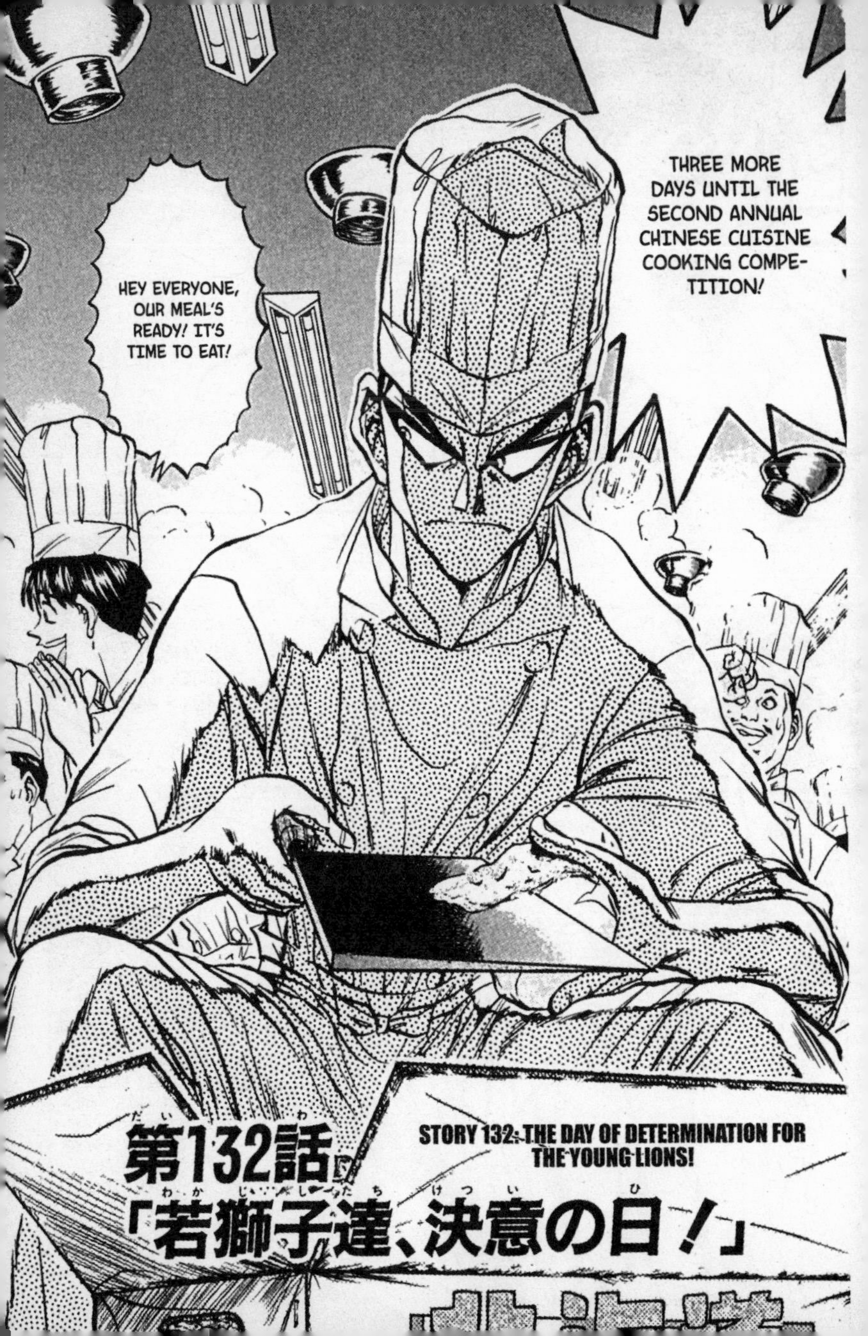
THREE MORE DAYS UNTIL THE SECOND ANNUAL CHINESE CUISINE COOKING COMPE-TITION!
HEY EVERYONE, OUR MEAL'S READY! IT'S TIME TO EAT!
STORY 132: THE DAY OF DETERMINATION FOR THE YOUNG LIONS!
第132話
「若獅子達、決意の日！」

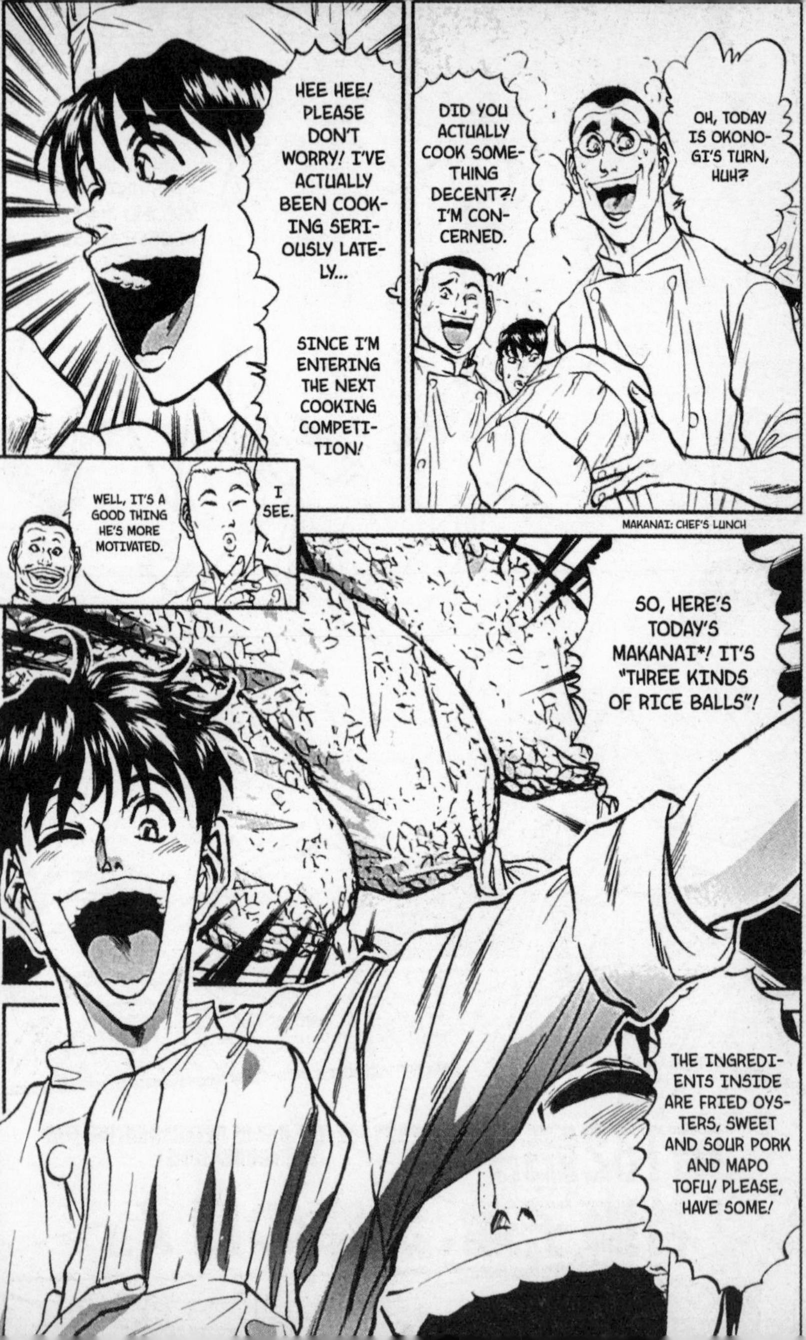
OH, TODAY IS OKONOGI'S TURN, HUH?
DID YOU ACTUALLY COOK SOMETHING DECENT?! I'M CONCERNED.
HEE HEE! PLEASE DON'T WORRY! I'VE ACTUALLY BEEN COOKING SERIOUSLY LATELY...
SINCE I'M ENTERING THE NEXT COOKING COMPETITION!
I SEE.
WELL, IT'S A GOOD THING HE'S MORE MOTIVATED.
SO, HERE'S TODAY'S MAKANAI*! IT'S "THREE KINDS OF RICE BALLS"!
THE INGREDIENTS INSIDE ARE FRIED OYSTERS, SWEET AND SOUR PORK AND MAPO TOFU! PLEASE, HAVE SOME!

MAKANAI: CHEF'S LUNCH

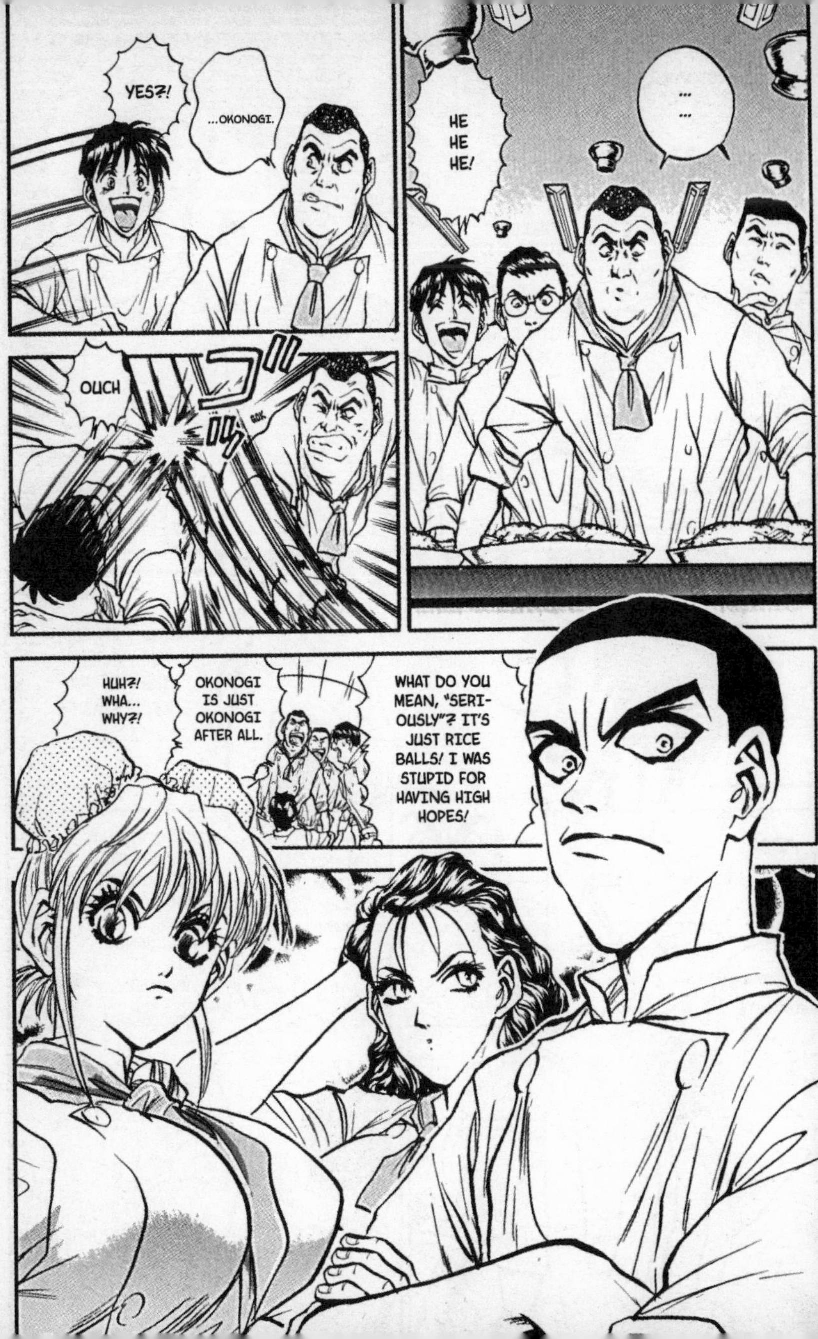
...
...
HE
HE
HE!
...OKONOGI.
YES?!
GOK
OUCH
WHAT DO YOU MEAN, "SERIOUSLY"? IT'S JUST RICE BALLS! I WAS STUPID FOR HAVING HIGH HOPES!
OKONOGI IS JUST OKONOGI AFTER ALL.
HUH?! WHA... WHY?!

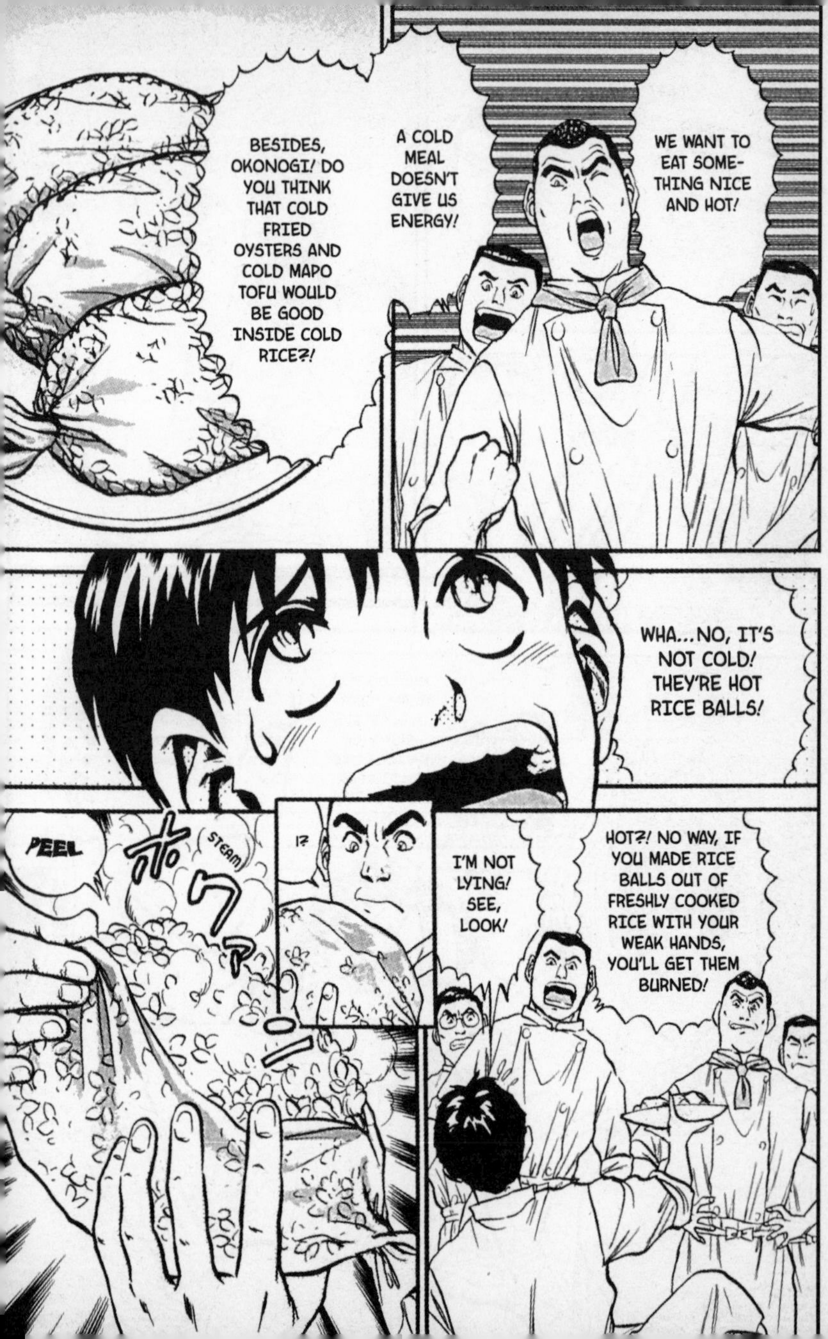
WE WANT TO EAT SOME-THING NICE AND HOT!
A COLD MEAL DOESN'T GIVE US ENERGY!
BESIDES, OKONOGI! DO YOU THINK THAT COLD FRIED OYSTERS AND COLD MAPO TOFU WOULD BE GOOD INSIDE COLD RICE?!
WHA...NO, IT'S NOT COLD! THEY'RE HOT RICE BALLS!
HOT?! NO WAY, IF YOU MADE RICE BALLS OUT OF FRESHLY COOKED RICE WITH YOUR WEAK HANDS, YOU'LL GET THEM BURNED!
I'M NOT LYING! SEE, LOOK!
!?
STEAM
PEEL

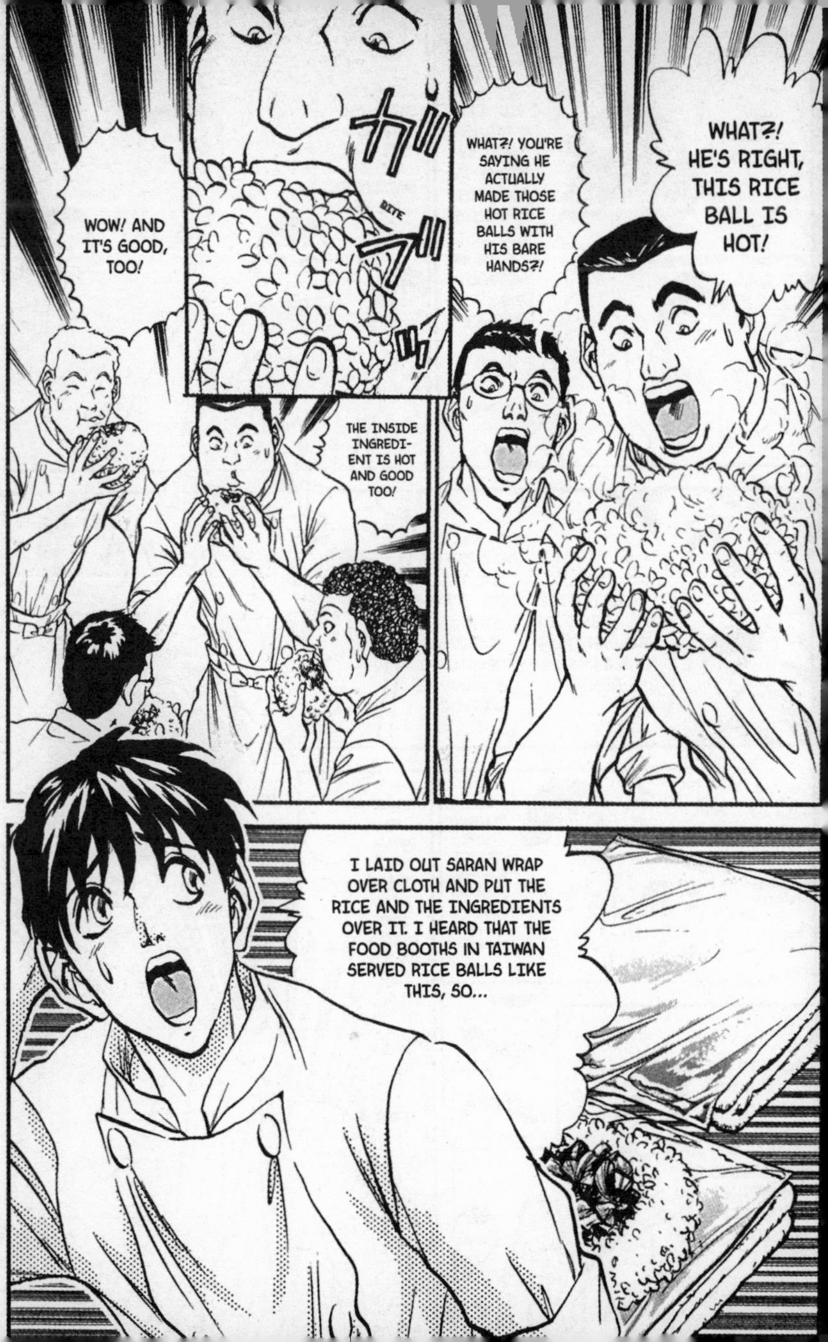
WHAT?! HE'S RIGHT, THIS RICE BALL IS HOT!
WHAT?! YOU'RE SAYING HE ACTUALLY MADE THOSE HOT RICE BALLS WITH HIS BARE HANDS?!
BITE
THE INSIDE INGREDI- ENT IS HOT AND GOOD TOO!
WOW! AND IT'S GOOD, TOO!
I LAID OUT SARAN WRAP OVER CLOTH AND PUT THE RICE AND THE INGREDIENTS OVER IT. I HEARD THAT THE FOOD BOOTHS IN TAIWAN SERVED RICE BALLS LIKE THIS, SO...

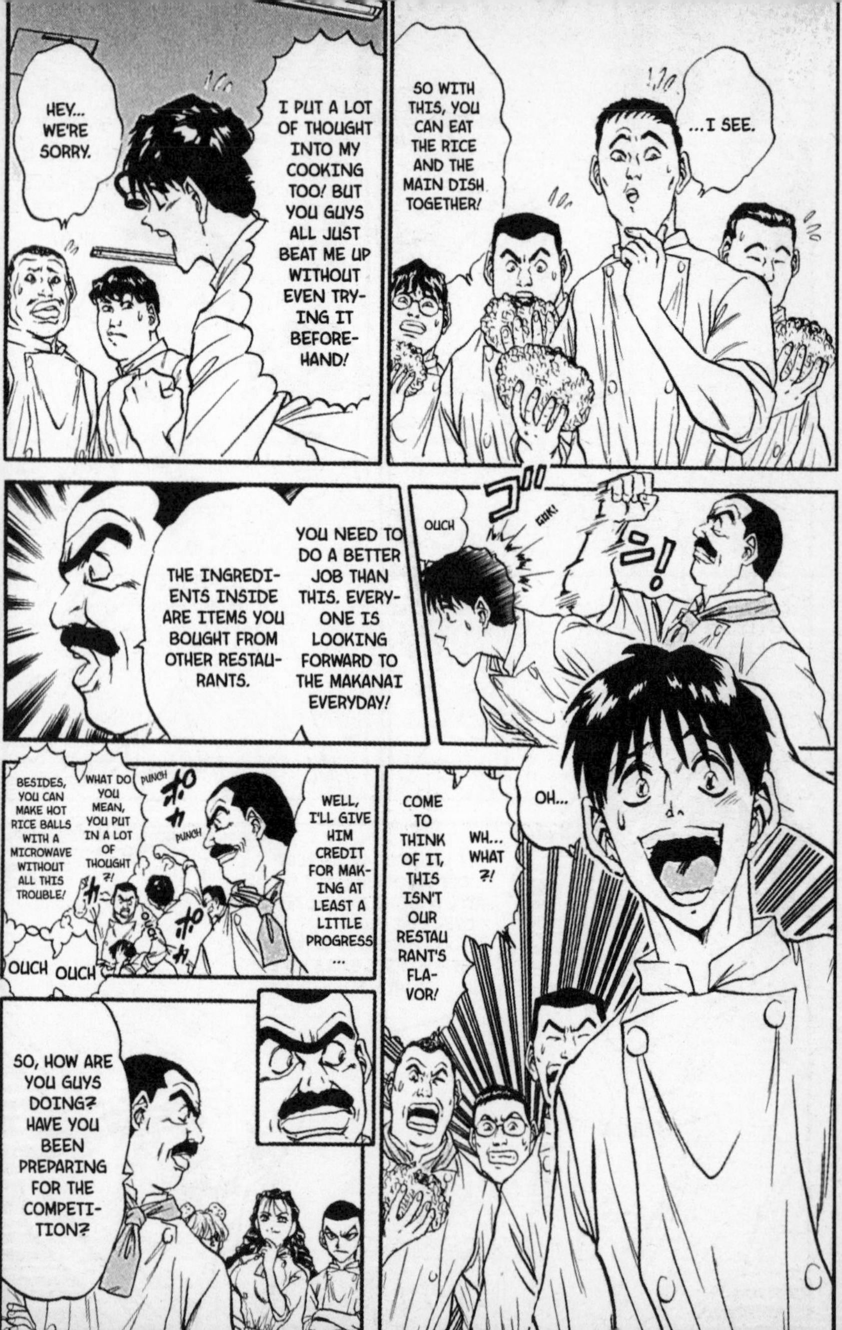
I PUT A LOT OF THOUGHT INTO MY COOKING TOO! BUT YOU GUYS ALL JUST BEAT ME UP WITHOUT EVEN TRYING IT BEFOREHAND!
HEY... WE'RE SORRY.
SO WITH THIS, YOU CAN EAT THE RICE AND THE MAIN DISH TOGETHER!
...I SEE.
THE INGREDIENTS INSIDE ARE ITEMS YOU BOUGHT FROM OTHER RESTAURANTS.
YOU NEED TO DO A BETTER JOB THAN THIS. EVERYONE IS LOOKING FORWARD TO THE MAKANAI EVERYDAY!
OUCH
GOK!
BESIDES, YOU CAN MAKE HOT RICE BALLS WITH A MICROWAVE WITHOUT ALL THIS TROUBLE!
WHAT DO YOU MEAN, YOU PUT IN A LOT OF THOUGHT?!
PUNCH
PUNCH
OUCH
OUCH OUCH
WELL, I'LL GIVE HIM CREDIT FOR MAKING AT LEAST A LITTLE PROGRESS...
OH...
COME TO THINK OF IT, THIS ISN'T OUR RESTAURANT'S FLAVOR!
WH... WHAT?!
SO, HOW ARE YOU GUYS DOING? HAVE YOU BEEN PREPARING FOR THE COMPETITION?

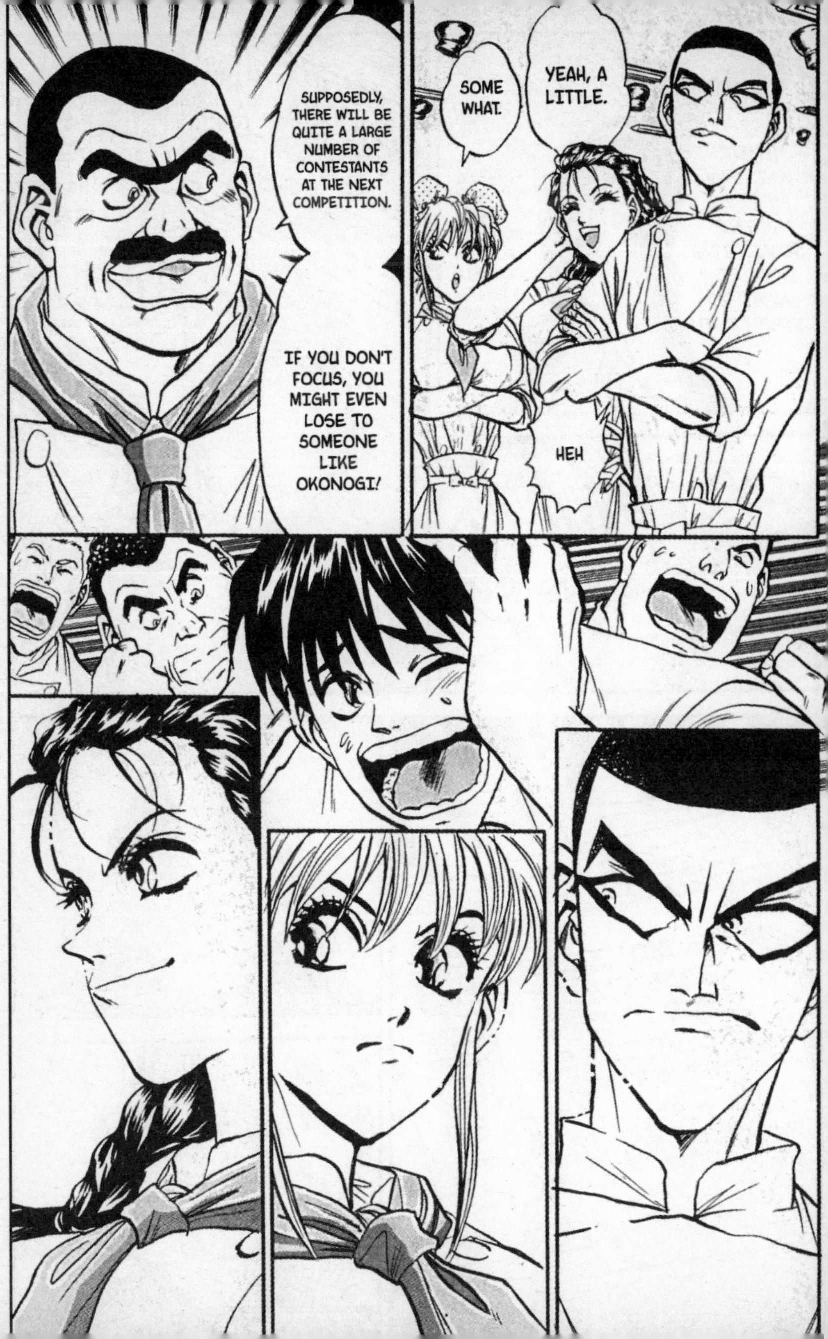
SUPPOSEDLY, THERE WILL BE QUITE A LARGE NUMBER OF CONTESTANTS AT THE NEXT COMPETITION.
IF YOU DON'T FOCUS, YOU MIGHT EVEN LOSE TO SOMEONE LIKE OKONOGI!
SOME WHAT.
YEAH, A LITTLE.
HEH

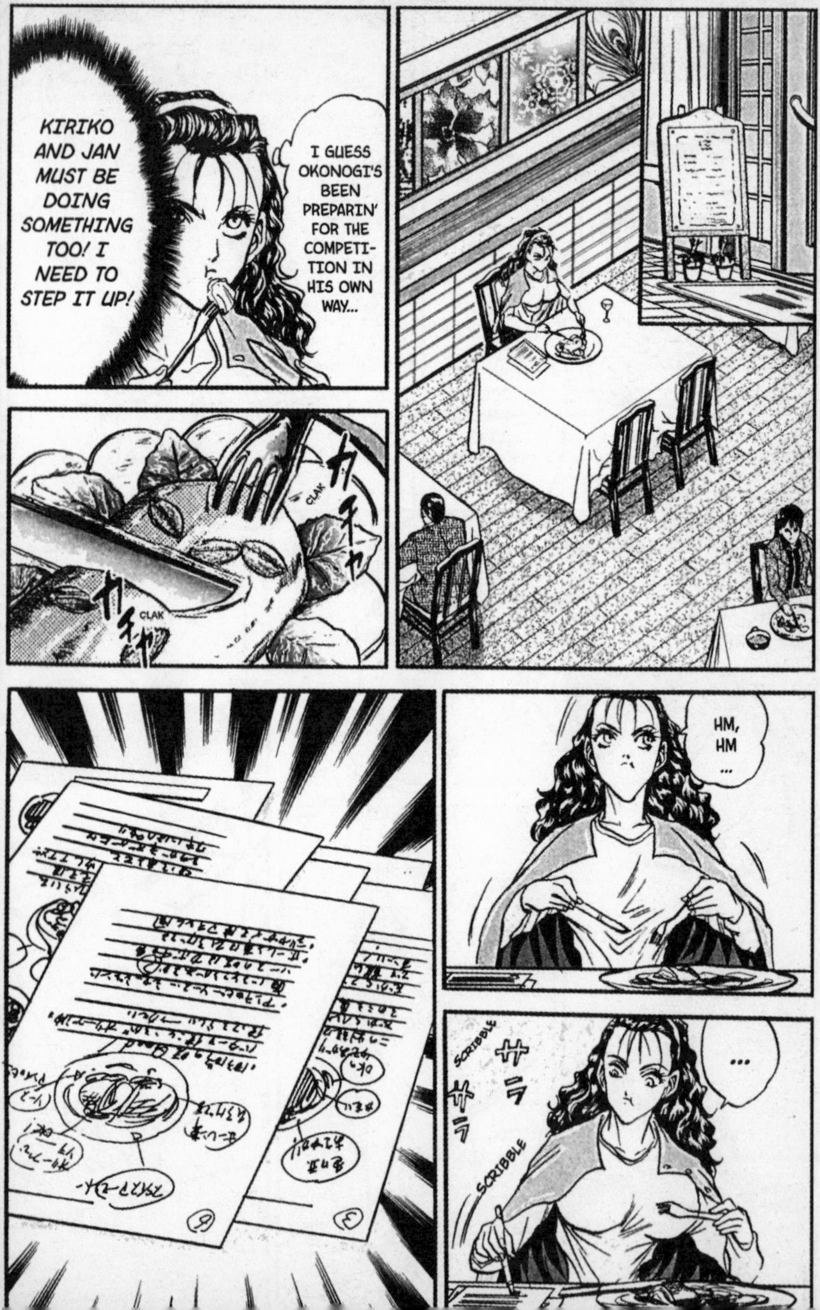
I GUESS OKONOGI'S BEEN PREPARIN' FOR THE COMPETITION IN HIS OWN WAY...
KIRIKO AND JAN MUST BE DOING SOMETHING TOO! I NEED TO STEP IT UP!
CLAK
CLAK
HM, HM ...
...
SCRIBBLE
SCRIBBLE

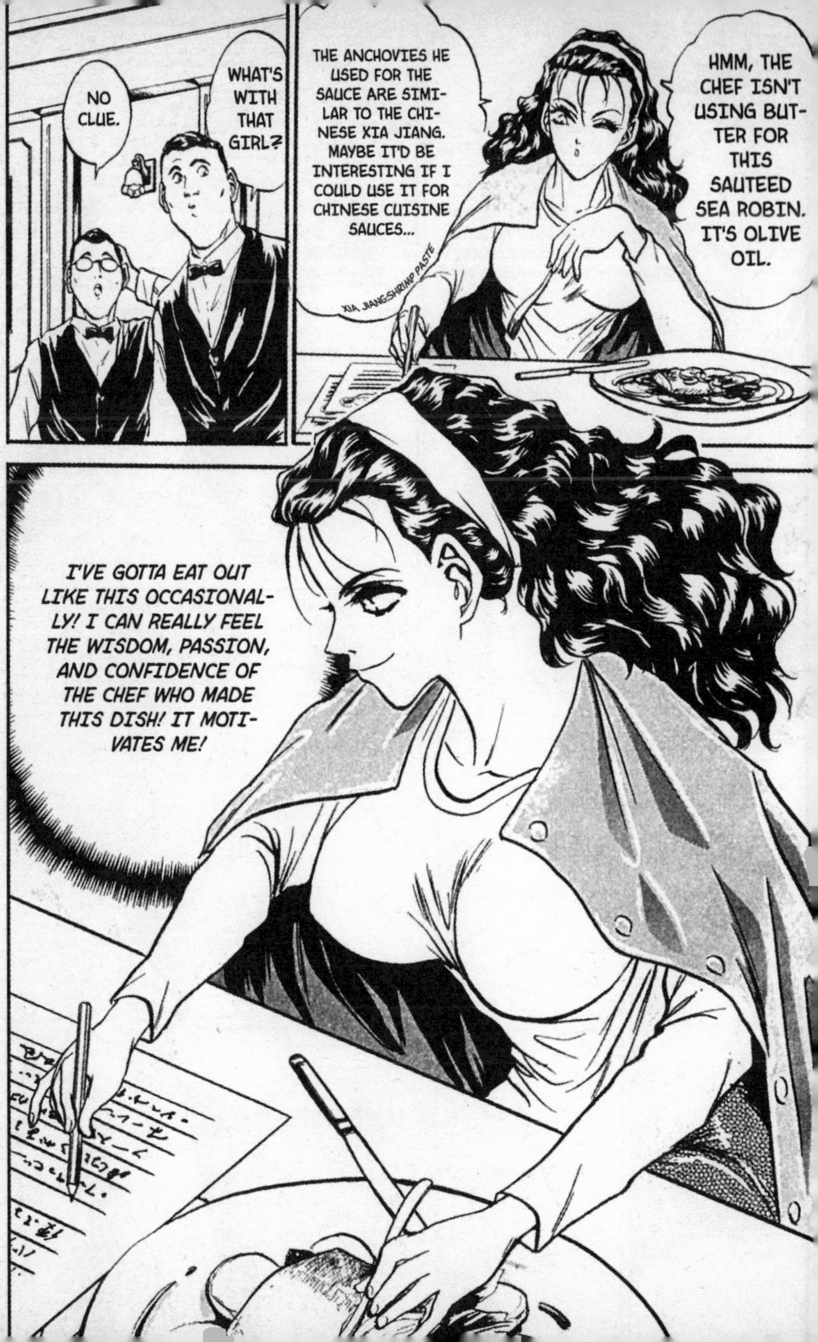
HMM, THE CHEF ISN'T USING BUTTER FOR THIS SAUTEED SEA ROBIN. IT'S OLIVE OIL.
THE ANCHOVIES HE USED FOR THE SAUCE ARE SIMILAR TO THE CHINESE XIA JIANG. MAYBE IT'D BE INTERESTING IF I COULD USE IT FOR CHINESE CUISINE SAUCES...
XIA JIANG-SHRIMP PASTE
WHAT'S WITH THAT GIRL?
NO CLUE.
I'VE GOTTA EAT OUT LIKE THIS OCCASIONALLY! I CAN REALLY FEEL THE WISDOM, PASSION, AND CONFIDENCE OF THE CHEF WHO MADE THIS DISH! IT MOTIVATES ME!

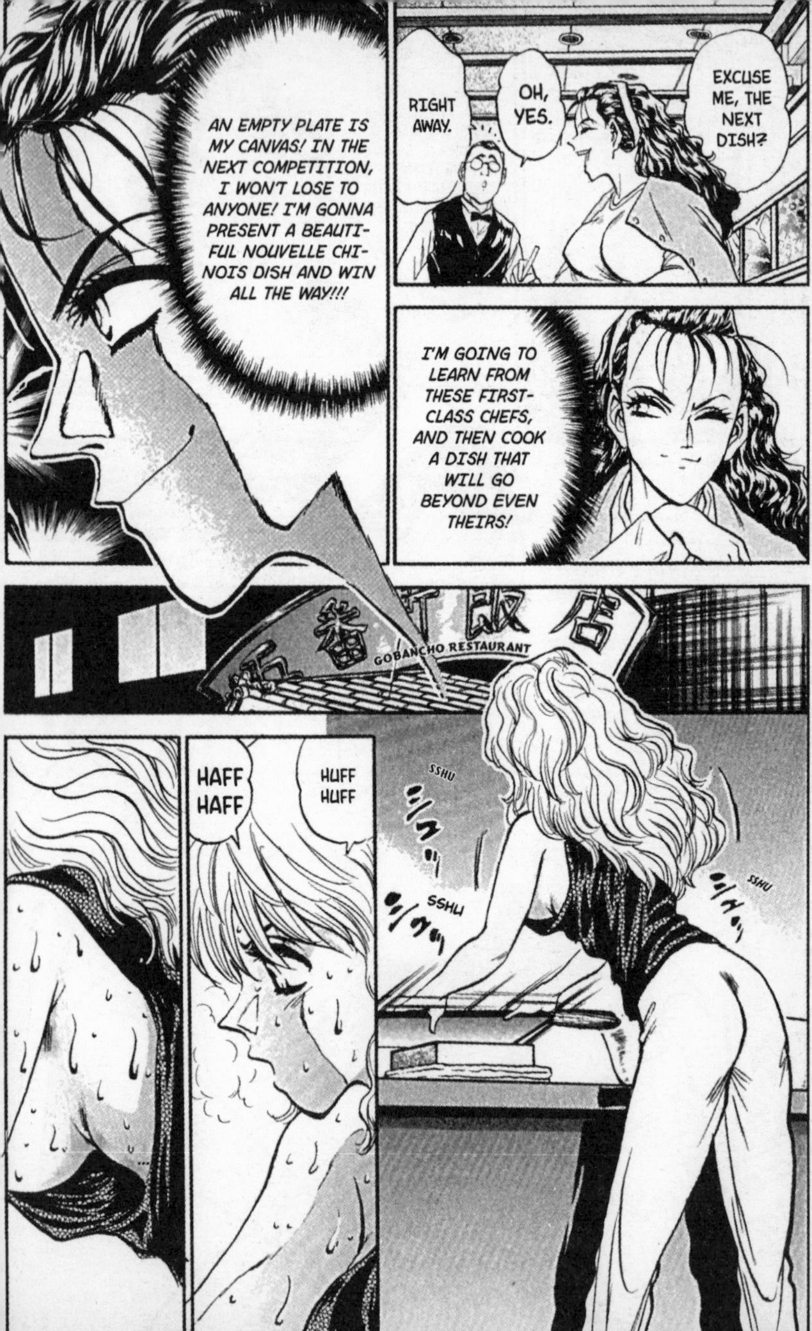
EXCUSE ME, THE NEXT DISH?
OH, YES.
RIGHT AWAY.
I'M GOING TO LEARN FROM THESE FIRST-CLASS CHEFS, AND THEN COOK A DISH THAT WILL GO BEYOND EVEN THEIRS!
AN EMPTY PLATE IS MY CANVAS! IN THE NEXT COMPETITION, I WON'T LOSE TO ANYONE! I'M GONNA PRESENT A BEAUTIFUL NOUVELLE CHINOIS DISH AND WIN ALL THE WAY!!!
GOBANCHO RESTAURANT
SSHU
SSHU
SSHU
HUFF HUFF
HAFF HAFF
...

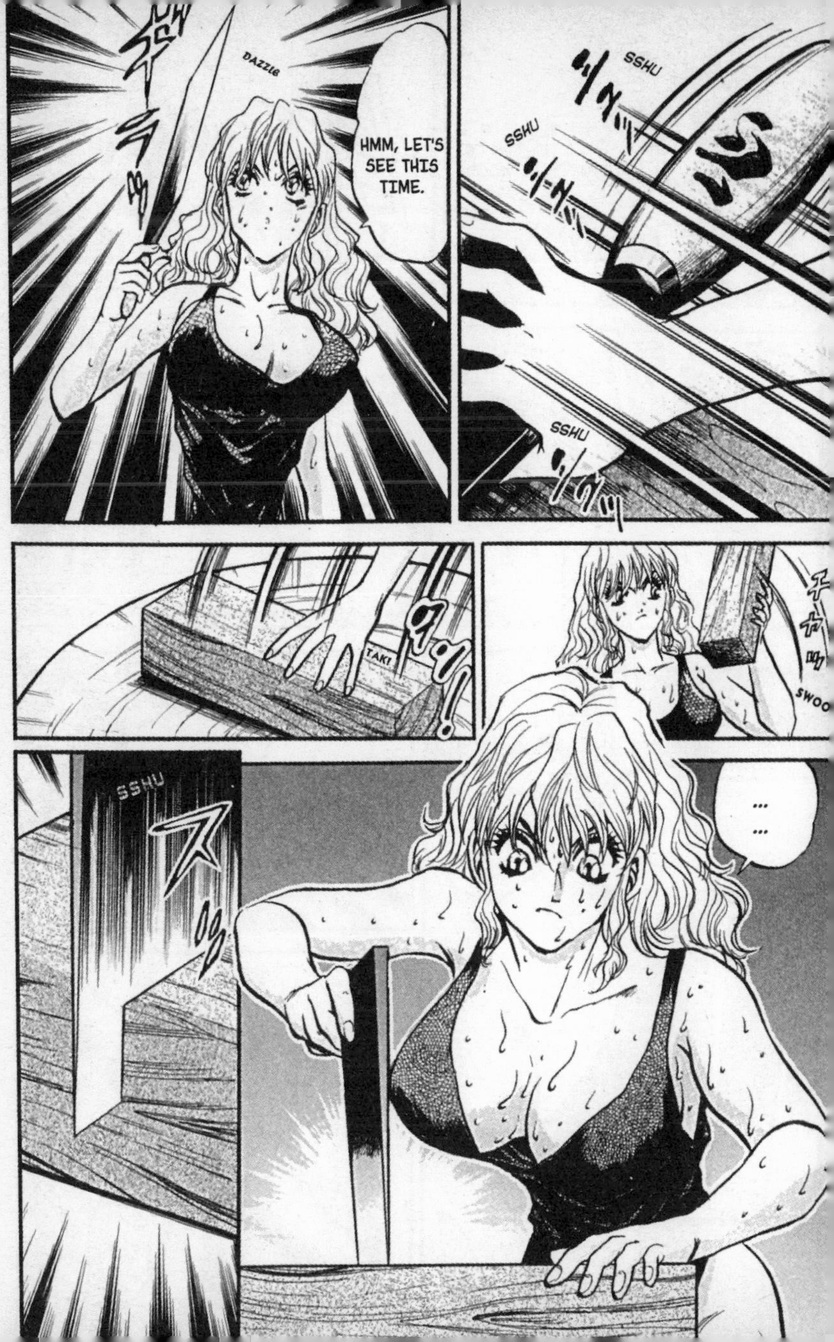
SSHU
SSHU
SSHU
DAZZLE
HMM, LET'S SEE THIS TIME.
SWOO
TAKI
SSHU
...
...

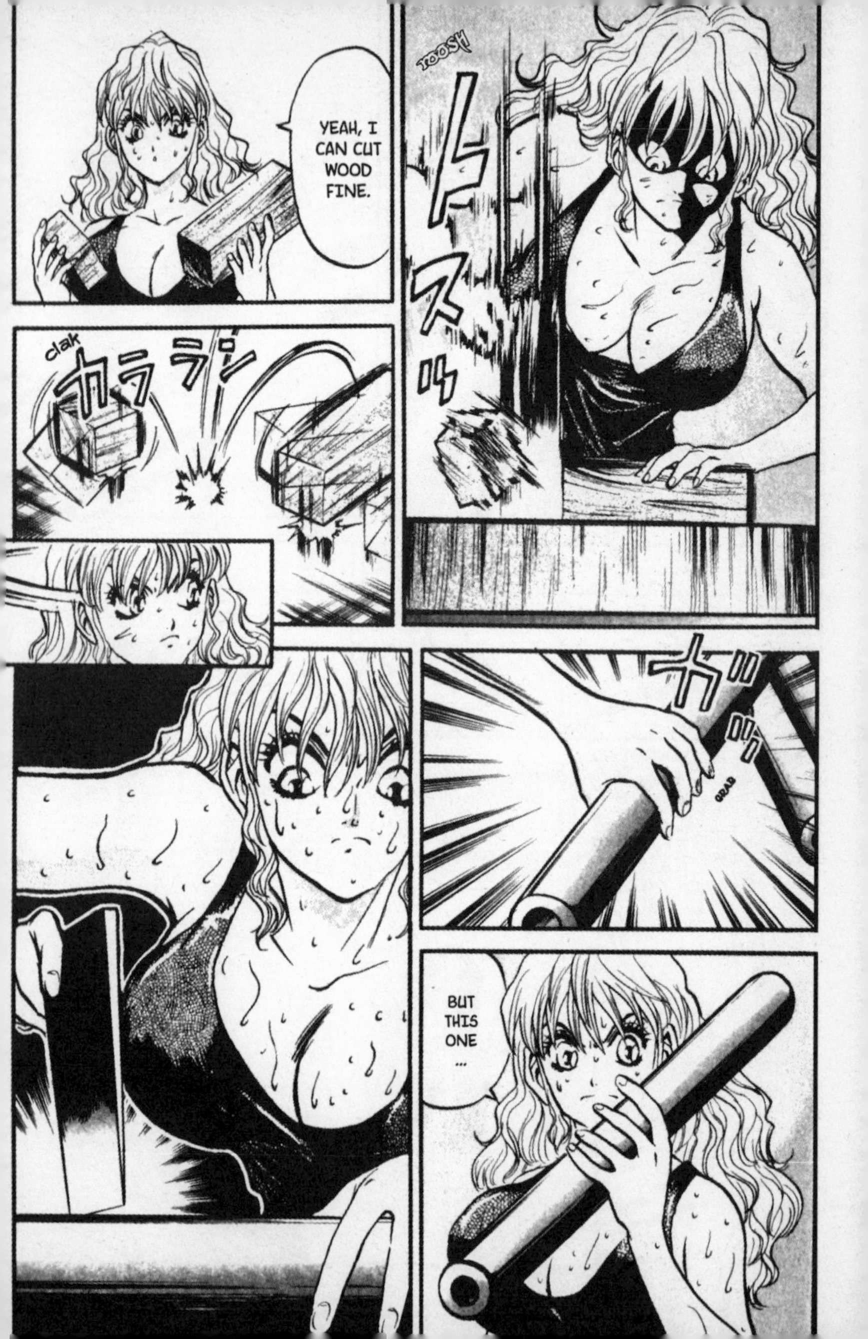
TOOSH
YEAH, I CAN CUT WOOD FINE.
clak
GRAB
BUT THIS ONE ...

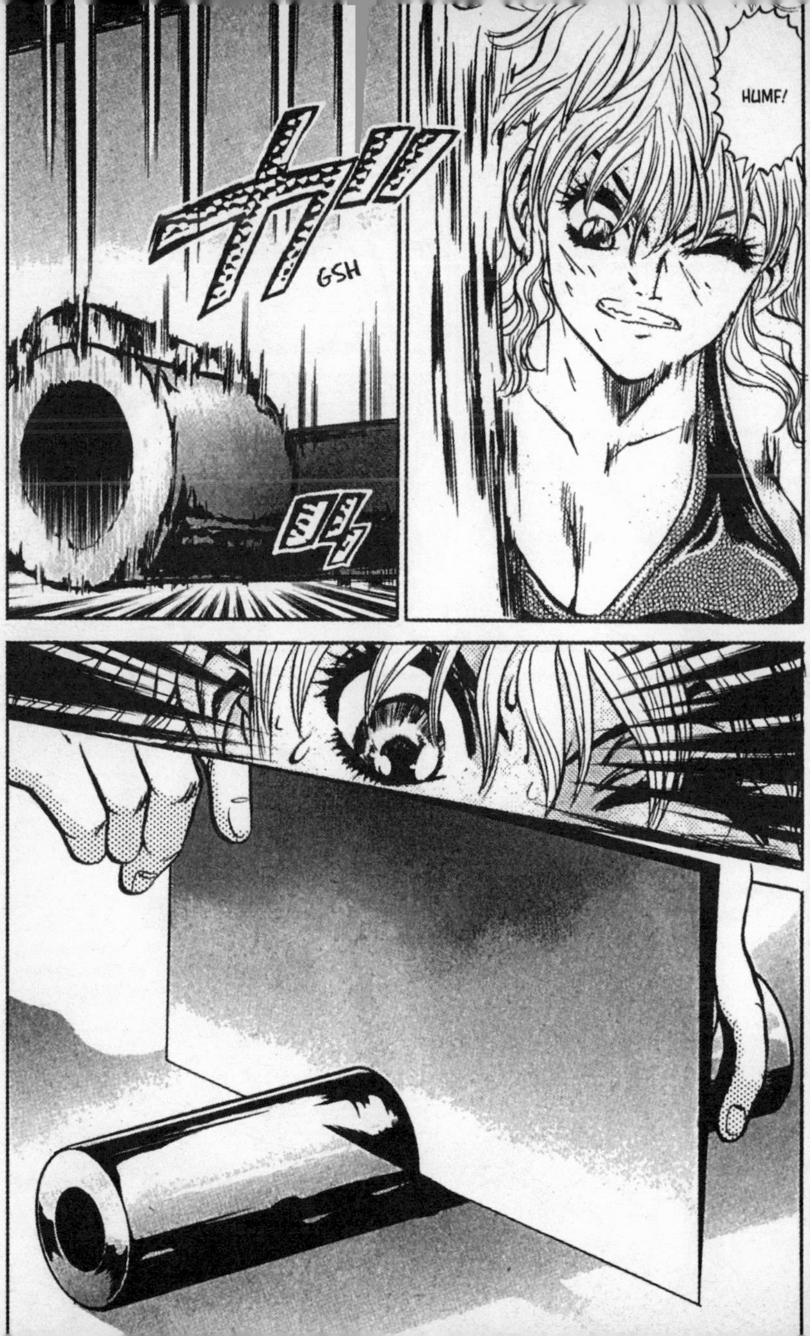
HUMF!
GSH

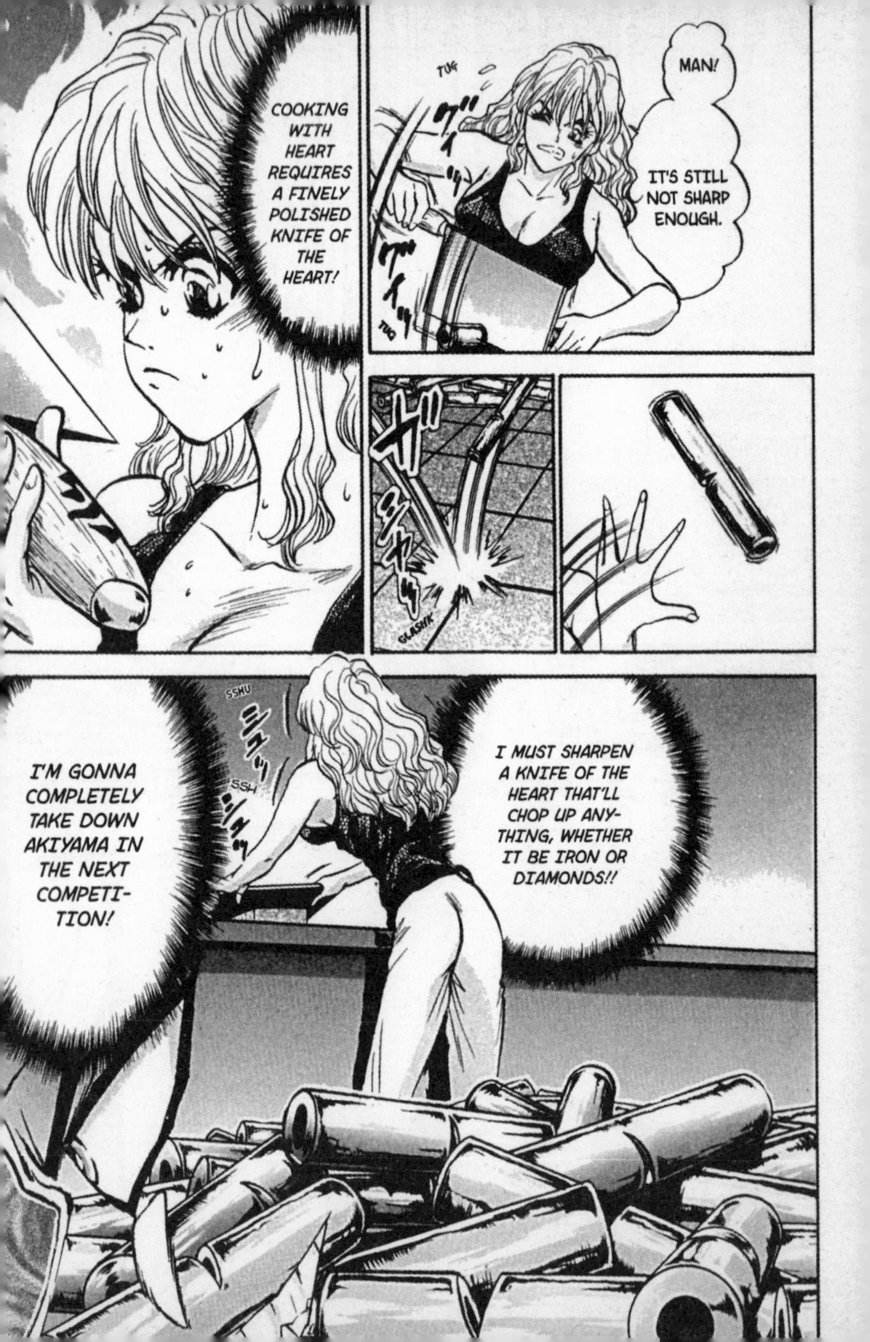

TUG
MAN!
IT'S STILL NOT SHARP ENOUGH.
TUG
COOKING WITH HEART REQUIRES A FINELY POLISHED KNIFE OF THE HEART!
GLASHK
SSHU
SSH
I MUST SHARPEN A KNIFE OF THE HEART THAT'LL CHOP UP ANY-THING, WHETHER IT BE IRON OR DIAMONDS!!
I'M GONNA COMPLETELY TAKE DOWN AKIYAMA IN THE NEXT COMPETI-TION!

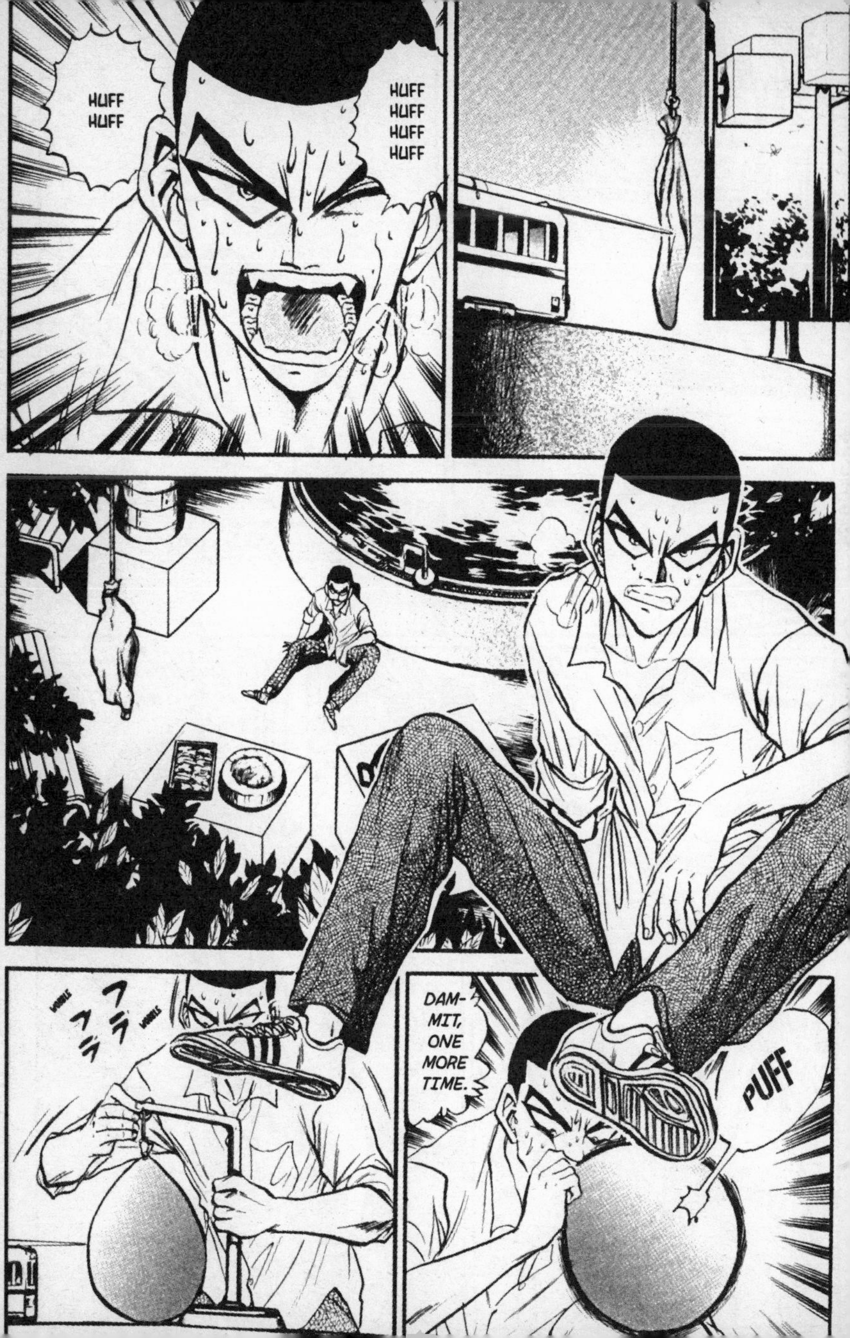
HUFF HUFF HUFF HUFF
HUFF HUFF
DAM-MIT, ONE MORE TIME.
PUFF
WOBBLE
WOBBLE

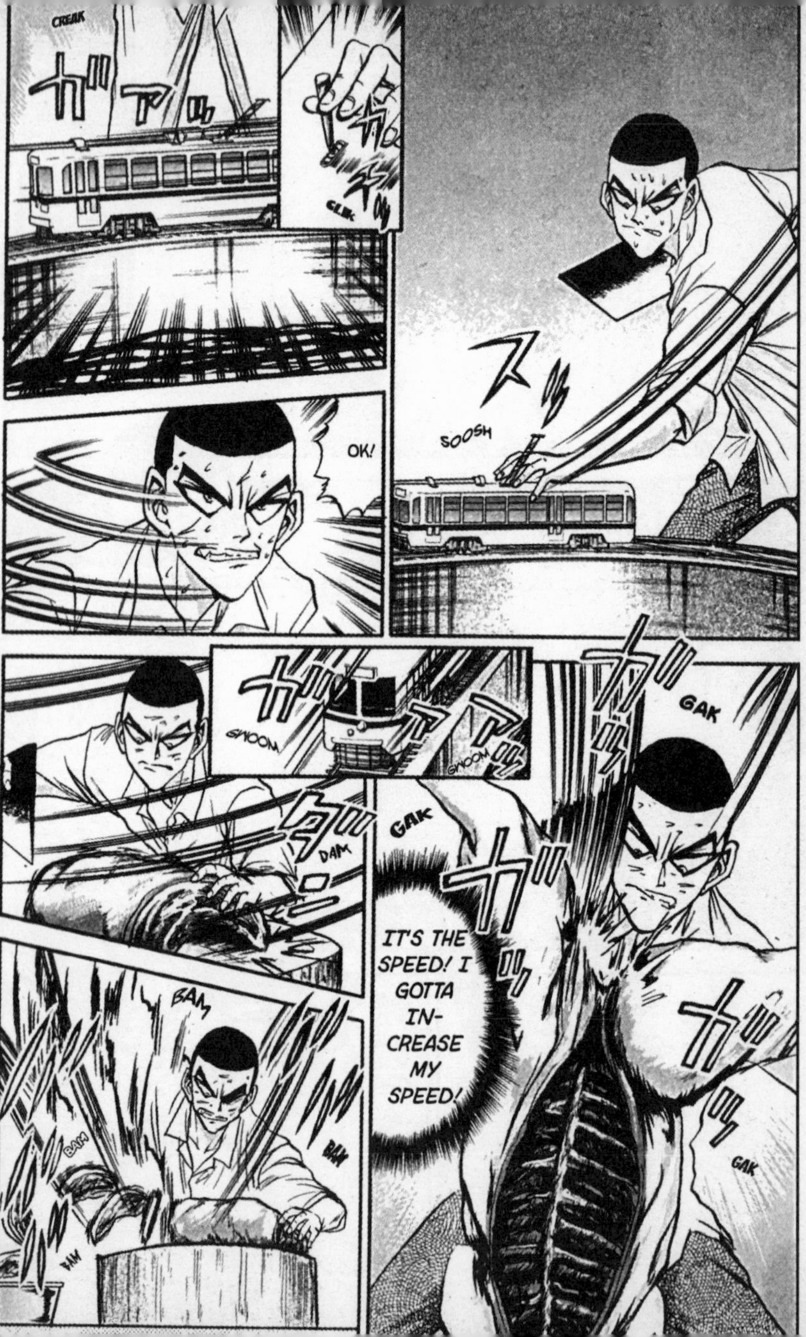
SOOSH
CLIK
CREAK
OK!
GAK
GAK
IT'S THE SPEED! I GOTTA IN-CREASE MY SPEED!
GAK
GWOOM
GWOOM
DAM
BAM
BAM
BAM
BAM

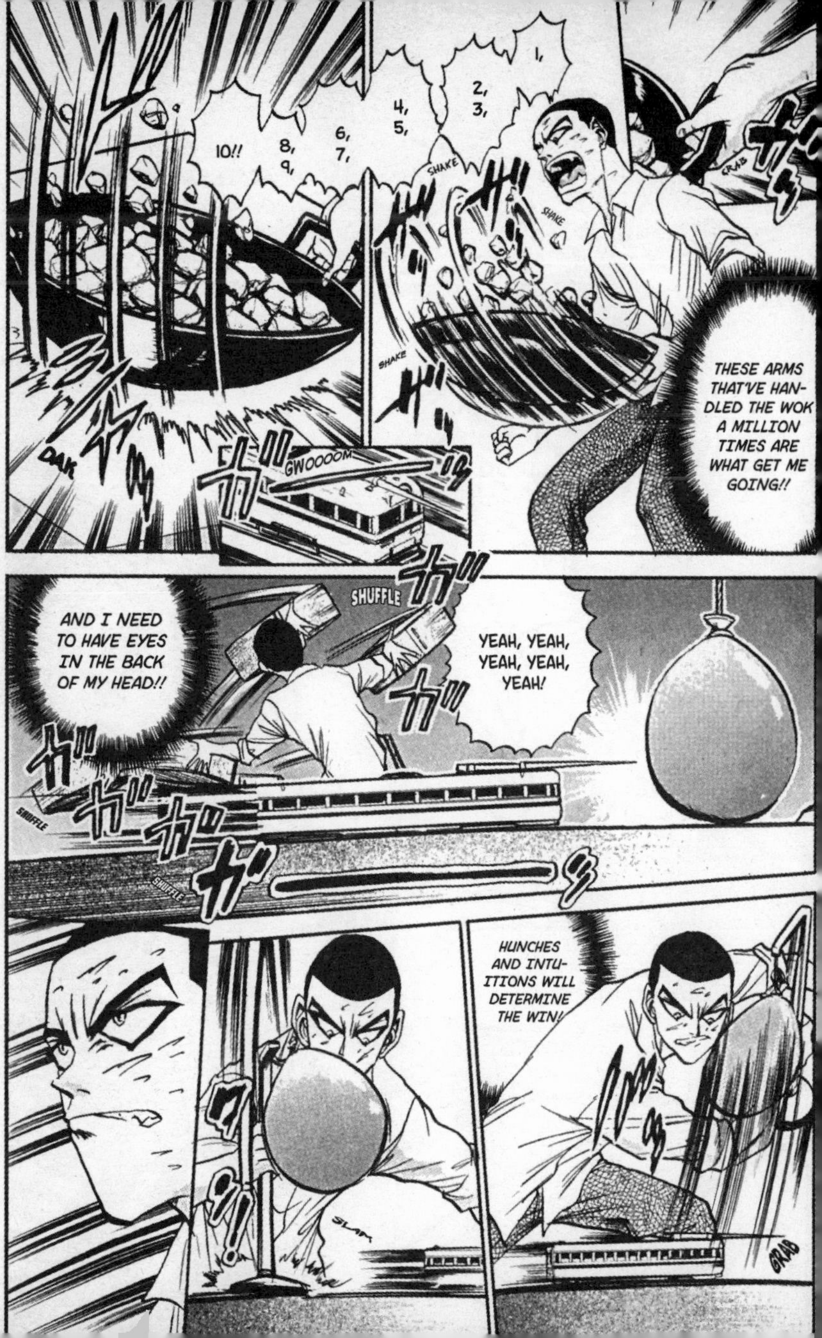
GRAB
SHAKE
SHAKE
1, 2, 3, 4, 5, 6, 7, 8, 9, 10!!
SHAKE
THESE ARMS THAT'VE HANDLED THE WOK A MILLION TIMES ARE WHAT GET ME GOING!!
DAK
GWOOOOM
YEAH, YEAH, YEAH, YEAH, YEAH!
SHUFFLE
AND I NEED TO HAVE EYES IN THE BACK OF MY HEAD!!
SHUFFLE
SHUFFLE
HUNCHES AND INTUITIONS WILL DETERMINE THE WIN!
GRAB
SLAM

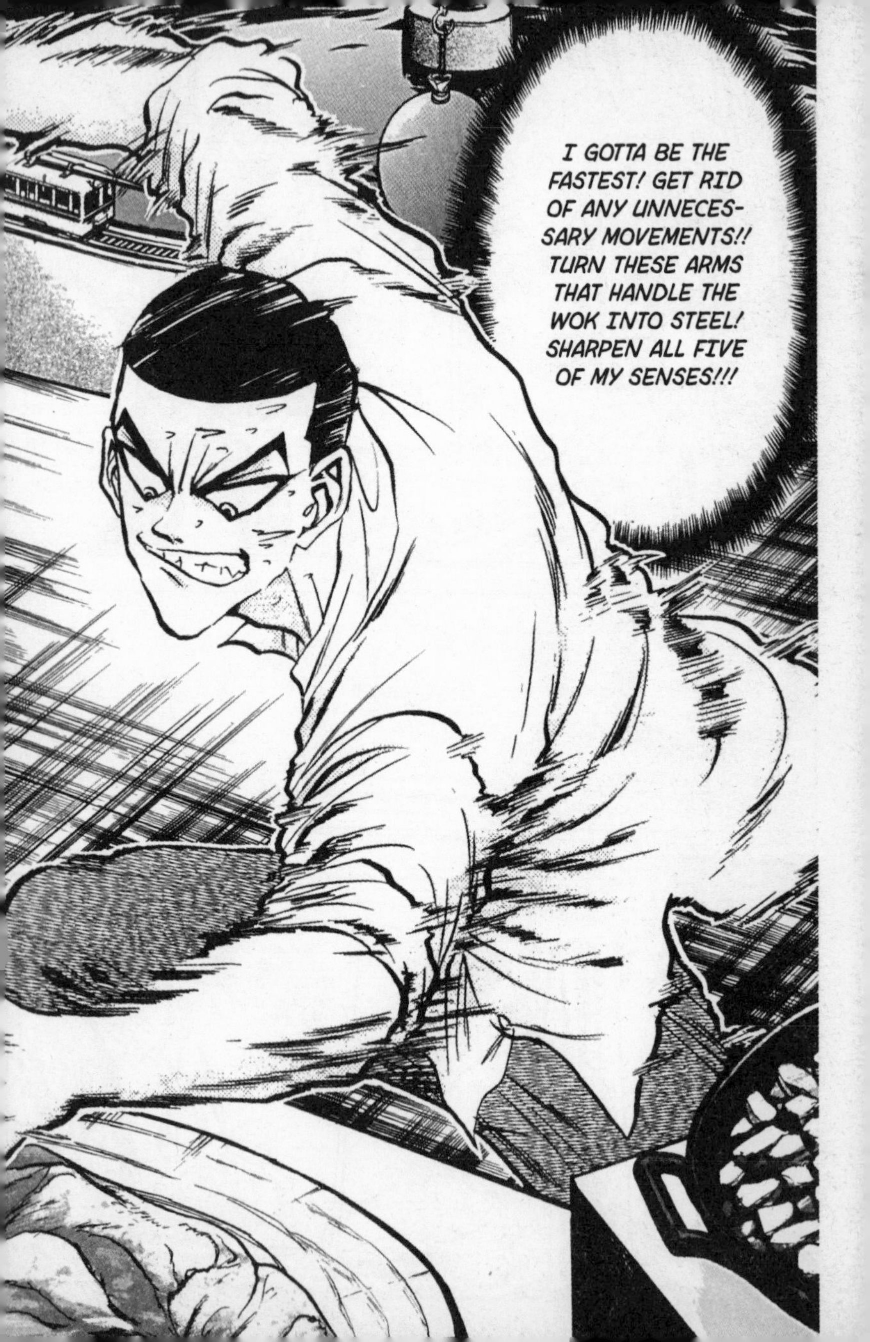
I GOTTA BE THE FASTEST! GET RID OF ANY UNNECES-SARY MOVEMENTS!! TURN THESE ARMS THAT HANDLE THE WOK INTO STEEL! SHARPEN ALL FIVE OF MY SENSES!!!

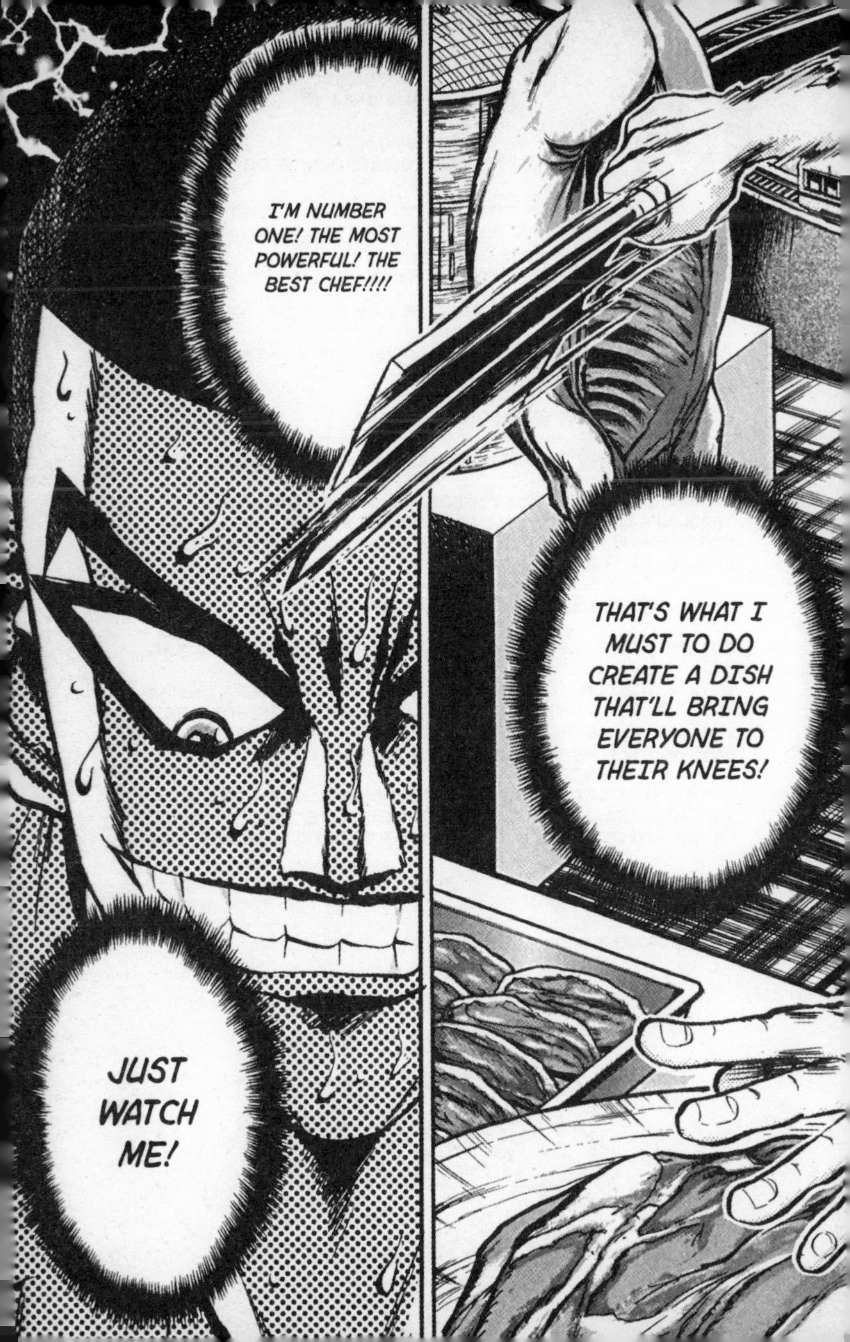
I'M NUMBER ONE! THE MOST POWERFUL! THE BEST CHEF!!!!
THAT'S WHAT I MUST TO DO CREATE A DISH THAT'LL BRING EVERYONE TO THEIR KNEES!
JUST WATCH ME!

 KIRIKO AND YANG'S

SI TIN CHAO MIAN
(INSTANT RAMEN NOODLES CHOW MEIN)

(Y) HEY KIRIKO, IS IT TRUE THAT YOU PULLED ONE OVER ON JAN RECENTLY?

(K) YUP. IT'S HIS FAULT FOR SPEAKING CRUDELY TO A LADY LIKE THAT.

(Y) OOH, I WANNA HEAR THE STORY. WHY DON'T WE HAVE A NIGHT-TIME SNACK WHILE YOU TELL ME ABOUT IT, SUGAH?

(K) OK, SURE (ALL I'VE BEEN DOING IS EATING).

(Y) THERE ARE ONLY INSTANT RAMEN NOODLES HERE. WHAT SHOULD WE DO?

(K) HOW ABOUT THIS? FIRST, YOU BOIL THE NOODLES THEN PUT IT THROUGH A STRAINER TO DRAIN THE WATER. NEXT, POUR SOME OIL IN A FRYING PAN, PUT THE BOILED NOODLES IN THERE, AND FLASH-FRY BOTH SIDES UNTIL IT TURNS BROWN.

(Y) OH, I GET IT. YOU'RE MAKIN' CHOW MEIN. IT SOUNDS FUN.

(K) ONCE BOTH SIDES ARE BROWN, TRANSFER THE NOODLES ONTO A PLATE...

(Y) NOW THIS TIME, COOK THE INGREDIENTS. SAUTE THE GREEN ONIONS AND GINGER IN A FRYIN' PAN. THEN, TOSS IN WHATEVER INGREDIENTS YOU LIKE, SUCH AS CARROTS, BAMBOO SHOOTS, GREEN PEPPERS, CHINESE CAB-BAGE, SHRIMP, PORK, AND SQUID.

(K) NEXT ADD HALF OF THE RAMEN SOUP POWDER THAT CAME WITH THE INSTANT NOODLES AND 1 CUP OF WATER. KEEP ADDING TO ADJUST TO TASTE. FINALLY, YOU ADD STARCH MIXED WITH WATER TO THICKEN THE SOUP.

(Y) POUR THE INGREDIENTS OVER THE NOODLES, AND IT'S DONE! HEY KIRIKO, HURRY, LET'S EAT!

(K) ... (I THOUGHT SHE WAS GOING TO LISTEN TO MY STORY?)

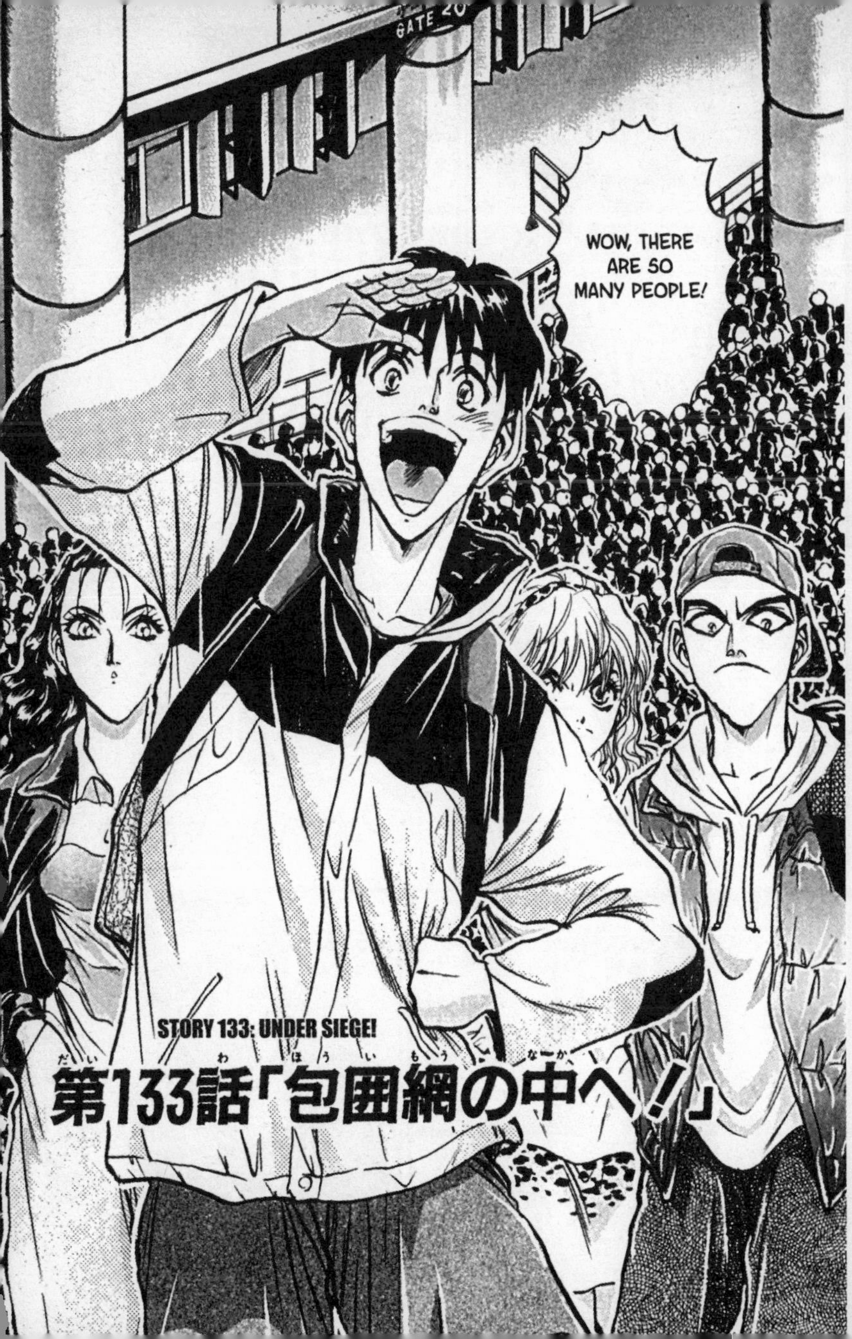
GATE 20
WOW, THERE ARE SO MANY PEOPLE!
STORY 133: UNDER SIEGE!
第133話「包囲網の中へ!」

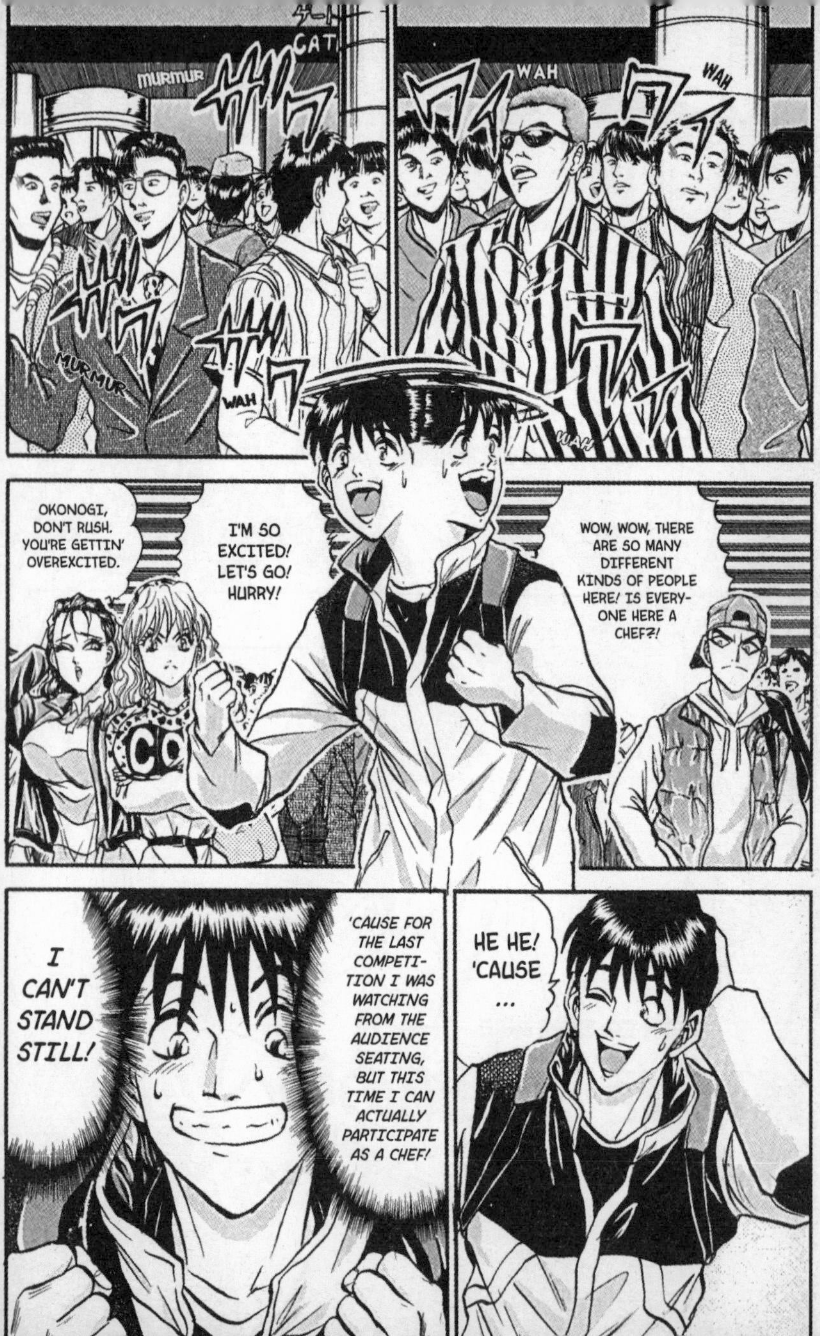
WAH
WAH
WAH
MURMUR
MURMUR
WAH
WOW, WOW, THERE ARE SO MANY DIFFERENT KINDS OF PEOPLE HERE! IS EVERYONE HERE A CHEF?!
I'M SO EXCITED! LET'S GO! HURRY!
OKONOGI, DON'T RUSH. YOU'RE GETTIN' OVEREXCITED.
HE HE! 'CAUSE ...
'CAUSE FOR THE LAST COMPETITION I WAS WATCHING FROM THE AUDIENCE SEATING, BUT THIS TIME I CAN ACTUALLY PARTICIPATE AS A CHEF!
I CAN'T STAND STILL!

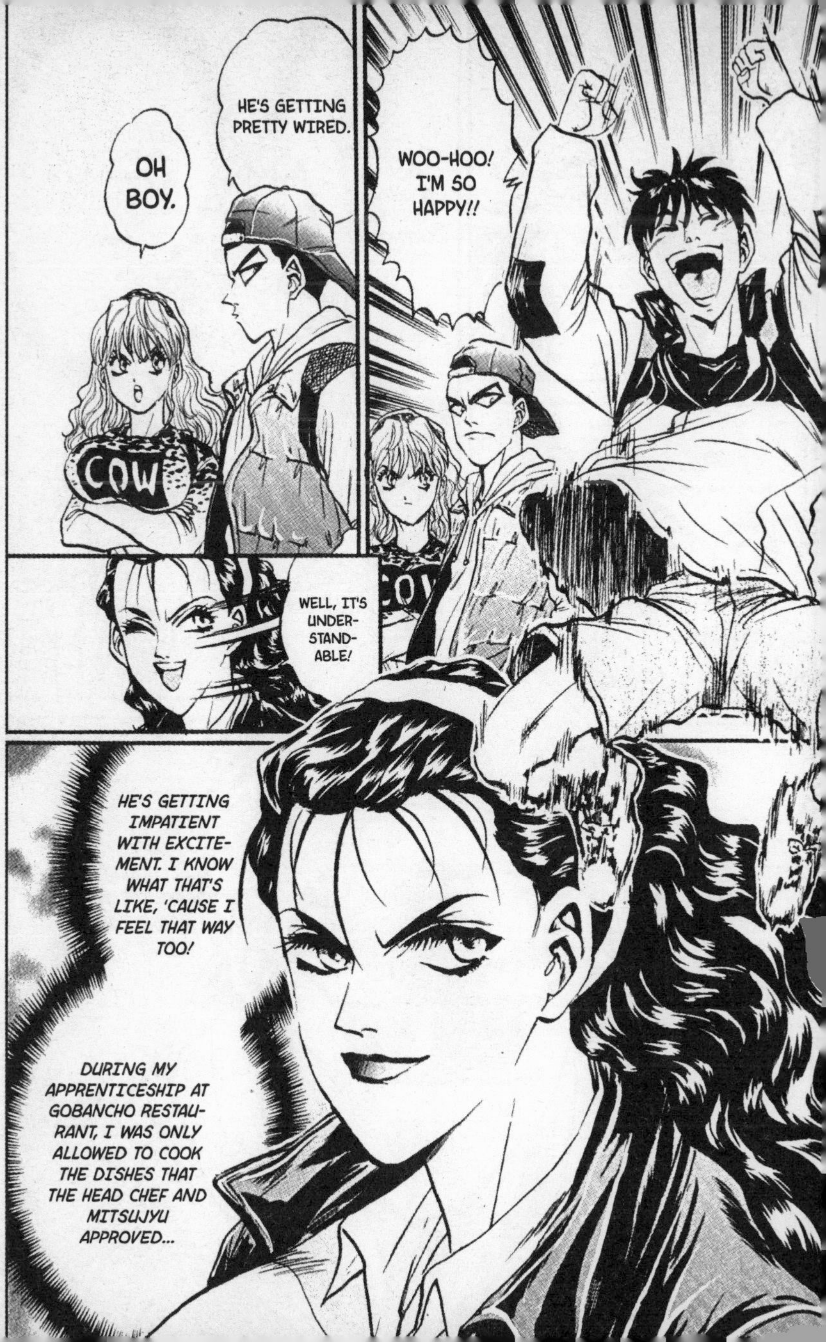
WOO-HOO! I'M SO HAPPY!!
HE'S GETTING PRETTY WIRED.
OH BOY.
WELL, IT'S UNDER-STAND-ABLE!
HE'S GETTING IMPATIENT WITH EXCITE-MENT. I KNOW WHAT THAT'S LIKE, 'CAUSE I FEEL THAT WAY TOO!
DURING MY APPRENTICESHIP AT GOBANCHO RESTAU-RANT, I WAS ONLY ALLOWED TO COOK THE DISHES THAT THE HEAD CHEF AND MITSUJYU APPROVED...

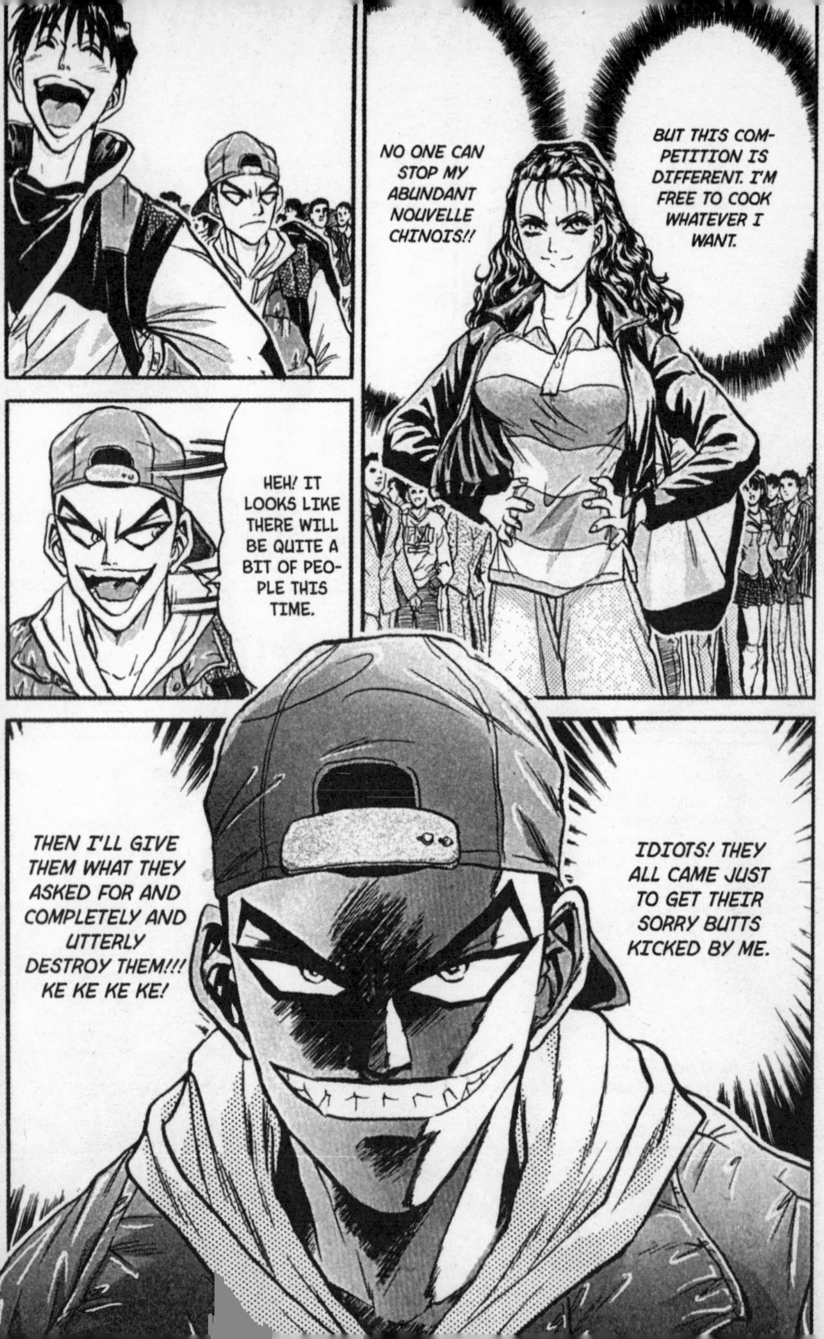
BUT THIS COMPETITION IS DIFFERENT. I'M FREE TO COOK WHATEVER I WANT.
NO ONE CAN STOP MY ABUNDANT NOUVELLE CHINOIS!!
HEH! IT LOOKS LIKE THERE WILL BE QUITE A BIT OF PEOPLE THIS TIME.
IDIOTS! THEY ALL CAME JUST TO GET THEIR SORRY BUTTS KICKED BY ME.
THEN I'LL GIVE THEM WHAT THEY ASKED FOR AND COMPLETELY AND UTTERLY DESTROY THEM!!! KE KE KE KE!

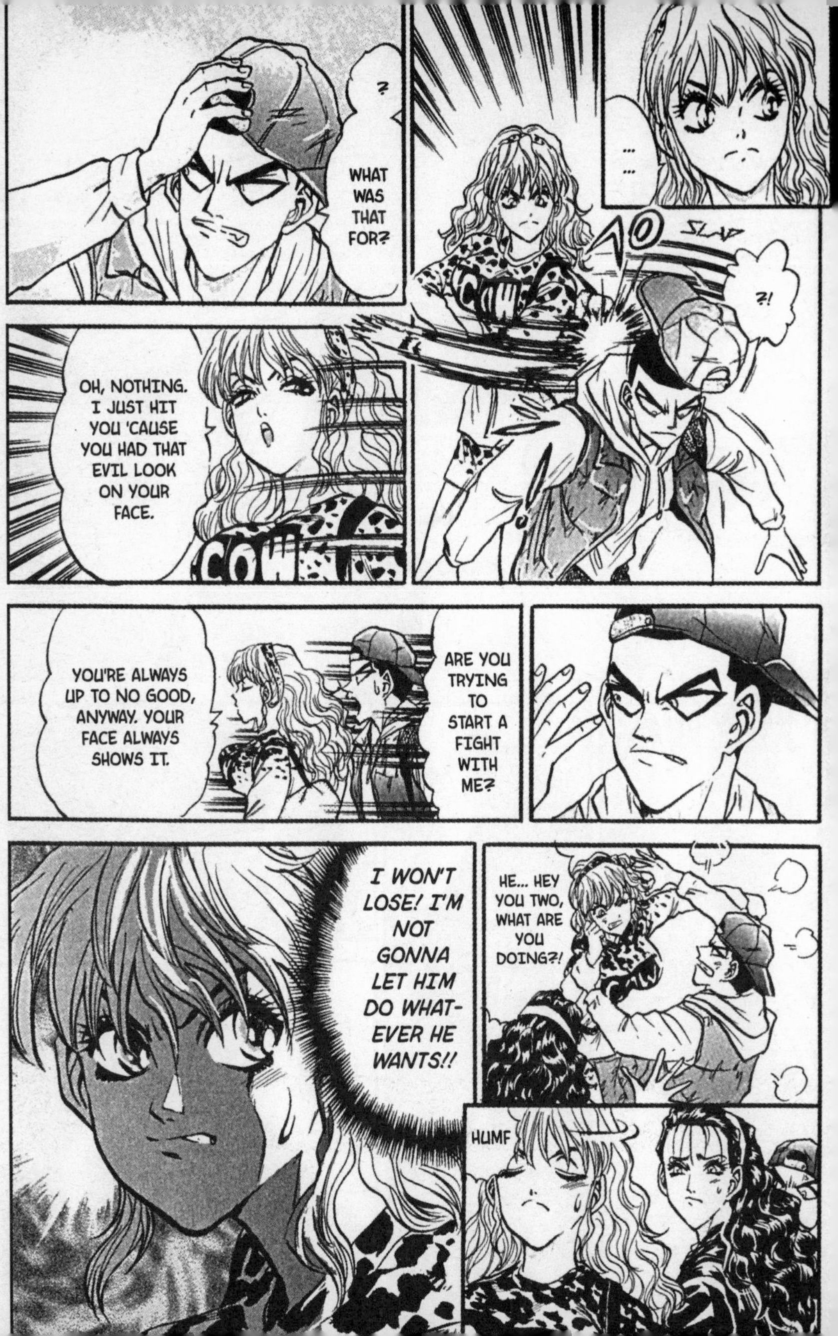
...
...
SLAP
?!
?
WHAT WAS THAT FOR?
OH, NOTHING. I JUST HIT YOU 'CAUSE YOU HAD THAT EVIL LOOK ON YOUR FACE.
ARE YOU TRYING TO START A FIGHT WITH ME?
YOU'RE ALWAYS UP TO NO GOOD, ANYWAY. YOUR FACE ALWAYS SHOWS IT.
HE... HEY YOU TWO, WHAT ARE YOU DOING?!
HUMF
I WON'T LOSE! I'M NOT GONNA LET HIM DO WHATEVER HE WANTS!!

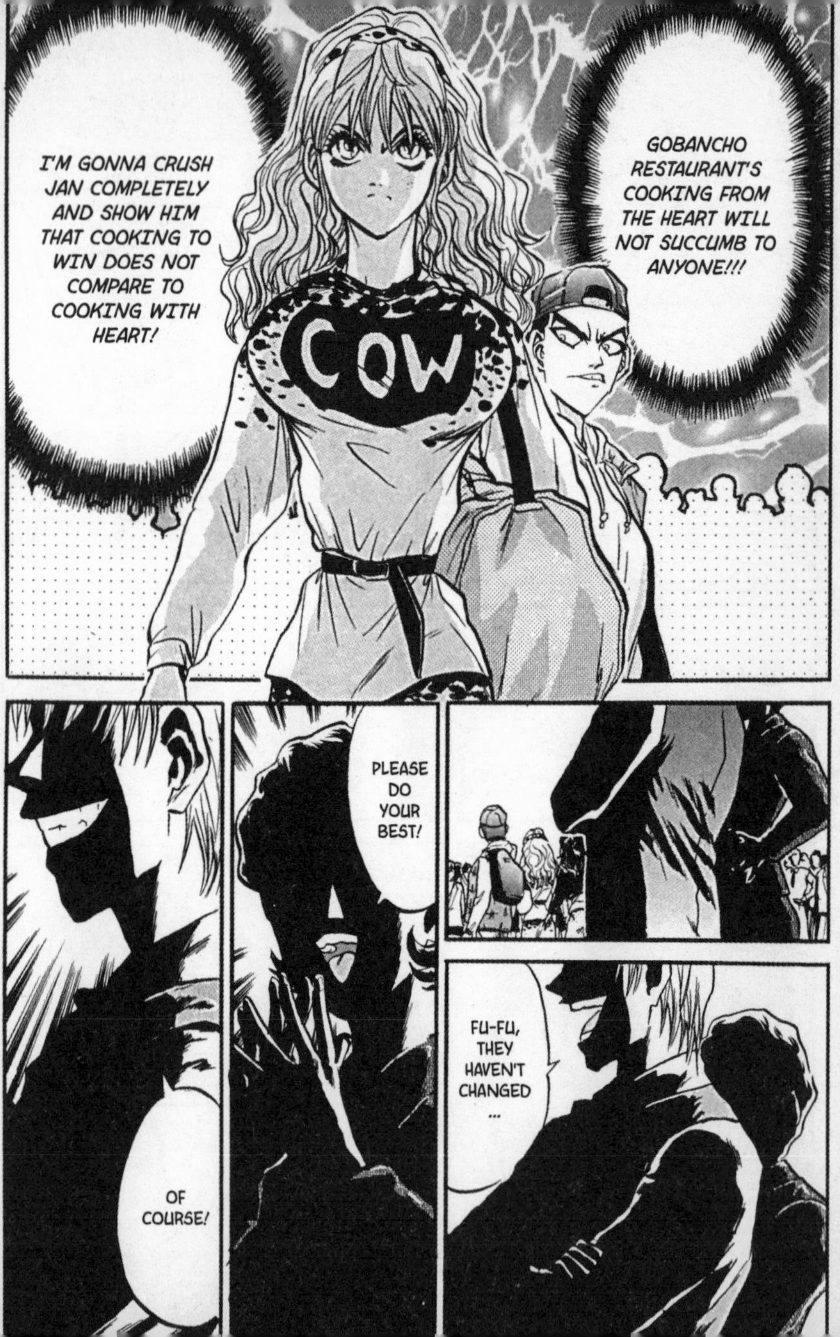
GOBANCHO RESTAURANT'S COOKING FROM THE HEART WILL NOT SUCCUMB TO ANYONE!!!
I'M GONNA CRUSH JAN COMPLETELY AND SHOW HIM THAT COOKING TO WIN DOES NOT COMPARE TO COOKING WITH HEART!
COW
FU-FU, THEY HAVEN'T CHANGED ...
PLEASE DO YOUR BEST!
OF COURSE!

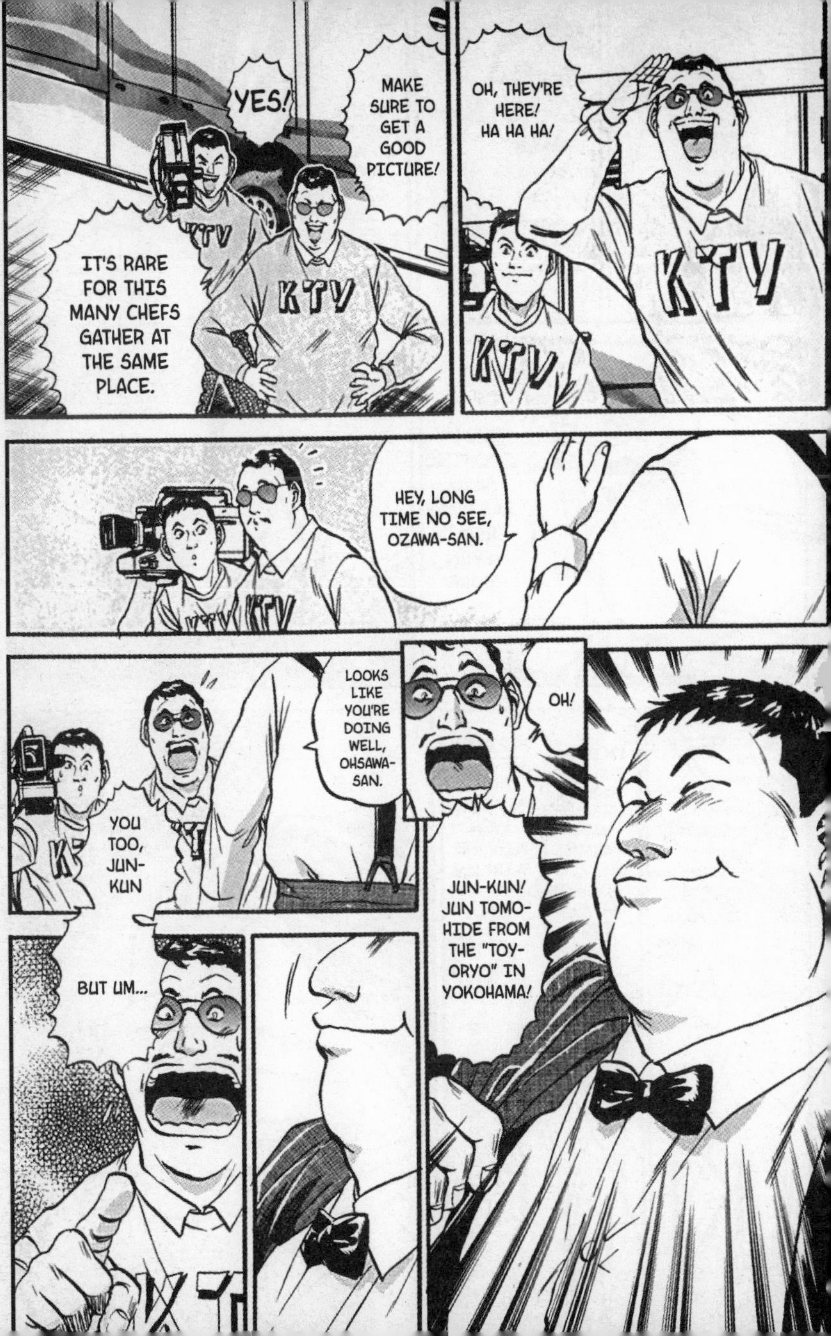
OH, THEY'RE HERE! HA HA HA!
MAKE SURE TO GET A GOOD PICTURE!
YES!
IT'S RARE FOR THIS MANY CHEFS GATHER AT THE SAME PLACE.
HEY, LONG TIME NO SEE, OZAWA-SAN.
LOOKS LIKE YOU'RE DOING WELL, OHSAWA-SAN.
YOU TOO, JUN-KUN
OH!
JUN-KUN! JUN TOMO-HIDE FROM THE "TOY-ORYO" IN YOKOHAMA!
BUT UM...

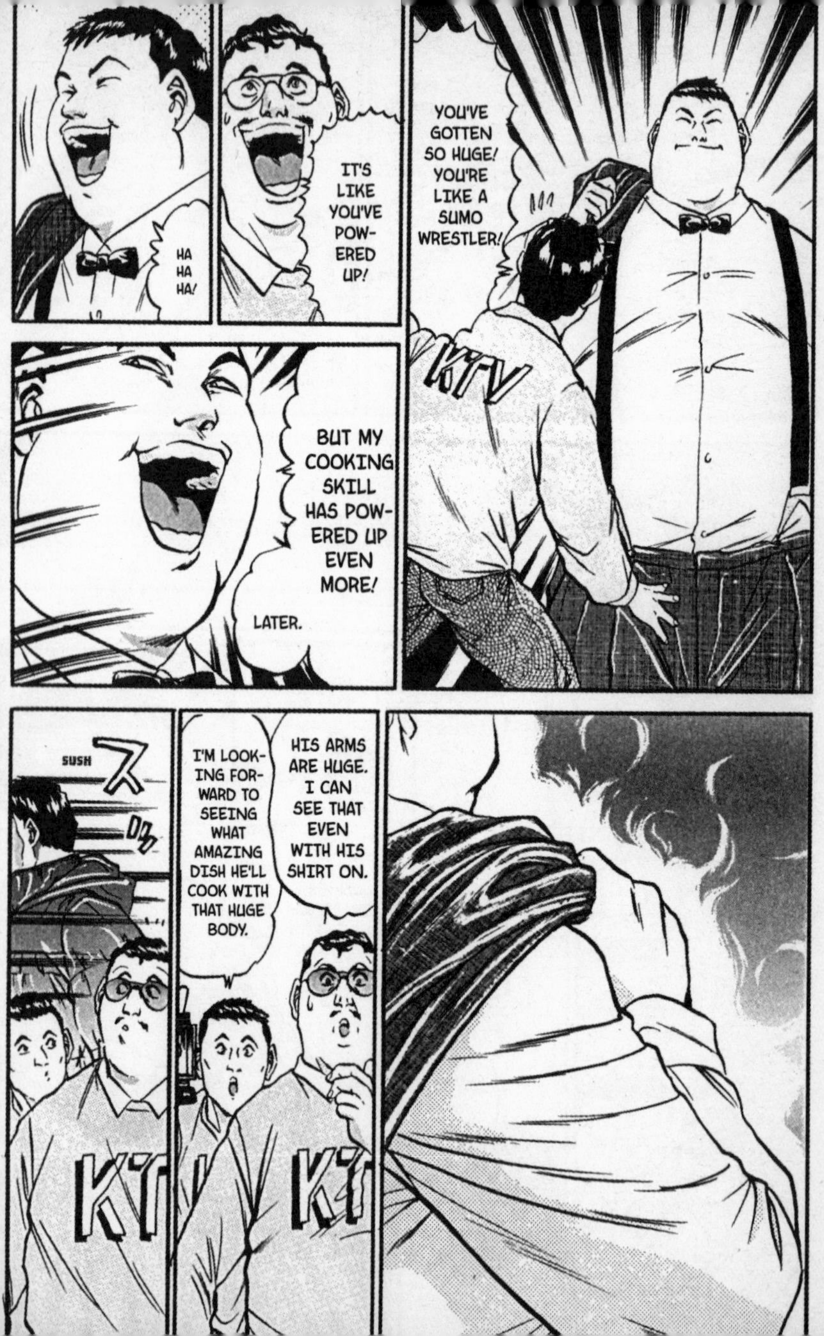
YOU'VE GOTTEN SO HUGE! YOU'RE LIKE A SUMO WRESTLER!
IT'S LIKE YOU'VE POW-ERED UP!
HA HA HA!
BUT MY COOKING SKILL HAS POW-ERED UP EVEN MORE!
LATER.
HIS ARMS ARE HUGE. I CAN SEE THAT EVEN WITH HIS SHIRT ON.
I'M LOOK-ING FOR-WARD TO SEEING WHAT AMAZING DISH HE'LL COOK WITH THAT HUGE BODY.
SUSH
ス

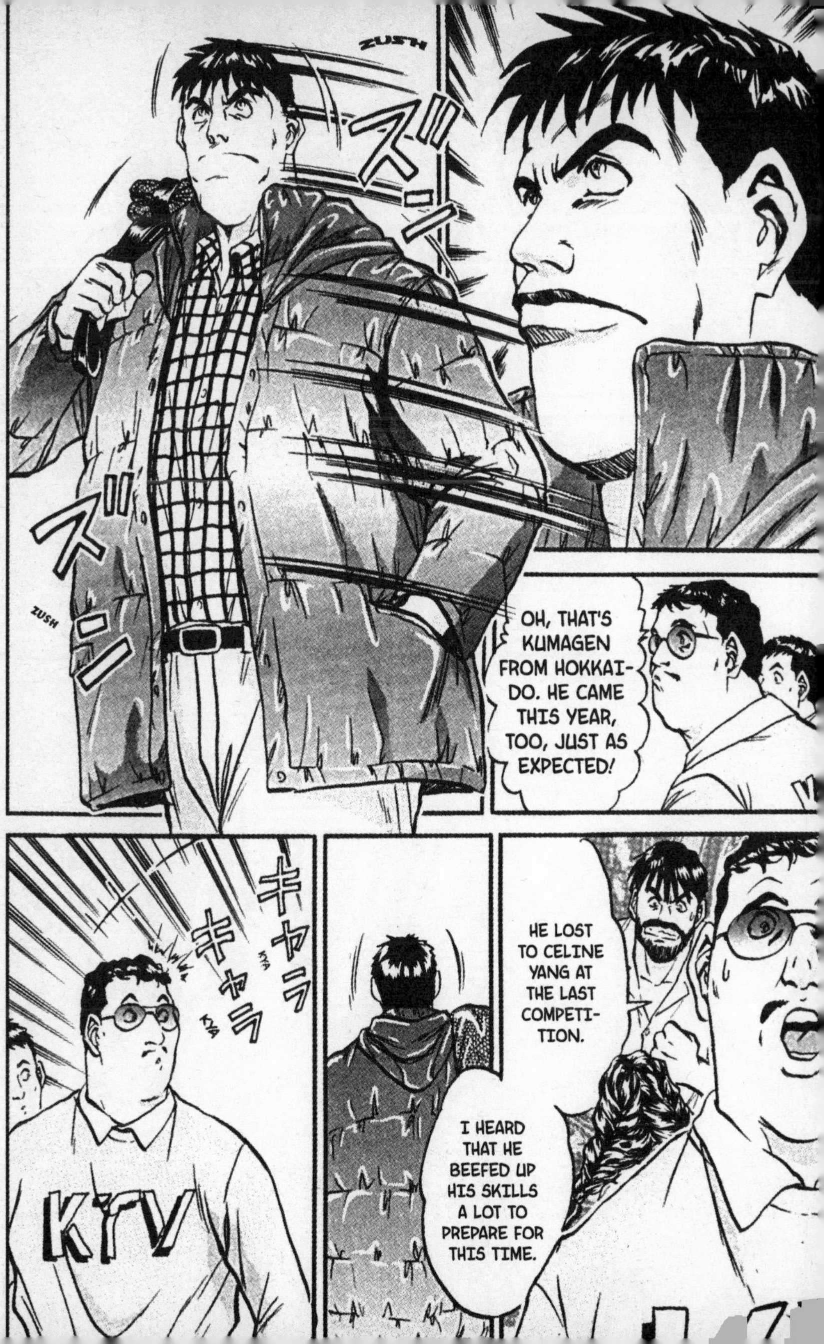
OH, THAT'S KUMAGEN FROM HOKKAIDO. HE CAME THIS YEAR, TOO, JUST AS EXPECTED!
ZUSH
ズーン
ZUSH
ズーン
HE LOST TO CELINE YANG AT THE LAST COMPETITION.
I HEARD THAT HE BEEFED UP HIS SKILLS A LOT TO PREPARE FOR THIS TIME.
キャラ
KYA
キャラ
KYA
KTV

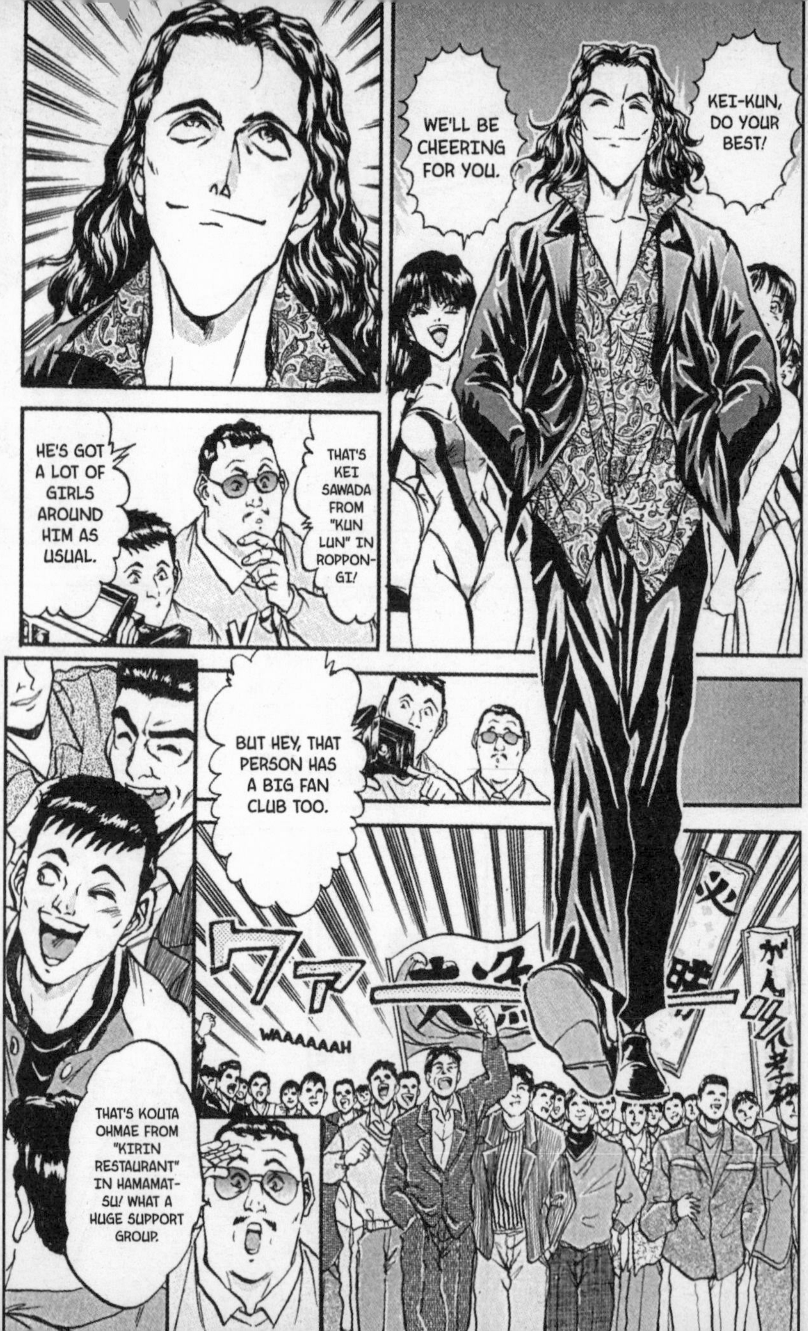
KEI-KUN, DO YOUR BEST!
WE'LL BE CHEERING FOR YOU.
THAT'S KEI SAWADA FROM "KUN LUN" IN ROPPONGI!
HE'S GOT A LOT OF GIRLS AROUND HIM AS USUAL.
BUT HEY, THAT PERSON HAS A BIG FAN CLUB TOO.
ウアー
WAAAAAAH
THAT'S KOUTA OHMAE FROM "KIRIN RESTAURANT" IN HAMAMATSU! WHAT A HUGE SUPPORT GROUP.

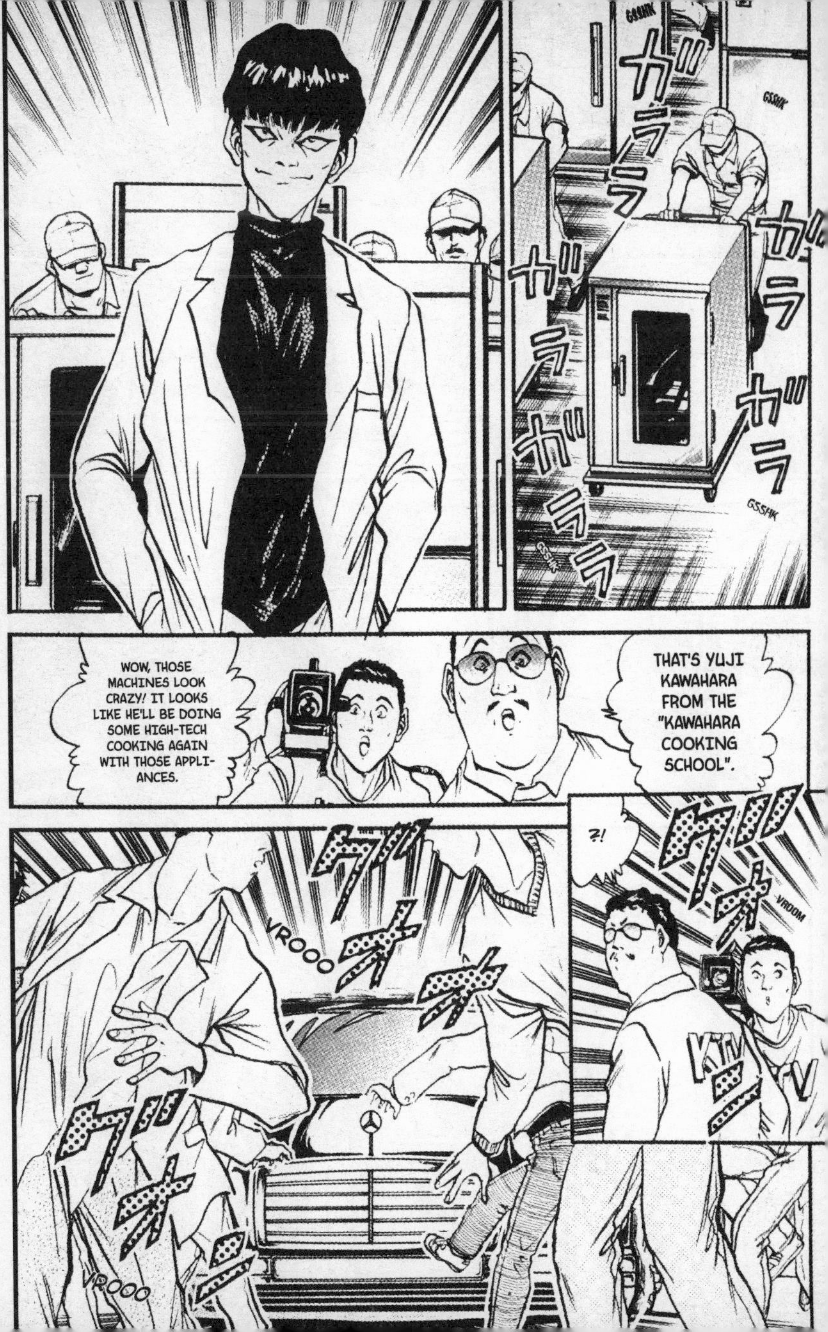
GSSHK
GSSHK
GSSHK
GSSHK
THAT'S YUJI KAWAHARA FROM THE "KAWAHARA COOKING SCHOOL".
WOW, THOSE MACHINES LOOK CRAZY! IT LOOKS LIKE HE'LL BE DOING SOME HIGH-TECH COOKING AGAIN WITH THOSE APPLI-ANCES.
?!
VROOM
KTV
VROOO
VROOO

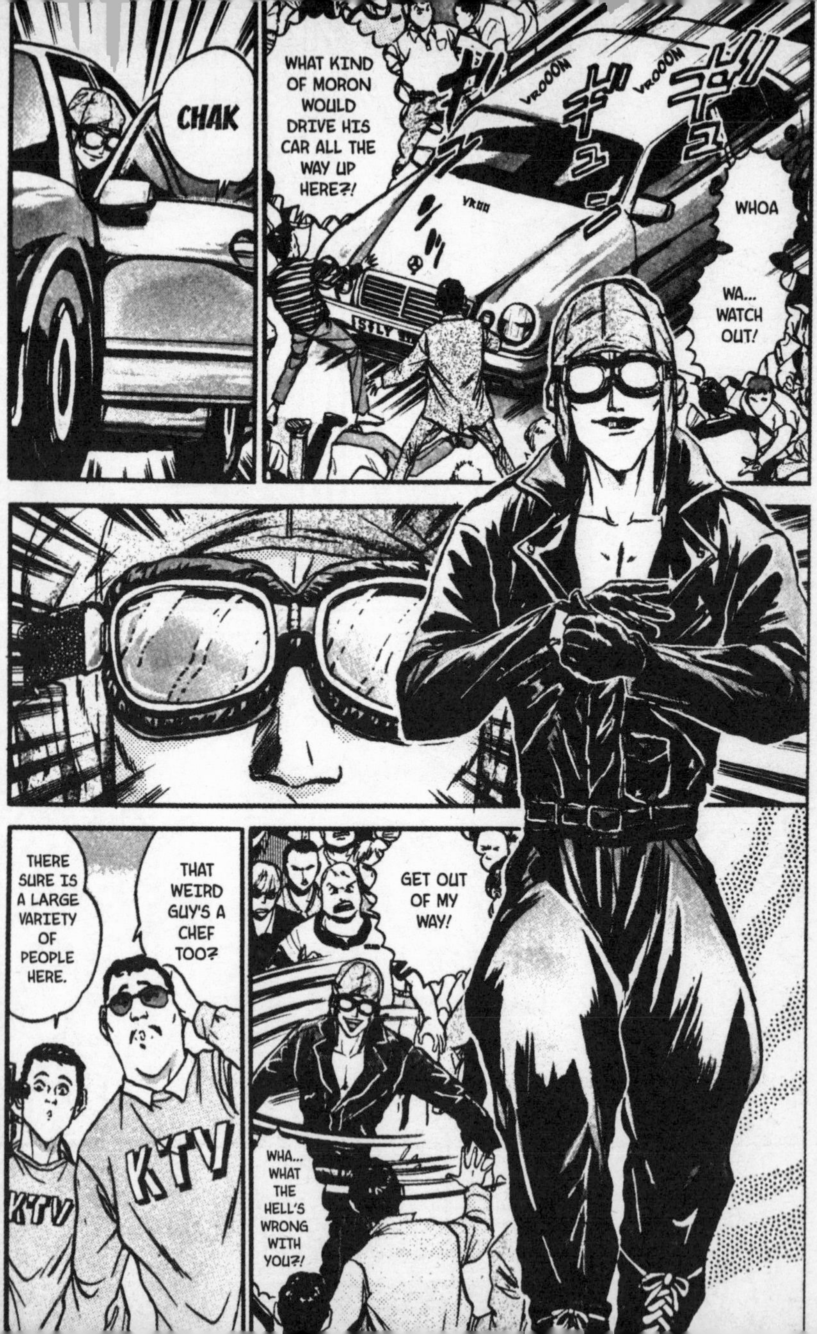
WHAT KIND OF MORON WOULD DRIVE HIS CAR ALL THE WAY UP HERE?!
VROOOM
VROOOM
VROO
WHOA
WA... WATCH OUT!
CHAK
GET OUT OF MY WAY!
WHA... WHAT THE HELL'S WRONG WITH YOU?!
THAT WEIRD GUY'S A CHEF TOO?
THERE SURE IS A LARGE VARIETY OF PEOPLE HERE.

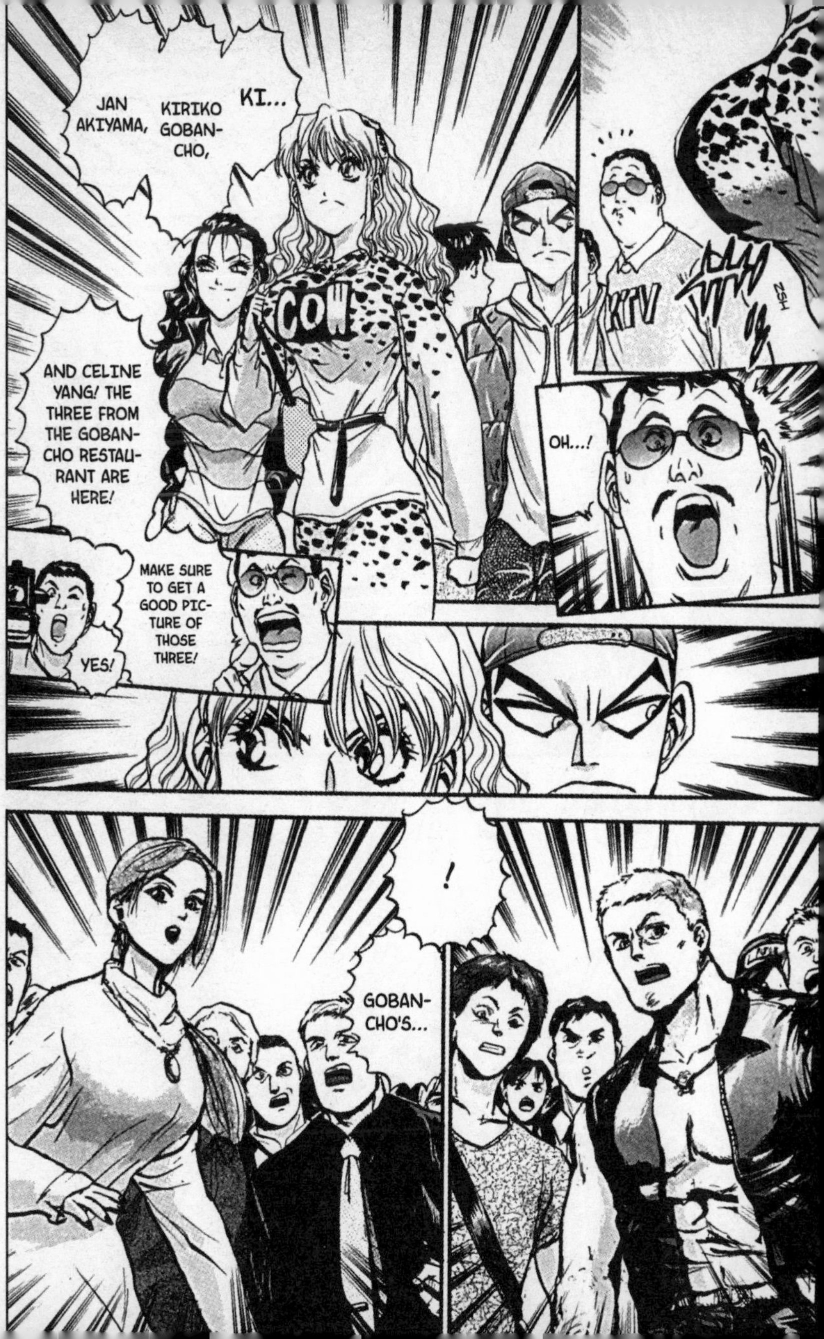
KI...
KIRIKO GOBAN-CHO,
JAN AKIYAMA,
AND CELINE YANG! THE THREE FROM THE GOBAN-CHO RESTAU-RANT ARE HERE!
OH...!
MAKE SURE TO GET A GOOD PIC-TURE OF THOSE THREE!
YES!
!
GOBAN-CHO'S...

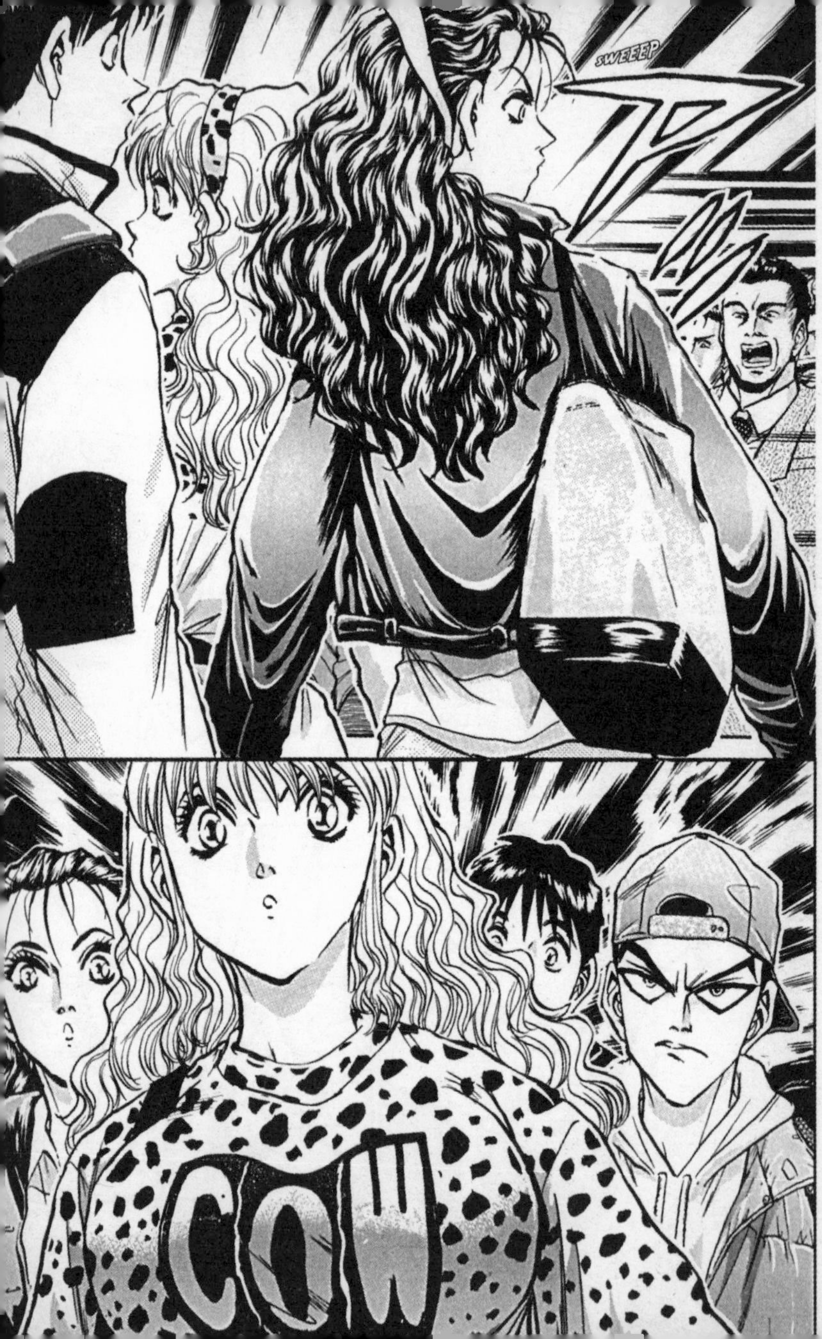
SWEEEP
COW

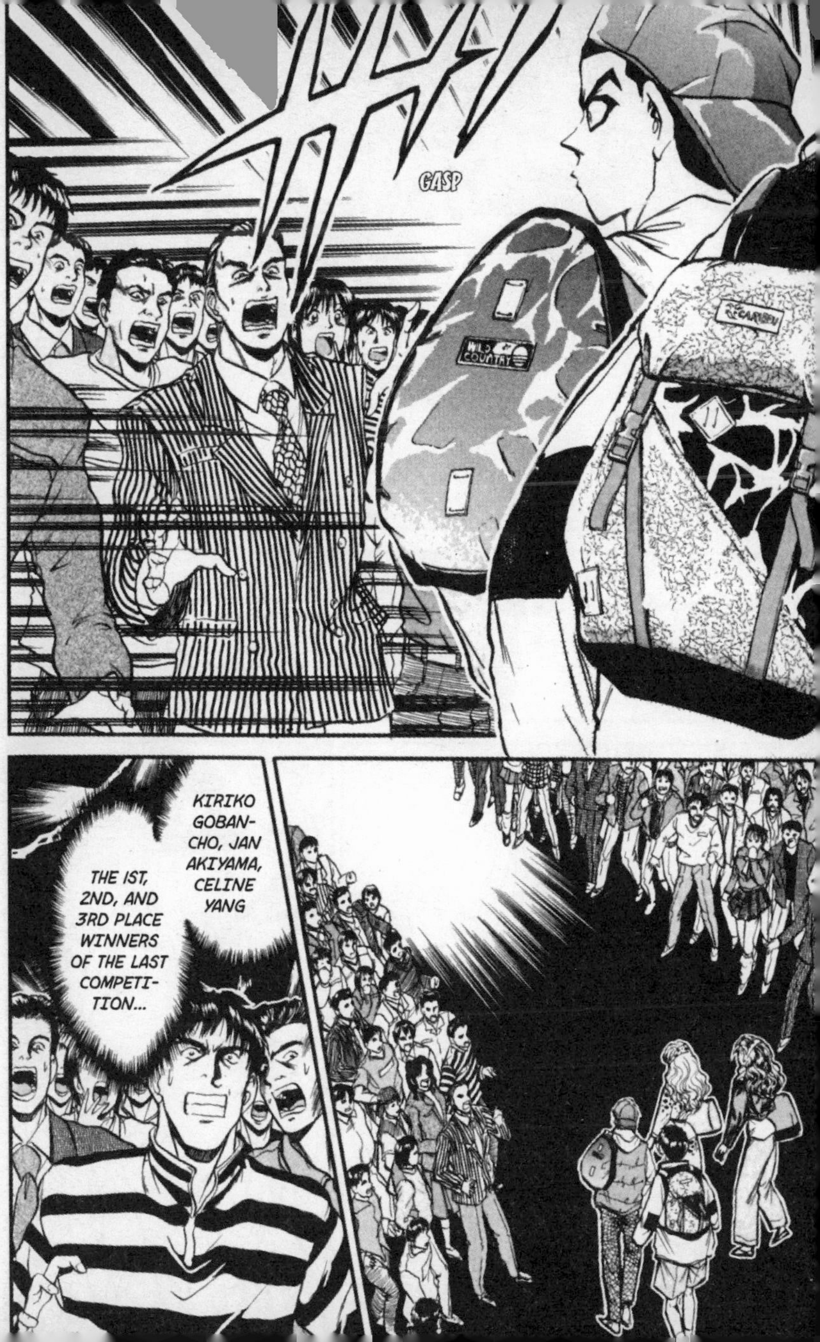
GASP
WILD COUNTRY
KIRIKO GOBAN-CHO, JAN AKIYAMA, CELINE YANG
THE 1ST, 2ND, AND 3RD PLACE WINNERS OF THE LAST COMPETI-TION...

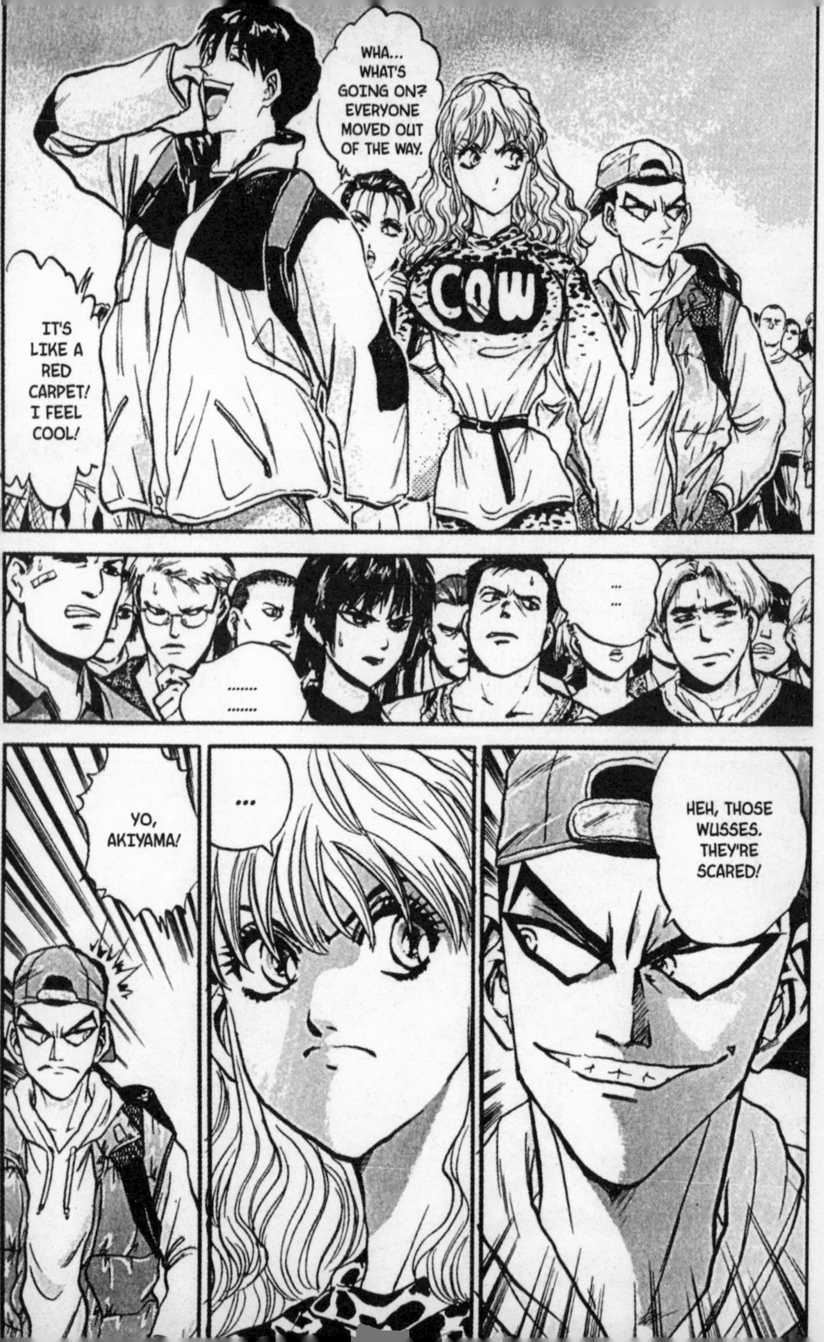
WHA... WHAT'S GOING ON? EVERYONE MOVED OUT OF THE WAY.
IT'S LIKE A RED CARPET! I FEEL COOL!
...
...
......
......
HEH, THOSE WUSSES. THEY'RE SCARED!
...
YO, AKIYAMA!

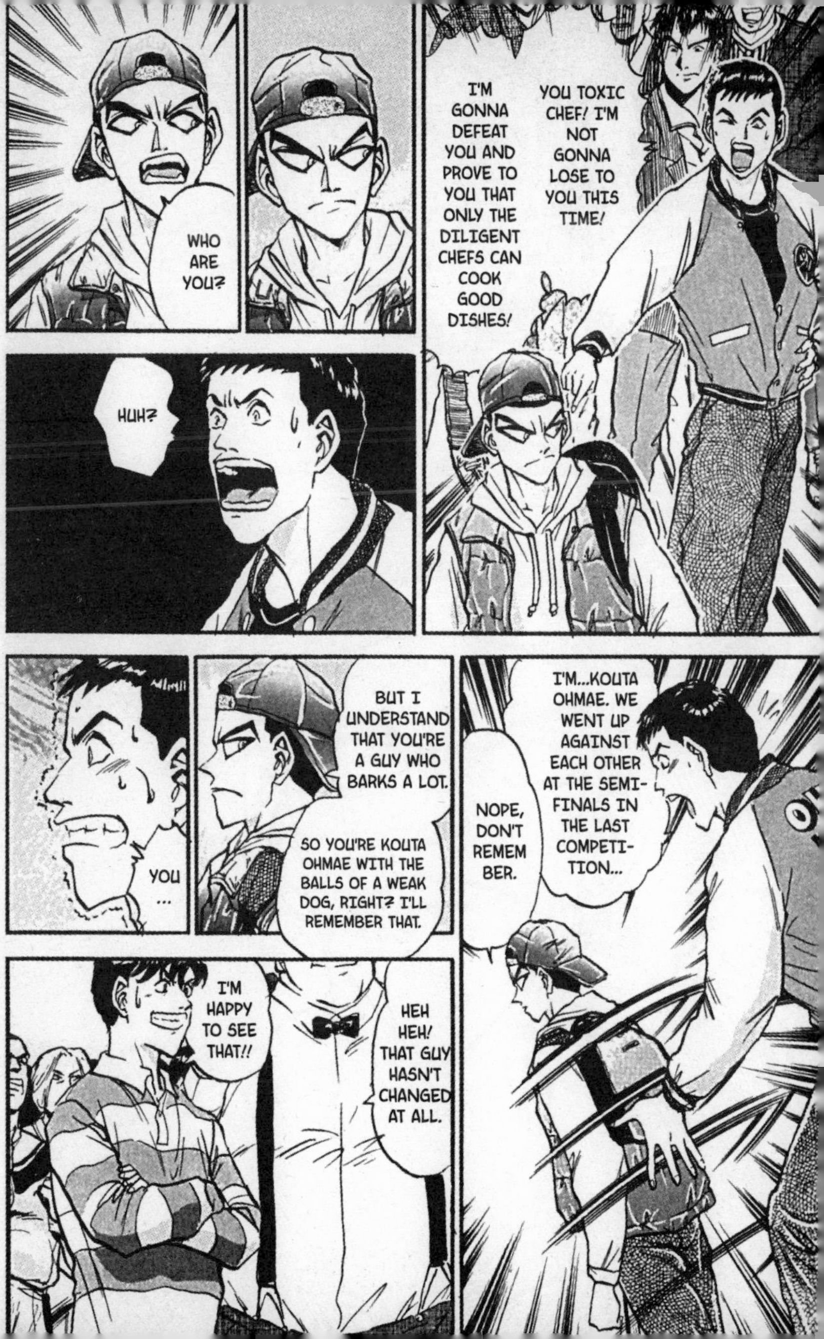
YOU TOXIC CHEF! I'M NOT GONNA LOSE TO YOU THIS TIME!
I'M GONNA DEFEAT YOU AND PROVE TO YOU THAT ONLY THE DILIGENT CHEFS CAN COOK GOOD DISHES!
WHO ARE YOU?
HUH?
I'M...KOUTA OHMAE. WE WENT UP AGAINST EACH OTHER AT THE SEMI-FINALS IN THE LAST COMPETITION...
NOPE, DON'T REMEMBER.
BUT I UNDERSTAND THAT YOU'RE A GUY WHO BARKS A LOT.
SO YOU'RE KOUTA OHMAE WITH THE BALLS OF A WEAK DOG, RIGHT? I'LL REMEMBER THAT.
YOU ...
HEH HEH! THAT GUY HASN'T CHANGED AT ALL.
I'M HAPPY TO SEE THAT!!

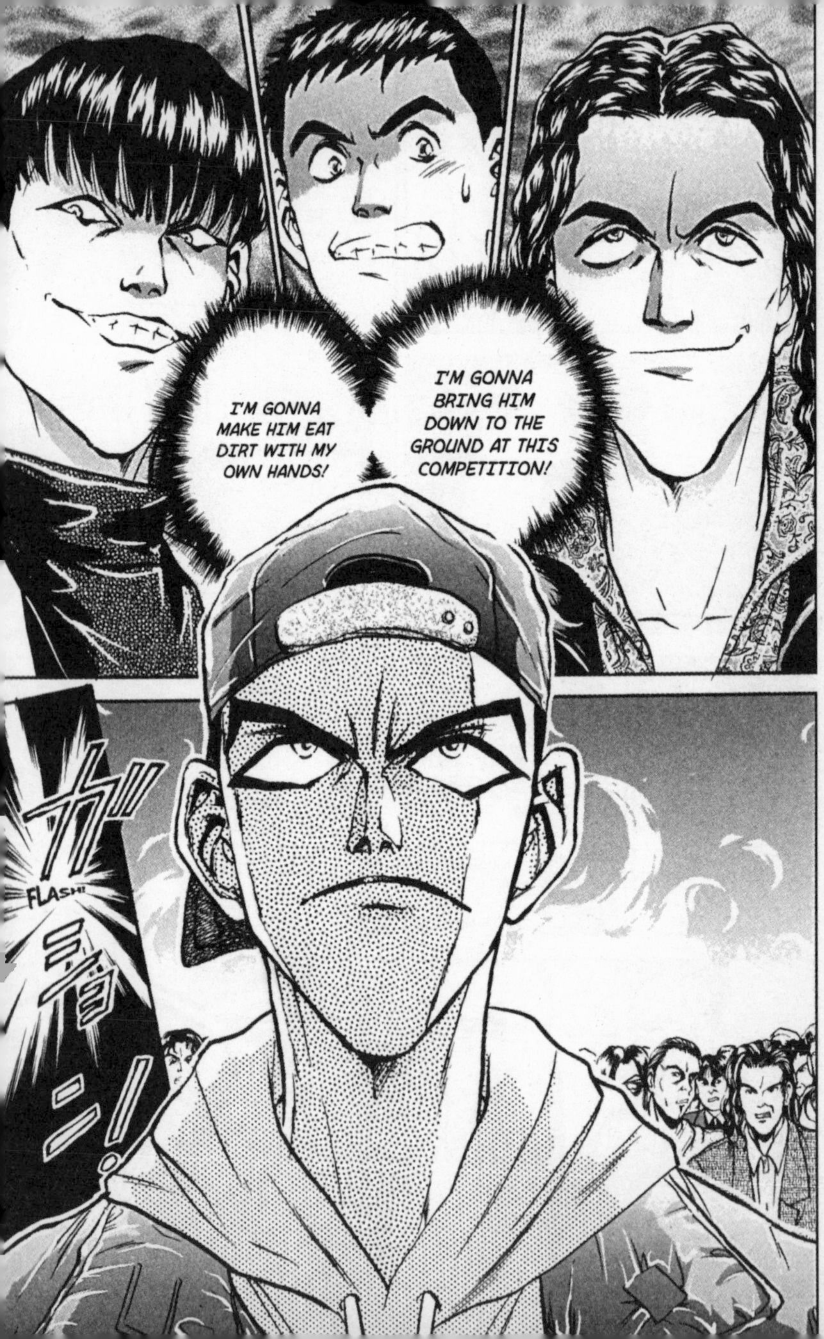
I'M GONNA BRING HIM DOWN TO THE GROUND AT THIS COMPETITION!
I'M GONNA MAKE HIM EAT DIRT WITH MY OWN HANDS!
FLASH!

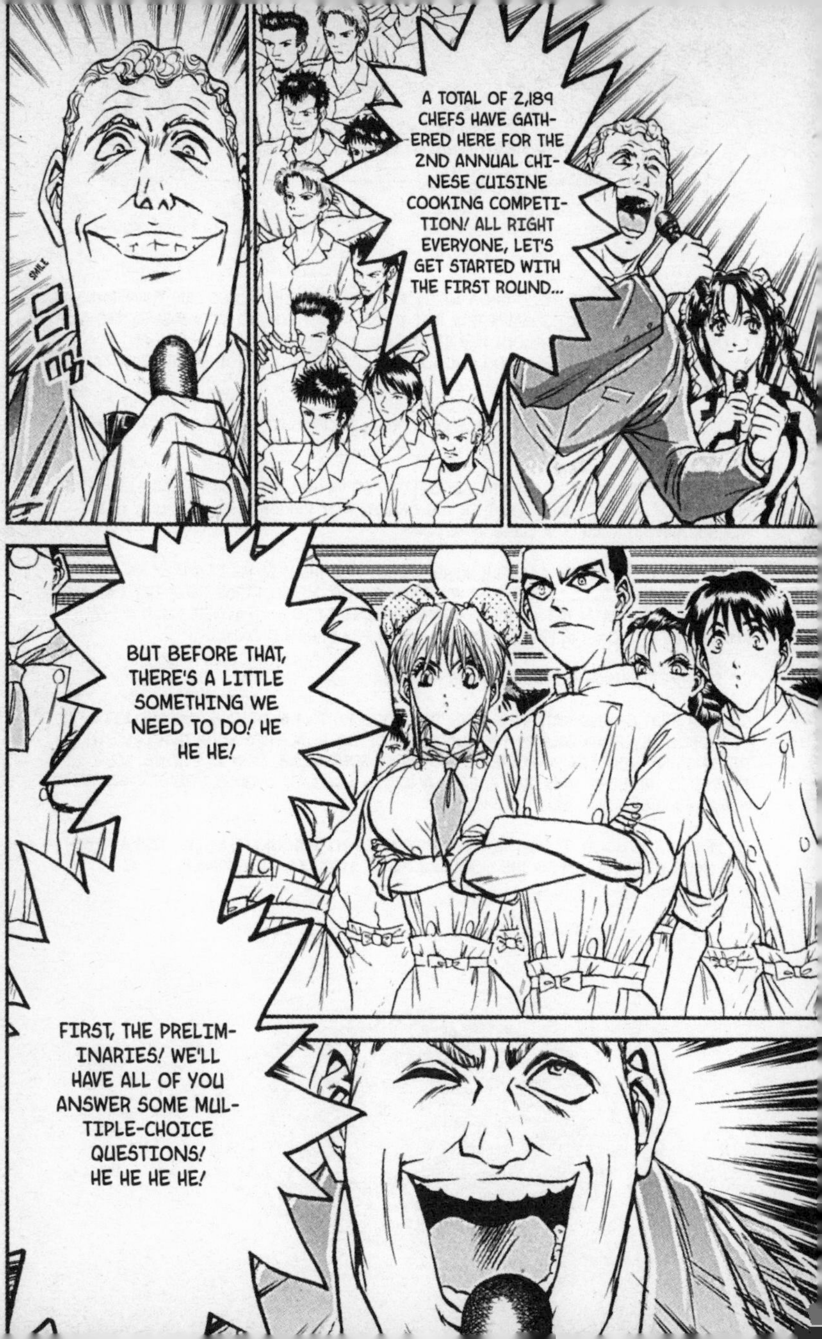
A TOTAL OF 2,189 CHEFS HAVE GATHERED HERE FOR THE 2ND ANNUAL CHINESE CUISINE COOKING COMPETITION! ALL RIGHT EVERYONE, LET'S GET STARTED WITH THE FIRST ROUND...
SMILE
BUT BEFORE THAT, THERE'S A LITTLE SOMETHING WE NEED TO DO! HE HE HE!
FIRST, THE PRELIMINARIES! WE'LL HAVE ALL OF YOU ANSWER SOME MULTIPLE-CHOICE QUESTIONS! HE HE HE HE!

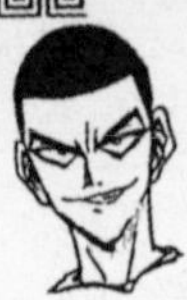

JAN AND YANG'S

CHAO MIAN
(STIR-FRIED INSTANT RAMEN NOODLES)

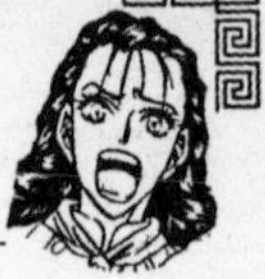

(Y) AHH, THAT WAS SOME GOOD CHOW MEIN. EVEN INSTANT NOODLES CAN TURN INTO A GOOD DISH IF IT'S COOKED PROPERLY. BUT I WAS TOO INVOLVED WITH MAH EATIN' THAT I FORGOT TO ASK KIRIKO ABOUT HER STORY. OH, PERFECT TIMIN', THERE'S JAN. HEY JAN, SO WHAT HAPPENED BETWEEN YOU AND KIRIKO EARLIER? I BET YA MADE SOME SARCASTIC REMARK TO HER.

(J) I DIDN'T SAY ANYTHING THAT BIG OF A DEAL. I JUST SAID THAT SHE'S LIKE A POTATO BECAUSE SHE EATS SO MUCH OF IT.

(Y) JAN, LISTEN TO ME. GIRLS ARE SENSITIVE, SO YA HAVE TO BE MORE CAREFUL WITH YOUR WORDS. WELL, I SHOULDN'T BE THE ONE TALKIN' HERE ABOUT CAREFULLY USIN' WORDS...ANYWAY, WHAT'D YA COME HERE FOR?

(J) I'M STARTING TO GET A LITTLE HUNGRY. JUST FOR THE HELL OF IT, I'M GONNA COOK SOMETHING THAT GOES UP AGAINST WHAT YOU GUYS COOKED. FIRST, BOIL THE INSTANT NOODLES AND DRAIN THE WATER BY TRANSFERRING IT TO A STRAINER. POUR A SMALL AMOUNT OF OIL ON THE FRYING PAN AND STIR-FRY GREEN ONIONS.

(Y) IT'S PRETTY MUCH THE SAME THING WE DID.

(J) JUST SHUT UP AND WATCH!! RETURN THE NOODLES TO THE FRYING PAN AND STIR-FRY IT THOROUGHLY. POUR HALF OF THE CONTENTS OF THE POWDERED SOUP THAT CAME WITH THE INSTANT NOODLES, AND THEN STIR-FRY IT SOME MORE. NOW IT'S DONE. SEE? SIMPLE IS THE BEST. IT'S QUICK, EASY, AND IT'S GOOD. OF COURSE, YOU CAN MIX IN WHATEVER VEGETABLES YOU LIKE WITH IT.

(Y) YEAH, IT IS GOOD. IF YOU'RE INEXPERIENCED WITH COOKIN', YA CAN USE A FRYIN' PAN MADE WITH TEFLON SO THE NOODLES WON'T STICK TO THE SURFACE.

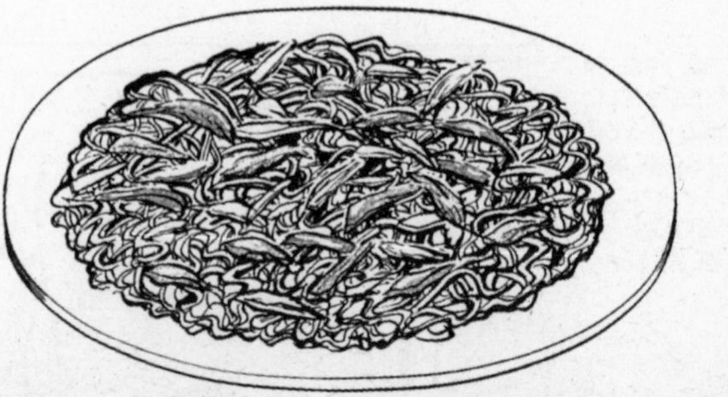

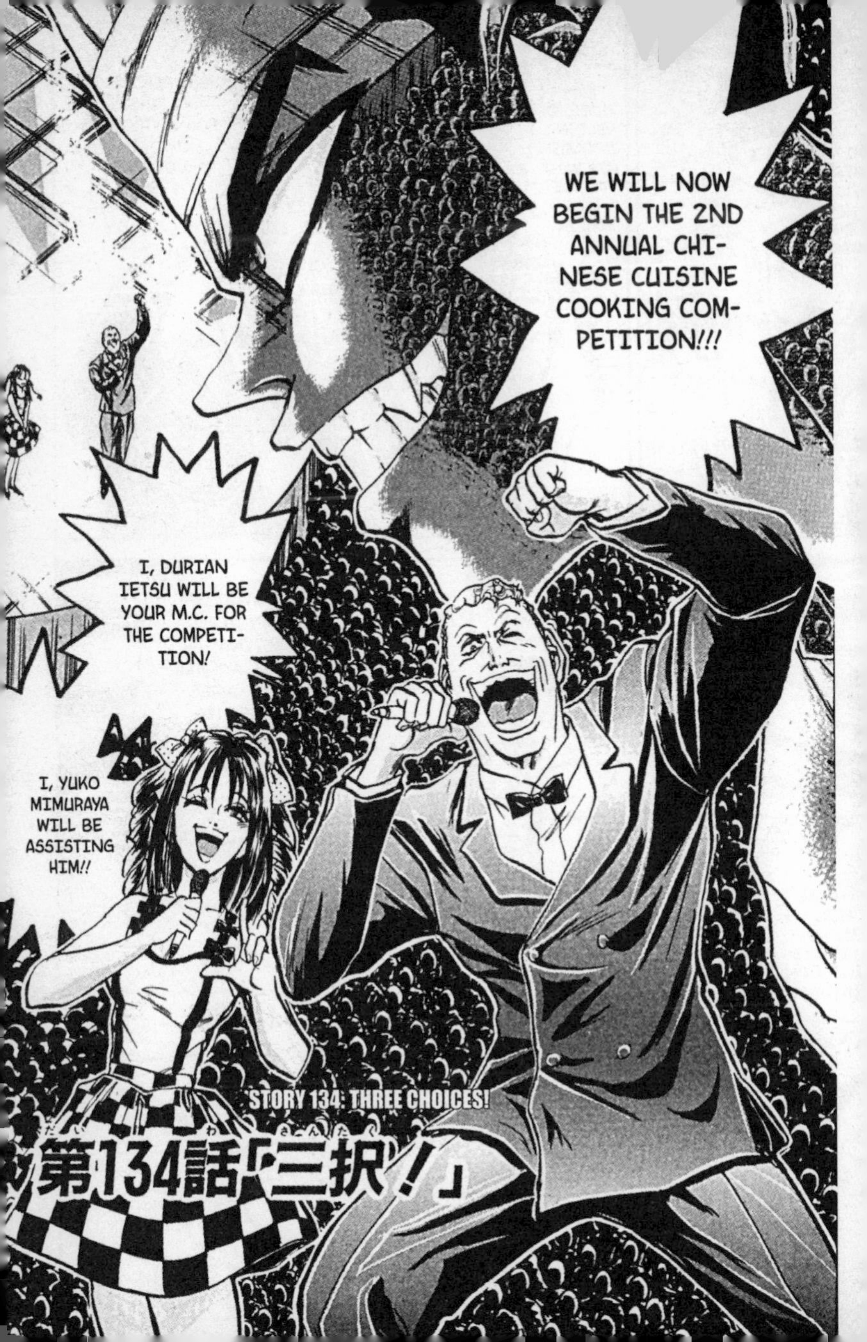
WE WILL NOW BEGIN THE 2ND ANNUAL CHI-NESE CUISINE COOKING COM-PETITION!!!
I, DURIAN IETSU WILL BE YOUR M.C. FOR THE COMPETI-TION!
I, YUKO MIMURAYA WILL BE ASSISTING HIM!!
STORY 134: THREE CHOICES!
第134話「三択！」

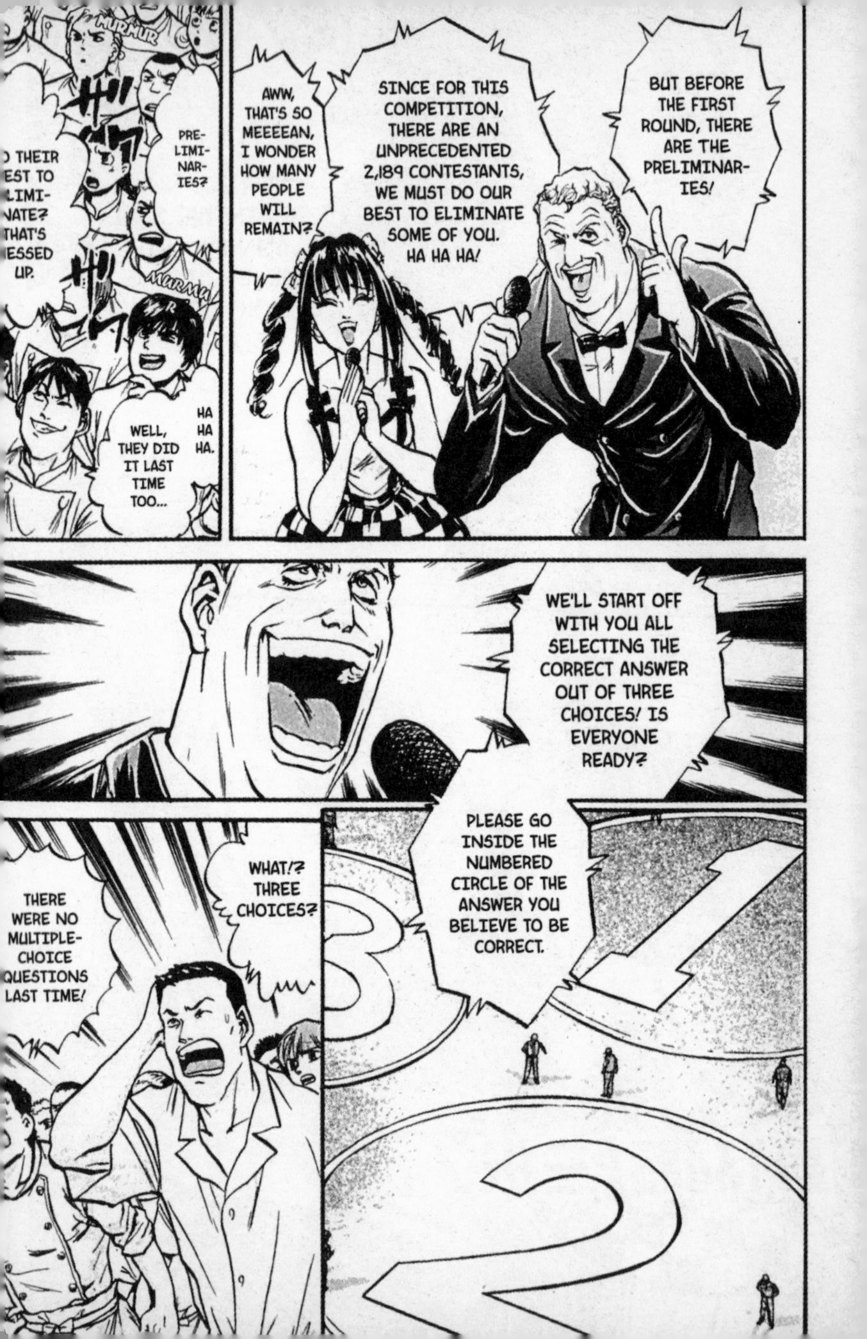
BUT BEFORE THE FIRST ROUND, THERE ARE THE PRELIMINARIES!
SINCE FOR THIS COMPETITION, THERE ARE AN UNPRECEDENTED 2,189 CONTESTANTS, WE MUST DO OUR BEST TO ELIMINATE SOME OF YOU. HA HA HA!
AWW, THAT'S SO MEEEEAN, I WONDER HOW MANY PEOPLE WILL REMAIN?
MURMUR
PRELIMINARIES?
O THEIR EST TO LIMINATE? THAT'S ESSED UP.
MURMUR
HA HA HA.
WELL, THEY DID IT LAST TIME TOO...
WE'LL START OFF WITH YOU ALL SELECTING THE CORRECT ANSWER OUT OF THREE CHOICES! IS EVERYONE READY?
PLEASE GO INSIDE THE NUMBERED CIRCLE OF THE ANSWER YOU BELIEVE TO BE CORRECT.
1
3
2
WHAT!? THREE CHOICES?
THERE WERE NO MULTIPLE-CHOICE QUESTIONS LAST TIME!

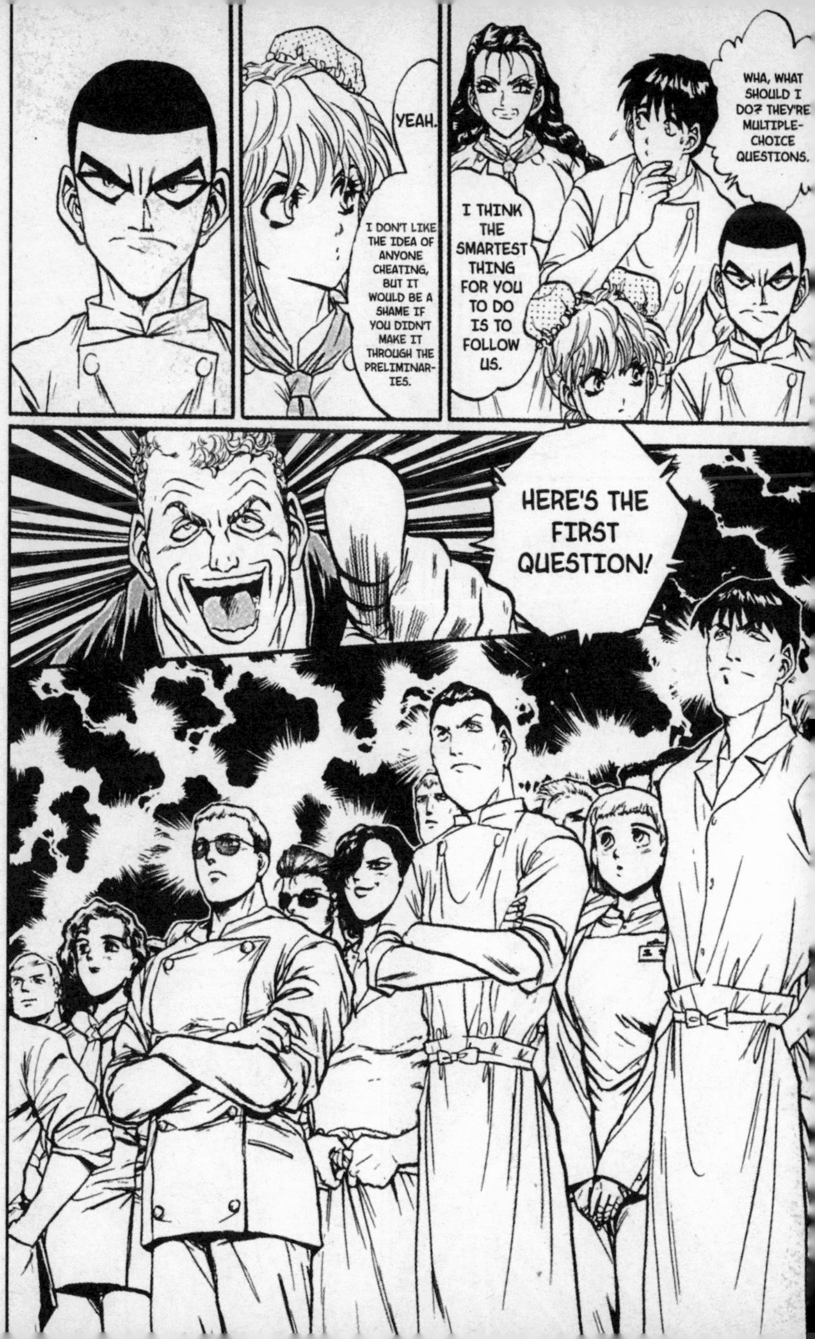
WHA, WHAT SHOULD I DO? THEY'RE MULTIPLE-CHOICE QUESTIONS.
I THINK THE SMARTEST THING FOR YOU TO DO IS TO FOLLOW US.
YEAH.
I DON'T LIKE THE IDEA OF ANYONE CHEATING, BUT IT WOULD BE A SHAME IF YOU DIDN'T MAKE IT THROUGH THE PRELIMINAR-IES.
HERE'S THE FIRST QUESTION!

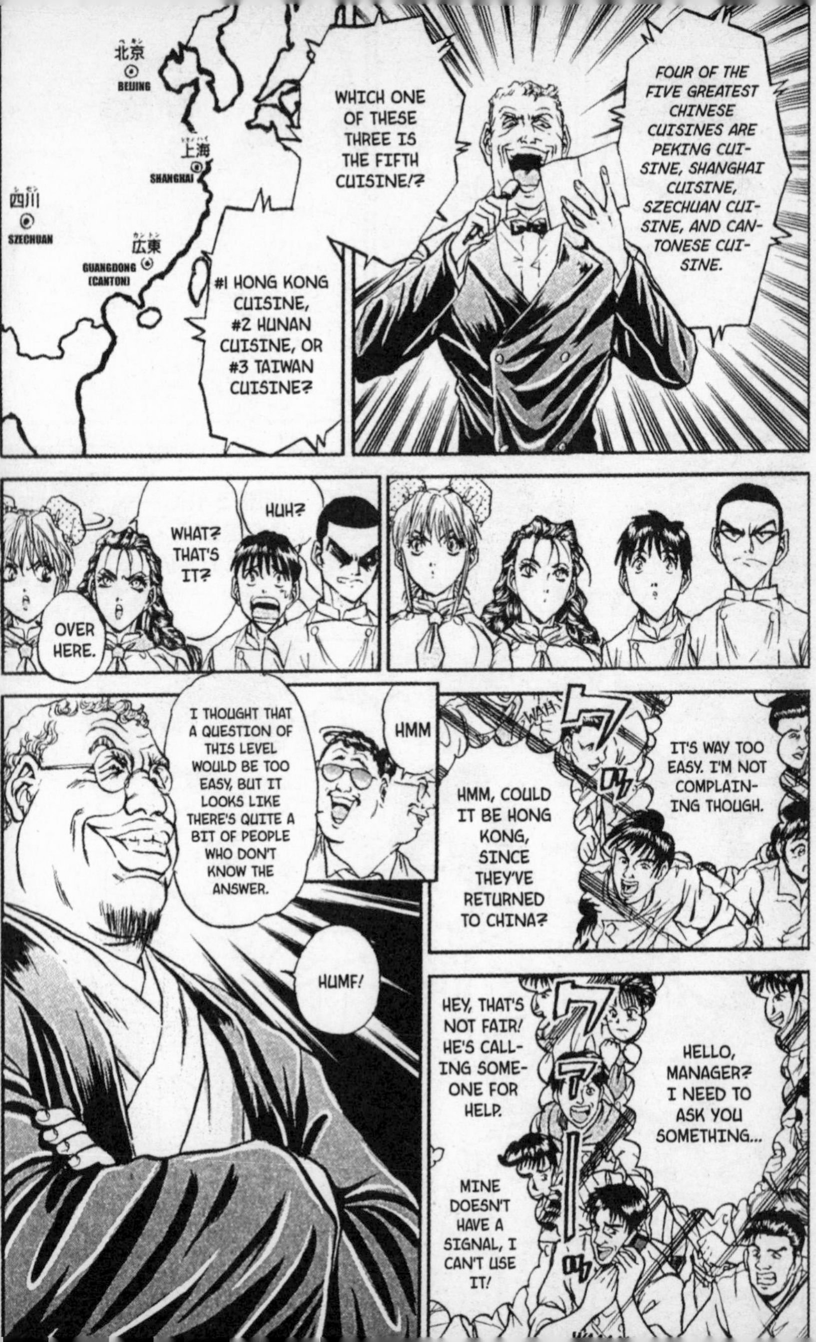
FOUR OF THE FIVE GREATEST CHINESE CUISINES ARE PEKING CUISINE, SHANGHAI CUISINE, SZECHUAN CUISINE, AND CANTONESE CUISINE.
WHICH ONE OF THESE THREE IS THE FIFTH CUISINE!?
#1 HONG KONG CUISINE, #2 HUNAN CUISINE, OR #3 TAIWAN CUISINE?
北京
BEIJING
上海
SHANGHAI
四川
SZECHUAN
広東
GUANGDONG (CANTON)
HUH?
WHAT? THAT'S IT?
OVER HERE.
WAH
IT'S WAY TOO EASY. I'M NOT COMPLAINING THOUGH.
HMM, COULD IT BE HONG KONG, SINCE THEY'VE RETURNED TO CHINA?
HELLO, MANAGER? I NEED TO ASK YOU SOMETHING...
HEY, THAT'S NOT FAIR! HE'S CALLING SOMEONE FOR HELP.
MINE DOESN'T HAVE A SIGNAL, I CAN'T USE IT!
HMM
I THOUGHT THAT A QUESTION OF THIS LEVEL WOULD BE TOO EASY, BUT IT LOOKS LIKE THERE'S QUITE A BIT OF PEOPLE WHO DON'T KNOW THE ANSWER.
HUMF!

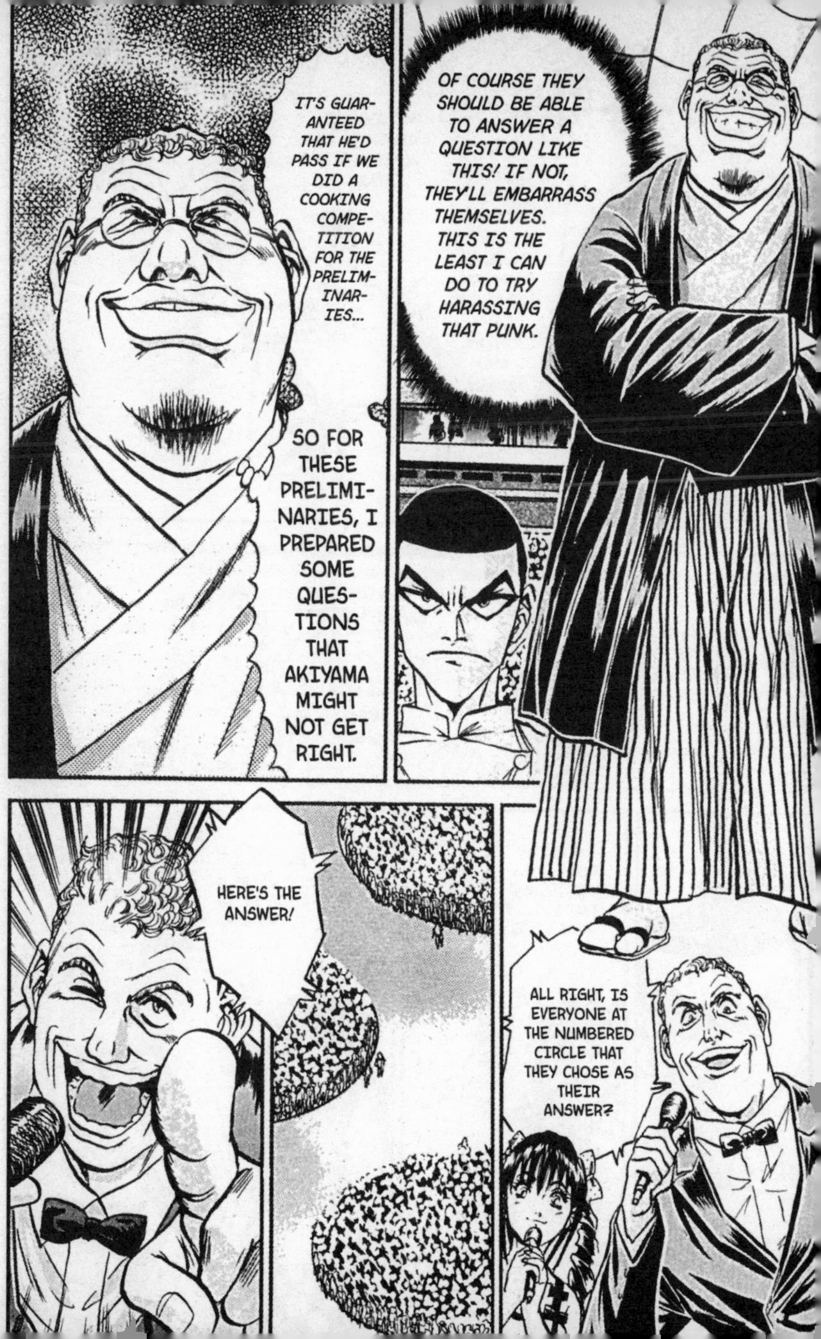
OF COURSE THEY SHOULD BE ABLE TO ANSWER A QUESTION LIKE THIS! IF NOT, THEY'LL EMBARRASS THEMSELVES. THIS IS THE LEAST I CAN DO TO TRY HARASSING THAT PUNK.
IT'S GUARANTEED THAT HE'D PASS IF WE DID A COOKING COMPETITION FOR THE PRELIMINARIES...
SO FOR THESE PRELIMINARIES, I PREPARED SOME QUESTIONS THAT AKIYAMA MIGHT NOT GET RIGHT.
ALL RIGHT, IS EVERYONE AT THE NUMBERED CIRCLE THAT THEY CHOSE AS THEIR ANSWER?
HERE'S THE ANSWER!

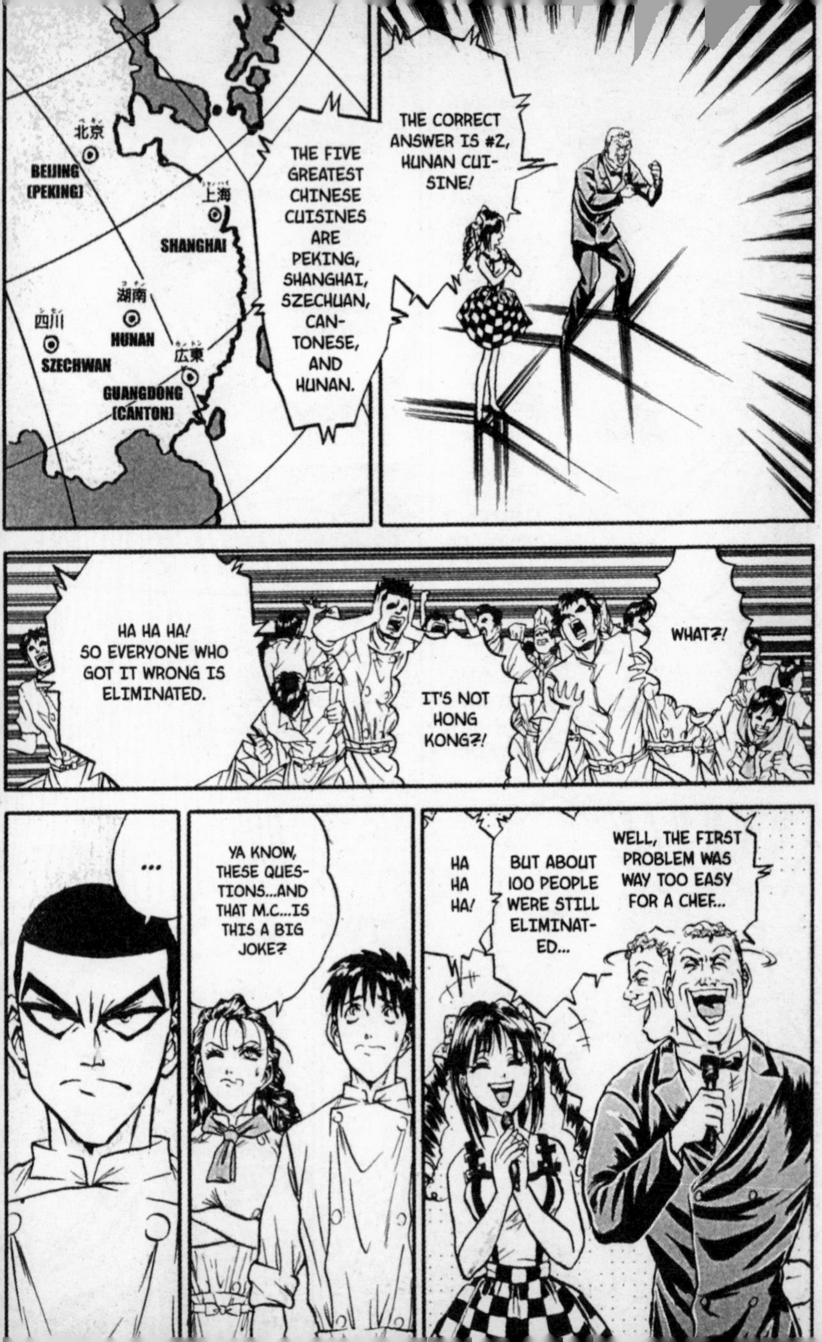
THE CORRECT ANSWER IS #2, HUNAN CUISINE!
THE FIVE GREATEST CHINESE CUISINES ARE PEKING, SHANGHAI, SZECHUAN, CANTONESE, AND HUNAN.
北京
BEIJING (PEKING)
上海
SHANGHAI
湖南
HUNAN
四川
SZECHWAN
広東
GUANGDONG (CANTON)
WHAT?!
IT'S NOT HONG KONG?!
HA HA HA! SO EVERYONE WHO GOT IT WRONG IS ELIMINATED.
WELL, THE FIRST PROBLEM WAS WAY TOO EASY FOR A CHEF...
BUT ABOUT 100 PEOPLE WERE STILL ELIMINATED...
HA HA HA!
YA KNOW, THESE QUESTIONS...AND THAT M.C...IS THIS A BIG JOKE?
...

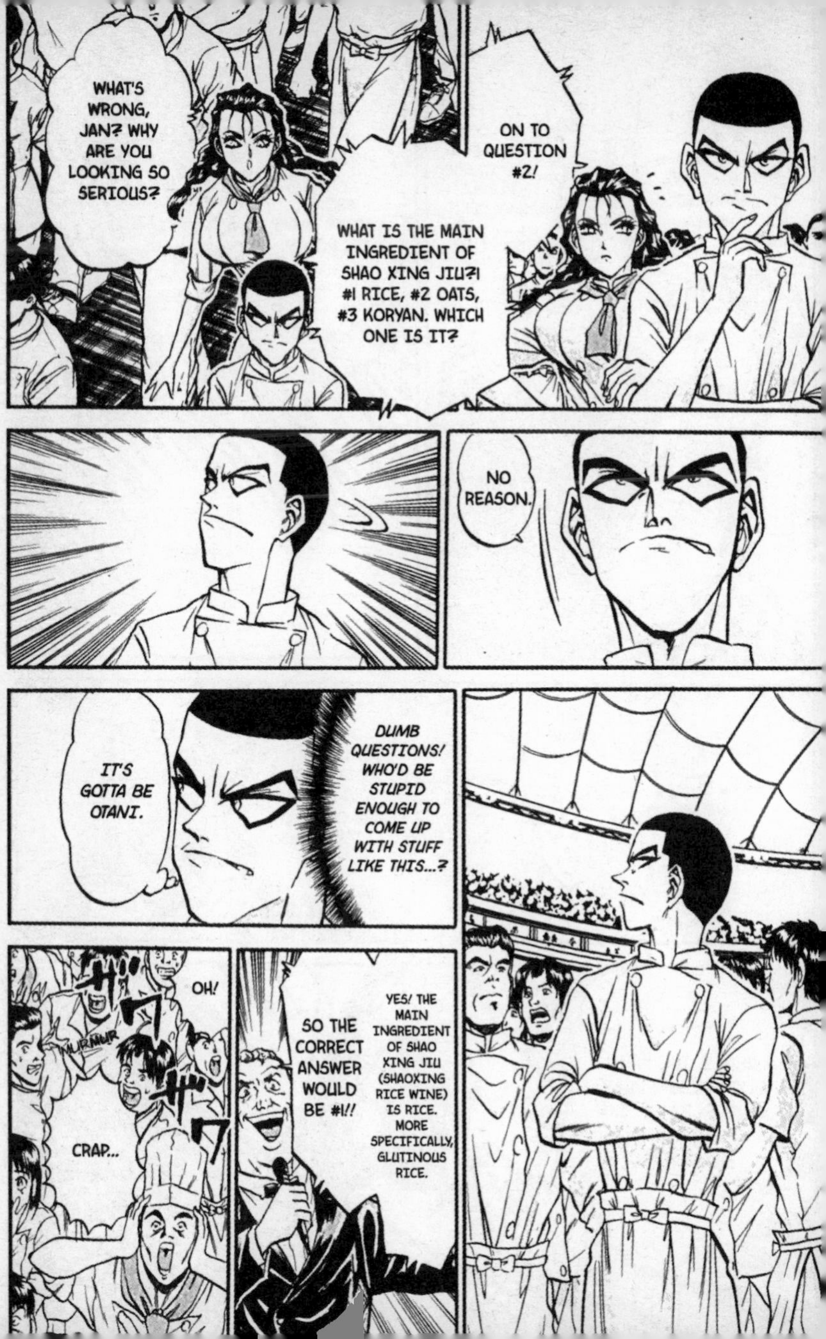
ON TO QUESTION #2!
WHAT IS THE MAIN INGREDIENT OF SHAO XING JIU?! #1 RICE, #2 OATS, #3 KORYAN. WHICH ONE IS IT?
WHAT'S WRONG, JAN? WHY ARE YOU LOOKING SO SERIOUS?
NO REASON.
DUMB QUESTIONS! WHO'D BE STUPID ENOUGH TO COME UP WITH STUFF LIKE THIS...?
IT'S GOTTA BE OTANI.
YES! THE MAIN INGREDIENT OF SHAO XING JIU (SHAOXING RICE WINE) IS RICE. MORE SPECIFICALLY, GLUTINOUS RICE.
SO THE CORRECT ANSWER WOULD BE #1!!
OH!
MURMUR
CRAP...

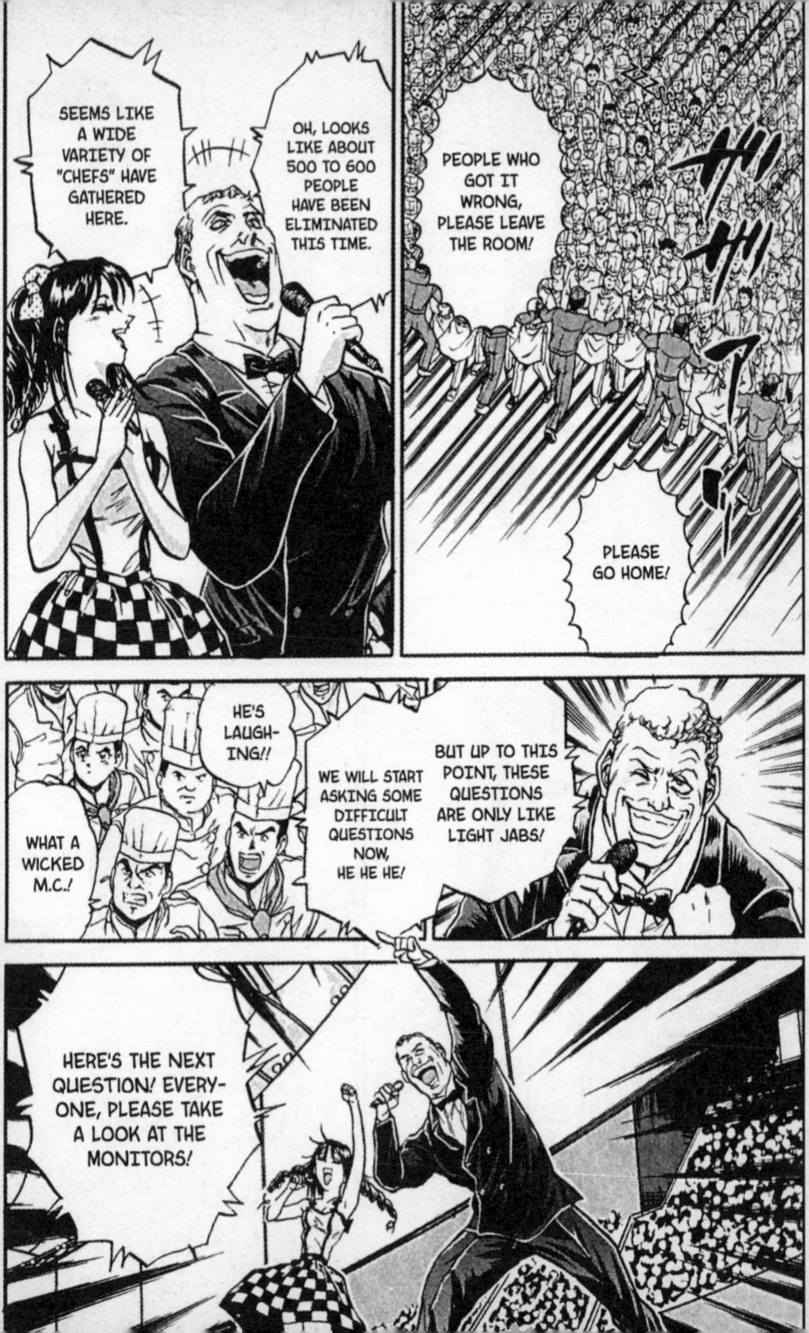
PEOPLE WHO GOT IT WRONG, PLEASE LEAVE THE ROOM!
PLEASE GO HOME!
OH, LOOKS LIKE ABOUT 500 TO 600 PEOPLE HAVE BEEN ELIMINATED THIS TIME.
SEEMS LIKE A WIDE VARIETY OF "CHEFS" HAVE GATHERED HERE.
BUT UP TO THIS POINT, THESE QUESTIONS ARE ONLY LIKE LIGHT JABS!
WE WILL START ASKING SOME DIFFICULT QUESTIONS NOW, HE HE HE!
HE'S LAUGHING!!
WHAT A WICKED M.C.!
HERE'S THE NEXT QUESTION! EVERYONE, PLEASE TAKE A LOOK AT THE MONITORS!

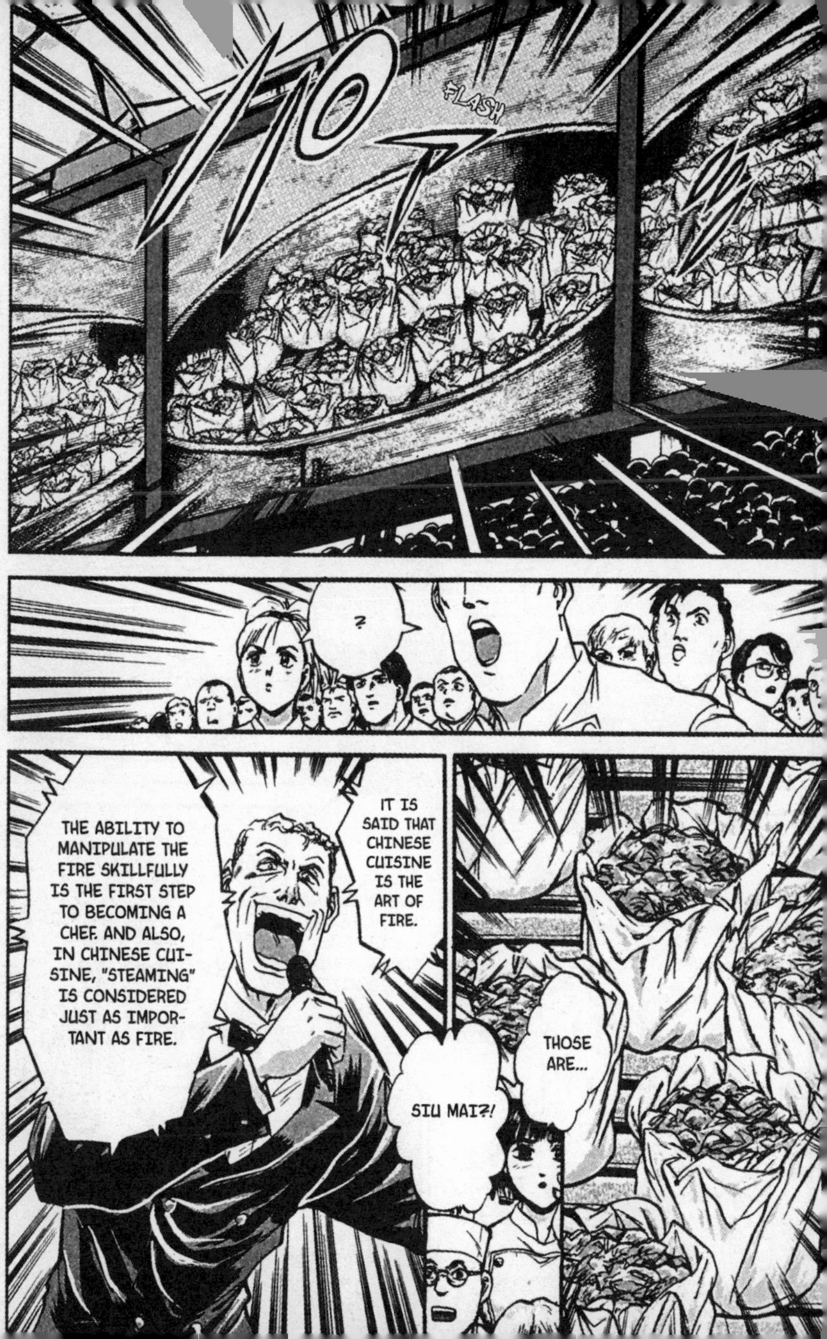
FLASH
?
IT IS SAID THAT CHINESE CUISINE IS THE ART OF FIRE.
THE ABILITY TO MANIPULATE THE FIRE SKILLFULLY IS THE FIRST STEP TO BECOMING A CHEF. AND ALSO, IN CHINESE CUISINE, "STEAMING" IS CONSIDERED JUST AS IMPORTANT AS FIRE.
THOSE ARE...
SIU MAI?!

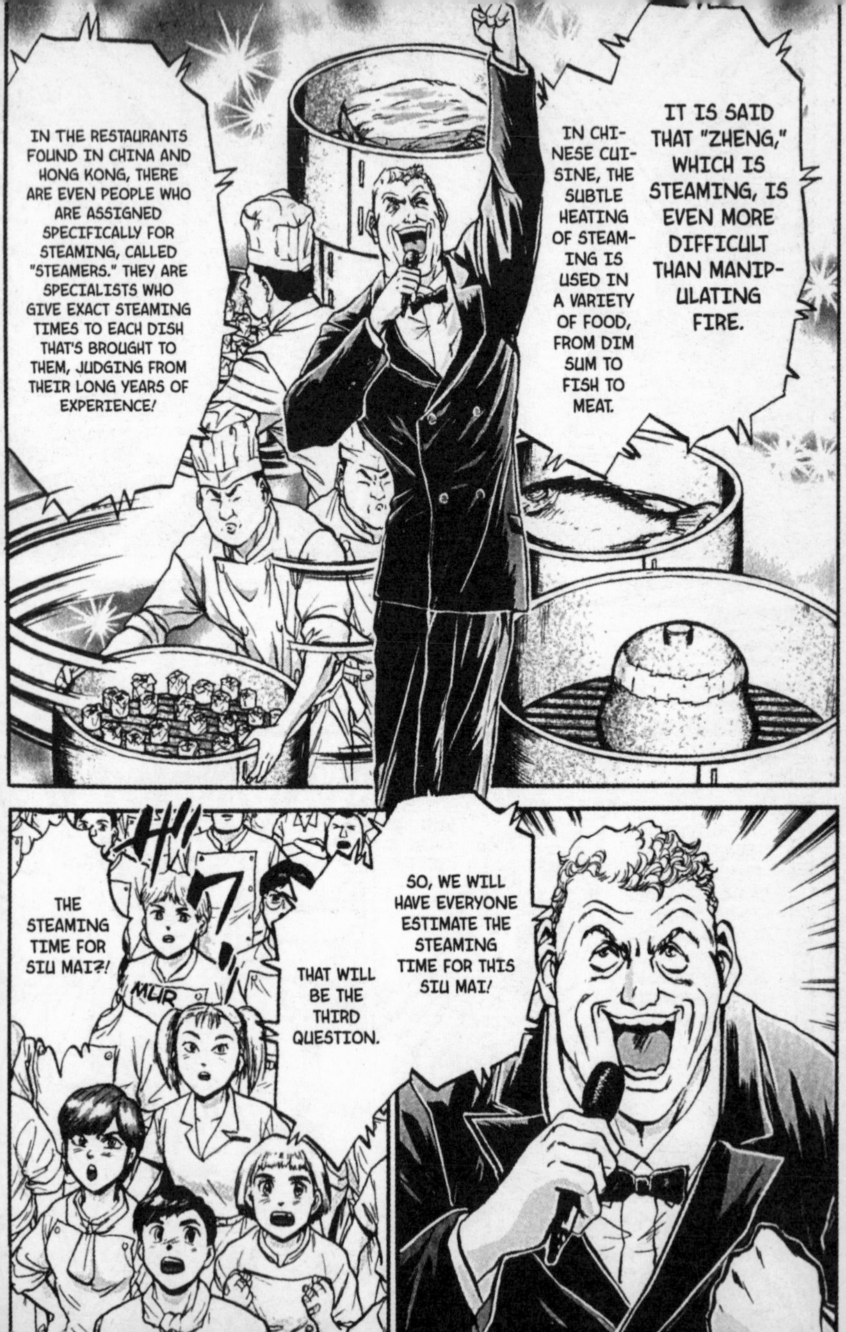
IT IS SAID THAT "ZHENG," WHICH IS STEAMING, IS EVEN MORE DIFFICULT THAN MANIPULATING FIRE.
IN CHINESE CUISINE, THE SUBTLE HEATING OF STEAMING IS USED IN A VARIETY OF FOOD, FROM DIM SUM TO FISH TO MEAT.
IN THE RESTAURANTS FOUND IN CHINA AND HONG KONG, THERE ARE EVEN PEOPLE WHO ARE ASSIGNED SPECIFICALLY FOR STEAMING, CALLED "STEAMERS." THEY ARE SPECIALISTS WHO GIVE EXACT STEAMING TIMES TO EACH DISH THAT'S BROUGHT TO THEM, JUDGING FROM THEIR LONG YEARS OF EXPERIENCE!
SO, WE WILL HAVE EVERYONE ESTIMATE THE STEAMING TIME FOR THIS SIU MAI!
THAT WILL BE THE THIRD QUESTION.
THE STEAMING TIME FOR SIU MAI?!

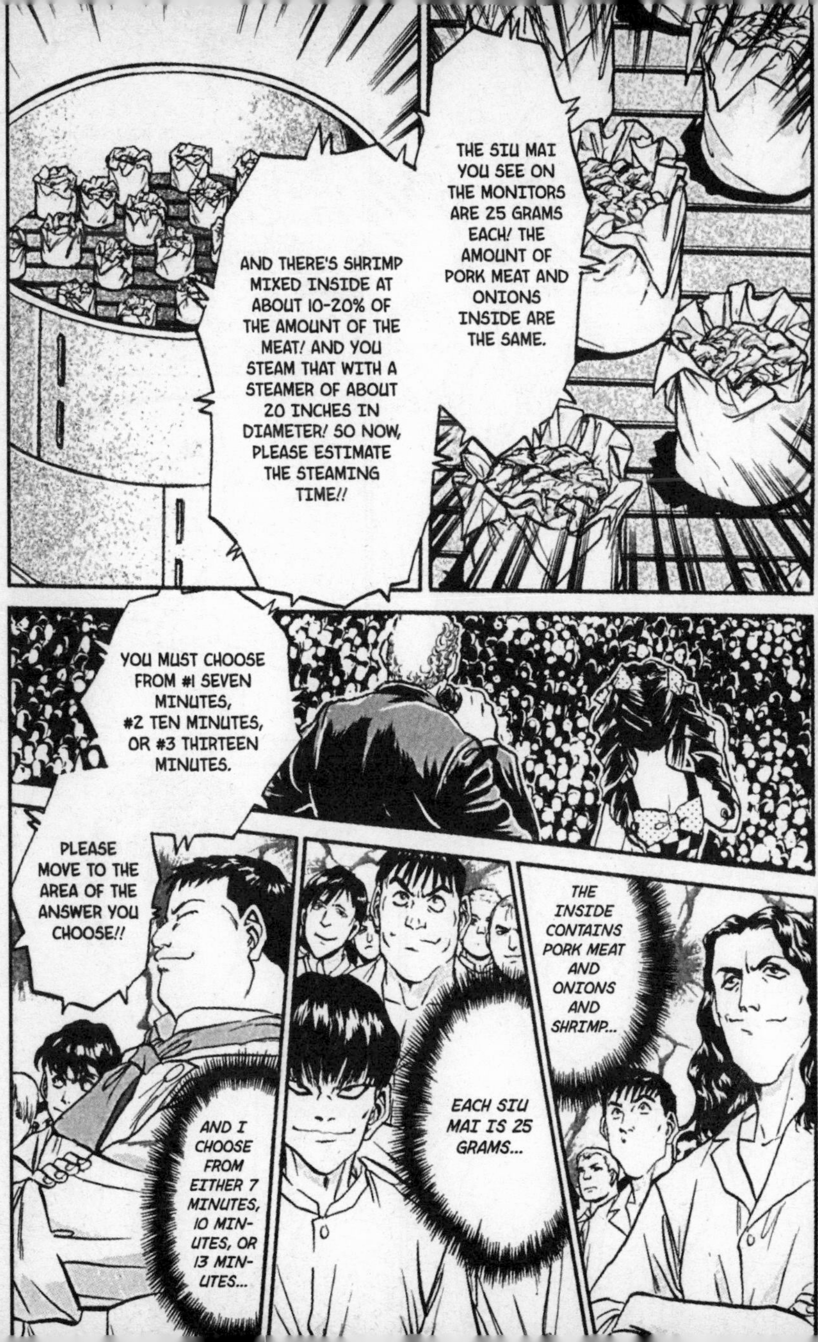
THE SIU MAI YOU SEE ON THE MONITORS ARE 25 GRAMS EACH! THE AMOUNT OF PORK MEAT AND ONIONS INSIDE ARE THE SAME.
AND THERE'S SHRIMP MIXED INSIDE AT ABOUT 10-20% OF THE AMOUNT OF THE MEAT! AND YOU STEAM THAT WITH A STEAMER OF ABOUT 20 INCHES IN DIAMETER! SO NOW, PLEASE ESTIMATE THE STEAMING TIME!!
YOU MUST CHOOSE FROM #1 SEVEN MINUTES, #2 TEN MINUTES, OR #3 THIRTEEN MINUTES.
PLEASE MOVE TO THE AREA OF THE ANSWER YOU CHOOSE!!
THE INSIDE CONTAINS PORK MEAT AND ONIONS AND SHRIMP...
EACH SIU MAI IS 25 GRAMS...
AND I CHOOSE FROM EITHER 7 MINUTES, 10 MINUTES, OR 13 MINUTES...

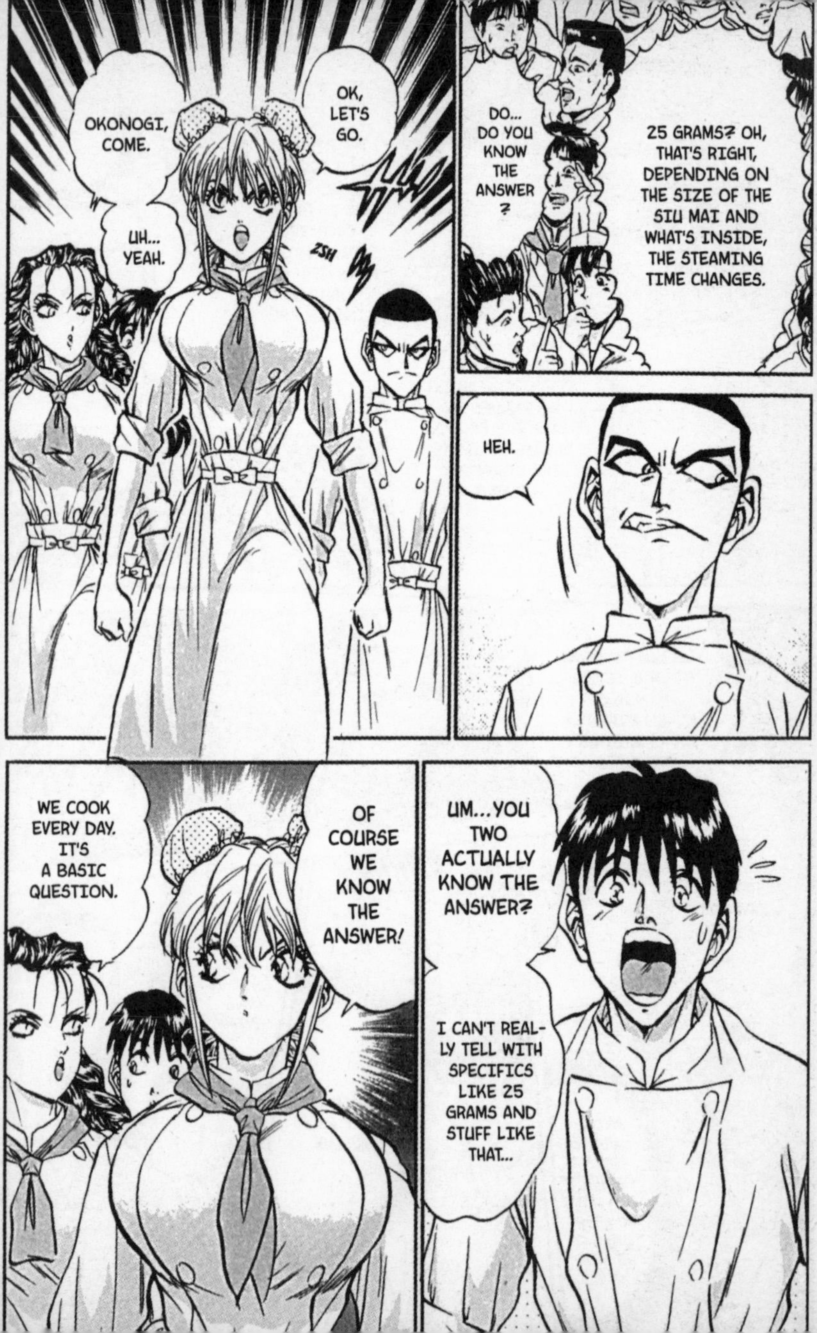
DO... DO YOU KNOW THE ANSWER?
25 GRAMS? OH, THAT'S RIGHT, DEPENDING ON THE SIZE OF THE SIU MAI AND WHAT'S INSIDE, THE STEAMING TIME CHANGES.
HEH.
OKONOGI, COME.
OK, LET'S GO.
UH... YEAH.
ZSH
UM...YOU TWO ACTUALLY KNOW THE ANSWER?
I CAN'T REALLY TELL WITH SPECIFICS LIKE 25 GRAMS AND STUFF LIKE THAT...
OF COURSE WE KNOW THE ANSWER!
WE COOK EVERY DAY. IT'S A BASIC QUESTION.

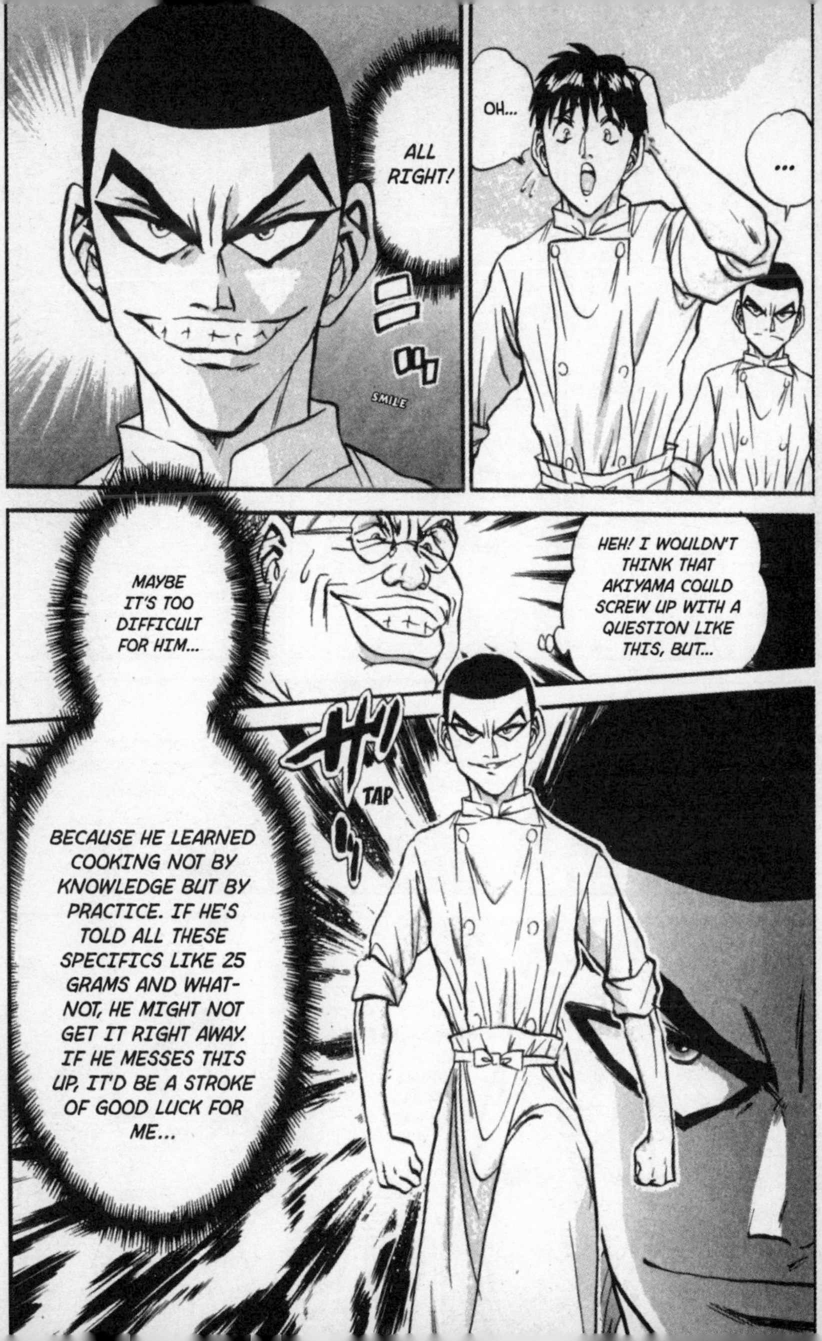
OH...
...
ALL RIGHT!
SMILE
HEH! I WOULDN'T THINK THAT AKIYAMA COULD SCREW UP WITH A QUESTION LIKE THIS, BUT...
MAYBE IT'S TOO DIFFICULT FOR HIM...
TAP
BECAUSE HE LEARNED COOKING NOT BY KNOWLEDGE BUT BY PRACTICE. IF HE'S TOLD ALL THESE SPECIFICS LIKE 25 GRAMS AND WHAT-NOT, HE MIGHT NOT GET IT RIGHT AWAY. IF HE MESSES THIS UP, IT'D BE A STROKE OF GOOD LUCK FOR ME...

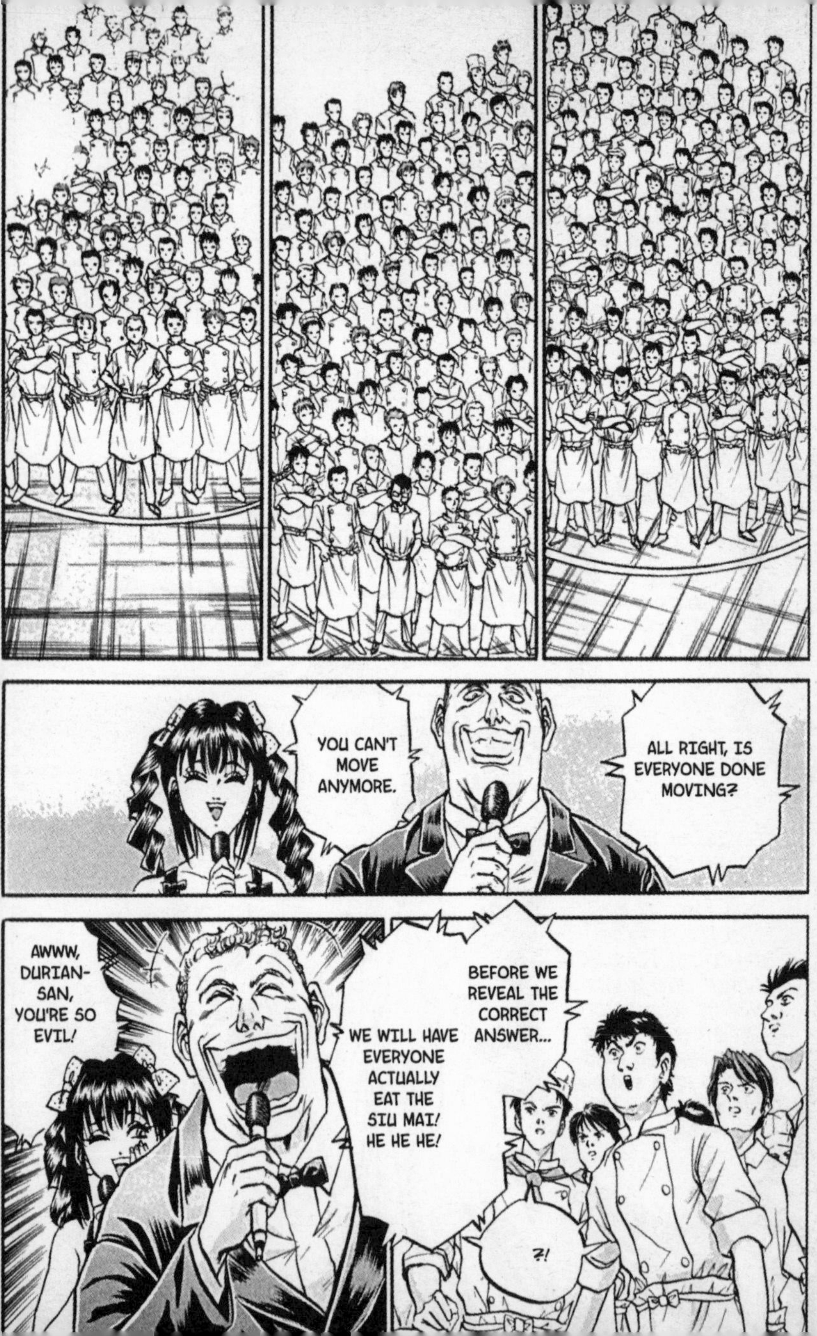
ALL RIGHT, IS EVERYONE DONE MOVING?
YOU CAN'T MOVE ANYMORE.
BEFORE WE REVEAL THE CORRECT ANSWER...
WE WILL HAVE EVERYONE ACTUALLY EAT THE SIU MAI! HE HE HE!
?!
AWWW, DURIAN-SAN, YOU'RE SO EVIL!

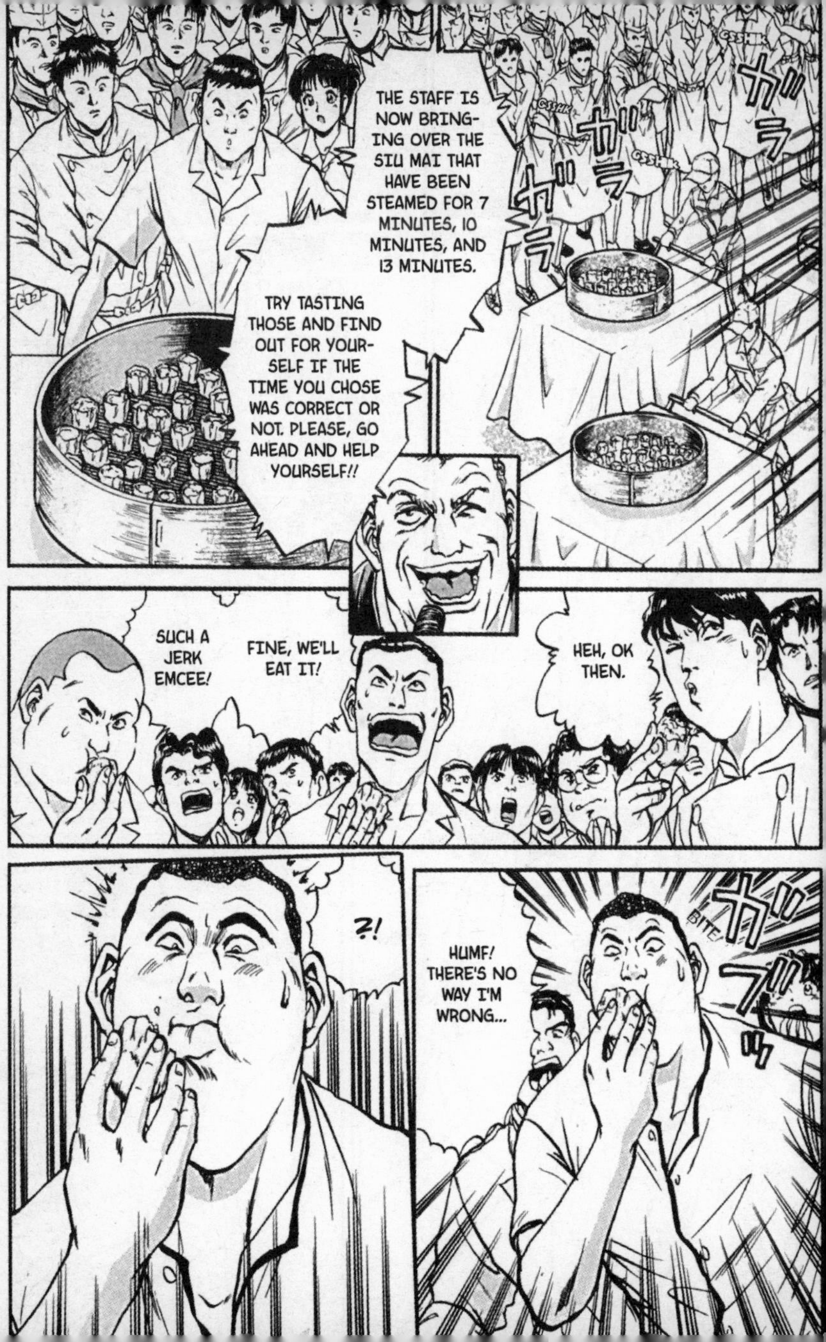
GSSHK
GSSHK
GSSHK
THE STAFF IS NOW BRINGING OVER THE SIU MAI THAT HAVE BEEN STEAMED FOR 7 MINUTES, 10 MINUTES, AND 13 MINUTES.
TRY TASTING THOSE AND FIND OUT FOR YOURSELF IF THE TIME YOU CHOSE WAS CORRECT OR NOT. PLEASE, GO AHEAD AND HELP YOURSELF!!
HEH, OK THEN.
FINE, WE'LL EAT IT!
SUCH A JERK EMCEE!
BITE
HUMF! THERE'S NO WAY I'M WRONG...
?!

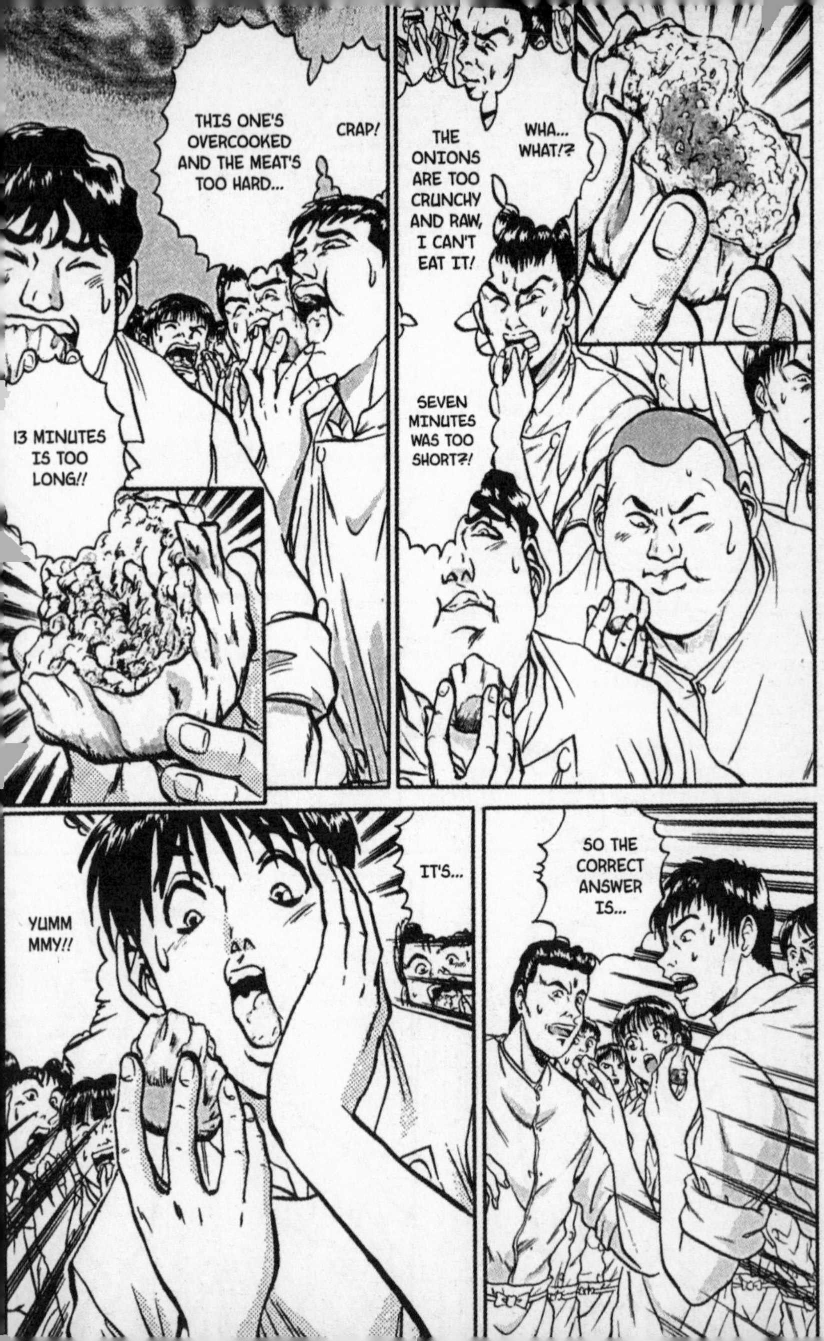
WHA... WHAT!?
THE ONIONS ARE TOO CRUNCHY AND RAW, I CAN'T EAT IT!
SEVEN MINUTES WAS TOO SHORT!?
CRAP!
THIS ONE'S OVERCOOKED AND THE MEAT'S TOO HARD...
13 MINUTES IS TOO LONG!!
SO THE CORRECT ANSWER IS...
IT'S...
YUMM MMY!!

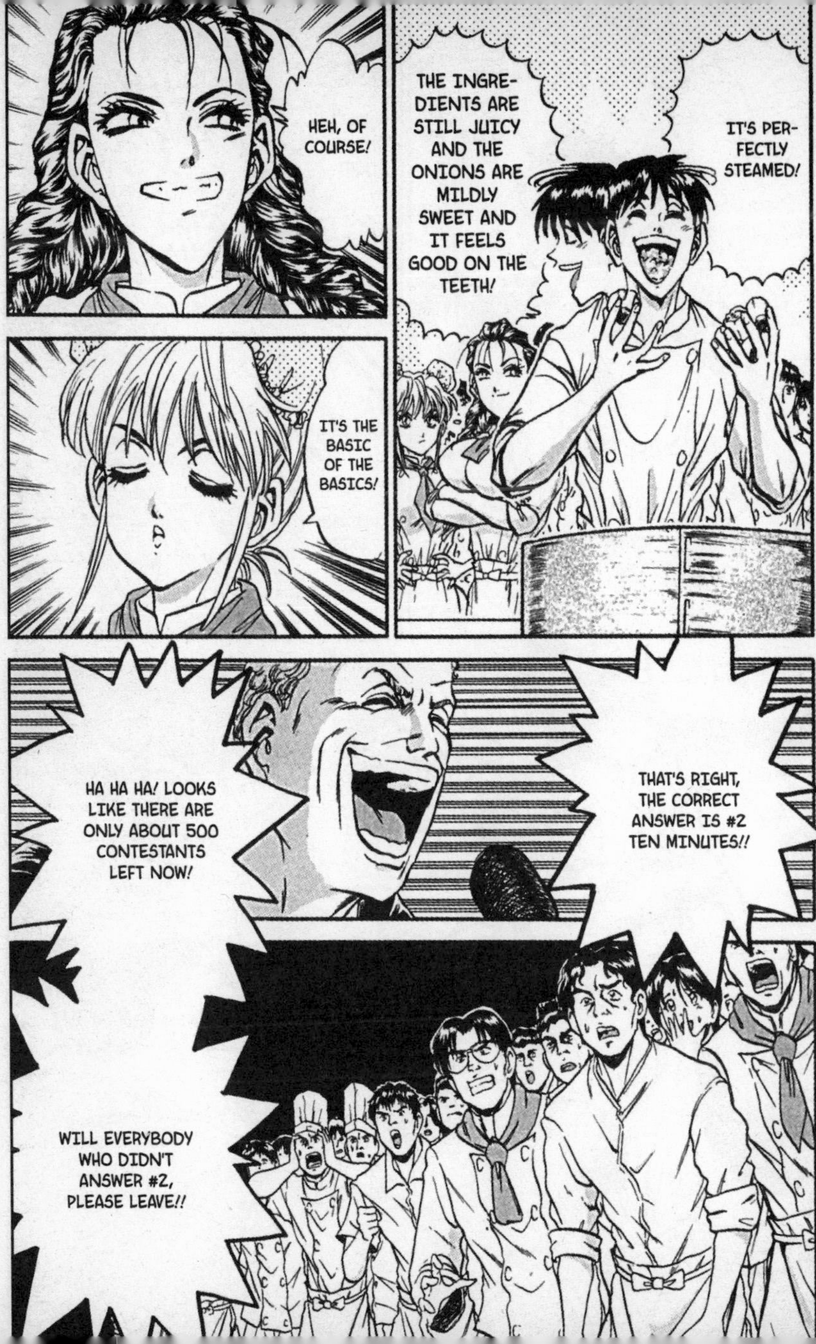
IT'S PERFECTLY STEAMED!
THE INGREDIENTS ARE STILL JUICY AND THE ONIONS ARE MILDLY SWEET AND IT FEELS GOOD ON THE TEETH!
HEH, OF COURSE!
IT'S THE BASIC OF THE BASICS!
THAT'S RIGHT, THE CORRECT ANSWER IS #2 TEN MINUTES!!
HA HA HA! LOOKS LIKE THERE ARE ONLY ABOUT 500 CONTESTANTS LEFT NOW!
WILL EVERYBODY WHO DIDN'T ANSWER #2, PLEASE LEAVE!!

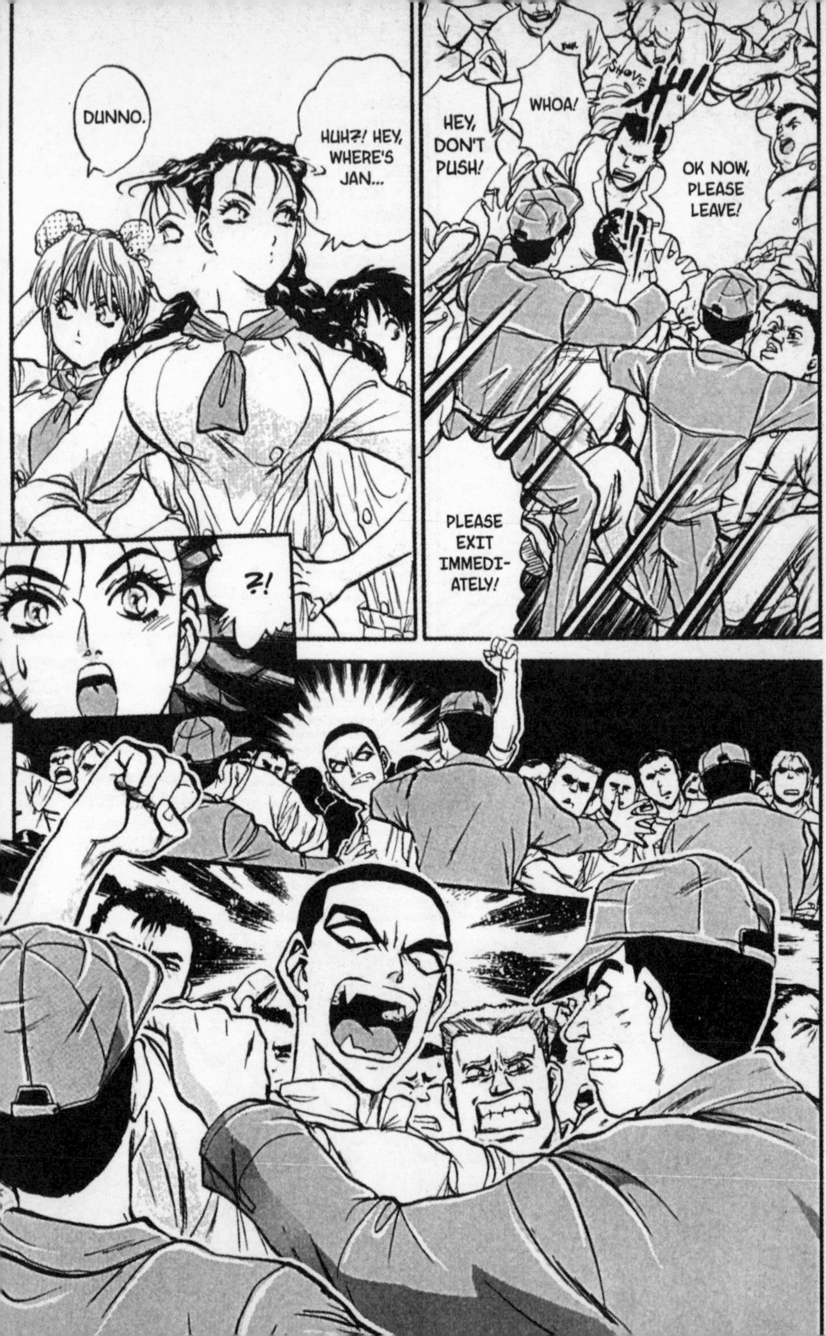
SHOVE
WHOA!
OK NOW, PLEASE LEAVE!
HEY, DON'T PUSH!
PLEASE EXIT IMMEDIATELY!
HUH?! HEY, WHERE'S JAN...
DUNNO.
?!

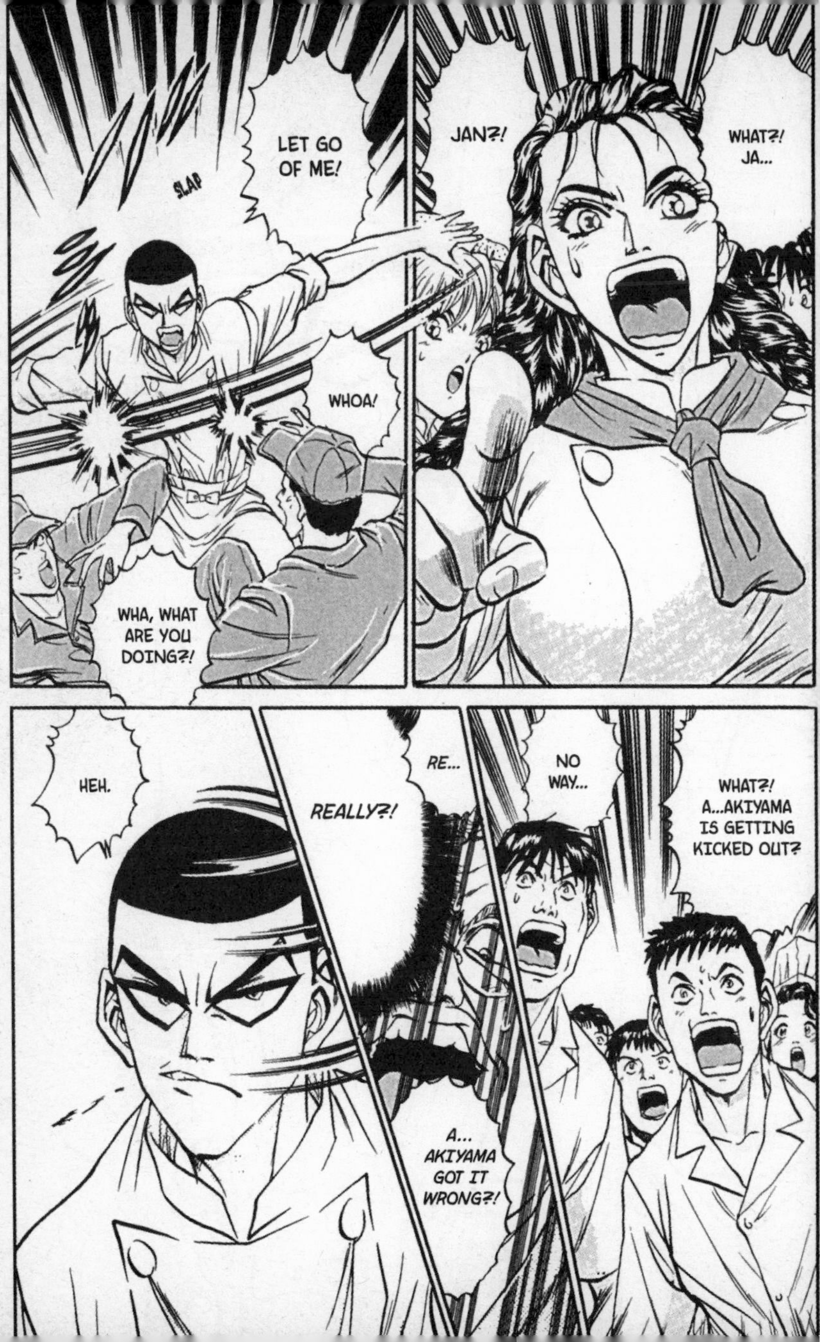
WHAT?! JA...
JAN?!
LET GO OF ME!
SLAP
WHOA!
WHA, WHAT ARE YOU DOING?!
WHAT?! A...AKIYAMA IS GETTING KICKED OUT?
NO WAY...
RE...
REALLY?!
A... AKIYAMA GOT IT WRONG?!
HEH.

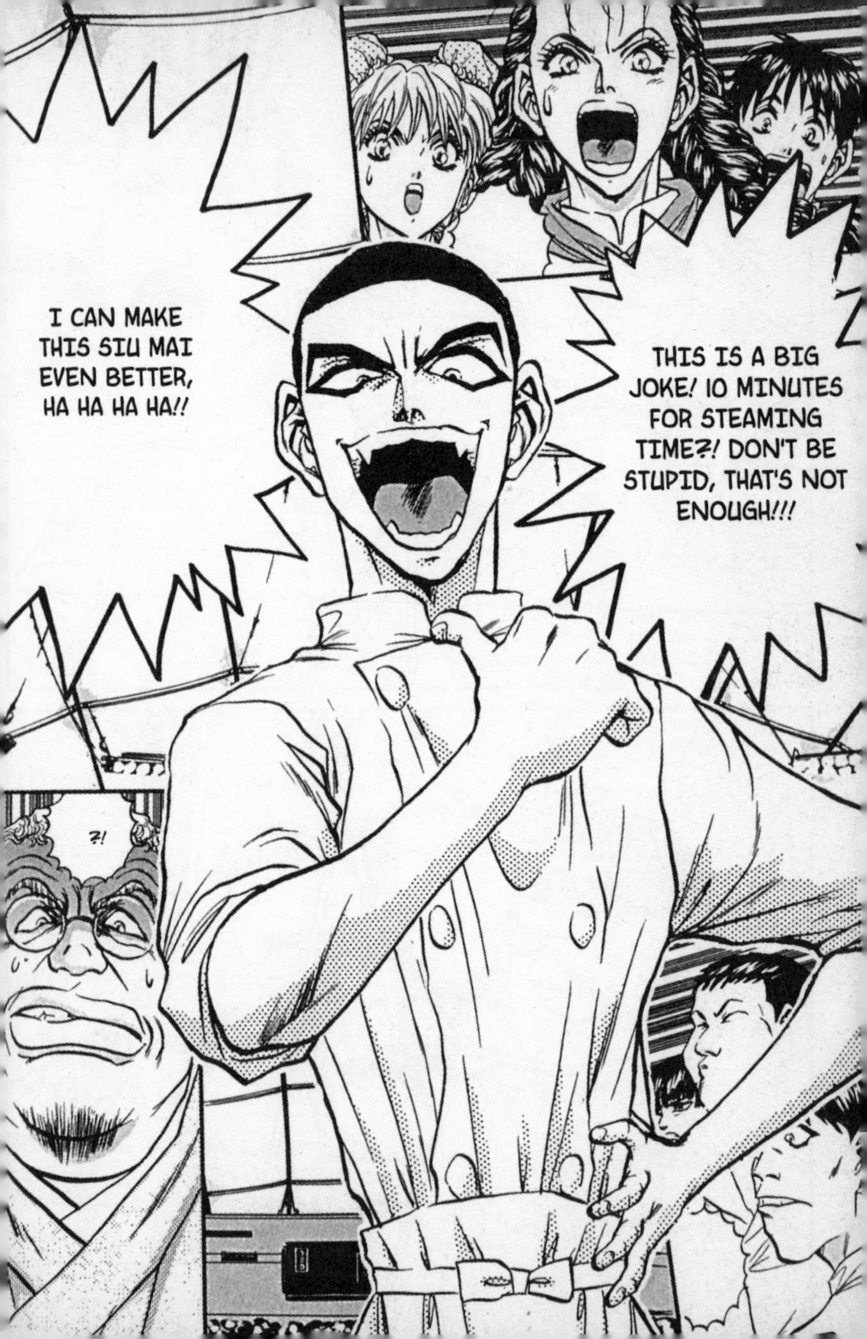
THIS IS A BIG JOKE! 10 MINUTES FOR STEAMING TIME?! DON'T BE STUPID, THAT'S NOT ENOUGH!!!
I CAN MAKE THIS SIU MAI EVEN BETTER, HA HA HA HA!!
?!

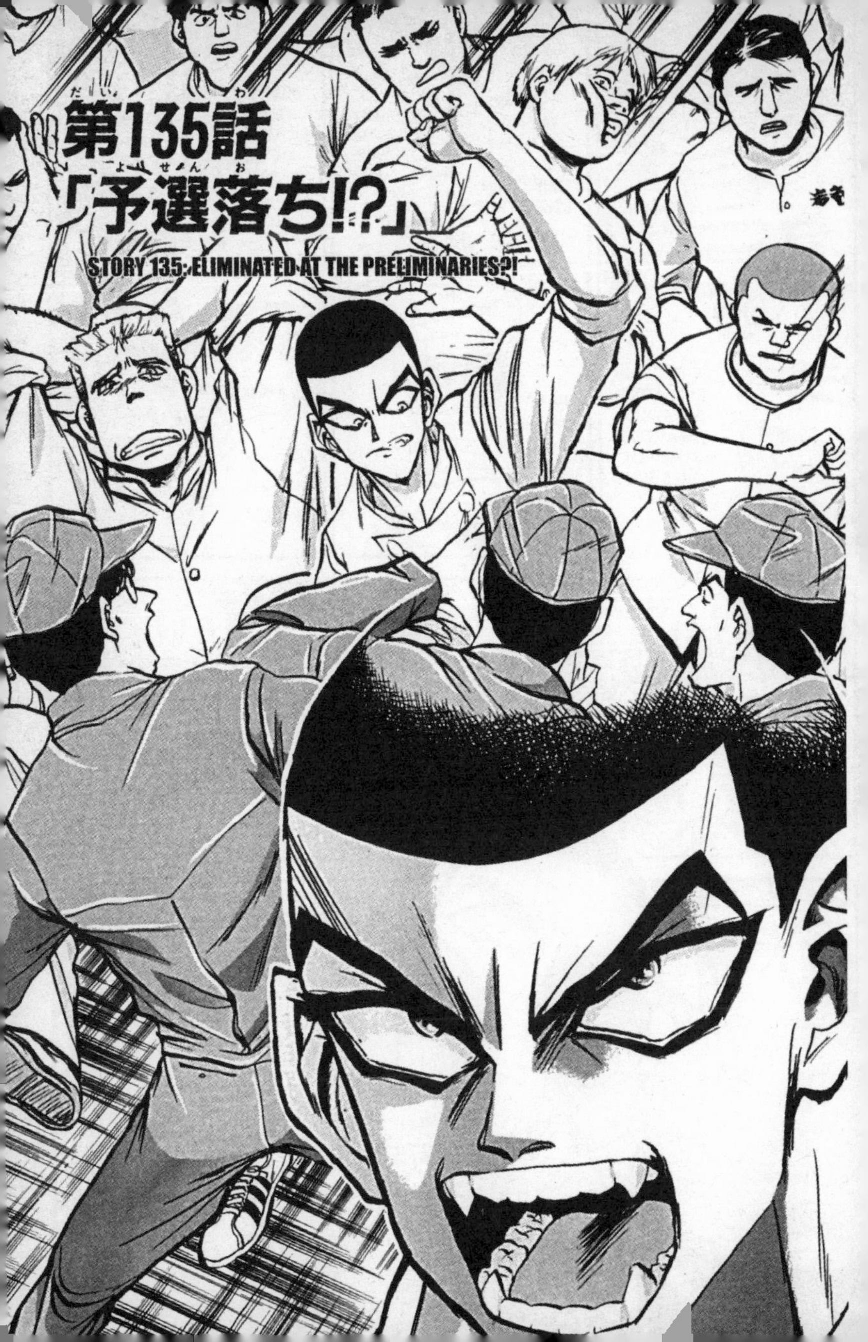
第135話
「予選落ち!?」
STORY 135: ELIMINATED AT THE PRELIMINARIES?!

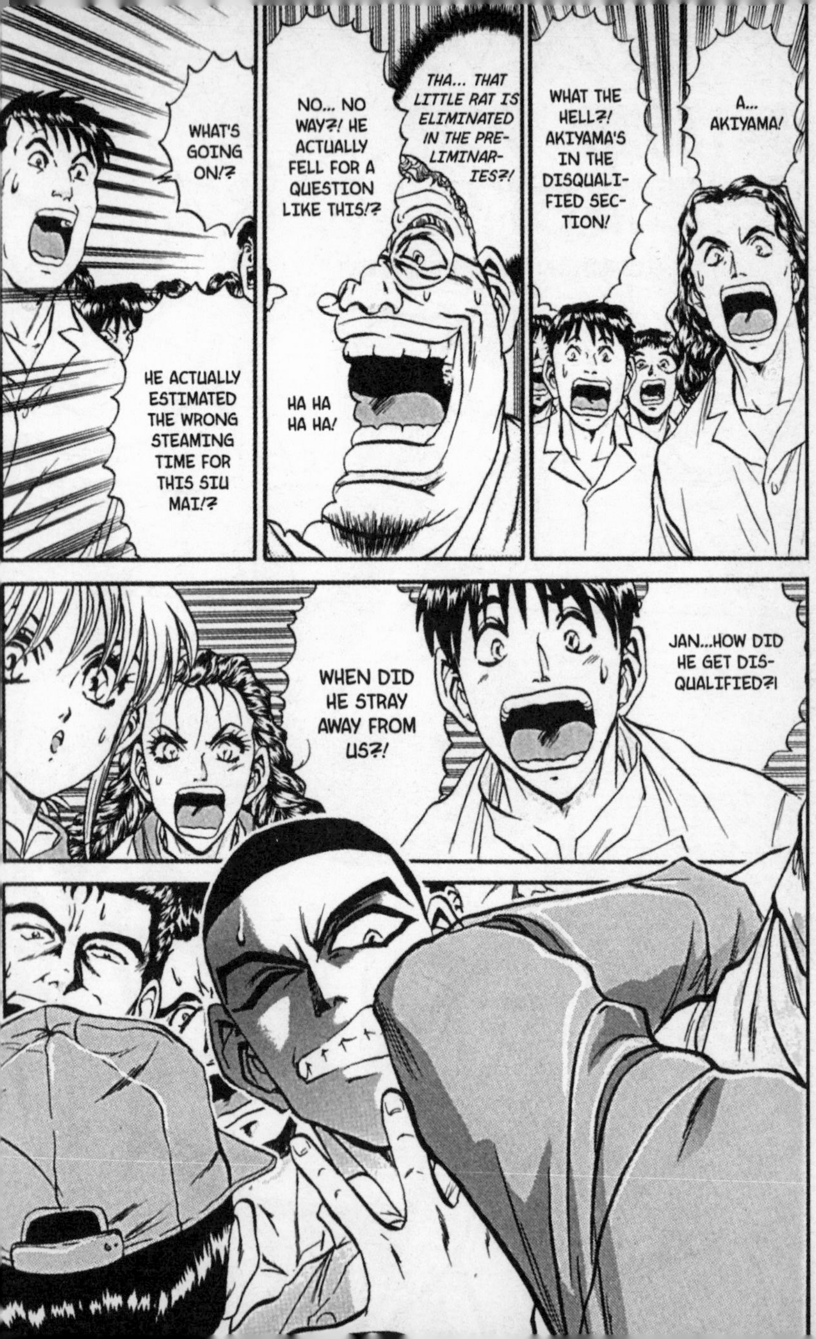
A... AKIYAMA!
WHAT THE HELL?! AKIYAMA'S IN THE DISQUALIFIED SECTION!
THA... THAT LITTLE RAT IS ELIMINATED IN THE PRELIMINARIES?!
NO... NO WAY?! HE ACTUALLY FELL FOR A QUESTION LIKE THIS!?
HA HA HA HA!
WHAT'S GOING ON!?
HE ACTUALLY ESTIMATED THE WRONG STEAMING TIME FOR THIS SIU MAI!?
JAN...HOW DID HE GET DISQUALIFIED?!
WHEN DID HE STRAY AWAY FROM US?!

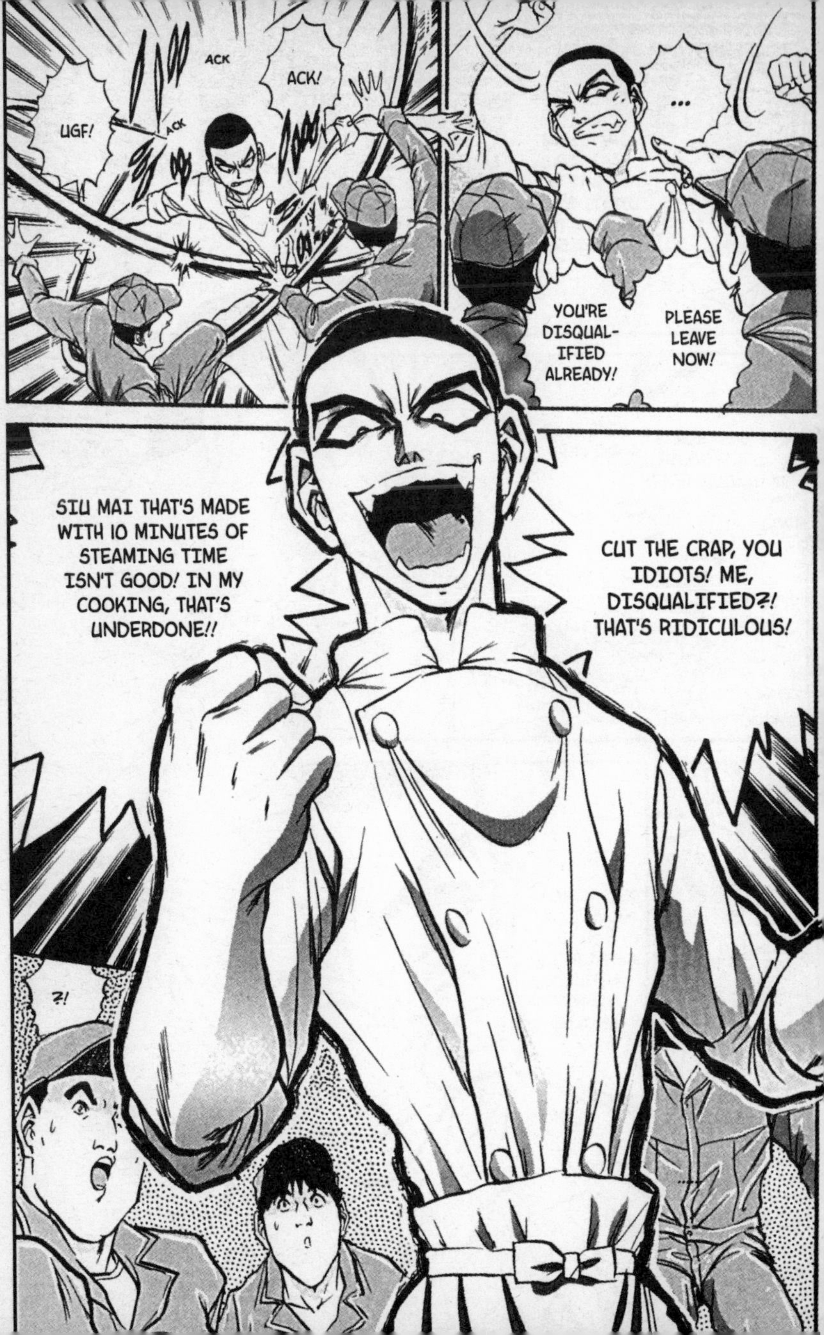
...
PLEASE LEAVE NOW!
YOU'RE DISQUAL-IFIED ALREADY!
ACK!
ACK
ACK
UGF!
CUT THE CRAP, YOU IDIOTS! ME, DISQUALIFIED?! THAT'S RIDICULOUS!
SIU MAI THAT'S MADE WITH 10 MINUTES OF STEAMING TIME ISN'T GOOD! IN MY COOKING, THAT'S UNDERDONE!!
?!

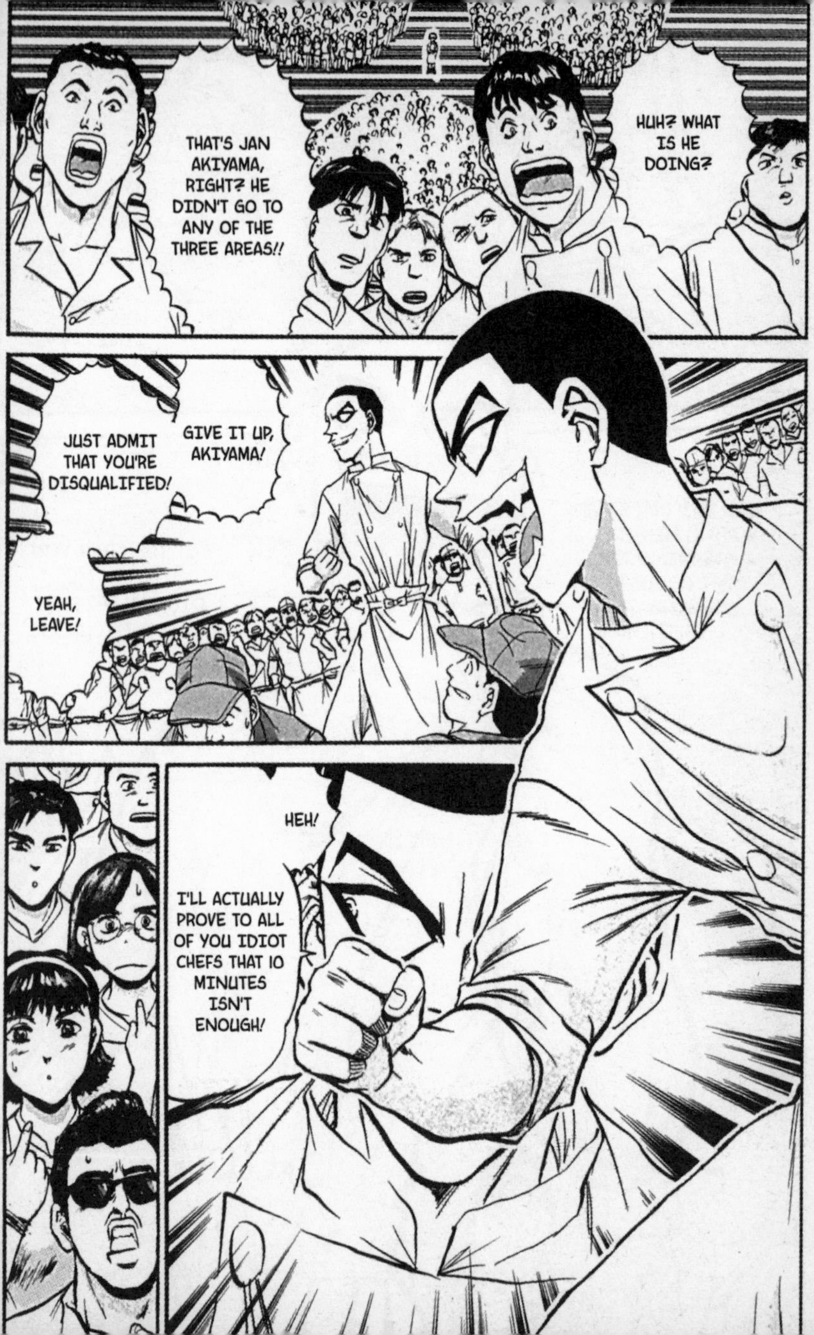
HUH? WHAT IS HE DOING?
THAT'S JAN AKIYAMA, RIGHT? HE DIDN'T GO TO ANY OF THE THREE AREAS!!
GIVE IT UP, AKIYAMA!
JUST ADMIT THAT YOU'RE DISQUALIFIED!
YEAH, LEAVE!
HEH!
I'LL ACTUALLY PROVE TO ALL OF YOU IDIOT CHEFS THAT 10 MINUTES ISN'T ENOUGH!

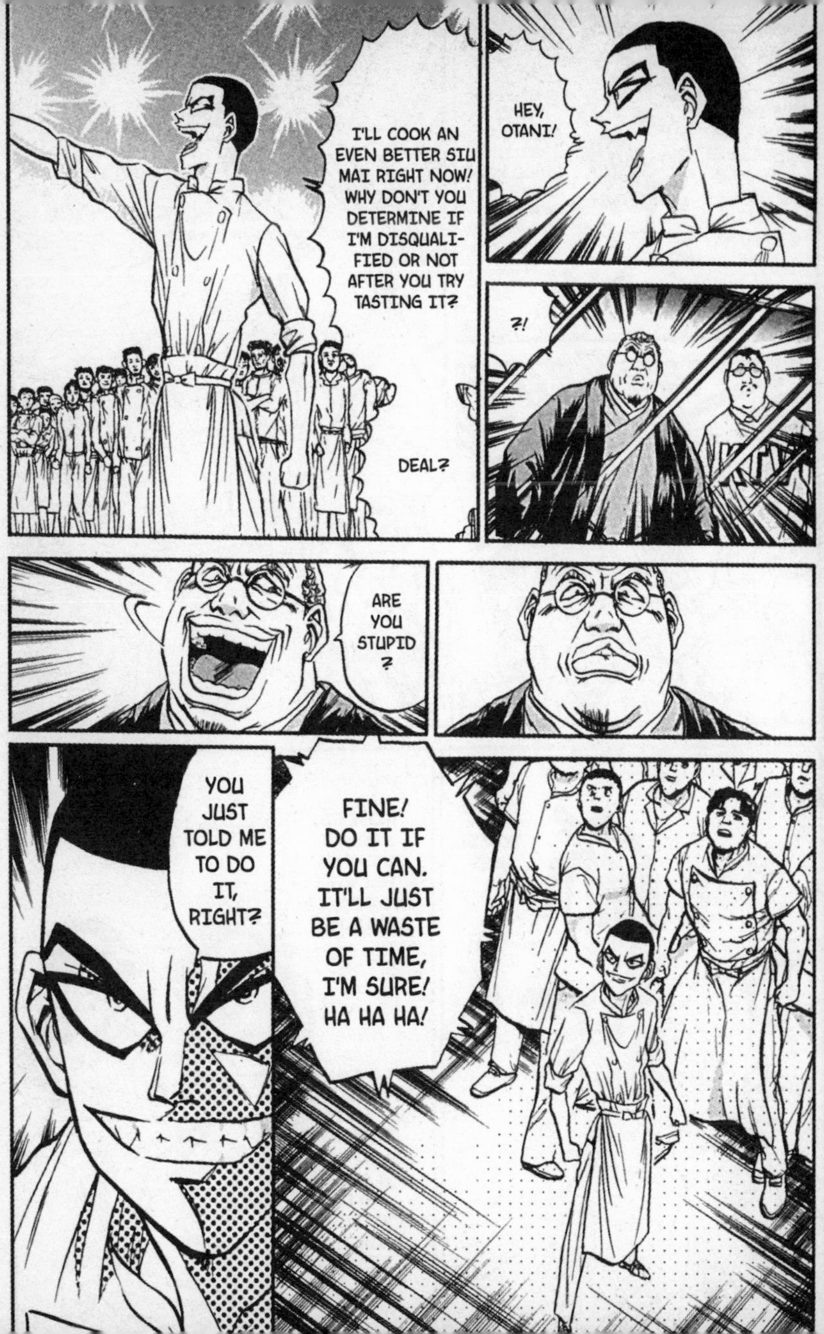
HEY, OTANI!
?!
I'LL COOK AN EVEN BETTER SIU MAI RIGHT NOW! WHY DON'T YOU DETERMINE IF I'M DISQUALIFIED OR NOT AFTER YOU TRY TASTING IT?
DEAL?
ARE YOU STUPID?
FINE! DO IT IF YOU CAN. IT'LL JUST BE A WASTE OF TIME, I'M SURE! HA HA HA!
YOU JUST TOLD ME TO DO IT, RIGHT?

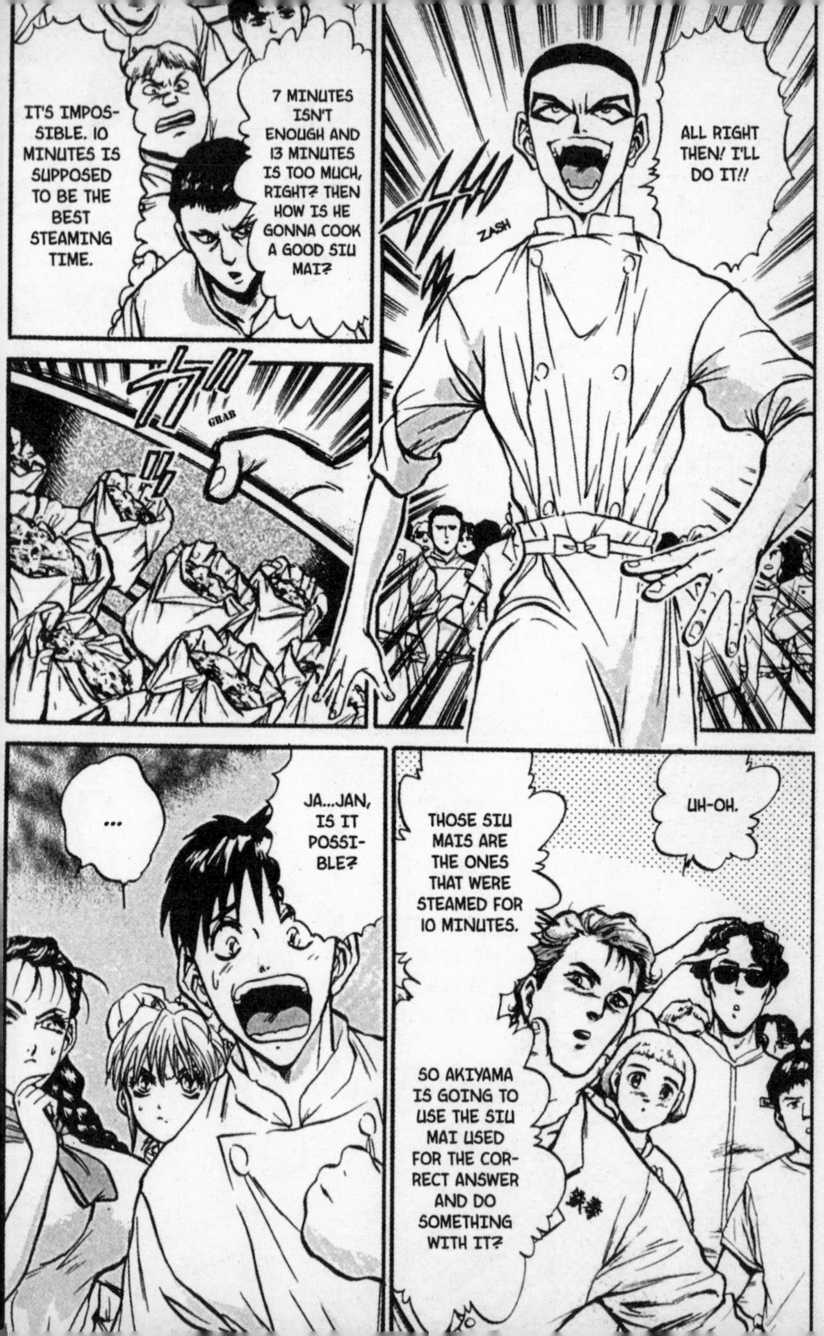
IT'S IMPOSSIBLE. 10 MINUTES IS SUPPOSED TO BE THE BEST STEAMING TIME.
7 MINUTES ISN'T ENOUGH AND 13 MINUTES IS TOO MUCH, RIGHT? THEN HOW IS HE GONNA COOK A GOOD SIU MAI?
ZASH
ALL RIGHT THEN! I'LL DO IT!!
GRAB
...
JA...JAN, IS IT POSSIBLE?
UH-OH.
THOSE SIU MAIS ARE THE ONES THAT WERE STEAMED FOR 10 MINUTES.
SO AKIYAMA IS GOING TO USE THE SIU MAI USED FOR THE CORRECT ANSWER AND DO SOMETHING WITH IT?

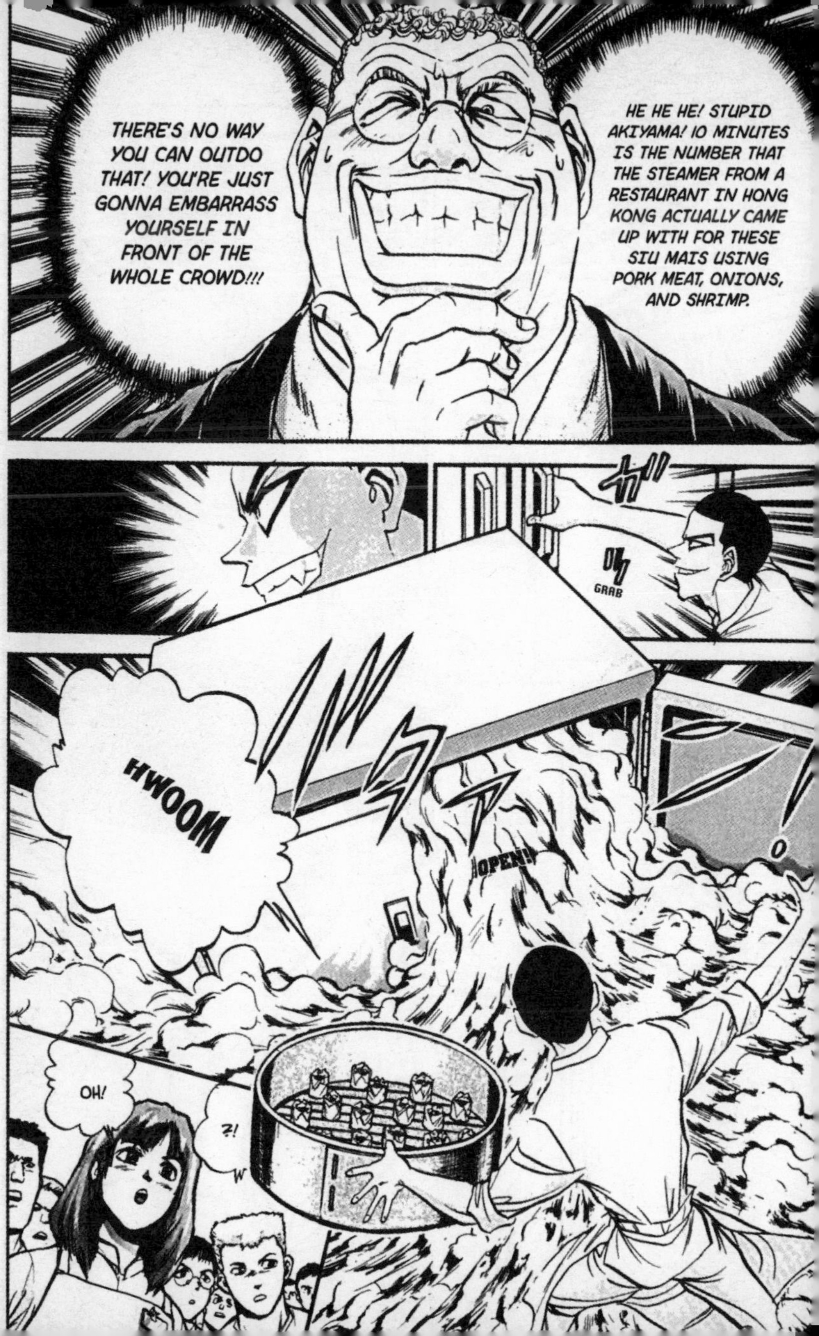
HE HE HE! STUPID AKIYAMA! 10 MINUTES IS THE NUMBER THAT THE STEAMER FROM A RESTAURANT IN HONG KONG ACTUALLY CAME UP WITH FOR THESE SIU MAIS USING PORK MEAT, ONIONS, AND SHRIMP.
THERE'S NO WAY YOU CAN OUTDO THAT! YOU'RE JUST GONNA EMBARRASS YOURSELF IN FRONT OF THE WHOLE CROWD!!!
GRAB
HWOOM
OPEN!
?!
OH!

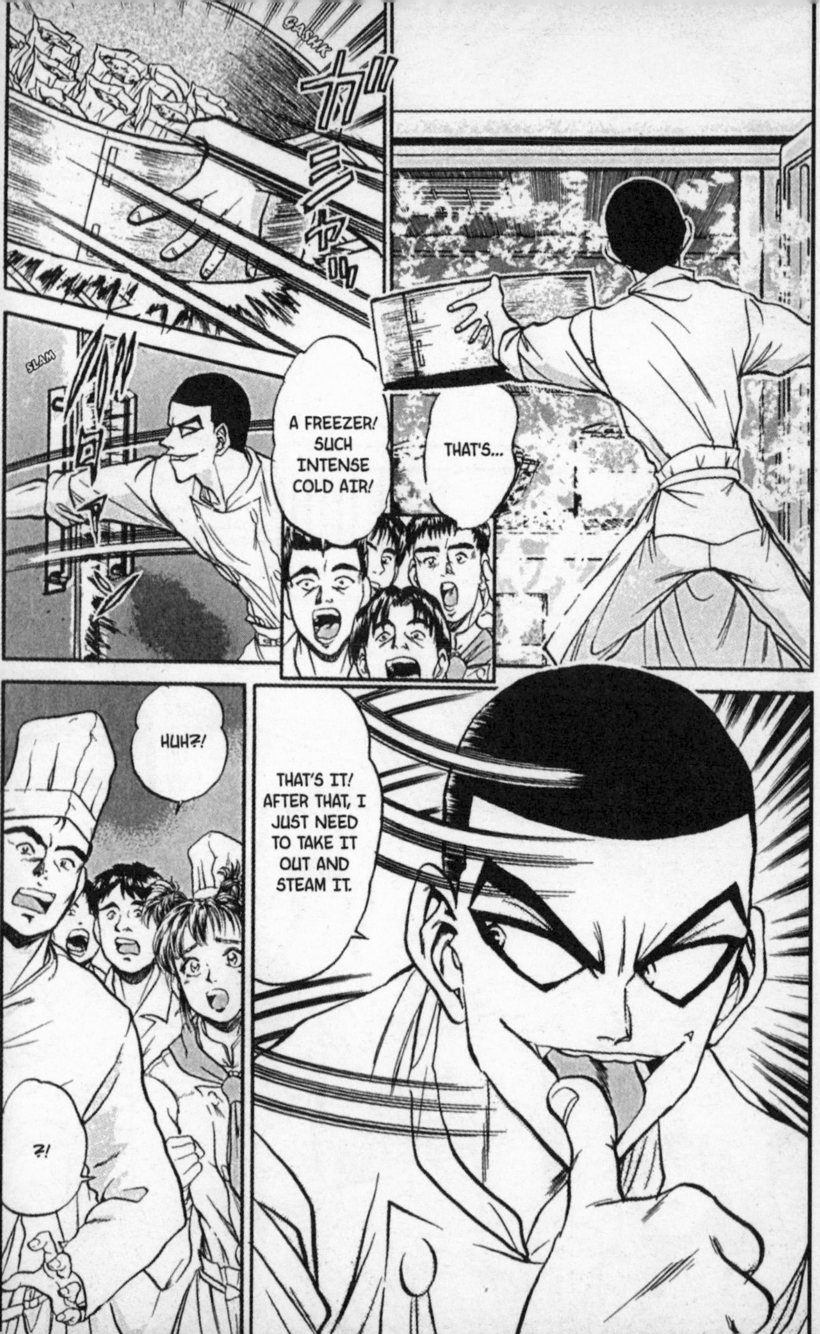
GASHK
SLAM
THAT'S...
A FREEZER! SUCH INTENSE COLD AIR!
THAT'S IT! AFTER THAT, I JUST NEED TO TAKE IT OUT AND STEAM IT.
HUH?!
?!

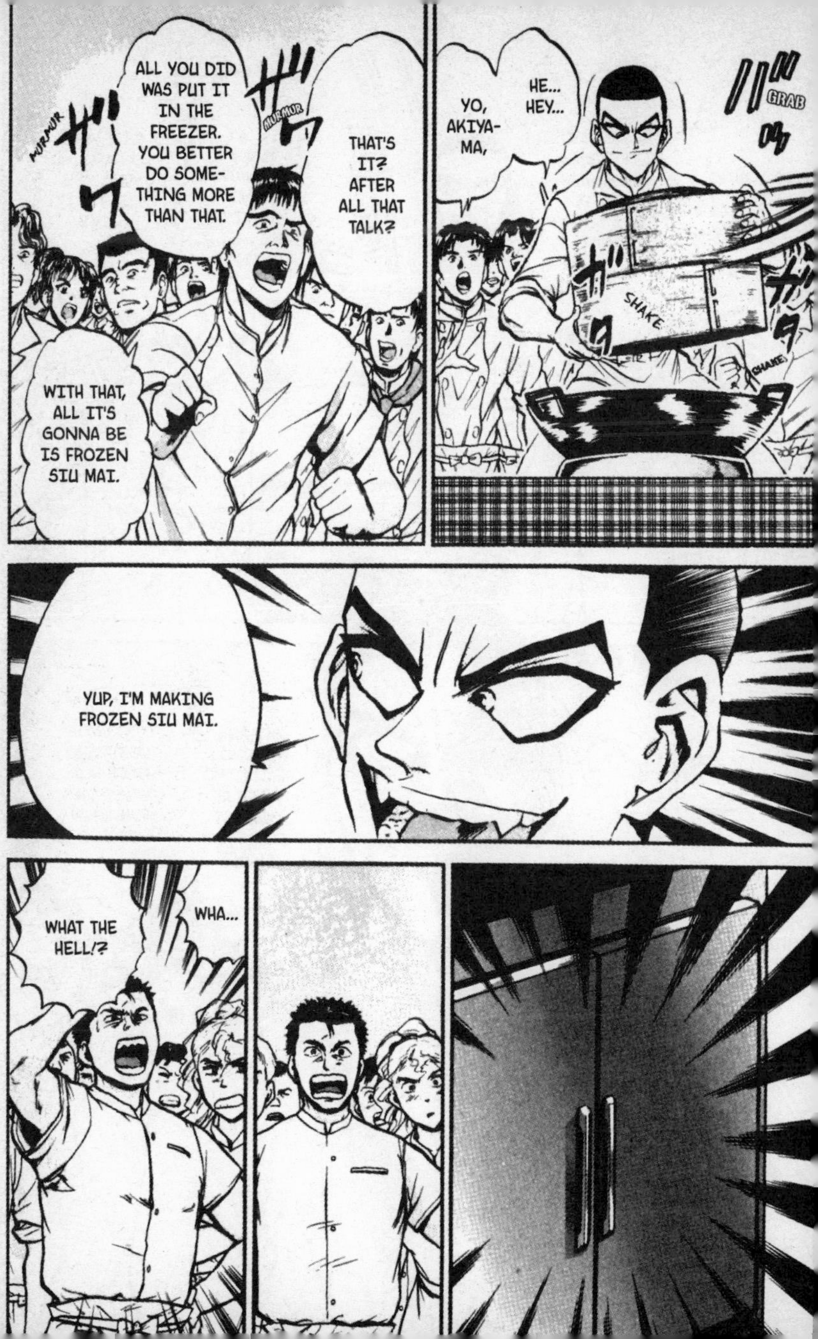
GRAB
HE... HEY...
YO, AKIYA-MA,
SHAKE
SHAKE
THAT'S IT? AFTER ALL THAT TALK?
MURMUR
ALL YOU DID WAS PUT IT IN THE FREEZER. YOU BETTER DO SOME-THING MORE THAN THAT.
MURMUR
WITH THAT, ALL IT'S GONNA BE IS FROZEN SIU MAI.
YUP, I'M MAKING FROZEN SIU MAI.
WHA...
WHAT THE HELL!?

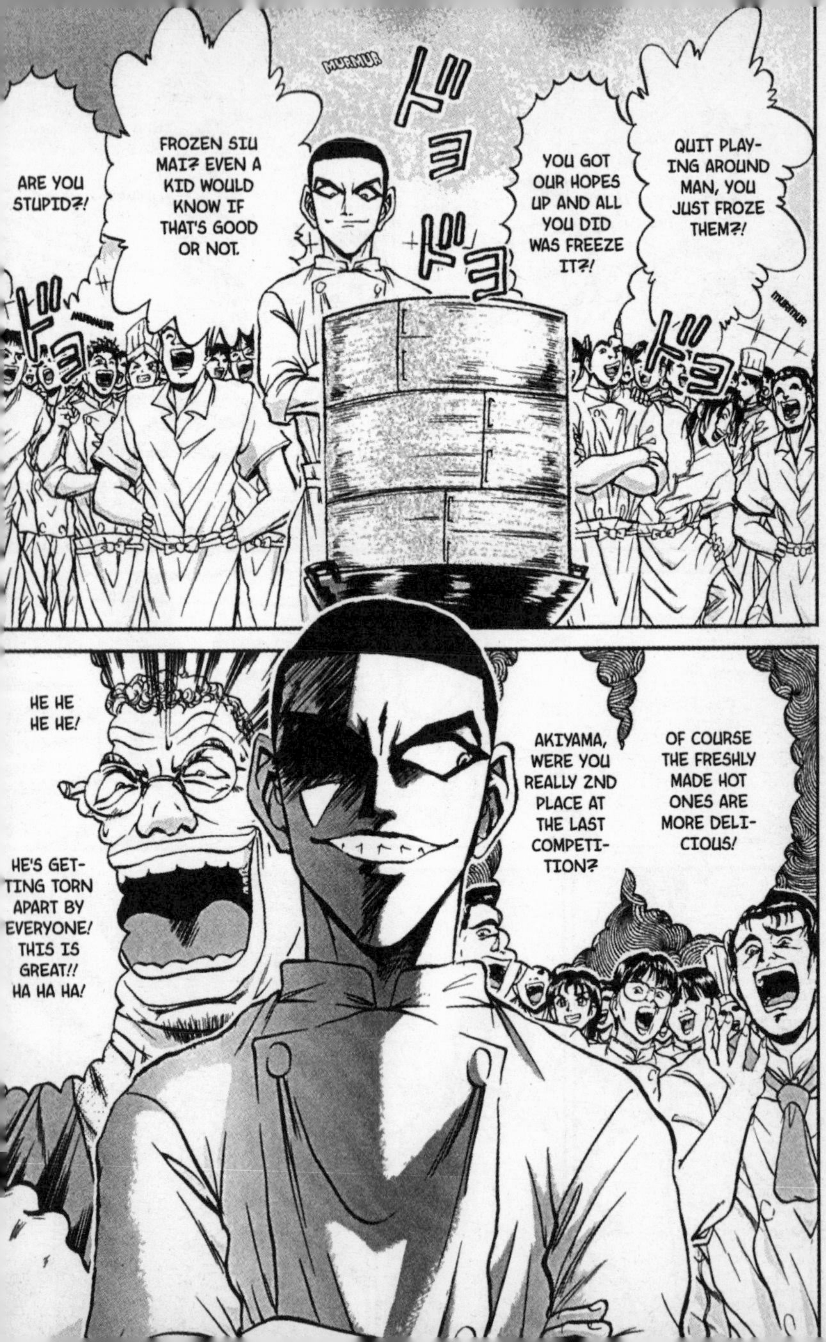
MURMUR
QUIT PLAYING AROUND MAN, YOU JUST FROZE THEM?!
YOU GOT OUR HOPES UP AND ALL YOU DID WAS FREEZE IT?!
ドヨドヨ
FROZEN SIU MAI? EVEN A KID WOULD KNOW IF THAT'S GOOD OR NOT.
ARE YOU STUPID?!
MURMUR
OF COURSE THE FRESHLY MADE HOT ONES ARE MORE DELICIOUS!
AKIYAMA, WERE YOU REALLY 2ND PLACE AT THE LAST COMPETITION?
HE HE HE HE!
HE'S GETTING TORN APART BY EVERYONE! THIS IS GREAT!! HA HA HA!

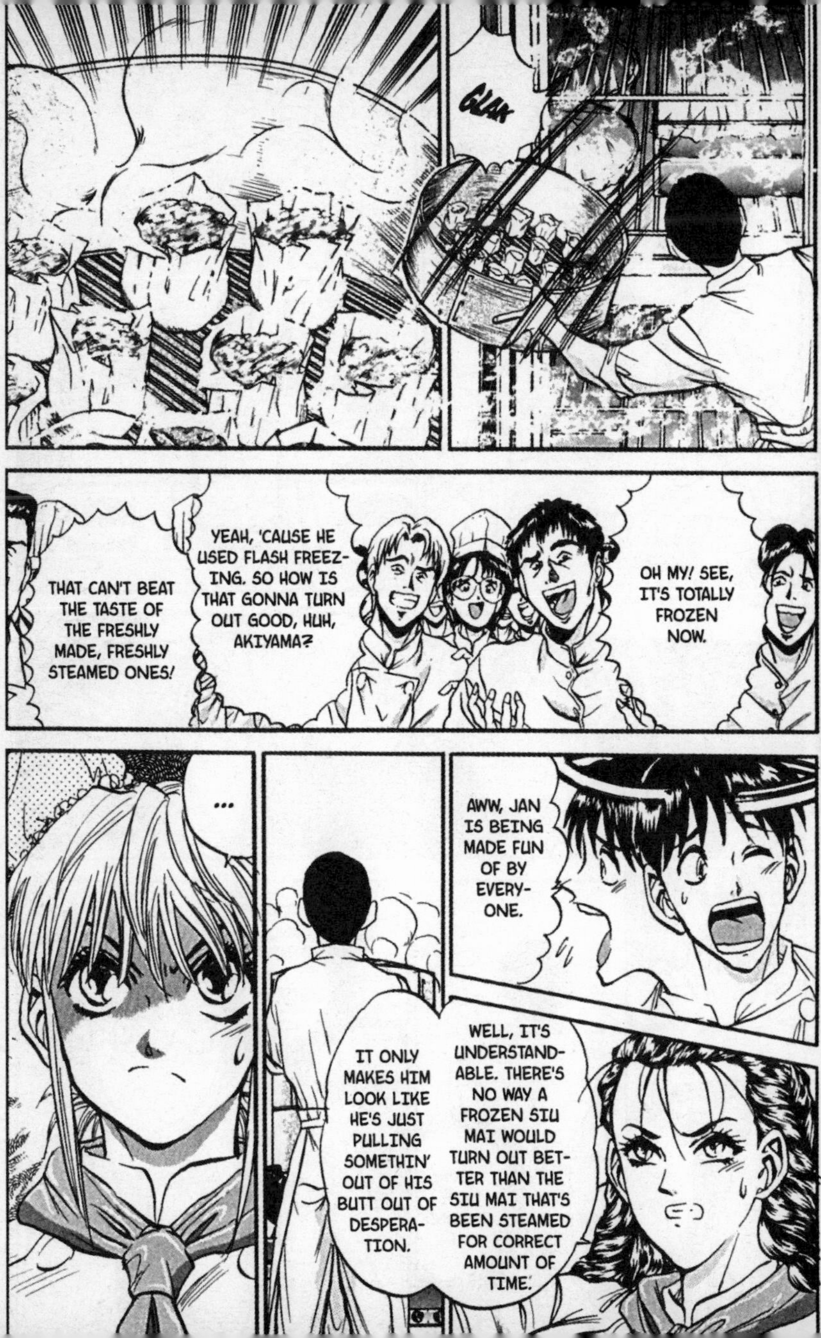
GLAK
OH MY! SEE, IT'S TOTALLY FROZEN NOW.
YEAH, 'CAUSE HE USED FLASH FREEZ-ING. SO HOW IS THAT GONNA TURN OUT GOOD, HUH, AKIYAMA?
THAT CAN'T BEAT THE TASTE OF THE FRESHLY MADE, FRESHLY STEAMED ONES!
AWW, JAN IS BEING MADE FUN OF BY EVERY-ONE.
WELL, IT'S UNDERSTAND-ABLE. THERE'S NO WAY A FROZEN SIU MAI WOULD TURN OUT BET-TER THAN THE SIU MAI THAT'S BEEN STEAMED FOR CORRECT AMOUNT OF TIME.
IT ONLY MAKES HIM LOOK LIKE HE'S JUST PULLING SOMETHIN' OUT OF HIS BUTT OUT OF DESPERA-TION.
...

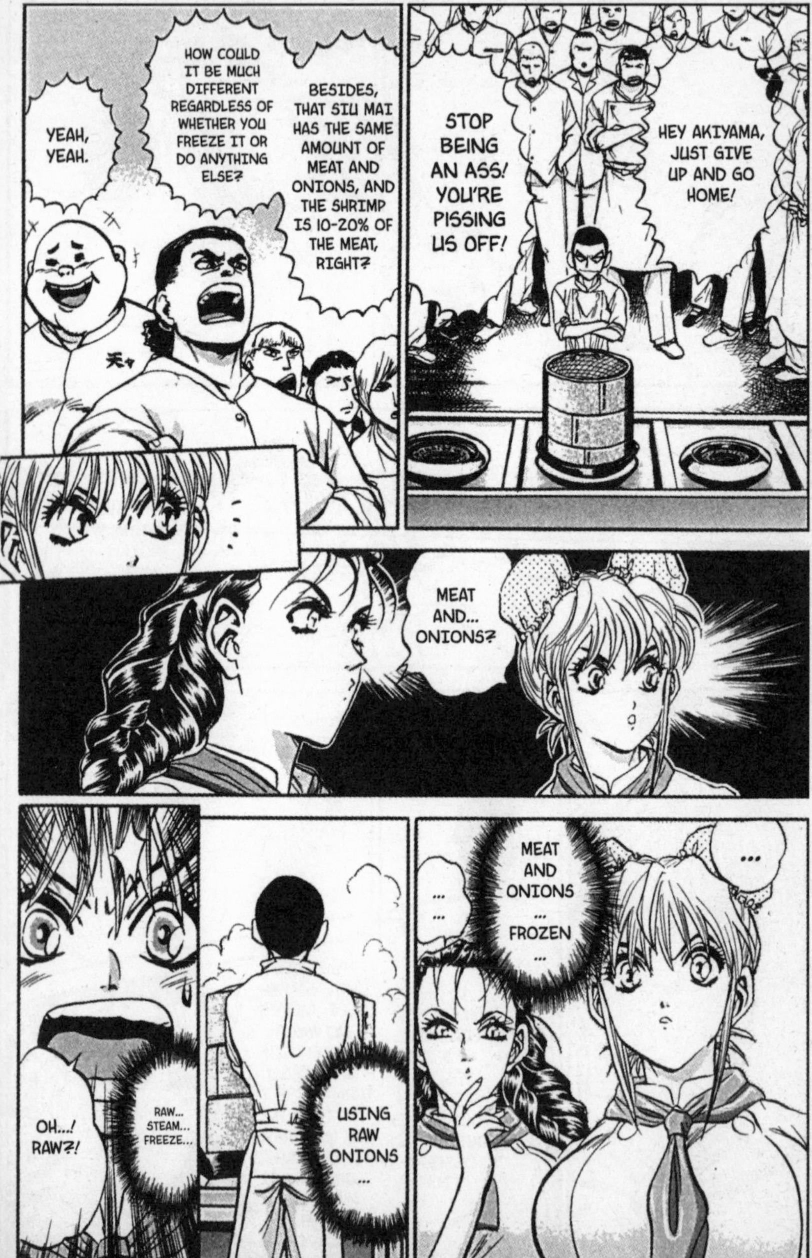
HEY AKIYAMA, JUST GIVE UP AND GO HOME!
STOP BEING AN ASS! YOU'RE PISSING US OFF!
BESIDES, THAT SIU MAI HAS THE SAME AMOUNT OF MEAT AND ONIONS, AND THE SHRIMP IS 10-20% OF THE MEAT, RIGHT?
HOW COULD IT BE MUCH DIFFERENT REGARDLESS OF WHETHER YOU FREEZE IT OR DO ANYTHING ELSE?
YEAH, YEAH.
...
MEAT AND... ONIONS?
...
MEAT AND ONIONS ... FROZEN ...
... ...
USING RAW ONIONS ...
RAW... STEAM... FREEZE...
OH...! RAW?!

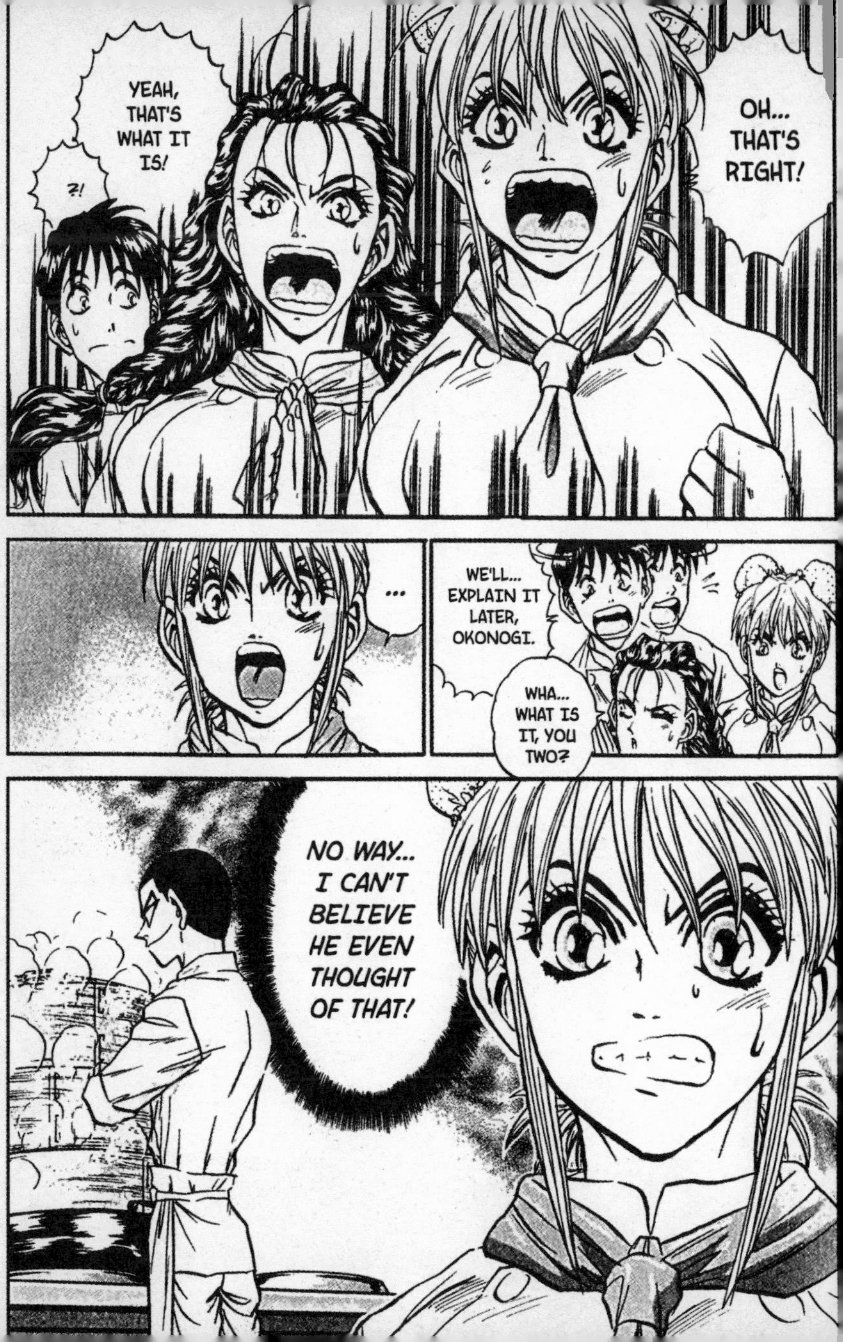
OH... THAT'S RIGHT!
YEAH, THAT'S WHAT IT IS!
?!
WE'LL... EXPLAIN IT LATER, OKONOGI.
WHA... WHAT IS IT, YOU TWO?
...
NO WAY... I CAN'T BELIEVE HE EVEN THOUGHT OF THAT!

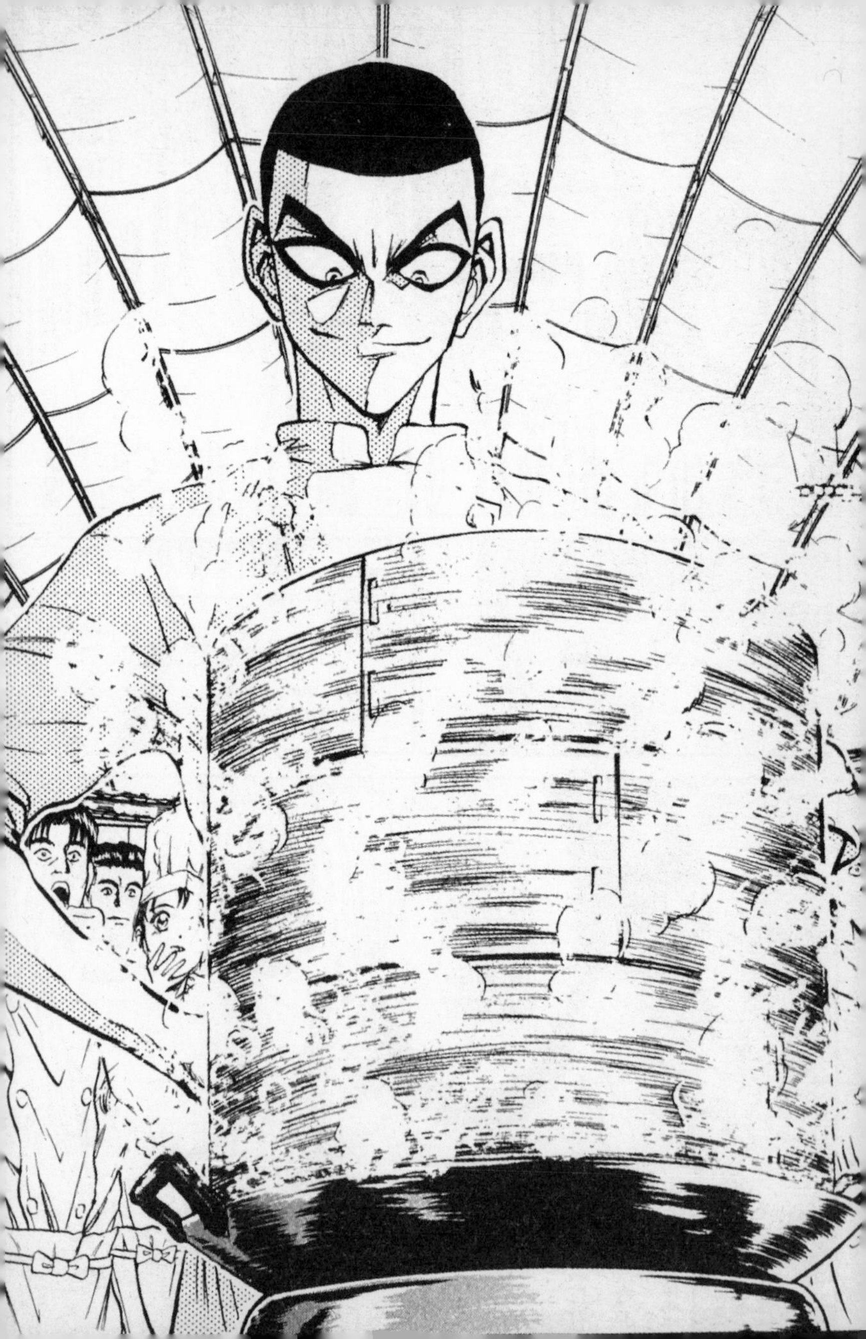

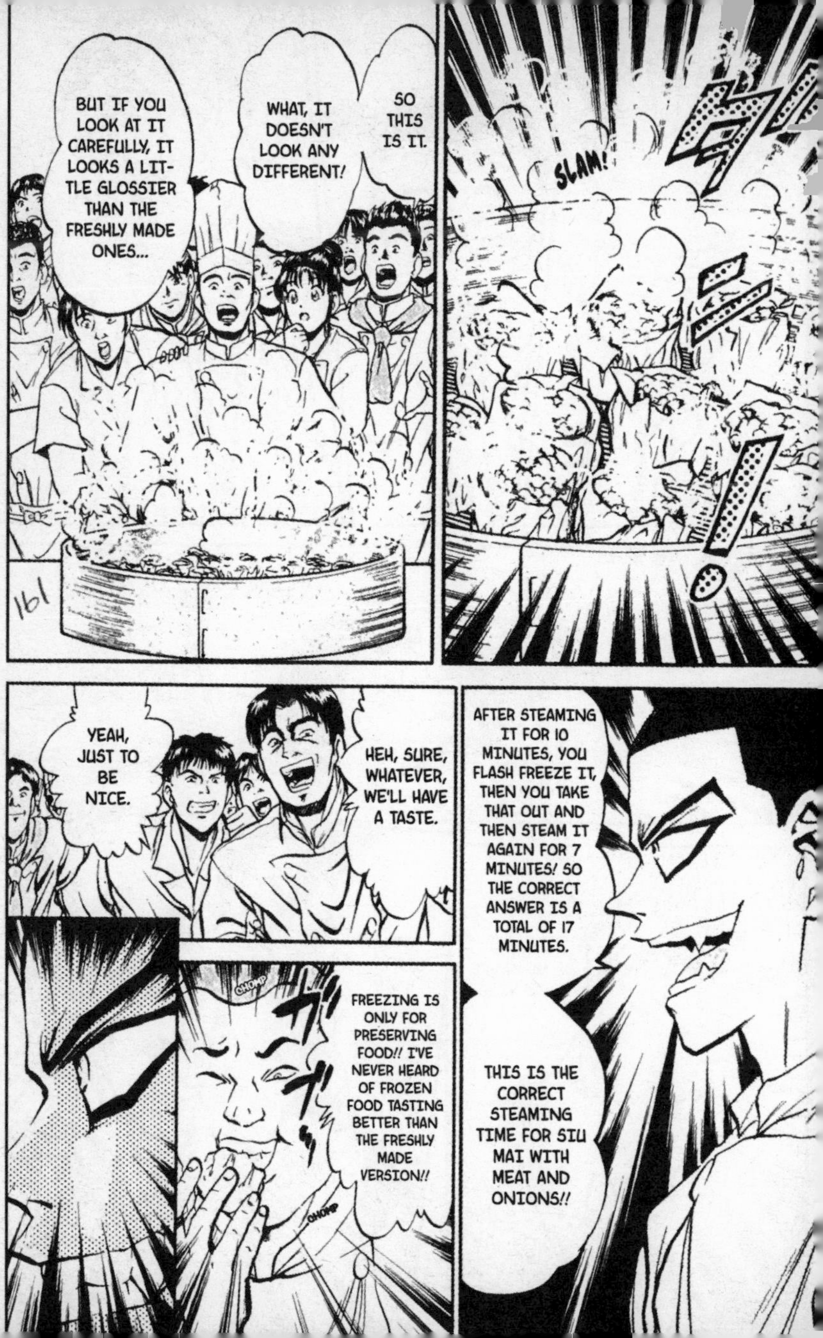
SLAM!
SO THIS IS IT.
WHAT, IT DOESN'T LOOK ANY DIFFERENT!
BUT IF YOU LOOK AT IT CAREFULLY, IT LOOKS A LIT-TLE GLOSSIER THAN THE FRESHLY MADE ONES...
AFTER STEAMING IT FOR 10 MINUTES, YOU FLASH FREEZE IT, THEN YOU TAKE THAT OUT AND THEN STEAM IT AGAIN FOR 7 MINUTES! SO THE CORRECT ANSWER IS A TOTAL OF 17 MINUTES.
THIS IS THE CORRECT STEAMING TIME FOR SIU MAI WITH MEAT AND ONIONS!!
HEH, SURE, WHATEVER, WE'LL HAVE A TASTE.
YEAH, JUST TO BE NICE.
CHOMP
FREEZING IS ONLY FOR PRESERVING FOOD!! I'VE NEVER HEARD OF FROZEN FOOD TASTING BETTER THAN THE FRESHLY MADE VERSION!!
CHOMP

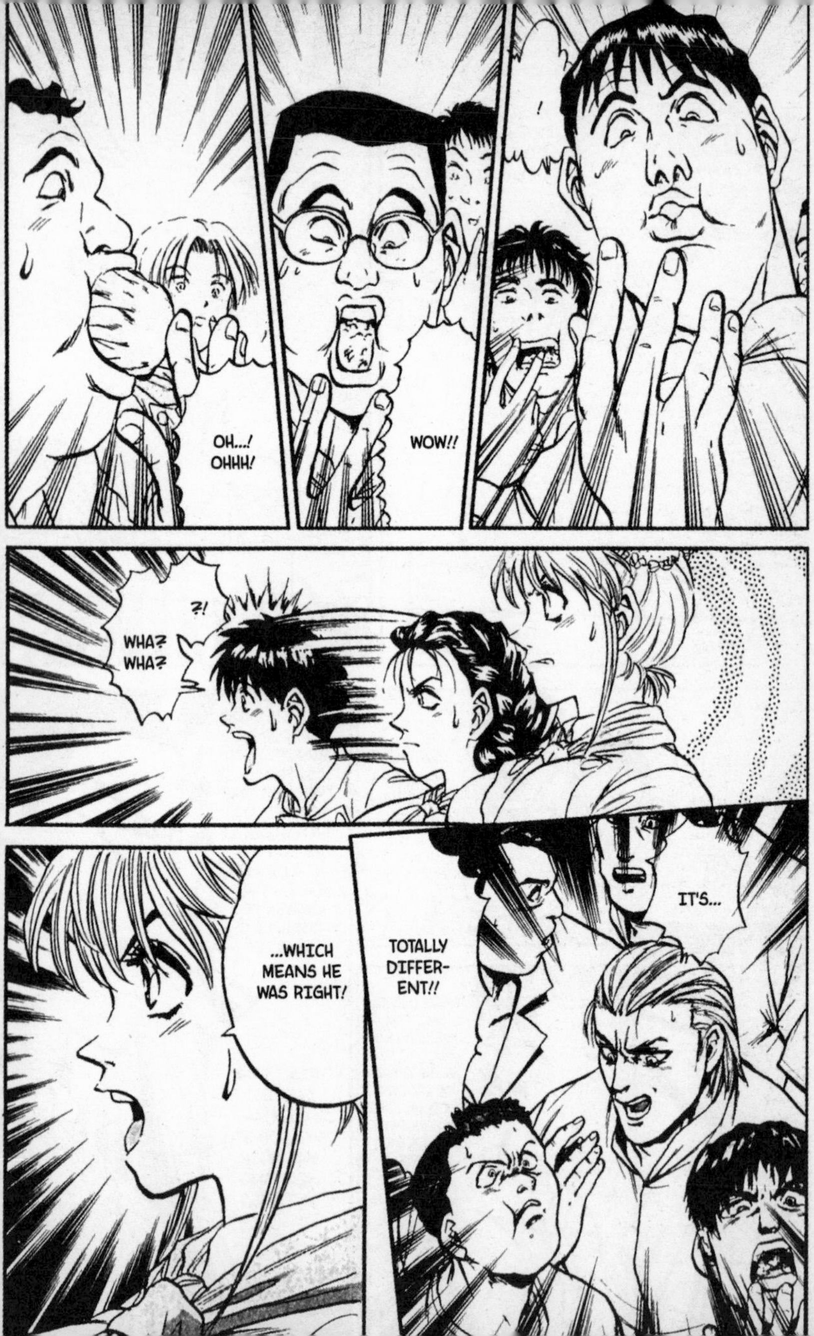
WOW!!
OH...! OHHH!
?!
WHA? WHA?
IT'S...
TOTALLY DIFFER-ENT!!
...WHICH MEANS HE WAS RIGHT!

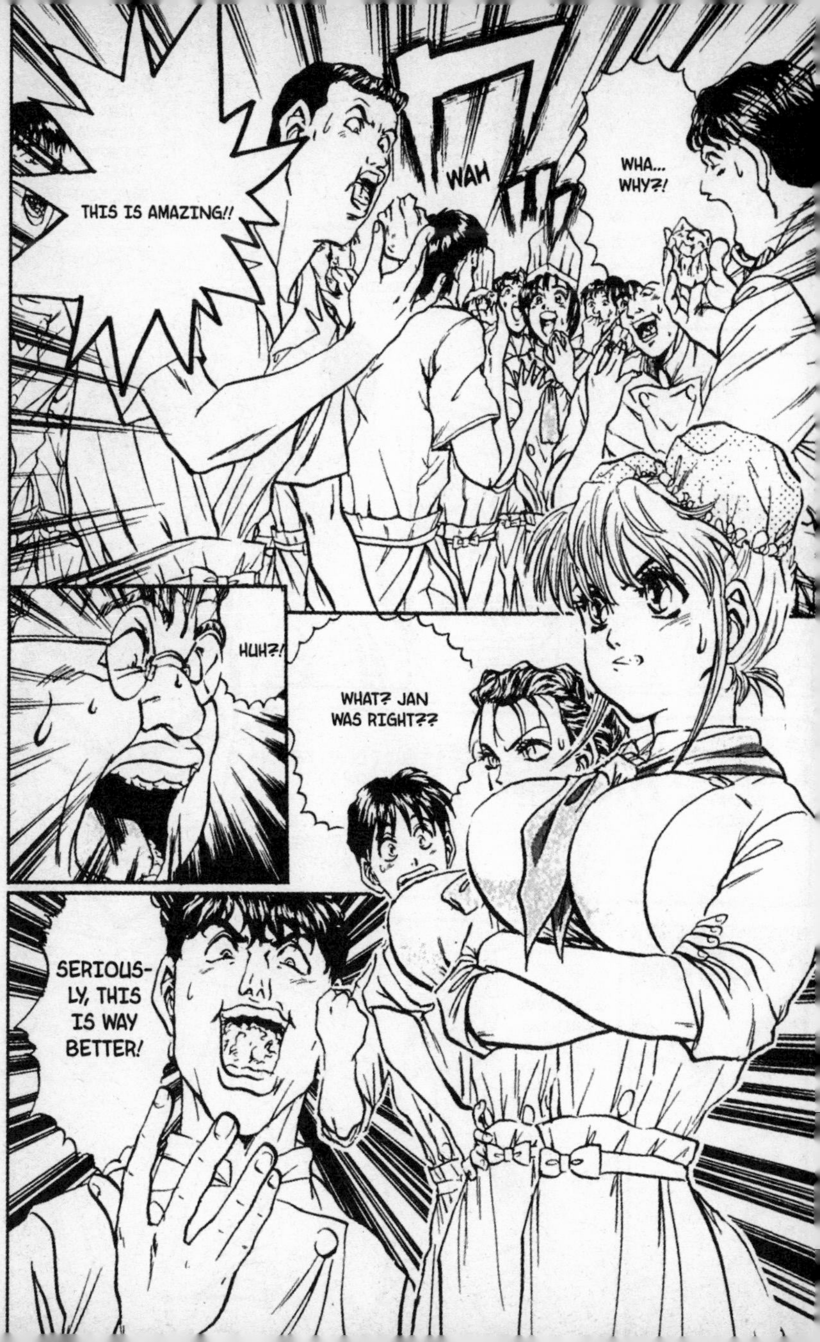
WHA... WHY?!
WAH
THIS IS AMAZING!!
WHAT? JAN WAS RIGHT??
HUH?!
SERIOUS-LY, THIS IS WAY BETTER!

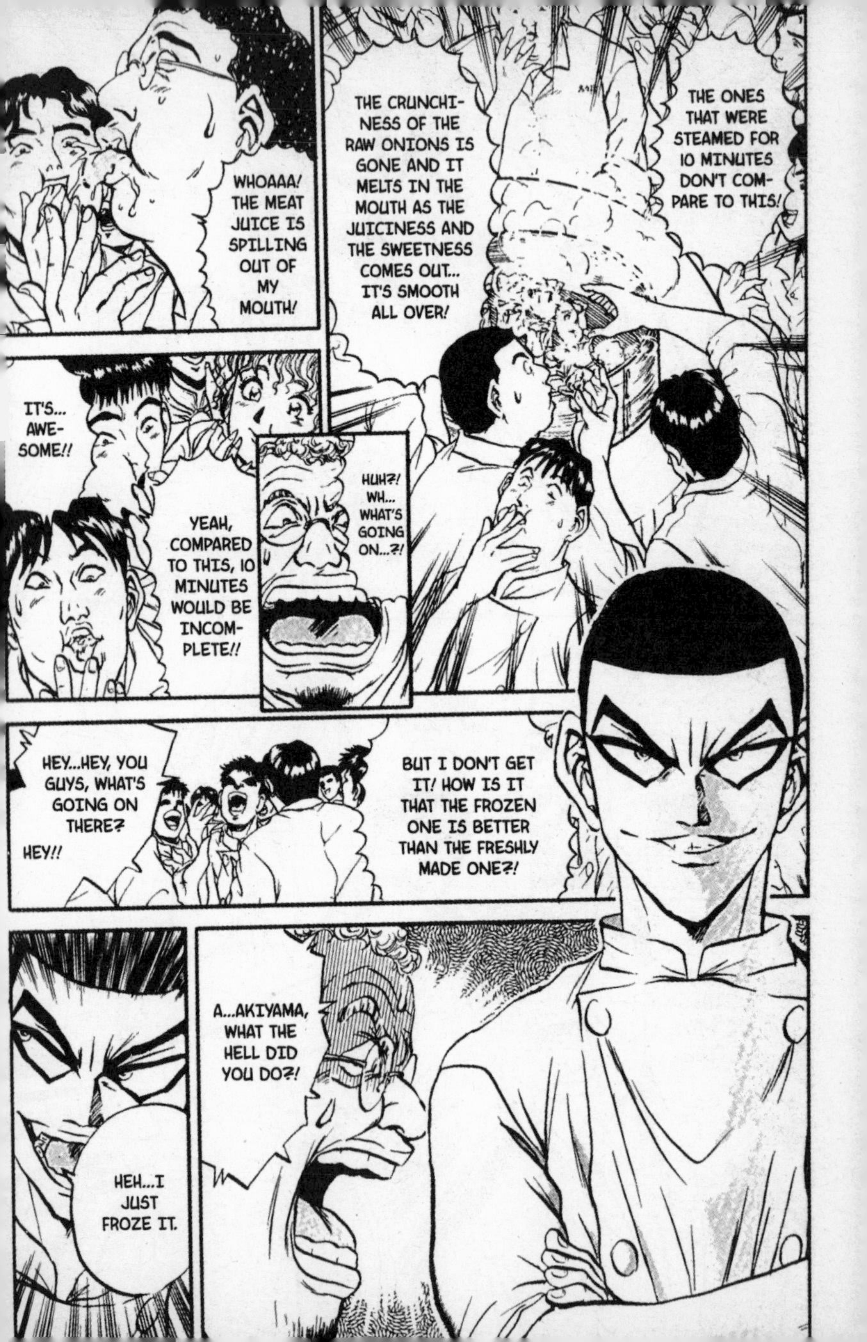
THE ONES THAT WERE STEAMED FOR 10 MINUTES DON'T COMPARE TO THIS!
THE CRUNCHINESS OF THE RAW ONIONS IS GONE AND IT MELTS IN THE MOUTH AS THE JUICINESS AND THE SWEETNESS COMES OUT... IT'S SMOOTH ALL OVER!
WHOAAA! THE MEAT JUICE IS SPILLING OUT OF MY MOUTH!
HUH?! WH... WHAT'S GOING ON...?!
IT'S... AWESOME!!
YEAH, COMPARED TO THIS, 10 MINUTES WOULD BE INCOMPLETE!!
BUT I DON'T GET IT! HOW IS IT THAT THE FROZEN ONE IS BETTER THAN THE FRESHLY MADE ONE?!
HEY...HEY, YOU GUYS, WHAT'S GOING ON THERE?
HEY!!
A...AKIYAMA, WHAT THE HELL DID YOU DO?!
HEH...I JUST FROZE IT.

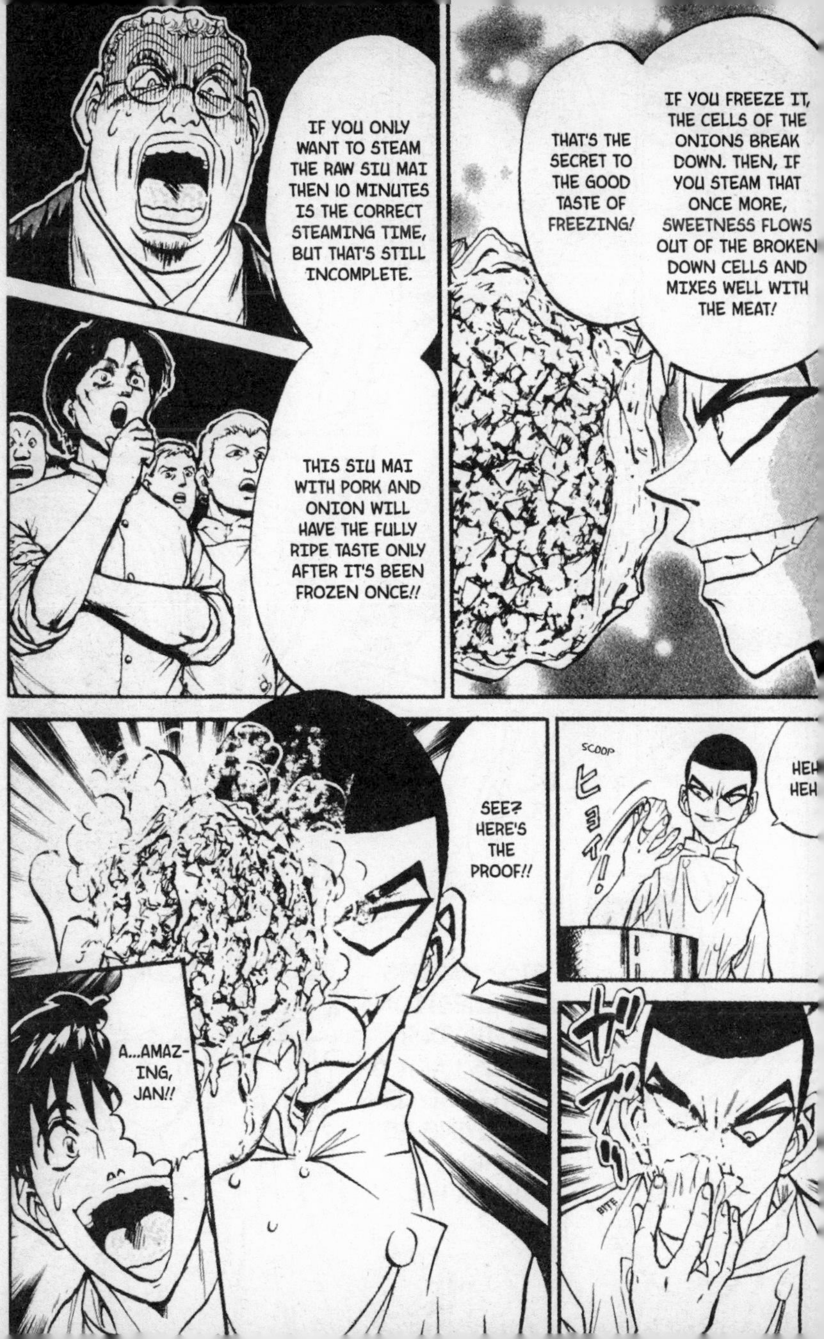
IF YOU FREEZE IT, THE CELLS OF THE ONIONS BREAK DOWN. THEN, IF YOU STEAM THAT ONCE MORE, SWEETNESS FLOWS OUT OF THE BROKEN DOWN CELLS AND MIXES WELL WITH THE MEAT!
THAT'S THE SECRET TO THE GOOD TASTE OF FREEZING!
IF YOU ONLY WANT TO STEAM THE RAW SIU MAI THEN 10 MINUTES IS THE CORRECT STEAMING TIME, BUT THAT'S STILL INCOMPLETE.
THIS SIU MAI WITH PORK AND ONION WILL HAVE THE FULLY RIPE TASTE ONLY AFTER IT'S BEEN FROZEN ONCE!!
HEH HEH
SCOOP
ヒョイ!
BITE
SEE? HERE'S THE PROOF!!
A...AMAZ-ING, JAN!!

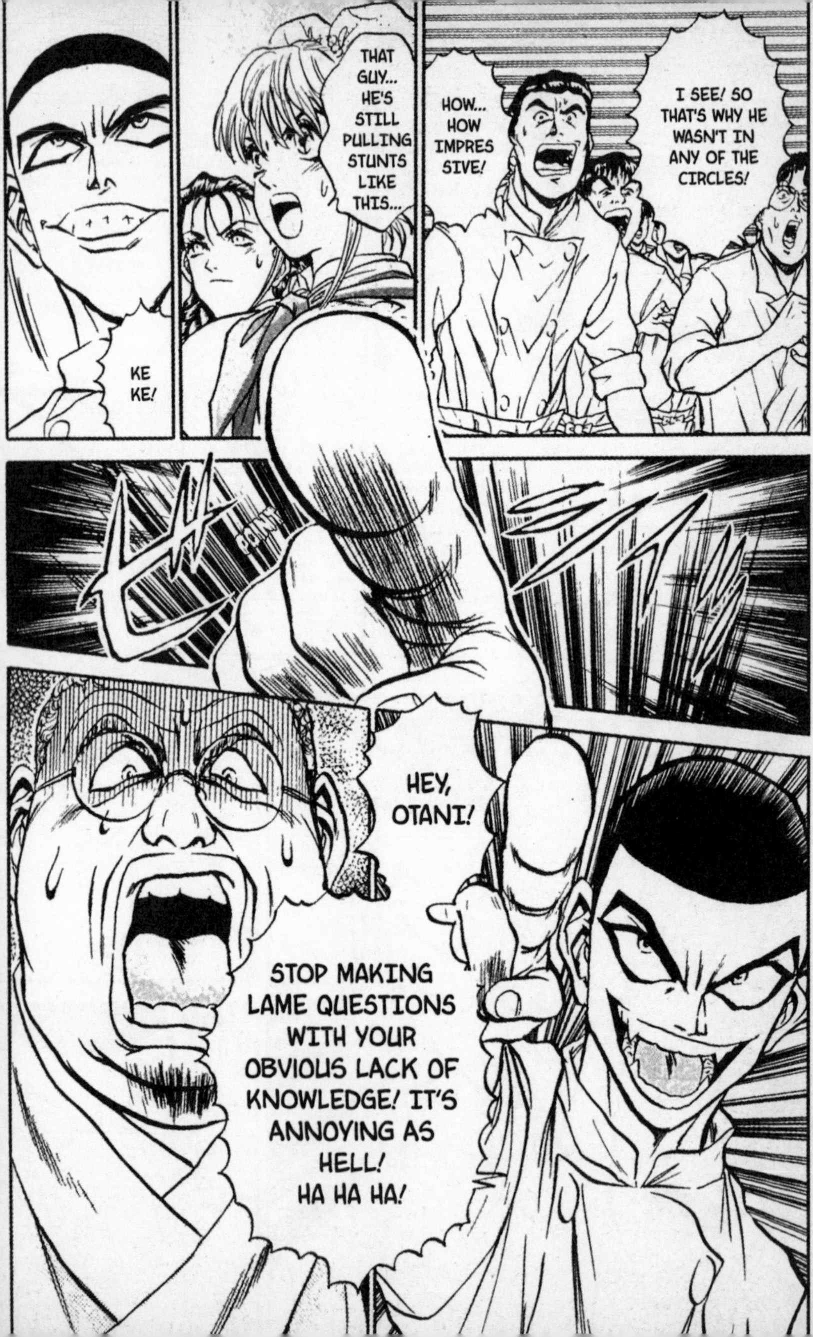
I SEE! SO THAT'S WHY HE WASN'T IN ANY OF THE CIRCLES!
HOW... HOW IMPRES SIVE!
THAT GUY... HE'S STILL PULLING STUNTS LIKE THIS...
KE KE!
POINT
HEY, OTANI!
STOP MAKING LAME QUESTIONS WITH YOUR OBVIOUS LACK OF KNOWLEDGE! IT'S ANNOYING AS HELL! HA HA HA!

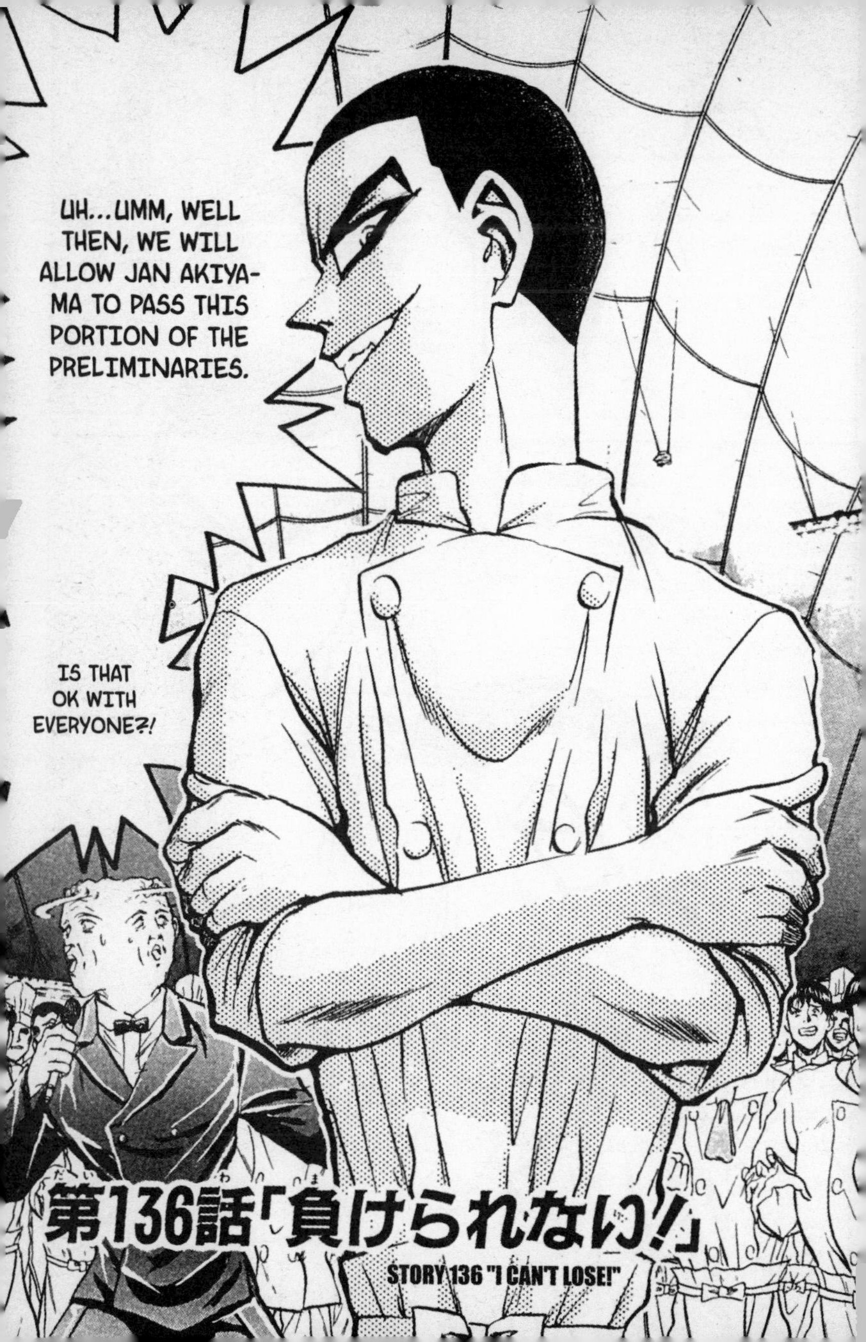
UH...UMM, WELL THEN, WE WILL ALLOW JAN AKIYA-MA TO PASS THIS PORTION OF THE PRELIMINARIES.
IS THAT OK WITH EVERYONE?!
第136話「負けられない!」
STORY 136 "I CAN'T LOSE!"

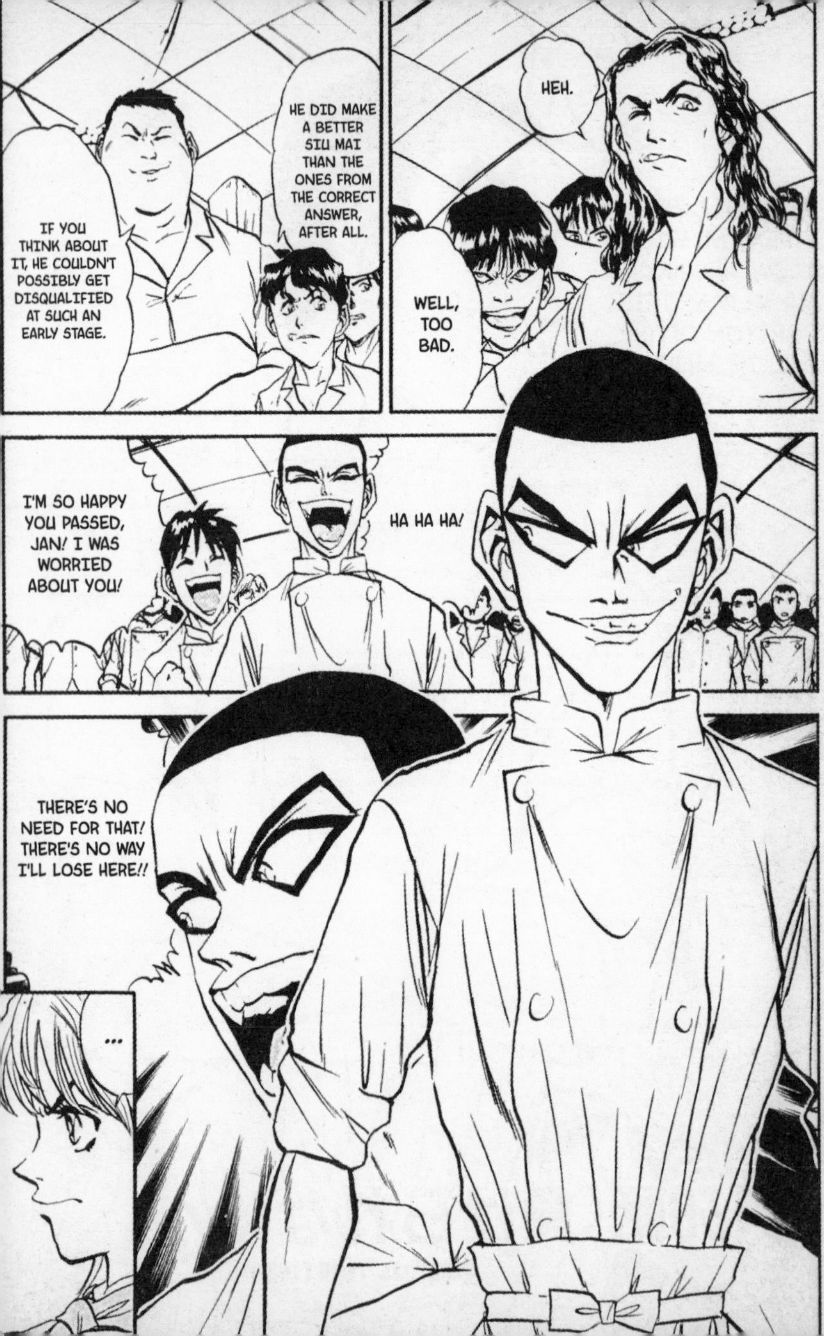
HEH.
WELL, TOO BAD.
HE DID MAKE A BETTER SIU MAI THAN THE ONES FROM THE CORRECT ANSWER, AFTER ALL.
IF YOU THINK ABOUT IT, HE COULDN'T POSSIBLY GET DISQUALIFIED AT SUCH AN EARLY STAGE.
HA HA HA!
I'M SO HAPPY YOU PASSED, JAN! I WAS WORRIED ABOUT YOU!
THERE'S NO NEED FOR THAT! THERE'S NO WAY I'LL LOSE HERE!!
...

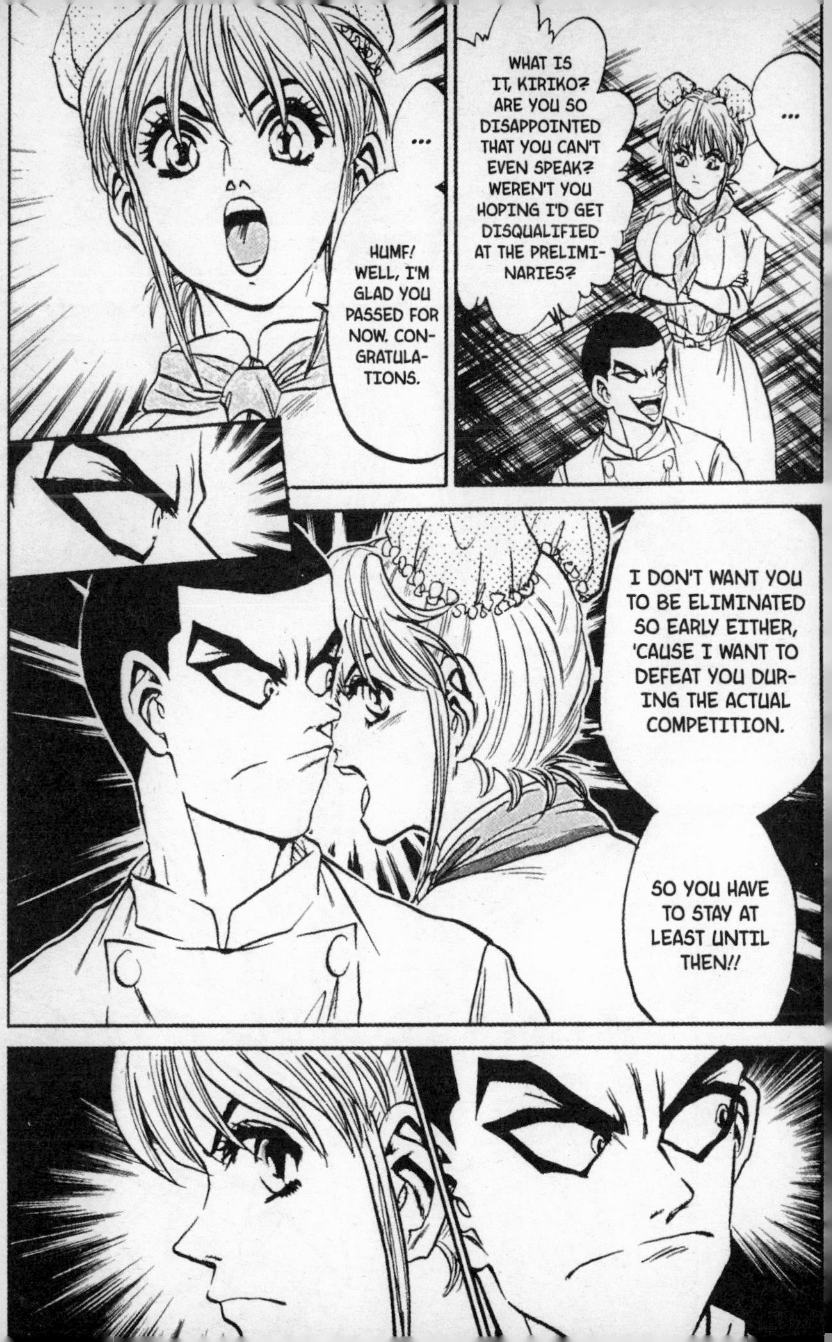
WHAT IS IT, KIRIKO? ARE YOU SO DISAPPOINTED THAT YOU CAN'T EVEN SPEAK? WEREN'T YOU HOPING I'D GET DISQUALIFIED AT THE PRELIMINARIES?
...
...
HUMF! WELL, I'M GLAD YOU PASSED FOR NOW. CONGRATULATIONS.
I DON'T WANT YOU TO BE ELIMINATED SO EARLY EITHER, 'CAUSE I WANT TO DEFEAT YOU DURING THE ACTUAL COMPETITION.
SO YOU HAVE TO STAY AT LEAST UNTIL THEN!!

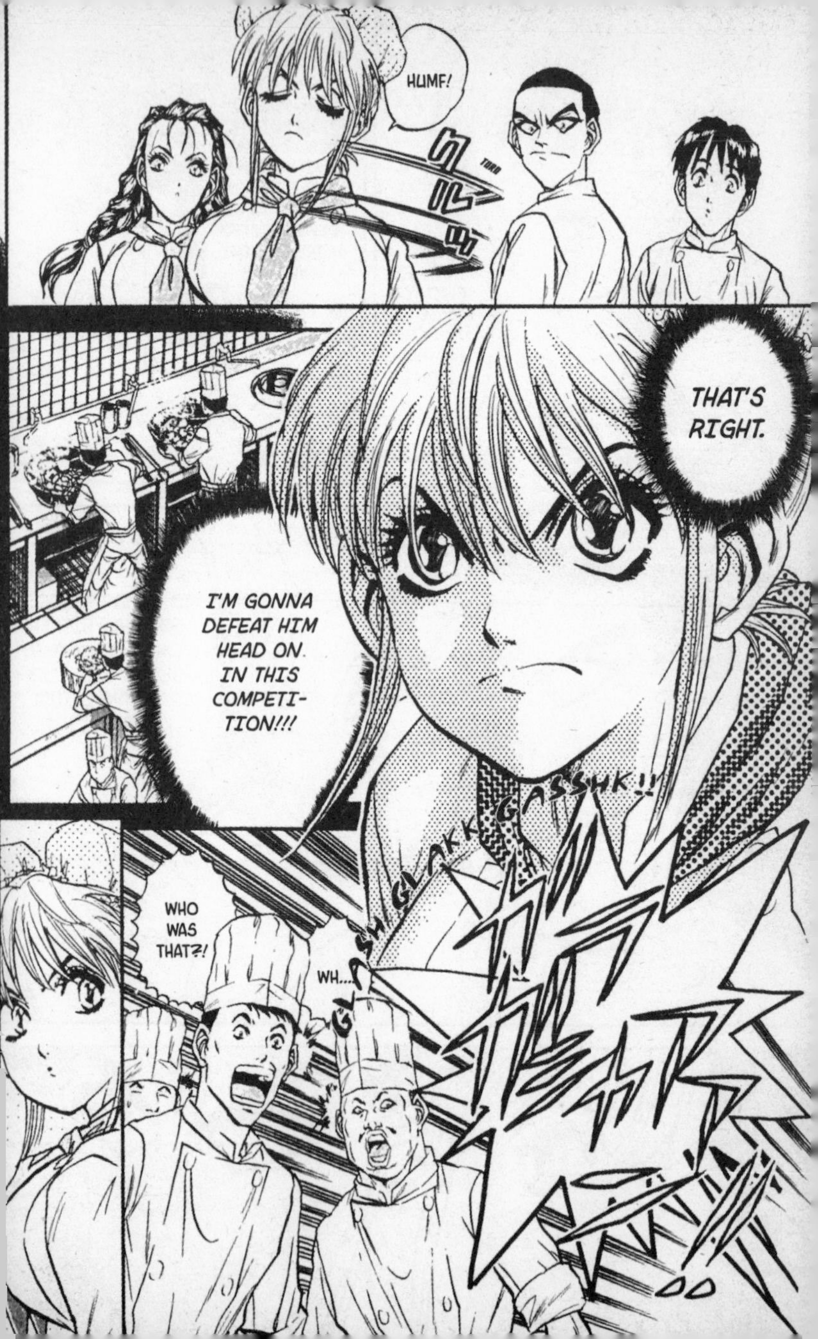
HUMF!
THAT'S RIGHT.
I'M GONNA DEFEAT HIM HEAD ON IN THIS COMPETITION!!!
GLAKK GASSHK!!
WH...
WHO WAS THAT?!

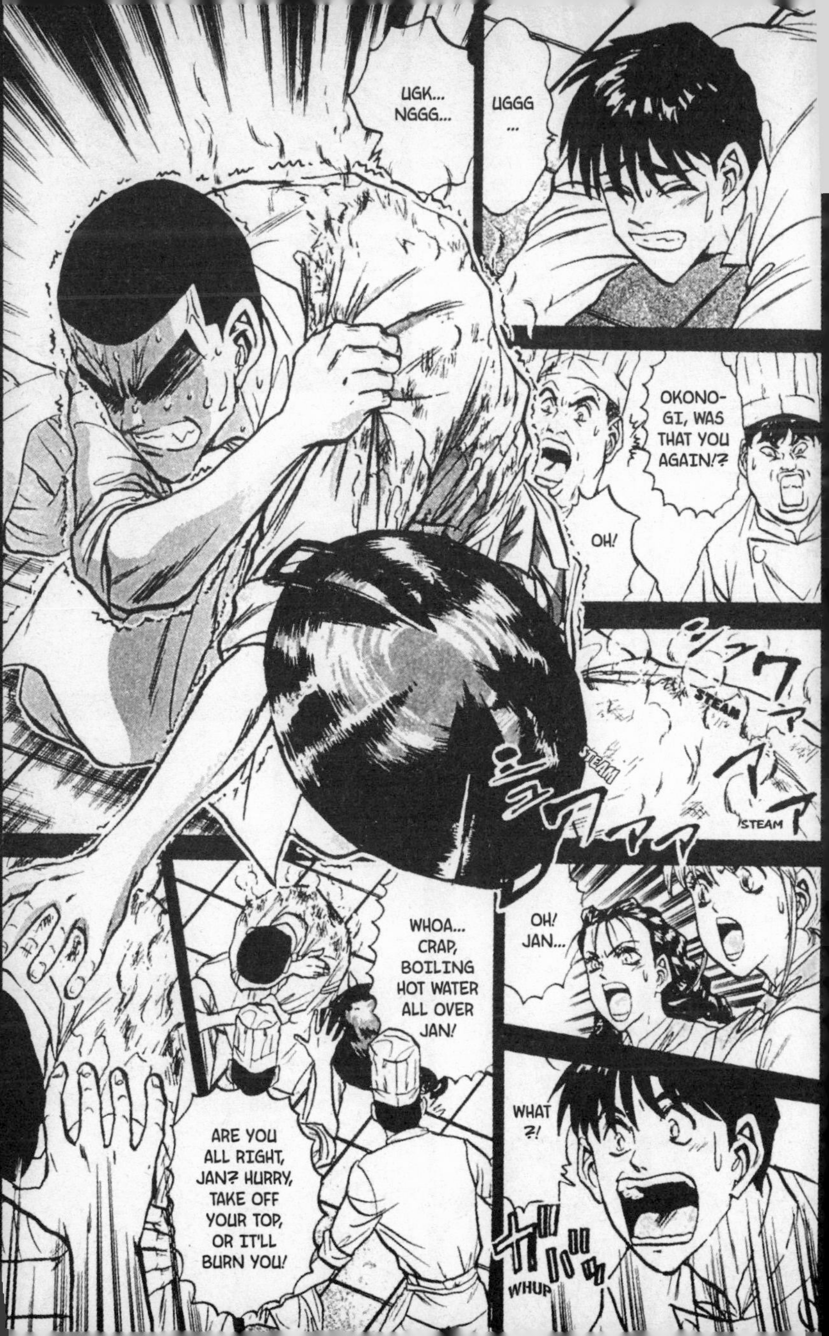
UGGG ...
UGK... NGGG...
OKONOGI, WAS THAT YOU AGAIN!?
OH!
STEAM
STEAM
STEAM
OH! JAN...
WHAT?!
WHUP
WHOA... CRAP, BOILING HOT WATER ALL OVER JAN!
ARE YOU ALL RIGHT, JAN? HURRY, TAKE OFF YOUR TOP, OR IT'LL BURN YOU!

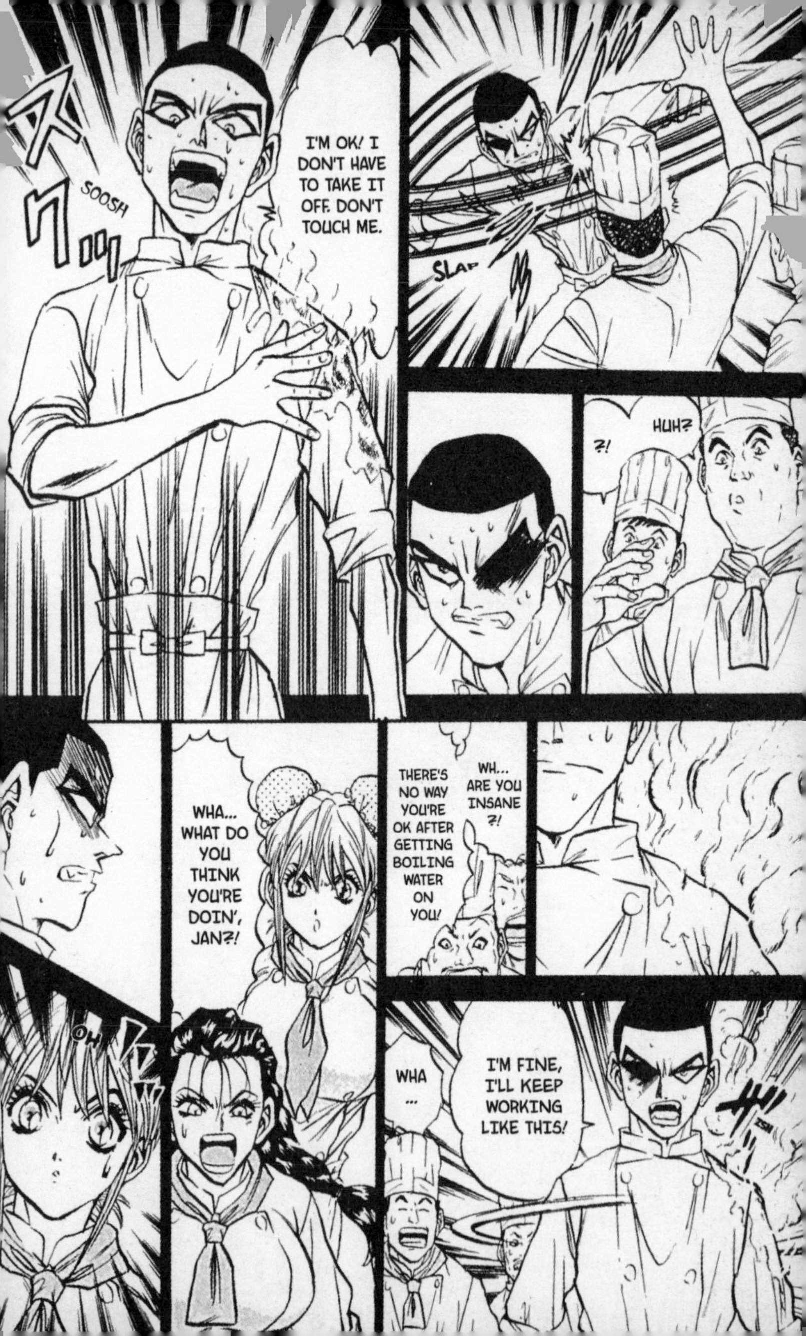
SLAP
HUH?
?!
I'M OK! I DON'T HAVE TO TAKE IT OFF. DON'T TOUCH ME.
SOOSH
WH... ARE YOU INSANE?!
THERE'S NO WAY YOU'RE OK AFTER GETTING BOILING WATER ON YOU!
I'M FINE, I'LL KEEP WORKING LIKE THIS!
WHA...
WHA... WHAT DO YOU THINK YOU'RE DOIN', JAN?!
OH

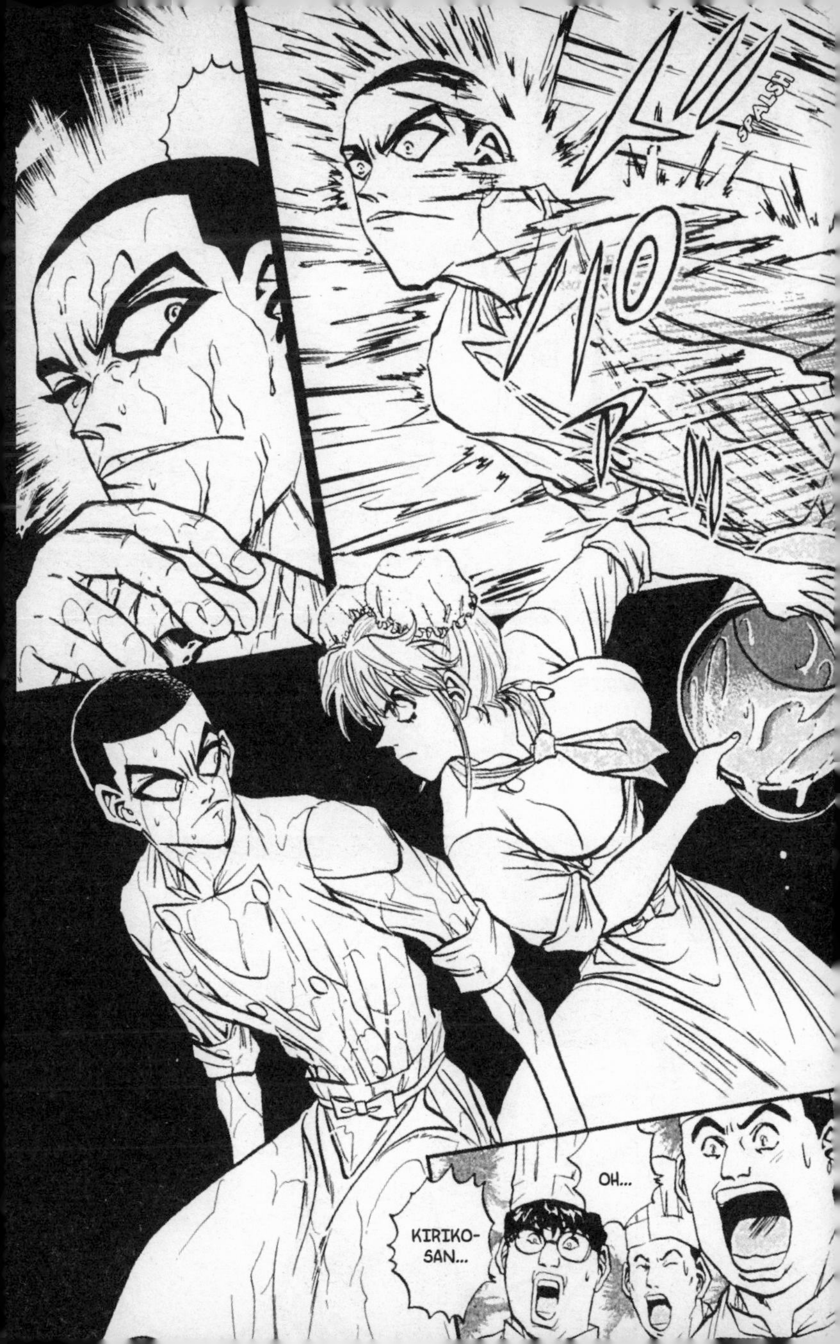
SPALSH
OH...
KIRIKO-SAN...

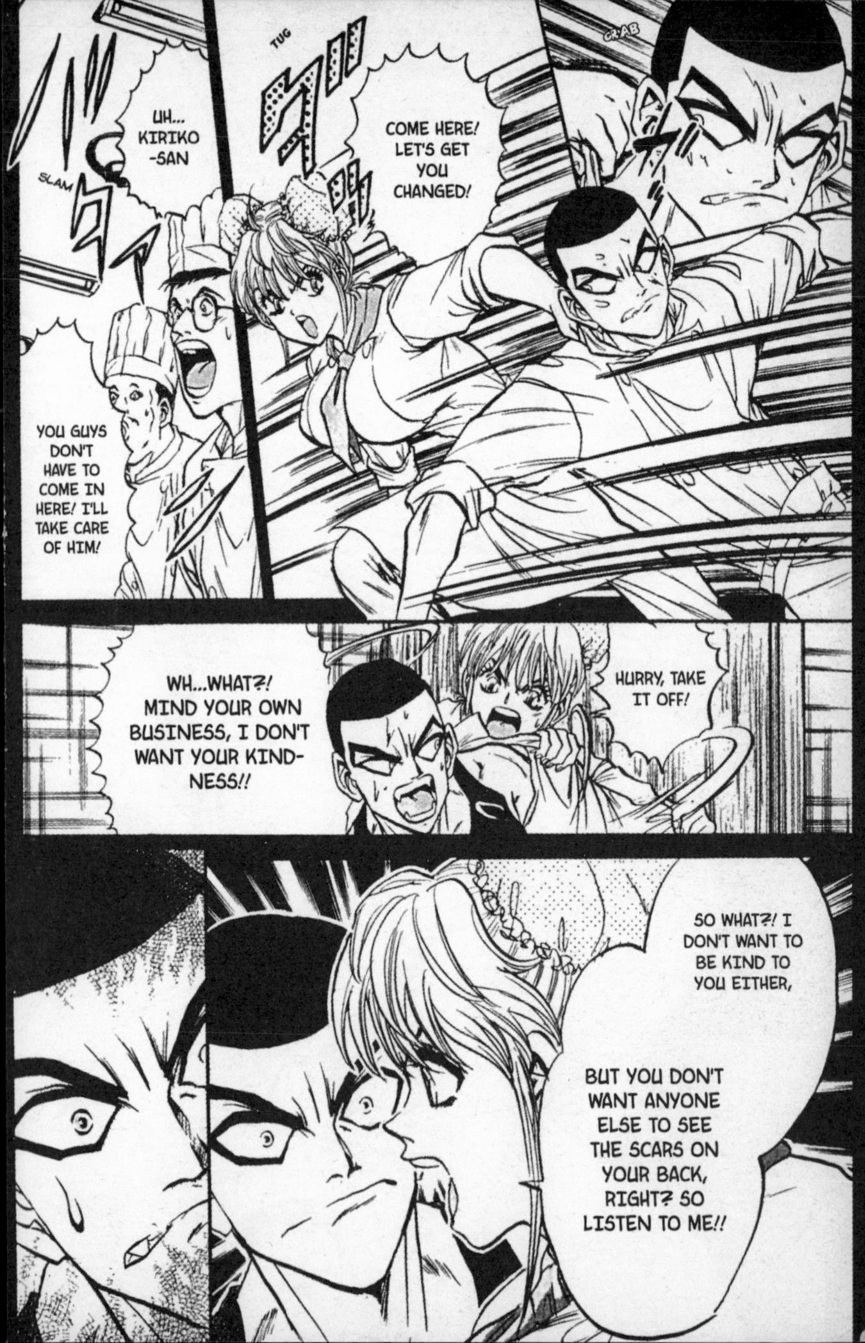
GRAB
TUG
COME HERE! LET'S GET YOU CHANGED!
SLAM
UH... KIRIKO -SAN
YOU GUYS DON'T HAVE TO COME IN HERE! I'LL TAKE CARE OF HIM!
HURRY, TAKE IT OFF!
WH...WHAT?! MIND YOUR OWN BUSINESS, I DON'T WANT YOUR KIND-NESS!!
SO WHAT?! I DON'T WANT TO BE KIND TO YOU EITHER,
BUT YOU DON'T WANT ANYONE ELSE TO SEE THE SCARS ON YOUR BACK, RIGHT? SO LISTEN TO ME!!

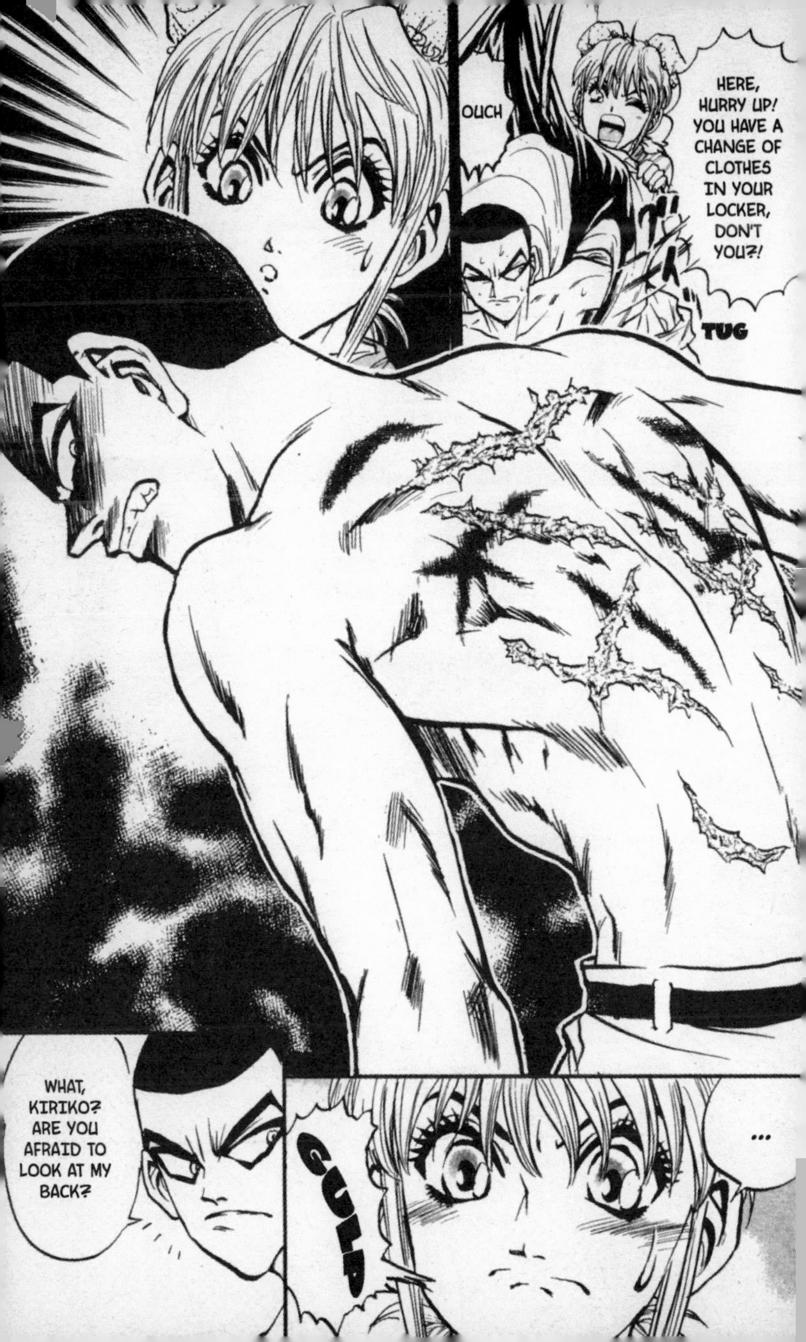
HERE, HURRY UP! YOU HAVE A CHANGE OF CLOTHES IN YOUR LOCKER, DON'T YOU?!
TUG
OUCH
...
GULP
WHAT, KIRIKO? ARE YOU AFRAID TO LOOK AT MY BACK?

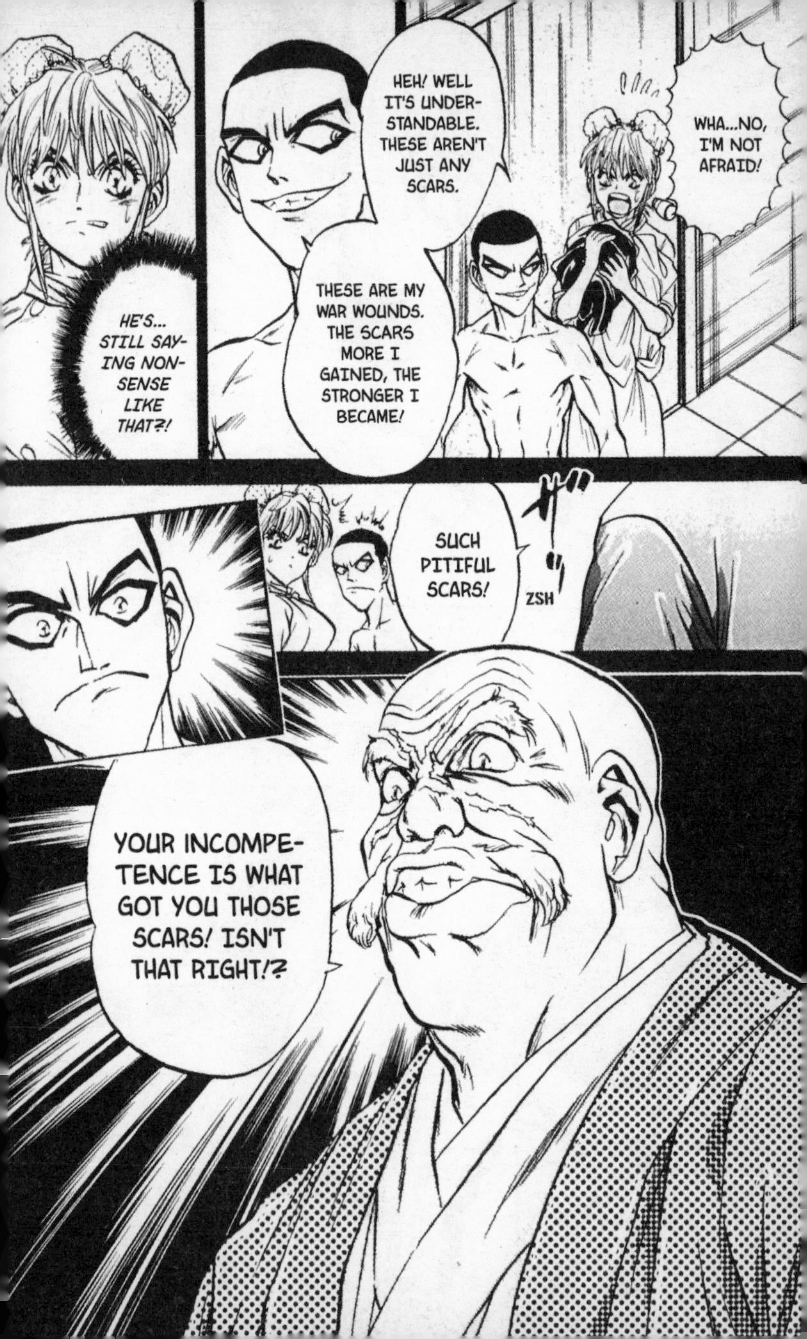
WHA...NO, I'M NOT AFRAID!
HEH! WELL IT'S UNDER-STANDABLE. THESE AREN'T JUST ANY SCARS.
THESE ARE MY WAR WOUNDS. THE SCARS MORE I GAINED, THE STRONGER I BECAME!
HE'S... STILL SAY-ING NON-SENSE LIKE THAT?!
ZSH
SUCH PITIFUL SCARS!
YOUR INCOMPE-TENCE IS WHAT GOT YOU THOSE SCARS! ISN'T THAT RIGHT!?

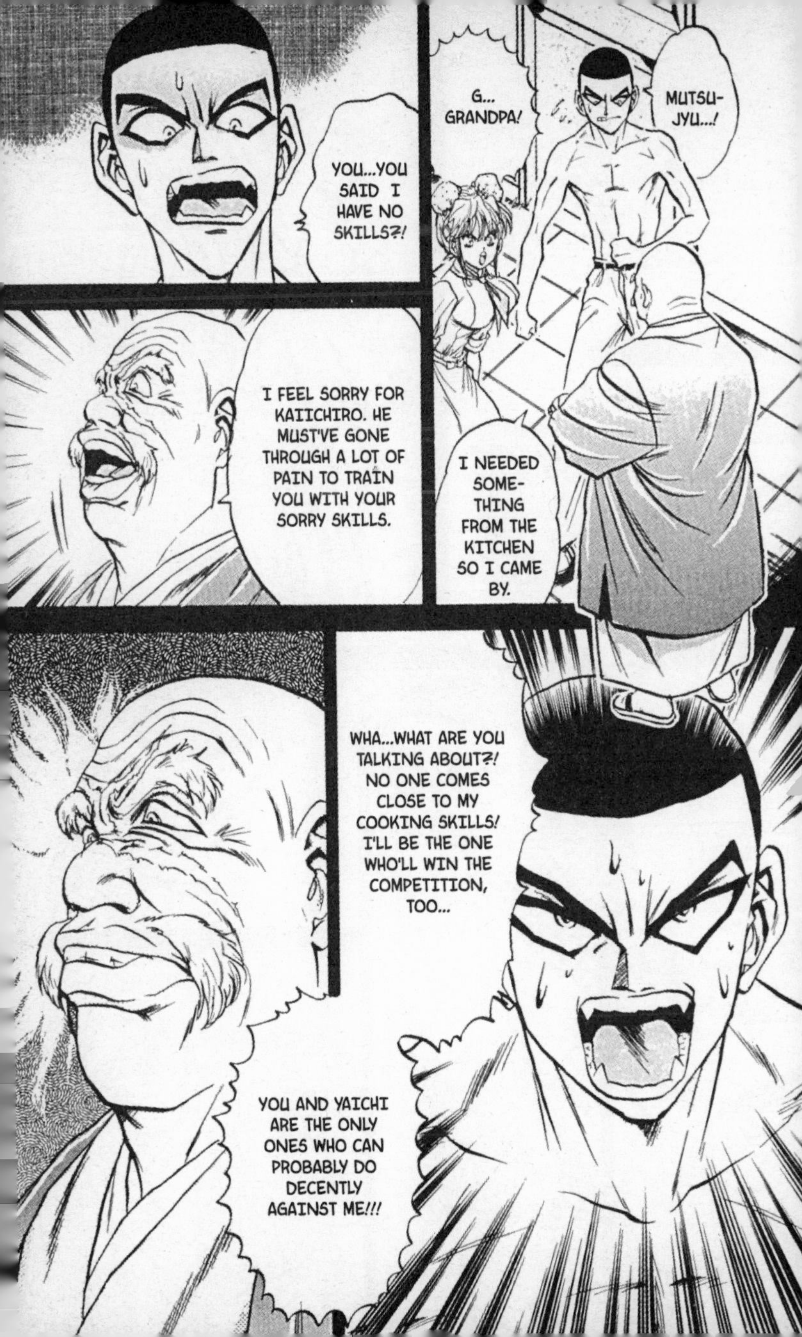
MUTSU-JYU...!
G... GRANDPA!
I NEEDED SOME-THING FROM THE KITCHEN SO I CAME BY.
YOU...YOU SAID I HAVE NO SKILLS?!
I FEEL SORRY FOR KAIICHIRO. HE MUST'VE GONE THROUGH A LOT OF PAIN TO TRAIN YOU WITH YOUR SORRY SKILLS.
WHA...WHAT ARE YOU TALKING ABOUT?! NO ONE COMES CLOSE TO MY COOKING SKILLS! I'LL BE THE ONE WHO'LL WIN THE COMPETITION, TOO...
YOU AND YAICHI ARE THE ONLY ONES WHO CAN PROBABLY DO DECENTLY AGAINST ME!!!

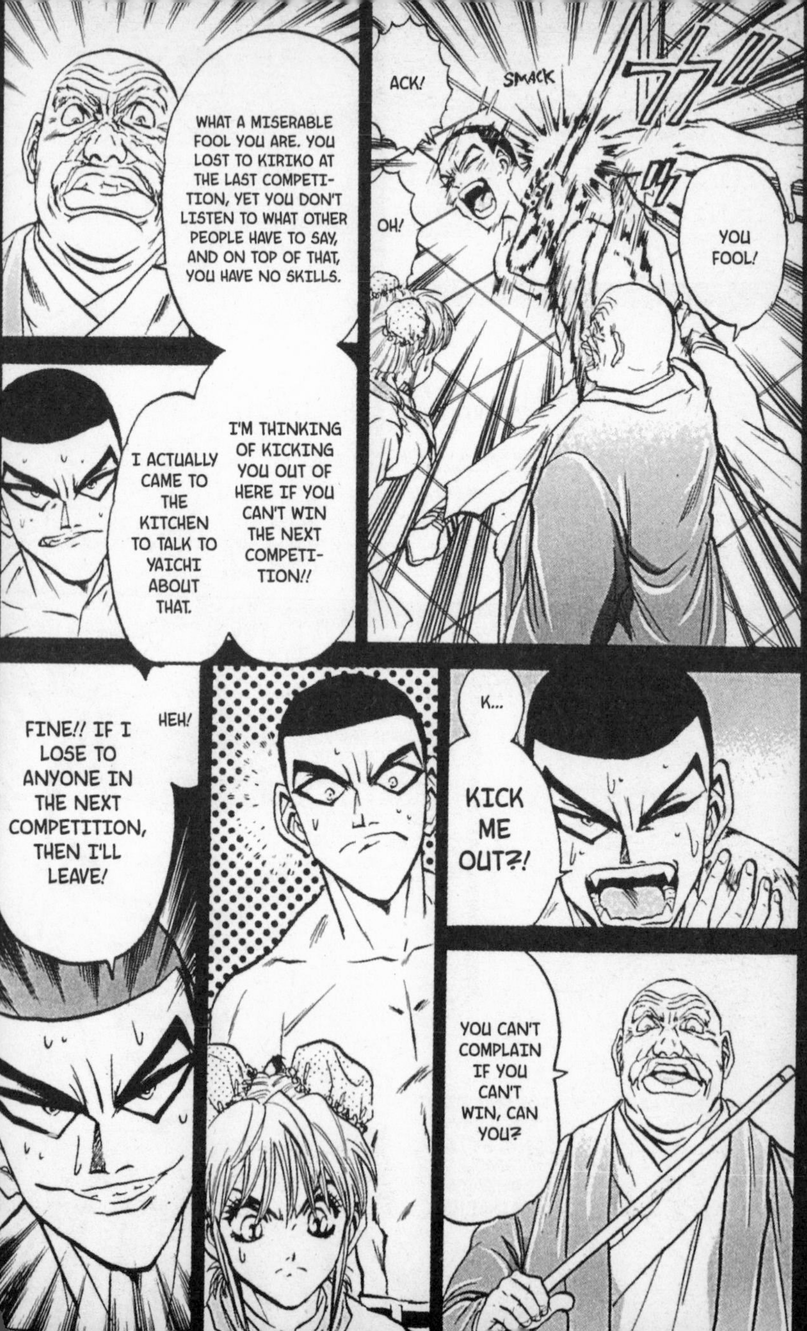
ACK!
SMACK
OH!
YOU FOOL!
WHAT A MISERABLE FOOL YOU ARE. YOU LOST TO KIRIKO AT THE LAST COMPETITION, YET YOU DON'T LISTEN TO WHAT OTHER PEOPLE HAVE TO SAY, AND ON TOP OF THAT, YOU HAVE NO SKILLS.
I'M THINKING OF KICKING YOU OUT OF HERE IF YOU CAN'T WIN THE NEXT COMPETITION!!
I ACTUALLY CAME TO THE KITCHEN TO TALK TO YAICHI ABOUT THAT.
K...
KICK ME OUT?!
YOU CAN'T COMPLAIN IF YOU CAN'T WIN, CAN YOU?
HEH!
FINE!! IF I LOSE TO ANYONE IN THE NEXT COMPETITION, THEN I'LL LEAVE!

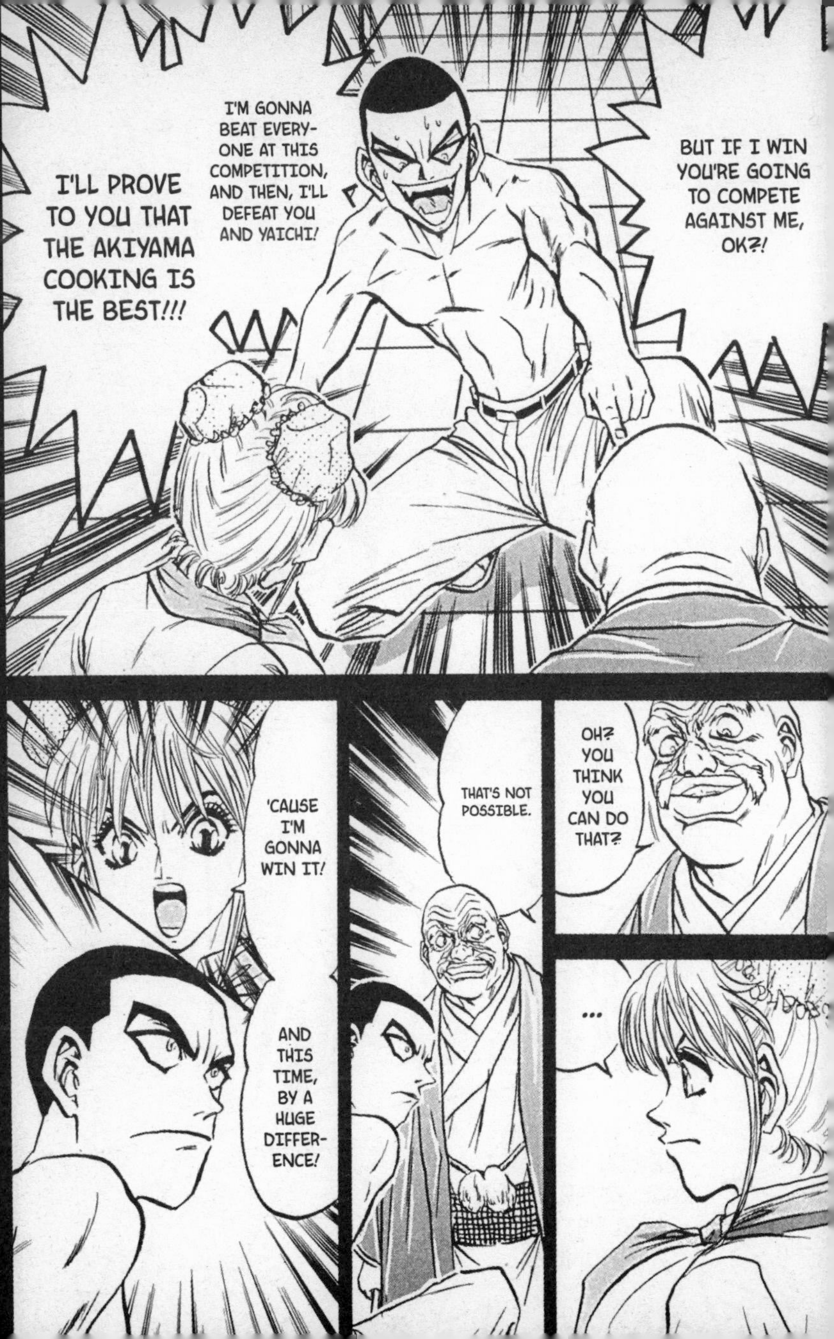
BUT IF I WIN YOU'RE GOING TO COMPETE AGAINST ME, OK?!
I'M GONNA BEAT EVERY-ONE AT THIS COMPETITION, AND THEN, I'LL DEFEAT YOU AND YAICHI!
I'LL PROVE TO YOU THAT THE AKIYAMA COOKING IS THE BEST!!!
OH? YOU THINK YOU CAN DO THAT?
...
THAT'S NOT POSSIBLE.
'CAUSE I'M GONNA WIN IT!
AND THIS TIME, BY A HUGE DIFFER-ENCE!

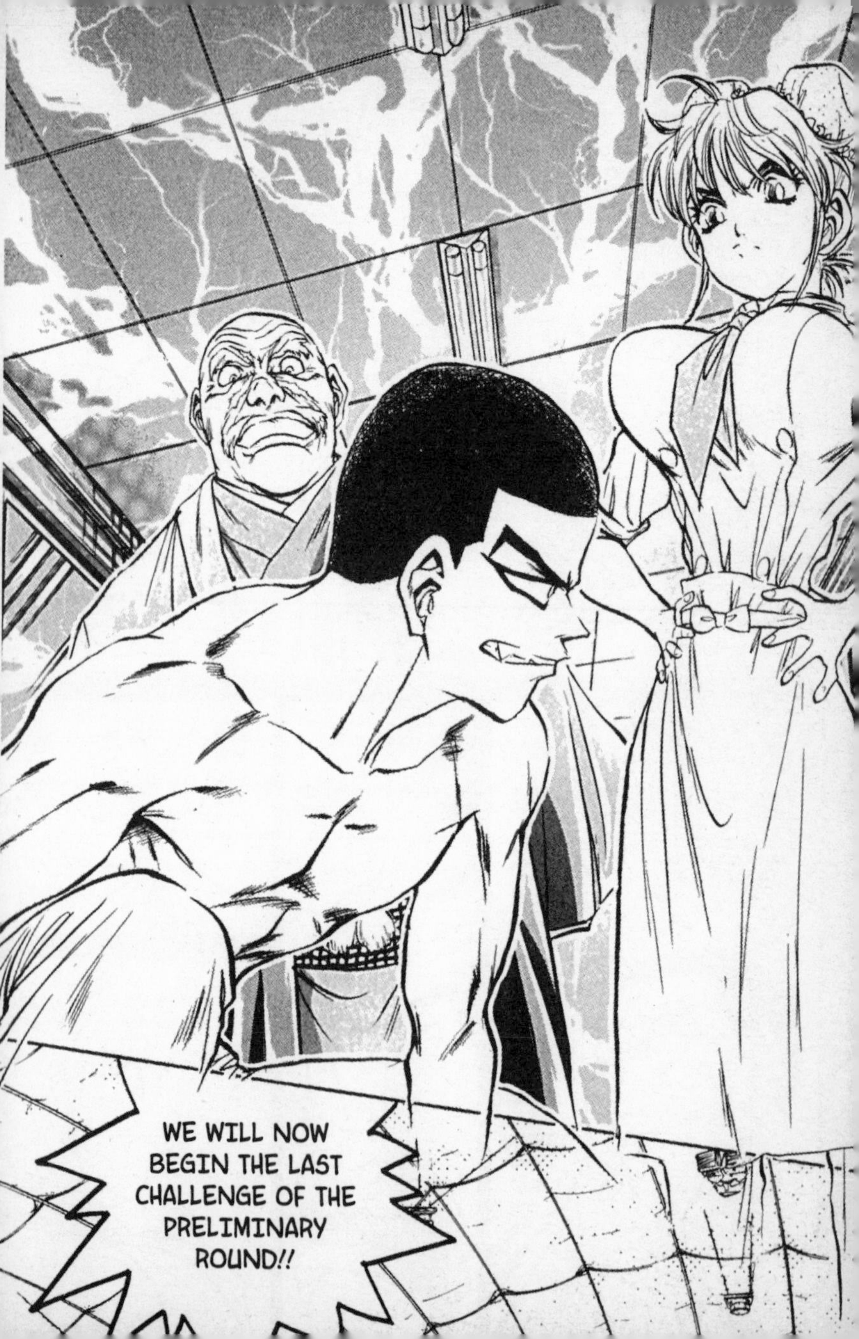
WE WILL NOW BEGIN THE LAST CHALLENGE OF THE PRELIMINARY ROUND!!

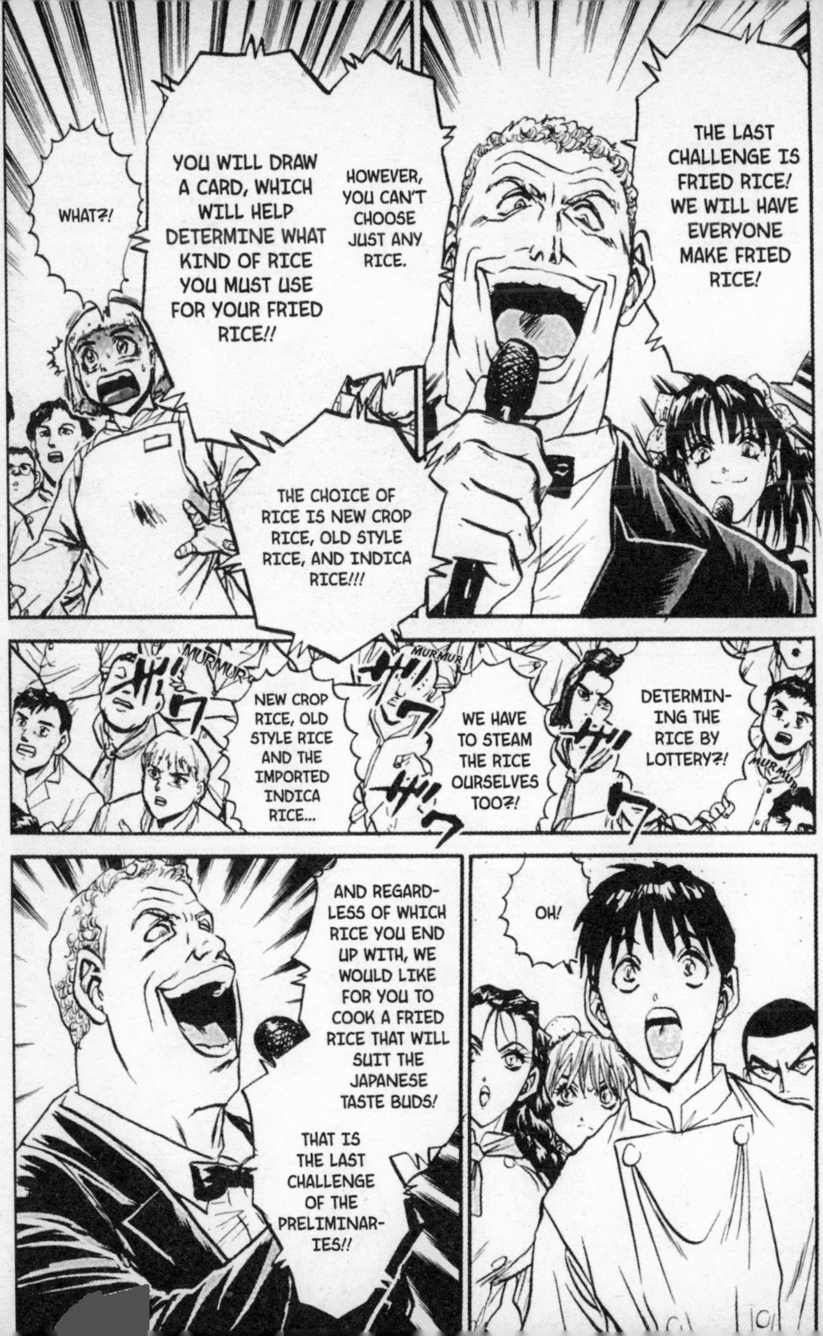
THE LAST CHALLENGE IS FRIED RICE! WE WILL HAVE EVERYONE MAKE FRIED RICE!
HOWEVER, YOU CAN'T CHOOSE JUST ANY RICE.
YOU WILL DRAW A CARD, WHICH WILL HELP DETERMINE WHAT KIND OF RICE YOU MUST USE FOR YOUR FRIED RICE!!
WHAT?!
THE CHOICE OF RICE IS NEW CROP RICE, OLD STYLE RICE, AND INDICA RICE!!!
MURMUR
DETERMINING THE RICE BY LOTTERY?!
WE HAVE TO STEAM THE RICE OURSELVES TOO?!
MURMUR
NEW CROP RICE, OLD STYLE RICE AND THE IMPORTED INDICA RICE...
MURMUR
OH!
AND REGARDLESS OF WHICH RICE YOU END UP WITH, WE WOULD LIKE FOR YOU TO COOK A FRIED RICE THAT WILL SUIT THE JAPANESE TASTE BUDS!
THAT IS THE LAST CHALLENGE OF THE PRELIMINARIES!!

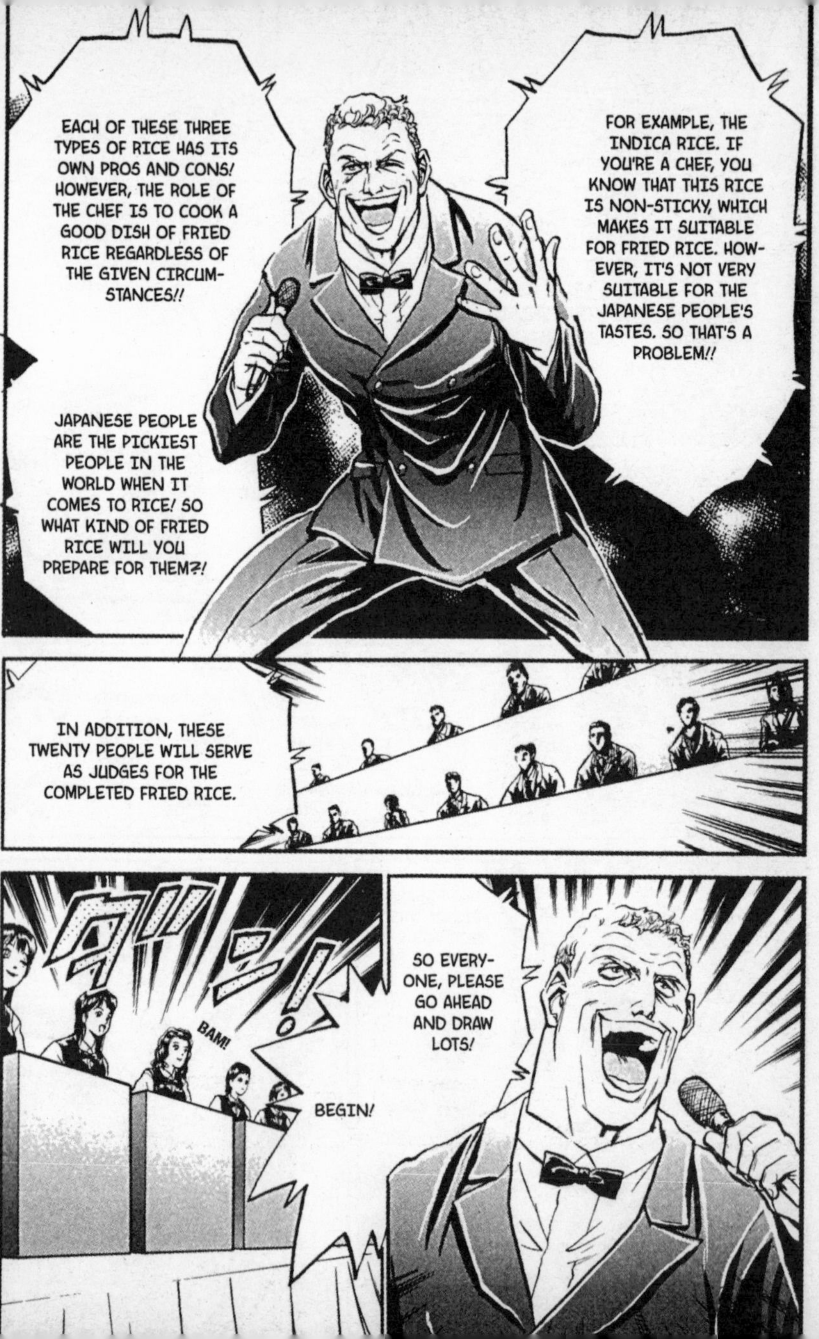

FOR EXAMPLE, THE INDICA RICE. IF YOU'RE A CHEF, YOU KNOW THAT THIS RICE IS NON-STICKY, WHICH MAKES IT SUITABLE FOR FRIED RICE. HOW-EVER, IT'S NOT VERY SUITABLE FOR THE JAPANESE PEOPLE'S TASTES. SO THAT'S A PROBLEM!!
EACH OF THESE THREE TYPES OF RICE HAS ITS OWN PROS AND CONS! HOWEVER, THE ROLE OF THE CHEF IS TO COOK A GOOD DISH OF FRIED RICE REGARDLESS OF THE GIVEN CIRCUM-STANCES!!
JAPANESE PEOPLE ARE THE PICKIEST PEOPLE IN THE WORLD WHEN IT COMES TO RICE! SO WHAT KIND OF FRIED RICE WILL YOU PREPARE FOR THEM?!
IN ADDITION, THESE TWENTY PEOPLE WILL SERVE AS JUDGES FOR THE COMPLETED FRIED RICE.
SO EVERY-ONE, PLEASE GO AHEAD AND DRAW LOTS!
BAM!
BEGIN!

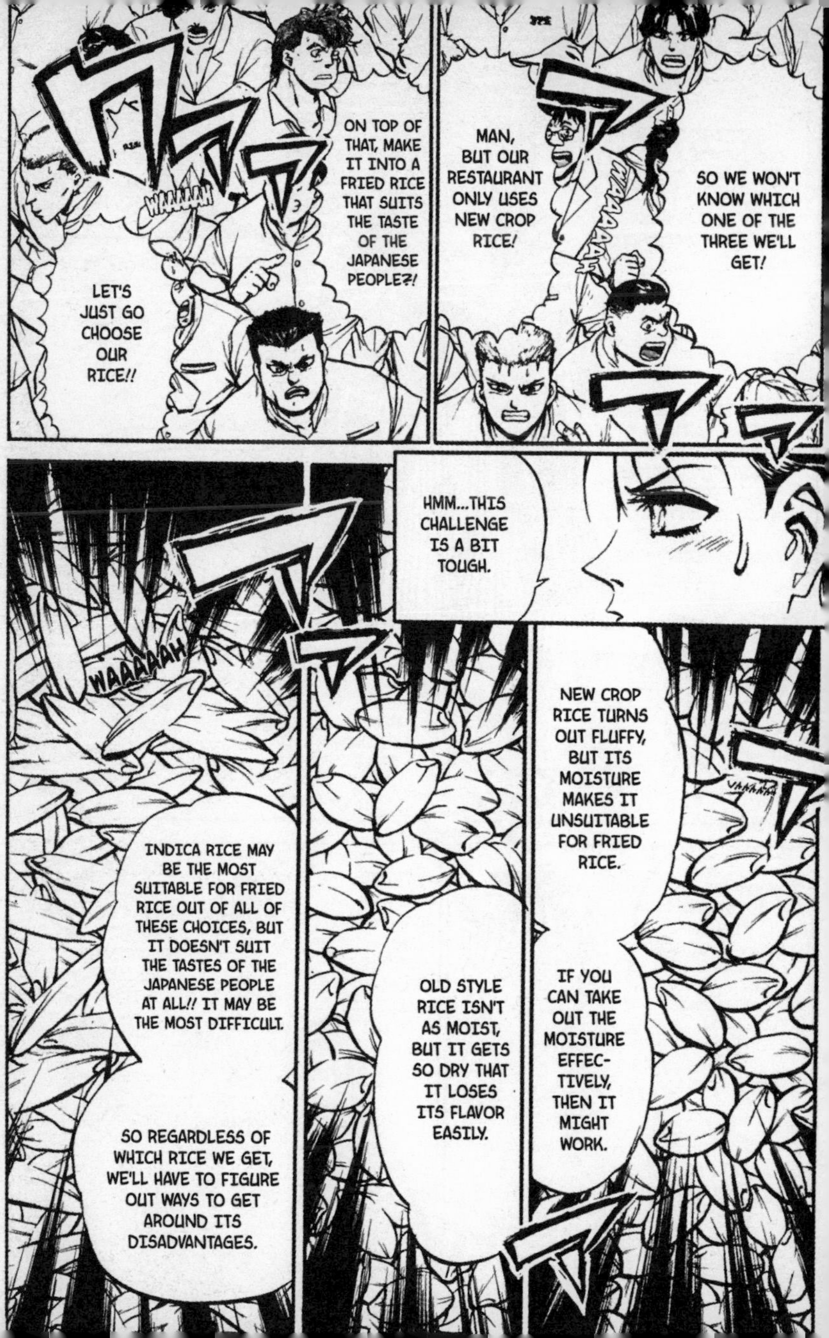

SO WE WON'T KNOW WHICH ONE OF THE THREE WE'LL GET!
MAN, BUT OUR RESTAURANT ONLY USES NEW CROP RICE!
WAAAAAH
ON TOP OF THAT, MAKE IT INTO A FRIED RICE THAT SUITS THE TASTE OF THE JAPANESE PEOPLE?!
WAAAAAH
LET'S JUST GO CHOOSE OUR RICE!!
HMM...THIS CHALLENGE IS A BIT TOUGH.
NEW CROP RICE TURNS OUT FLUFFY, BUT ITS MOISTURE MAKES IT UNSUITABLE FOR FRIED RICE.
IF YOU CAN TAKE OUT THE MOISTURE EFFEC-TIVELY, THEN IT MIGHT WORK.
OLD STYLE RICE ISN'T AS MOIST, BUT IT GETS SO DRY THAT IT LOSES ITS FLAVOR EASILY.
WAAAAAH
INDICA RICE MAY BE THE MOST SUITABLE FOR FRIED RICE OUT OF ALL OF THESE CHOICES, BUT IT DOESN'T SUIT THE TASTES OF THE JAPANESE PEOPLE AT ALL!! IT MAY BE THE MOST DIFFICULT.
SO REGARDLESS OF WHICH RICE WE GET, WE'LL HAVE TO FIGURE OUT WAYS TO GET AROUND ITS DISADVANTAGES.

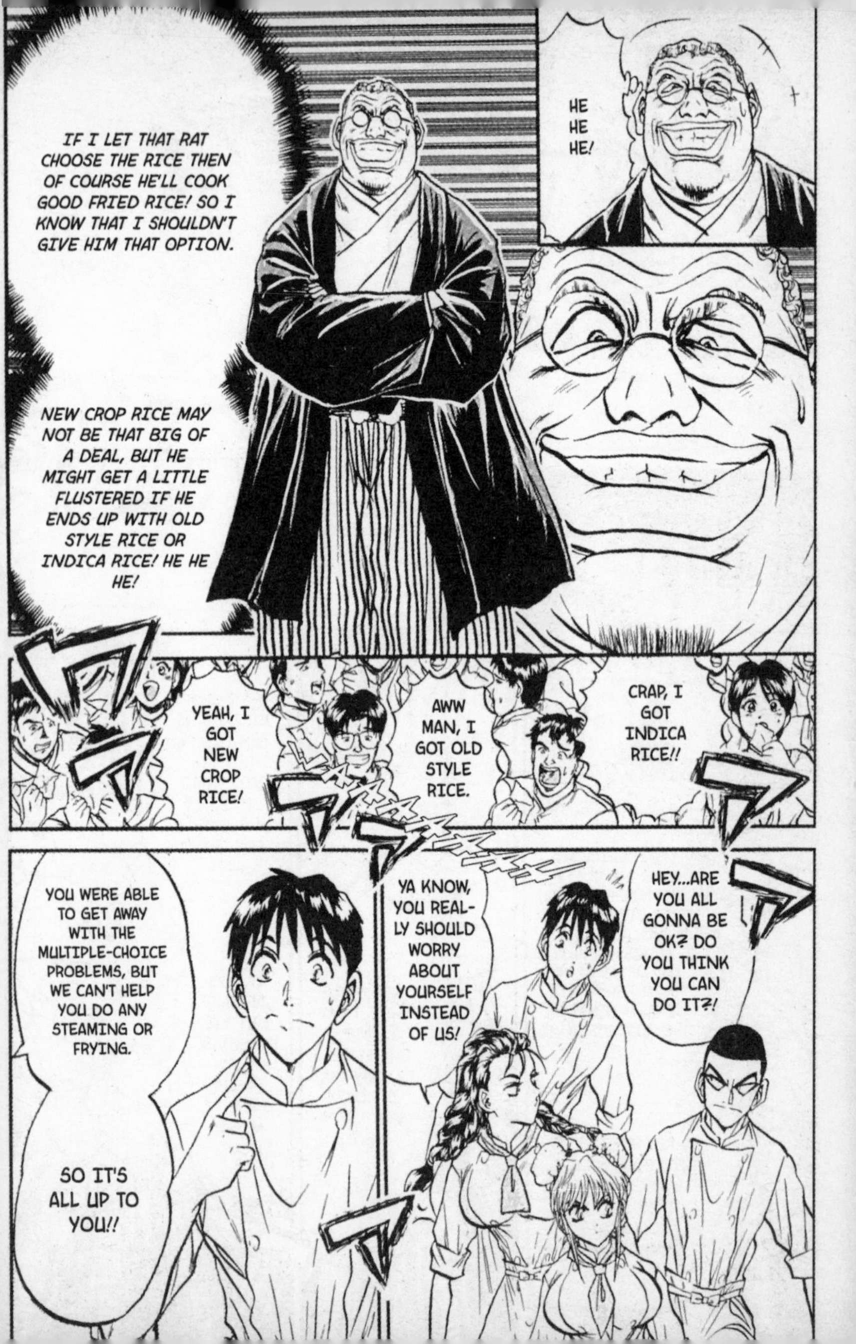
HE HE HE!
IF I LET THAT RAT CHOOSE THE RICE THEN OF COURSE HE'LL COOK GOOD FRIED RICE! SO I KNOW THAT I SHOULDN'T GIVE HIM THAT OPTION.
NEW CROP RICE MAY NOT BE THAT BIG OF A DEAL, BUT HE MIGHT GET A LITTLE FLUSTERED IF HE ENDS UP WITH OLD STYLE RICE OR INDICA RICE! HE HE HE!
CRAP, I GOT INDICA RICE!!
AWW MAN, I GOT OLD STYLE RICE.
YEAH, I GOT NEW CROP RICE!
HEY...ARE YOU ALL GONNA BE OK? DO YOU THINK YOU CAN DO IT?!
YA KNOW, YOU REAL-LY SHOULD WORRY ABOUT YOURSELF INSTEAD OF US!
YOU WERE ABLE TO GET AWAY WITH THE MULTIPLE-CHOICE PROBLEMS, BUT WE CAN'T HELP YOU DO ANY STEAMING OR FRYING.
SO IT'S ALL UP TO YOU!!

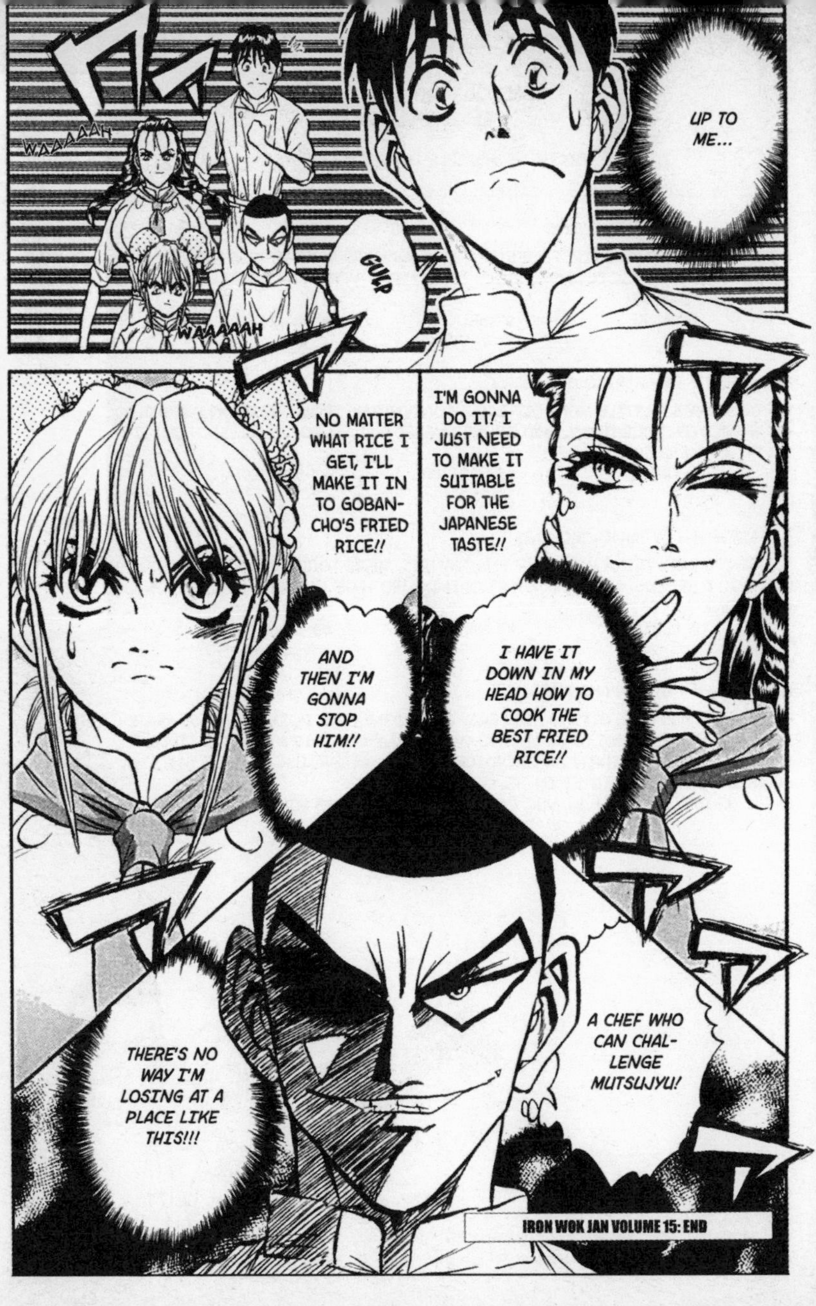
UP TO ME...
GULP
WAAAAAH
WAAAAAH
I'M GONNA DO IT! I JUST NEED TO MAKE IT SUITABLE FOR THE JAPANESE TASTE!!
NO MATTER WHAT RICE I GET, I'LL MAKE IT IN TO GOBAN-CHO'S FRIED RICE!!
I HAVE IT DOWN IN MY HEAD HOW TO COOK THE BEST FRIED RICE!!
AND THEN I'M GONNA STOP HIM!!
A CHEF WHO CAN CHAL-LENGE MUTSUJYU!
THERE'S NO WAY I'M LOSING AT A PLACE LIKE THIS!!!
IRON WOK JAN VOLUME 15: END

CAN YOU MAKE IT PAST THE PRELIMINARIES?!

TRY THESE MULTIPLE-CHOICE PROBLEMS!!

QUESTION 1 - BY CELINE YANG

(Y) ARE YA READY?! THE FIRST QUESTION IS A WARM-UP. WHAT IS THIS INGREDIENT USED IN THE CHINESE CUISINE, WHICH IS CALLED A "VIPER" IN THE KANSAI REGION IN JAPAN?!

#1 SNAKE #2 EEL #3 GARLIC

QUESTION 2 - BY KIRIKO GOBANCHO

(K) THIS ONE'S A LITTLE MORE DIFFICULT. CONTINUING FROM QUESTION 1, IT'S ALSO AN INGREDIENT QUESTION. WHAT IS THE INGREDIENT, WHICH IS CALLED "TIAN JI" IN THE CHINESE CUISINE?

#1 FROGS #2 LOBSTERS #3 SPARROW

QUESTION 3 - BY TAKAO OKONOGI

(O) MINE'S EASY. THINK HARD, OK? IN JAPANESE, THESE FOUR WORDS: A PEANUT, A PADLOCK, A BEDBUG, AND TAMASUDARE ORIGINATED FROM ONE OF THESE REGIONS. WHICH ONE IS IT?

#1 PEKING #2 NANKING #3 TONKIO

QUESTION 4 - BY JAN AKIYAMA

(J) WHY ARE YOU GUYS GIVING SUCH EASY QUESTIONS? THE POINT OF THESE MULTIPLE-CHOICE QUESTIONS IS TO GET RID OF AS MANY CONTESTANTS AS POSSIBLE. ALRIGHT, LET'S GO. WITHIN THESE CHOICES, ______ IS INCLUDED IN THE THREE GREATEST TASTING TEXTURES IN THE CHINESE CUISINE:

#1 CUI (CRISPY TEXTURE) #2 NUO (MOIST AND STICKY) #3 HUA (THICK AND SYRUPY)

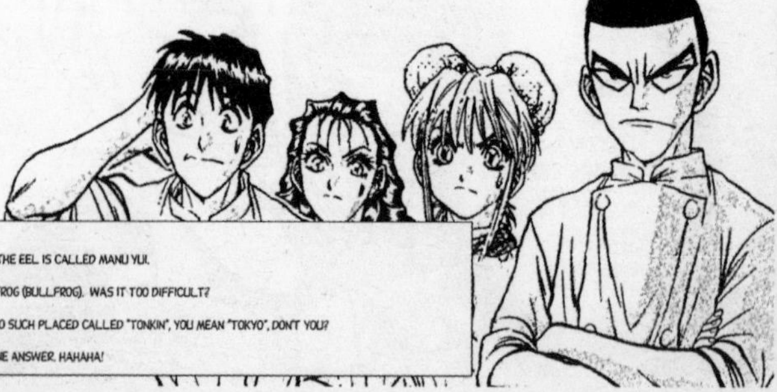

QUESTION 1 - ANSWER 2
(Y) BY THE WAY, IN CHINESE CUISINE THE EEL IS CALLED MANU YUI.
QUESTION 2- ANSWER 1
(K) MORE SPECIFICALLY, AN EDIBLE FROG (BULLFROG). WAS IT TOO DIFFICULT?
QUESTION 3- ANSWER 2
(O) WAS IT EASY? (J) HEY, THERE'S NO SUCH PLACED CALLED "TONKIN", YOU MEAN "TOKYO", DON'T YOU?
QUESTION 4- ANSWER 1, 2, 3
(J) I NEVER SAID THERE WAS ONLY ONE ANSWER. HAHAHA!

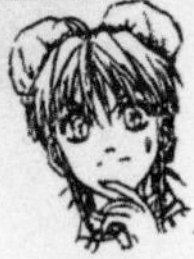

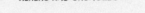

KIRIKO AND OKONOGI'S

BEI QIU SHAO MAI (SCALLOP EYE SIU MAI)

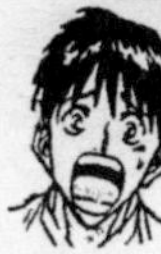

(O) KIRIKO-SAN, LATELY IT SEEMS LIKE YOU'RE ONLY MAKING SIU MAI ALL THE TIME.

(K) YEAH, YOU'RE RIGHT. AFTER I DID THAT SIU MAI STEAMING TIME ESTIMATING QUESTION AT THE COMPETITION, I GOT ALL INTO IT.

(O) WELL, SIU MAI SURE IS GOOD.

(K) THEN WHEN I'M DONE, WOULD YOU MIND TASTING SOME OF WHAT I'M MAKING RIGHT NOW?

(O) YAAAAY! OF COURSE. THE INGREDIENTS ARE 16 SIU MAI SKINS, 10 PIECES OF SCALLOP SASHIMI, 80 GRAMS OF CANNED ARROWHEAD BULBS, 40 GRAMS OF RAW SHI-ITAKE MUSHROOMS, 30 GRAMS OF GREEN PEAS, AND 1 TABLESPOON OF STARCH. I SEE.

(K) DON'T PRETEND LIKE YOU HAVE IT ALL FIGURED OUT. FIRST, FOR THE SCALLOPS, REMOVE THE THIN LAYER OF SKIN AROUND IT AND CUT IT IN HALF-INCH CUBES. CUT THE SHITTAKE MUSHROOMS IN THE SAME SIZE, AND CUT THE ARROWHEAD BULBS IN EVEN SMALLER CUBES. NEXT, YOU MAKE THE SEASONING BY MIXING ALL OF THE INGREDIENTS (SEE BELOW) TOGETHER, ADD THE CHOPPED SCALLOPS TO IT, AND KEEP MIXING UNTIL IT GETS STICKY. WHEN IT DOES, ADD THE REMAINING INGREDIENTS. DIVIDE THE MIXTURE INTO 16 PORTIONS AND PLACE EACH MIXTURE IN THE MIDDLE OF THE SIU MAI SKIN. ONCE YOU FOLD UP THE SIU MAI AND MAKE EACH OF THEM IN TO CYLINDRICAL SHAPES, YOU PLACE THEM IN THE STEAMER AFTER YOU SPREAD A THIN LAYER OF OIL OVER THE SURFACE. STEAM FOR 5 MINUTES. NOW IT'S DONE. ENJOY IT WITH SOME GINGER SAUCE.

(O) WOW, IT'S LIGHTLY REFRESHING AND YUMMY!

(K) THE SCALLOPS ARE RAW, SO IF YOU STEAM IT TOO LONG IT WILL GET TOO HARD, SO WATCH OUT FOR THAT. AND OF COURSE, YOU CAN'T STEAM IT TWICE...

(O) IT'S GOOD IF YOU FRY IT TOO, RIGHT? LET'S MAKE IT AGAIN.

SEASONINGS

COOKING SAKE	2 TEASPOONS
SALT	1/2 TEASPOONS
PEPPER	A PINCH
MSG	A PINCH
EGG WHITES	1 TABLESPOON

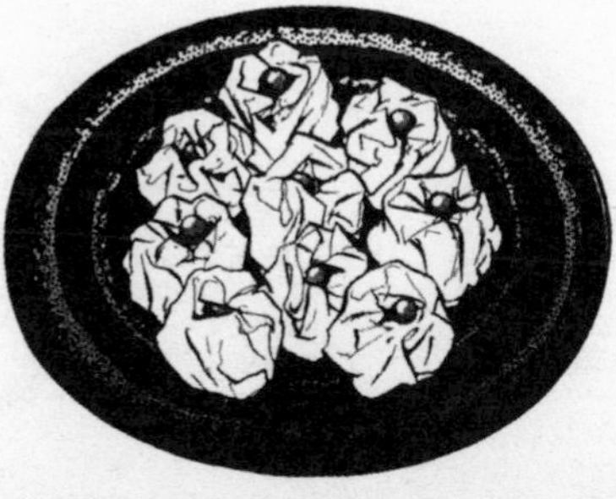

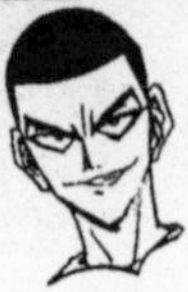

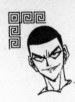

JAN AND OKONOGI'S

SHAO MAI (SIU MAI)

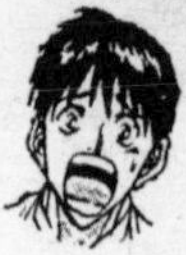

(O) HEY JAN, KIRIKO-SAN MADE SOME REALLY GOOD SIU MAI. I TRIED SOME, AND IT'S THE BEST SIU MAI I'VE EVER HAD.

(J) HEY, I DON'T KNOW ABOUT THAT. ALL RIGHT THEN, OKONOGI, I'M GONNA MAKE THE MOST AMAZING SIU MAI RIGHT NOW, SO TASTE IT AND COMPARE IT WITH KIRIKO'S.

(O) OH, SURE (*YAY!*).

(J) THE INGREDIENTS ARE 200 GRAMS OF GROUND PORK MEAT, 380 GRAMS OF ONIONS, 40 GRAMS OF BABY SHRIMPS, HALF OF AN EGG, 15 GRAMS OF GINGER, 8 TABLESPOONS OF STARCH AND 36 PIECES OF SIU MAI SKIN.

(O) (*YAY! THAT MEANS HE'S MAKING 20 MORE THAN KIRIKO-SAN DID.*)

(J) FIRST, YOU CHOP THE ONIONS FINELY AND SPRINKLE STARCH OVER IT. YOU MINCE THE GINGER AS WELL. THEN, YOU PEEL THE SKINS OFF THE BABY SHRIMPS, TAKE OUT THE SAND VEIN, AND SMASH IT WITH THE CUTTING KNIFE. GET A BIG BOWL AND PUT IN THE GROUND PORK MEAT, CHOPPED GINGER, EGG AND BABY SHRIMP. MIX IT WELL AND ADJUST THE TASTE WITH THE SEASONING (SEE BELOW). ADD THE ONIONS SPRINKLED WITH STARCH IN THIS BOWL AND MIX EVERYTHING TOGETHER BUT DON'T KNEAD IT. WRAP THE MIXTURE WITH THE SIU MAI SKINS AND STEAM IT WITH A STEAMER FOR 10 MINUTES, AND IT'S DONE. HERE, EAT IT.

(O) MMMM. IT'S THE BEST, JAN! (*MY STRATEGY WORKED! AS LONG AS I KEEP STIRRING UP THE COMPETITION BETWEEN JAN AND KIRIKO, I CAN KEEP EATING YUMMY THINGS FOR THE REST OF MY LIFE*).

(J) HEY, I KNOW WHAT YOU'RE THINKING, OKONOGI. USE YOUR BRAINS ON SOMETHING ELSE INSTEAD.

SEASONINGS

COOKING SAKE	1 TABLESPOON
SALT	1/2 TEASPOON
SOY SAUCE	1 TABLESPOON
SUGAR	1 TABLESPOON
PEPPER	A PINCH
MSG	A PINCH

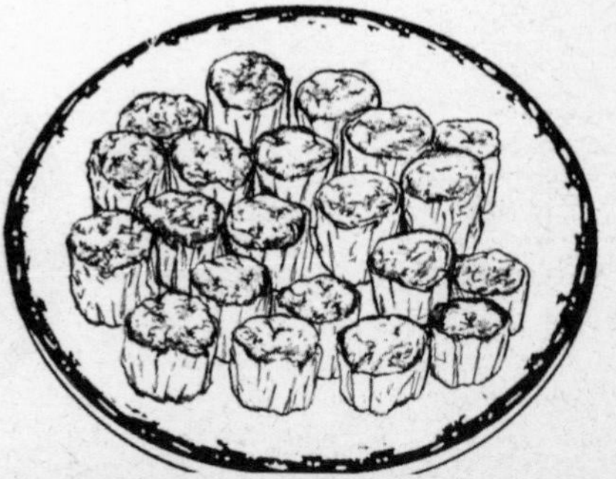

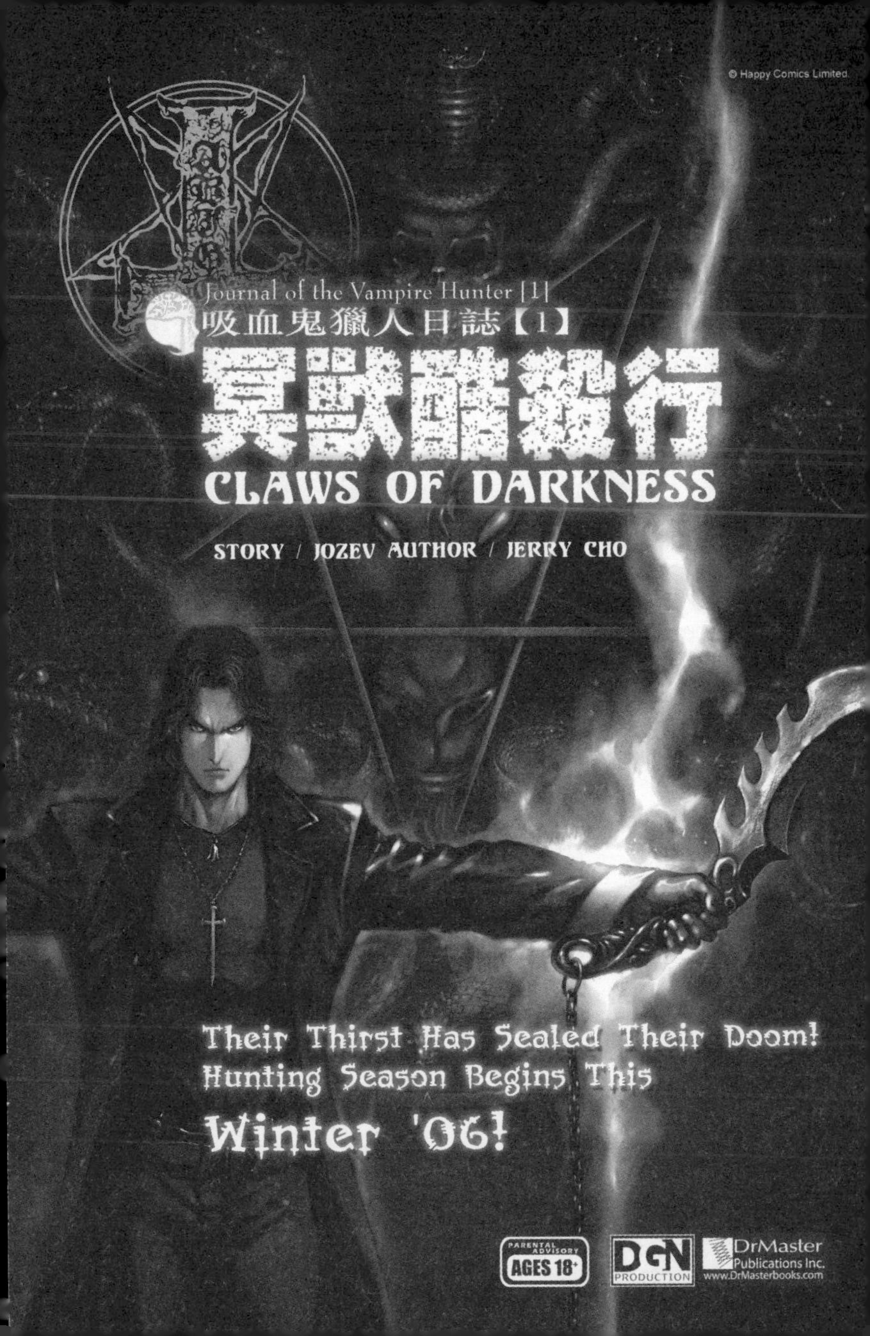

© Happy Comics Limited.
Journal of the Vampire Hunter [1]
吸血鬼獵人日誌【1】
冥獸酷殺行
CLAWS OF DARKNESS
STORY / JOZEV AUTHOR / JERRY CHO
Their Thirst Has Sealed Their Doom!
Hunting Season Begins This
Winter '06!
PARENTAL ADVISORY AGES 18+
DGN PRODUCTION
DrMaster Publications Inc.
www.DrMasterbooks.com

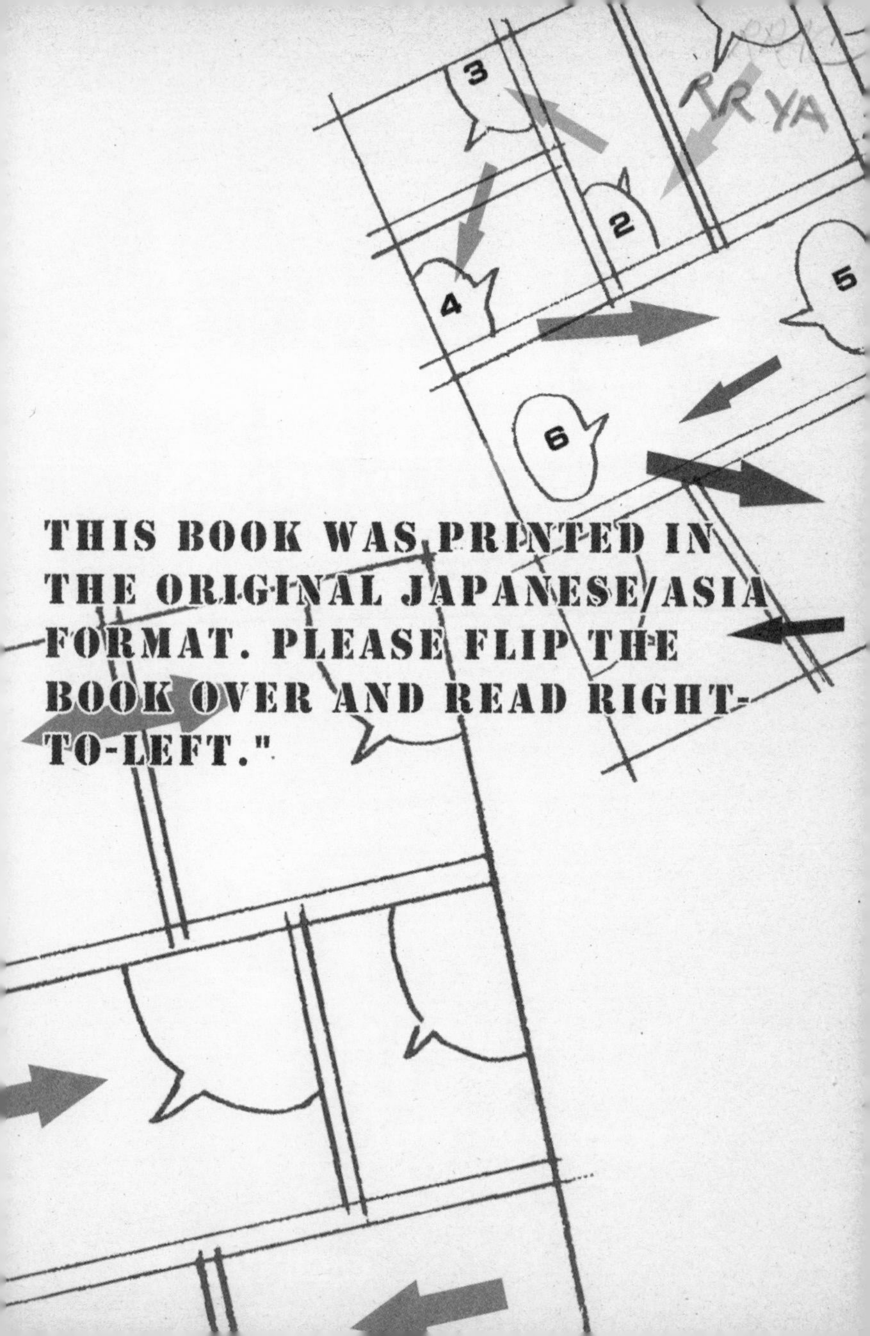

THIS BOOK WAS PRINTED IN THE ORIGINAL JAPANESE/ASIA FORMAT. PLEASE FLIP THE BOOK OVER AND READ RIGHT-TO-LEFT."